FIELDS OF REVOLUTION

Pitt Latin American Series

Catherine M. Conaghan, Editor

FIELDS OF REVOLUTION

Agrarian Reform *and* Rural State Formation *in* Bolivia, 1935–1964

CARMEN SOLIZ

University of Pittsburgh Press

Published by the University of Pittsburgh Press, Pittsburgh, Pa., 15260

Manufactured in the United States of America
Printed on acid-free paper
10 9 8 7 6 5 4 3 2 1

Cataloging-in-Publication data is available from the Library of Congress

ISBN 13: 978-0-8229-4665-6
ISBN 10: 0-8229-4665-3

Cover art: María Luis Pacheco, *Siembra*, La Paz, 1953. Óleo-lienzo. Museo Tambo Quirquincha, Museos Municipales, La Paz. Fotografía Pedro Querejazu.
Cover design: Melissa Dias-Mandoly

A Andrés Soliz, a quien le hubiera gustado leer este libro
A Silvia Urrutia, quien ha acompañado la escritura de cada una de estas páginas

CONTENTS

Acknowledgments ix

List of Acronyms xiii

Introduction 3

Chapter One: The Liberal Project in the Countryside 19

Chapter Two: The Indian Problem and the Agrarian Question under Debate 46

Chapter Three: Revolution Comes to the Countryside 70

Chapter Four: Redistribute Land Soon 94

Chapter Five: Land to Its Original Owners 120

Chapter Six: Land for Those Who Work It 141

Epilogue: Everyday Forms of Revolution 171

Notes 183

Bibliography 231

Index 259

ACKNOWLEDGMENTS

It is a pleasure to acknowledge all of those who helped me in the long process of writing this book. Financial support for my research was provided by one year's research fellowship from the Social Science Research Council, summer funding in 2008 and 2009 from the Center for Latin American and Caribbean Studies at New York University, a dissertation completion fellowship from the Mellon Foundation and Graduate School of Arts and Sciences at NYU, a Summer Stipend from the National Endowment for the Humanities, a Faculty Research Summer Grant from UNC-Charlotte, and a Junior Faculty Development Award from UNC-Charlotte.

I wish to express my deep gratitude to my advisor, Sinclair Thomson, who was by my side from the moment I started drafting this project and writing my dissertation. He continued to accompany the process of turning the dissertation into a book years after my graduation from NYU. His guidance and patience made this work possible. I am grateful to Dylan Yeats for their encouragement, support, and advice over years. He has been a sounding board for many of the ideas collected in this book. I am indebted to Ernesto Semán, James Dunkerley, Jennifer Adair, and Rachel Nolan, for their invaluable suggestions on tone and style. All of them are close friends whose kindness and generosity made this book possible.

I had the privilege to receive the pointed comments and warm advice from Ada Ferrer, Laura Gotkowitz, Greg Grandin, Brooke Larson, Barbara Weinstein, and Kevin Young. My work is deeply indebted to their own work, which has helped to frame my questions on peasant political activism, the role of rural elites, and the process of state formation. I also owe this book to the advice, support, and provocative questions of Allison Bigelow, Nancy Egan, Susan Ellison, Thomas Field, Matt Gildner, Mariana Heredia, Sarah Hines, Ben Nobbs-Thiessen, Nicole Pacino, Hernán Pruden, Marian Schlotterbeck, Elizabeth Shesko, and Karl Swineheart. I have also enjoyed the comradeship from my dear friends from graduate school: Michelle Chase, Greg Childs, Marcela Echeverri, Anne Eller, Josh Frens-

String, Laura Honsberger, Shira Klein, Allan Amanik, Sarah Kozameh, Yuko Miki, Kate Mulry, Federico Sor, and Martin Sivak.

In Bolivia, my first intellectual debt is to Rossana Barragán who has been my professor, guide, and dearest friend since my years as undergraduate. Working with her has been one of the most delightful times in my life and I have enjoyed it immensely. Much of my own desire to understand and rethink Bolivia state formation came from Rossana's own work. I was also privileged to be a part of a group of intellectuals in Bolivia who greatly contributed to my formation. My thanks go to Clara López Beltrán, Cristina Machicado, Ximena Medinacelli, Pilar Mendieta, Ramiro Molina Rivero, Silvina Montenegro, Mario Murillo, Ximena Soruco, Silvia Rivera Cusicanqui, Cecilia Salazar, Ricardo Asebey, Roger Mamani, Magdalena Cajías, Thomas Grissaffi, Amy Kennemore, Alice Soarez Guimaraez, Maria Luisa Soux, and Maria Isabel Villagomez mother and daughter.

I would also like to thank the librarians and staff of the Bolivian archives who made my research possible. Research at the National Agrarian Institute in La Paz and Cochabamba was a wonderful experience because it gave me the chance not only to learn about agrarian conflicts in the past but also to engage with the current political dilemmas over land redistribution. I want to thank the La Paz Archive and the long list of friends who worked there, including Nilda Llanqui Quispe, Lupe Mamani, Santusa Marca, Elisa Ticona, and Daniela Troche. I spent months at the Bolivian National Archive in Sucre where I found a professional staff on a par with any library in the world. My thanks to Ivanna Campos, Nelva Delgadillo, and Oscar Hurtado. I spent almost every US summer since 2009 at the Biblioteca y Archivo Histórico de la Asamblea Legislativa Plurinacional. I have enjoyed the professionalism of the director Luis Oporto and the archive's personnel Rolando Álvarez, Rene Mérida, and Ruby Portugal.

I relish the friendship of many who opened their homes and hearts to me in La Paz, New York, and Charlotte, North Carolina: Estela Alarcón, Marcela Alarcón, Carwil Bjork-James, Sophie Bjork-James, Pamela Calla, Estelle Davis, Greg Fogie, Sarah Fogie, Tom Kruse, Soledad Marambio, Miguel Peraita, Seemin Qayum, Steven Ross, Irene Vidal, and Vannia Villegas.

Since 2014, my colleagues—and now friends—at University of North Carolina at Charlotte welcomed and offer support at every step as a faculty. My greatest debt is to Professors John David Smith and Lyman Johnson. I received the support and guidance of the chair of my department, Jurgen Buchenau, as well as the friendship and welcoming generosity of Amanda Binder, Chris Cameron, Dan Cozart, Erika Edwards, Maren Ehlers, Emek Ergun, Ella Fratantuono, Christine Haynes, Cheryl Hicks, Steve Hyland, Gabi Kuenzli, Oscar Lansen, Jill Massino, Ritika Prasad, Oscar de la Torre, and Mark Wilson. I also thank to the dedicated work of editors who spent hours improving different versions of this manuscript: Isis Sadek, Katherine Tingelstald, the anonymous reviewers of this book, the detailed and careful work of the copyeditor Pippa Letsky, Amy Sherman, and Joshua Shanholtzer, editors of Pittsburgh University Press.

My deepest thanks go to my family, the stronghold of my life and my work. My mom, Silvia Urrutia, has been an engine behind this and every project. I was both nourished and enriched by her work as a lawyer of indigenous people and their claims for territory in the 1990s and by her sharp meditations about Bolivian politics, life, and everything else. My father, Andrés Soliz, an inveterate Bolivian nationalist, passed away in 2016 when I was still writing this book. He was an unstoppable supporter of all my projects and an endless source of provocative ideas and new materials. My brothers, Sergio and Jorge, are the bedrock on which I stand. They have closely followed, encouraged, and supported what has often seemed like an endless project.

LIST OF ACRONYMS

BAH-ALP — Biblioteca y Archivo Histórico de la Asamblea Legislativa Plurinacional (Library and Historical Archive at the Plurinational Legislative Assembly)

CIDOB — Confederación Indígena del Oriente Boliviano (Indigenous Federation of Eastern Bolivia)

CNRA — Consejo Nacional de Reforma Agraria (National Council of Agrarian Reform)

CNTCB — Confederación Nacional de Trabajadores Campesinos de Bolivia (National Confederation of Peasant Workers of Bolivia)

COB — Central Obrera Boliviana (Bolivian Workers Federation)

FAD — Federación Agraria Departamental (Departmental Agrarian Federation)

FAO — Food and Agricultural Organization

FDA — Frente Democrático Antifascista (Antifascist Democratic Front)

FOL — Federación Obrera Local (Local Workers Federation)

FOS – Federación Obrera Sindical (Workers Union Federation)

FRC —Federación Rural de Cochabamba (Rural Federation of Cochabamba)

FSB — Falange Socialista Boliviana (Bolivian Socialist Falange)

LTC — Land Tenure Center, University of Wisconsin, Madison

MAC — Ministerio de Asuntos Campesinos (Ministry of Peasant Affairs)

MNR — Movimiento Nacionalista Revolucionario (Revolutionary Nationalist Movement)

PIR — Partido de la Izquierda Revolucionaria (Left Revolutionary Party)

POR — Partido Obrero Revolucionario (Trotskyist Revolutionary Workers' Party)

SNRA — Servicio Nacional de Reforma Agraria (National Agricultural Reform Service)

SRB — Sociedad Rural Boliviana (Bolivian Rural Society)

SPY — Sociedad de Propietarios de los Yungas (Yungas Landlords Society)

THOA — Taller de Historia Oral Andina (Andean Oral History Workshop)

FIELDS OF REVOLUTION

INTRODUCTION

"Today, the second of August of 1953, ends four hundred years of oppression. . . . Today, more than two million peasants have become part of the nation."[1] With these words, President Víctor Paz Estenssoro, the leader of the Movimiento Nacionalista Revolucionario (MNR), the Revolutionary Nationalist Movement, announced the decree of agrarian reform that abolished personal labor services by indigenous tenants and redistributed estates among peasants. This agrarian reform, along with the nationalization of mines and the extension of suffrage to women and Indians, constituted the three most important transformations of the 1952 Bolivian National Revolution, placing it within the pantheon of the great social revolutions in twentieth-century Latin America.[2]

The Bolivian revolution was a very unusual political process in Latin American terms. It was as profound and far-reaching as the revolution in Mexico, yet its agrarian reform did not take decades to be implemented, as the one in Mexico did. Instead, de facto peasant land distribution started a year after the 1952 National Revolution and acquired rapid momentum. The Bolivian revolution occurred at the same time that President Jacobo Arbenz in Guatemala was implementing a similar program of agrarian reform. Yet, unlike Guatemala's revolution, Bolivia's was not overthrown by covert CIA operations. It preceded the Cuban revolution by only seven years, but the MNR openly distanced itself from the Soviet Union. The Bolivian agrarian reform was as radical as the reforms led by General Juan Velasco Alvarado in Peru in 1968 and by Salvador Allende in Chile in 1970, yet its achievements in terms of land redistribution in the highlands and the valleys were never undone by conservative reaction, as in those countries.

The transformations in terms of land tenure and power begun in 1952 continue to shape Bolivia's contemporary politics, which makes this country a unique example in Latin America. The revolution and the agrarian reform brought a profound democratization of the state apparatus, the erosion of landlords' formal and informal means of power, and the expropriation of hundreds of haciendas in the most densely populated areas in the country (the highlands, the valleys, and the subtropical ecoregion of Yungas).[3] Unlike other countries in Latin America such as Guatemala, Peru, or Chile, reactionary military regimes did not dare to undermine those conquests. The subsequent civilian and military regimes that followed the MNR's overthrow in 1964 sought to seal their alliance with the peasantry in order to secure their own political stability. In the late 1990s, when the influence of the Central Obrera Boliviana (COB), the once strong mineworkers' Bolivian Workers Federation, faded away and the traditional party system felt apart, the territorial control that peasant unions had in the countryside secured them national outreach. These peasant unions constituted one of the most critical factors in reshaping the balance of political power in the nation in the late 1990s and early 2000s. It is impossible to understand the surprising emergence of Evo Morales and the ongoing political weight of peasants in today's politics without tracing the roots of this radical transformation. Although concentration of land in few hands continues to be a predominant factor in the profound inequality in Latin America today, and rural landed societies are still a decisive actor in countries such as Brazil, Argentina, or Paraguay, agrarian reform is no longer—as it was in the 1960s—a subject of discussion in the region.[4] Yet, the legacies of agrarian reform in Bolivia, and its profound political consequences in the makeup of the country's political map, reveal the enduring importance of this issue for Bolivia and the rest of Latin America.

Who was the engine behind this transformative change? In the first years after the revolution, the familiar image of Paz Estenssoro signing the Agrarian Reform Decree-Law in front of thousands of peasants in the community of Ucureña reinforced the idea that the will of the president and legal fiat were sufficient to break the powerful hold of traditional landowning elites.[5] Peasant and Indian petitions and struggles to obtain land and transform power relations at the time of the revolution are at the center of the story. By looking at the fraught encounter between landlords, Indians, and peasants, we can see how central government policies were shaped, negotiated, and transformed at the local level. My findings reveal that the timing, depth, and final outcome of the land reform—a process ostensibly carried out by the revolutionary party—was fundamentally defined by local and community forces.

Reassessing Peasants Role in the National Revolution

From the start of revolution, the MNR spread the idea that the party was the leading force for change in the countryside. This suggested that the peasants were the passive and grateful beneficiaries of the agrarian reform. Party officials argued that, although the nationalization of the mines was a product of mineworkers' widespread mobilization, peasants received land almost without a fight. The MNR used a strong multimedia apparatus (newspapers, booklets, statistics, paintings, murals, and videos) to reinforce this top-down depiction of the agrarian reform.[6] This representation shaped scholarly interpretations of the agrarian reform for decades. Echoing this view, political scientist Robert Alexander wrote one of the earliest accounts of the Bolivian revolution in English. He states that the MNR's leadership was unquestionable: "For the first time, the Indians had a protector of their interests.[7]

Against this view, in the late 1950s anthropologist Richard Patch argues that the agrarian reform was not the result of government initiative but, rather, of intense social pressure sparked by the self-organized unions in the valleys of Cochabamba where, immediately after the revolution, peasants began to seize large estates. This movement quickly spread through the valleys, forcing the government to decree land reform one year after the MNR took power.[8] On the other hand, the comparative work of anthropologists Dwight Heath, Charles Erasmus, and Hans Buechler states: "The idea of Bolivia's land reform as having been the product of grassroots action on the part of the illiterate Indian majority is not supported."[9] These authors argue that peasants only started to organize politically when the MNR launched a national program for peasant unionization. In their view, the peasant union was not based on any previous peasant or Indian structure existing in either haciendas or free communities but, rather, was modeled on industrial labor unions, slightly modified to fit the agrarian context.[10] Reinforcing their view that the revolution was a force that spread to the countryside from the top down, they assert that no one in Bolivia would agree with Patch. However, these authors do not fully endorse the MNR's position either. They argue: "The Bolivian agrarian reform was the result of many subtle, interlocking forces. To assert it originated only from above or from below would be to ignore the fact that without leaders there are merely aimless mobs and that leaders without followers are impotent."[11] Despite their division over which forces were behind the agrarian reform, in both perspectives Ucureña (situated in the valley of Cochabamba) was at the center of peasant political mobilization.

A new set of scholarly works from the 1970s reexamine the sources of the political mobilization in the countryside, and they all agree it started at the top and worked down. Anthropologist Jorge Dandler demonstrates that peasants organized the first peasant unions in the valleys of Cochabamba more than a decade prior to the revolution. Yet, for him, neither the peasants nor the MNR were the engines behind peasant political mobilization but, rather, political brokers (using Eric Wolf's concept) such as rural teachers and left-leaning political party activists such as those in the Partido de la Izquierda Revolucionaria (PIR), the Party of the Revolutionary Left. Dandler argues that nonpeasants' active support was vital in connecting parochial peasant demands with emergent national ideologies.[12] According to Dandler, peasant in the valleys caught on to the idea of organizing a union sooner than other peasants because of the specific cultural and social distinctions of this region. According to Dandler distinctions between Indians and mixed-race people had been softening since the nineteenth century in the valleys of Cochabamba, in contrast to the altiplano where social distinctions between Indians and whites were more sharply defined.[13]

In a similar vein, political scientist James Malloy highlights the distinctiveness of the peasant political mobilization in Cochabamba (and Ucureña in particular). Malloy argues that Indian migration from the countryside to the city and especially to the mines was especially important. According to Malloy, this context allowed the development of a small but real peasant class of Indian smallholders who could distance themselves from the uniform condition of vassalage experienced by their racial brothers.[14]

These studies challenge the MNR's self-proclaimed role in leading the agrarian reform and bestowing land upon Indians. They offer a denser depiction of the political dynamics of the decades before and during the revolution and enlarge the view beyond the MNR's official narrative. However, all of them stress that Ucureña was the one place where this early peasant politicization took place. These works assert the unique role of this region within a sea of unorganized and depoliticized indigenous and peasant communities.[15] These authors limit political organization to the frame of the peasant union, and all other forms of political action fade from their view.[16]

Beginning in the early 1980s (though at a remove from the debates over the Bolivian revolution and the agrarian reform), scholars and activists gathered around the Taller de Historia Oral Andina (THOA), the Andean Oral History Workshop, have explored more deeply both Indian and peasant political struggles.[17] Silvia Rivera Cusicanqui, Carlos Mamani, Roberto Choque, and Esteban Ticona (among others) uncover silenced accounts of Indian and peasant struggles since the late nineteenth century and throughout the first half of the twentieth century.[18] Ramiro Condarco Morales had already revealed in the 1960s that the powerful Indian mobilization led by Pablo Zárate Willka in 1899 was a response to the expansion of large agricultural estates.[19] Silvia Rivera Cusicanqui points out that after the 1910s, although defeated by the military, a network of Indian leaders known as *caciques apoderados* battled landlords in the courts by presenting titles conferred by the Spanish Crown to demonstrate community ownership of the land.[20]

Inspired by this new work, Laura Gotkowitz reframes the 1952 national revolution as the culmination of rural struggles dating back to the 1880s.

She locates peasant and Indian politics at the center of national debates and places the 1952 revolution in the context of prior rebellions that took place in 1899, 1921, 1927, and 1947. For Gotkowitz, the two most remarkable political projects over this period were the development of transregional networks of Indian community leaders (the movement of the caciques apoderados) and the 1945 National Indigenous Congress. She shows how this long cycle of mobilization, involving both legal efforts and direct action, directly shaped the events of 1952. This work challenges previous conceptions of Indians and peasants as marginal political actors.[21] Yet, the work of Laura Gotkowitz ends in 1947, and we still need to understand the role that peasant and Indian communities played at the time of the revolution, and that is the story at the center of this book.

When analyzing the role of peasant and Indian communities at the time of the revolution, THOA academics were very critical of the role of the MNR in the countryside. As in the scholarship of the 1960s and 1970s, they endorse the view that the agrarian reform was a program implemented from above. They point out that the organization of peasant unions and the individual distribution of land among peasants undermined autonomous organization and traditional systems of Indian authority. For them, the 1952 revolution was more a continuation than a rupture with previous modernization projects. One of the most critical views of the policies of the 1950s was best articulated by anthropologist Tristan Platt, who held that the agrarian reform of 1953 was a continuation of the privatization policies that started in 1874 (the Disentailment Law) under the Liberals. Platt argues that both laws aimed to privatize land and to undermine the control of land by indigenous communities. Yet, his analysis is so focused on the role of the state and of the indigenous communities that it downplays the political and economic role played by the landlord elite before 1952. The agrarian policy of 1874 allowed the concentration of land in the country in few hands; the agrarian policy of 1953, on the other hand, distributed the land among the peasants, at the expense of the former landlords.[22] Also critical of the agrarian reform of the 1950s, sociologist Silvia Rivera Cusicanqui holds that MNR "clientelist" policies in the countryside in the 1950s turned peasants from "economic *pongos*" (indentured servants) to political *pongos* (subordinated political clients). According to Rivera Cusicanqui, the agrarian reform gave the MNR the unconditional political support of the peasantry, which allowed the nationalist party to remain in power for twelve years (1952–1964).[23]

The literature about the revolution became increasingly critical of the role of the MNR in the countryside. Since the 1980s most scholars have described the MNR as a reactionary force whose ultimate goal was to dismantle long-standing autonomous Indian political struggles. We seem to be facing a contradiction in the trend of this literature. Although scholars have come to emphasize peasant and Indian political agency prior to the revolution, they have reinforced the view that peasants, outside of Ucureña, passively implemented the MNR's agrarian political agenda after the revolution. With the exception of the early work of Richard Patch, most scholars saw the process of unionization and the agrarian reform as programs imposed to peasants from the top.[24]

One of the latest works to depart from this tendency is the study by José Gordillo who analyzes peasant political mobilization of the valleys of Cochabamba in the first years of the revolution. Although he views the MNR leadership as politically moderate, he argues that peasant political identity was not shaped from above by governmental policies but was forged by pre- and postrevolutionary struggles, and that this allowed peasants to marshal an important degree of political autonomy.[25] Yet, Gordillo's work, is primarily rooted in analysis of the MNR and peasant leaders' rhetoric. In contrast, my aim is to analyze MNR's policies on the ground, to research the impact they had on ordinary people, and to show that the party had to constantly negotiate with and adapt to multiple local demands. My focus is on the revolutionary cycle that started again after 1952, and I examine how peasant and Indian communities radically transformed relations of property and power in the countryside, a process that has long-lasting effects in present Bolivia.

Redefining Relations of Power and Property from the Bottom-Up

In this book I challenge revisionist analyses that have understood peasant unions as obediently implementing the MNR's political program in the countryside. The demand to organize unions in the countryside predated the revolution. In the late 1930s, for example, *colonos* (laborers who work for a landlord in exchange for farming a small parcel of land within the estate) from several haciendas in La Paz, Cochabamba, and Tarija sought to organize unions.[26] Conservative governments shut them down because they were afraid of colonos' organizing politically on the haciendas.[27] This previous history explains why, as soon as the MNR decreed peasant union organization in 1952, thousands of colonos and *comunarios* (members of still existing corporate Indian communities mostly concentrated in the altiplano of La Paz, Oruro, and Potosí), following the contours of the haciendas and communities, organized hundreds of territorialized unions.[28] According to the government's own reports from Cochabamba, already in 1952, the MNR controlled only 10 percent of the unions.[29] The leader of each union—elected yearly on a rotational basis, a principle that followed the Andean principles of political organization—was in charge of dealing with the heavy agrarian reform bureaucracy, both in their provinces and in the capital city of La Paz. These unions became the most important actors in the implementation of the agrarian reform. They allowed peasants to fight land expropriation as a group rather than as individuals. These practices shaped state-peasant/Indians relations in the countryside. As it was the case prior to the revolution, Indian and peasants understood that only collective action would make them visible to the state and that collective pressure would improve the chances that the government would accept their petitions. Thus, the implementation of the agrarian reform emboldened peasants' communal ties as a means to secure their property and to negotiate with the state. Rather than imposing an individualized experience of citizenship—as revisionist scholars have argued—the unions reinforced a collective relation with the state.[30]

In terms of property relations, my study shows the radical political role played by hacienda workers and indigenous communities in the implementation of the agrarian reform. First, in contrast to what the MNR presumed, I found that, soon after the revolution, the government was reluctant to begin a generalized program of land redistribution and tried instead to introduce a wage system on the haciendas. In the context of the revolution, many landowners were willing to implement this system, but my work reveals that peasants refused any new arrangement without redistribution. By 1954 the government had to give up on the project for rural proletarianization. Over the course of the implementation of the agrarian reform, colonos expanded the limits of land redistribution beyond the large unproductive estates. As a result, many medium-sized and productive properties were also expropriated because of peasant pressure.

Second, I argue that peasant unions led the process of land distribution among the beneficiaries as the government quickly lost control of the process. In the agrarian courts landlords often denounced the continual growth of the number of peasants demanding land. Many landlords complained that not only the colonos on the estates but also their landless relatives were acquiring parcels of land, at the expense of plots that should have remained in the landlords' hands. In many legal cases, the local judges and the Consejo Nacional de Reforma Agraria (CNRA), the National Council of Agrarian Reform, restricted land redistribution only to the colonos. Yet in his verdict, acknowledging how difficult it was to expel peasants who were already occupying the hacienda, the president often ruled differently, declaring the expropriation of the property in favor of all "settlers," whether they were colonos, temporary workers, or landless peasants. The MNR yielded to the peasant unions and allowed them to define the distribution of land among peasants.

Third, my work also reveals the distinct political agenda of ex-comunarios (members of former indigenous communities who had lost their land to the expansion of the hacienda and who had become a dependent labor force on the land they used to work or on neighboring haciendas). I explore how leaders of indigenous communities, who led one of the most important campaigns for land restitution prior to the revolution, adapted the nationalist discourse after the revolution to reclaim their lands. Uneasy with a government agenda that proclaimed "land for those who work it," ex-comunarios proclaimed "land to the original owners." Ex-comunario political action after the revolution succeeded in reshaping the government agrarian agenda, and ex-comunarios used the new legislation to regain lands lost to hacienda landlords since 1900, and in some cases even prior to 1900. In this study I uncover some of the disputes over land that emerged between colonos and ex-comunarios after the agrarian reform. Colonos rightly feared that the ex-comunario principle of "land to the original owners" threatened their own rights to land. Ex-comunarios' struggles for the restitution of their lands and the occasional conflicts with the colonos on the altiplano expose crucial economic differences among peasants after the revolution, a subject scarcely analyzed by previous literature in Bolivia, which often refers to the peasantry as a flat category.[31] The implementation of claims of land restitution also shows that ex-comunarios, when successful, were able to consolidate considerably larger plots of land than colonos.

My analysis of court cases on land distribution shows that the state had only a limited voice and ability in defining the process of land distribution among peasants. The final outcome of this process created a map comprised of both individually and collectively owned plots in a variety of different shapes, sizes, and uses. In fact, the very chaotic and uneven character of this map reveals the strength of bottom-up decisions relative to top-down governmental planning.[32] The government preferred to accept and endorse peasant union plans for land distribution that were rooted in earlier practices rather than risk sparking political conflict in the countryside. Considering the political pressure that the government faced almost from the start of the revolution from the mine and urban workers to radicalize the revolution and from conservative sectors in Bolivia and from the United States to restrained it, the MNR sought to consolidate its alliance with the peasantry by accommodating its nationalist discourse to local political forces.[33] The government signed for the expropriation of a property but then played little role in the internal organization of land redistribution. In the absence of maps or censuses and with very little effective control of Bolivia's territory, official authorities relied heavily on union leaders and communal authorities to implement the long, tedious, and politically less profitable process of land distribution among peasants. In this new political scenario, peasant unions and Indian communities won a major new role in defining land redistribution and mediating the new conflicts among peasants.

The files on agrarian reform show that, over time, peasant unions won legitimacy among their members beyond issues about land. Union leaders began serving as mediators on a number of disputes over property boundaries, rights to pasturelands and water, and even family conflicts. Court cases in the altiplano, the valleys, and the Yungas show the role of communal authorities and union leaders in solving judicial conflicts among peasants and in tying peasants' individual choices to communal decisions. Numerous cases reveal that communal authorities' decisions often outweighed those of local state officials and demonstrate that plaintiffs realized that agreements hammered out locally were the most useful, since the state—whose presence was more nominal than real—had no effective capacity to enforce its edicts. Despite the Bolivian state's weakness, or precisely because of it, peasant unions and peasant communities became powerful political actors in the countryside over the second half of the twentieth century, gaining effective territorial and political control in the countryside.

Finally, in this book I rethink the role of the revolutionary nationalist movement and government in the countryside. Although the MNR showed caution before launching a general program of land distribution, the party undertook critical decisions soon after the revolution that changed the balance of power in the countryside. First, Víctor Paz Estenssoro, afraid of landlords' political maneuvers, dismantled their association known as the Sociedad Rural Boliviana (SRB), Bolivian Rural Society, undermining their capacity to respond as a class. Second, the MNR deactivated the rural councils (the entities that represented the most "notable" neighbors in the province), which before 1952 had been the mediators at the local level between the state and rural society, and replaced them with peasant unions. The elimination of the rural councils and the institution of the unions as a mechanism of political control transformed everyday politics in the countryside. Third, the MNR challenged the church, one of the most important landlords in Bolivia. Fourth, Paz Estenssoro—more pragmatic than dogmatic—signed the decree for community land restitution in 1954, as a state response to Indian political pressures. This last decree clearly diverged from orthodox notions of modernization in nationalist and left circles. These four decisions were political landmarks that contributed toward the radicalization of the political process.

Rethinking the Timing of the Revolution in the Countryside

I also rethink the timing of the revolution in the countryside. A number of scholars have identified that the revolutionary process ended in 1964 when General René Barrientos overthrew the Paz Estenssoro government.[34] Barrientos's regime started a new era of tumultuous military regimes that ended in 1982 when Bolivia returned to democracy. Other scholars have also argued that the MNR became a moderate force if not conservative as early as in 1955. Sergio Almaraz, James Dunkerley, and James Malloy, along with Kevin Young and Steven Cote in their more recent works, state that the decline of the revolution had already begun in 1955 when the MNR shifted to the right. These studies point to the fact that the government approved a new code on hydrocarbons, which opened up investments by US oil companies in 1955, passed an austerity plan for monetary stabilization in 1956, and launched the Triangular Plan, which gave the government a new opportunity to discipline the combatant workers' movement in the mines in 1960.[35] Although these policy changes are key to understanding the course of the revolution, particularly in terms of the government's relation to the United States in the midst of the Cold War, the timing of the revolution in the countryside does not parallel the timing of the revolution in the mines and in the cities. Peasant land seizures started at the end of 1952, yet peasant legal claims for land expropriation began only at the end of 1954. Although president Paz Estenssoro signed few cases of land expropriation in 1955, it was in his second presidency that Paz Estenssoro (1960–1964) boosted land expropriation in favor of former colonos even further than his predecessor President Hernán Siles Zuazo (1956–1960) as a way to consolidate his alliance with the peasants.

After 1964, General René Barrientos (1964–1969), who aggressively repressed the combative miners, as soon as he took power was also eager to secure his alliance with the peasantry. He enacted the Military-Peasant Pact. Scholars such as René Zavaleta Mercado and Rivera Cusicanqui have highlighted that the Military-Peasant Pact favored the military because it have guaranteed peasant subordinated support, we might reconsider the importance of the pact for peasants. When Barrientos took power, dozens of former landlords petitioned the new president to review the last twelve years of agrarian reform.[36] They argued that the MNR had illegally expropriated medium- and small-sized properties as well as those that had significant capital investment. But neither Barrientos nor the more violent regime of General Hugo Bánzer (1971–1978) reversed those processes. In fact, Barrientos enacted key decrees that prohibited any revision of lands already granted to peasants, and in 1975 General Bánzer ended the economic compensation that peasants had to pay to landlords for the land they received as a result of an expropriation.[37] Although most of these decrees simply reinforced a reality that was already in place, the military, unlike other cases in Latin America (Guatemala, Chile, or Peru) were not able to reverse the process of land reform that started in the 1950s. Under the Military-Peasant Pact, peasant unions' control of internal affairs in the countryside continued.

Despite the subordinated relation that peasantry had at the national level, as a number of authors point out, agrarian court cases show it was in the 1960s, 1970s, and 1980s that landlords, unable to recover their old power, sold or abandoned the lands that the government granted them as medium-sized properties because of the continued pressure of the peasant unions. This pressure was applied through everyday forms of revolution, such as former colonos' rejection of work for the former landlord in spite of wage offers, their stealing of livestock, their burning of hacienda houses, which all ended up pushing landlords out of the countryside. It was over the course of 1960s–1980s that the peasant unions won full political and territorial control of the countryside. The countryside became predominantly indigenous. The unions exercised control over all local state positions.

Everyday Forms of Revolution

To track day-to-day peasant struggles within revolutionary times, I adapt James Scott's notion of "everyday forms of resistance" to "everyday forms of revolution."[38] My own notion refers to the ways in which rural actors followed news about the unfolding events of the revolution, how they understood what the revolution was about, and how they accordingly redefined their political engagements. Also, the notion of everyday forms of revolution applies to the almost two decades of legal and political struggles that followed the enactment of the agrarian reform legislation. The signing of the decree led to years of hacienda seizures, livestock theft, union organizing, public auctions, legal disputes, geographic measuring and mapmaking, and government lobbying that went on through sustained small-scale efforts. The notion of everyday forms of revolution challenges the view that the revolutionary state fought for, designed, and pushed through the agrarian reform on its own initiative.[39]

My conception of everyday forms of revolution both stems from and diverges from Scott's call for understanding peasant political practices outside the moment of political rupture, beyond the revolutionary event. Scott understandably sought to foreground everyday resistance as the ordinary mode of peasant struggle in history, arguing against the tradition in peasant studies of focusing on the rare moments of radical and overt peasant revolt, which he also considered less effective in advancing peasant interests. I too am interested in the ordinary and day-to-day agency of peasant political actors. But my work also draws from Sinclair Thomson's critique of Scott. Thomson argues that Scott's emphasis on informal, isolated, petty, and covert acts of resistance unnecessarily privileges "resistance without protest and without organization." This tendency, Thomson continues, plays down the importance of direct action and overt mobilization against the ruling order, which have been recurrent if less constant forms of peasant struggle. I believe that Scott's attention to the quotidian dimension of peasant politics can be productively applied to revolutionary processes as well as nonrevolutionary periods in history.[40]

In the spirit of Scott, and based on innumerable reports from landlords beginning in the late 1930s, my research shows, for example, how before the revolution colonos refused to work the amount of hours expected by landlords, or they gave less of the amount of the harvest than landlords required. All such quotidian, small-scale, and cumulative individual actions weakened the peonage system before the revolution. However, like Thomson, I challenge the idea that these everyday individual actions counted for more than the organized collective action on the part of colonos and Indian community members that was carried out through ongoing and often invisible campaigns to advance their cause in the courts, to pressure political authorities, and to secure and defend the lands they claimed.

Tracking the Voices of the Peasant Actors of the Agrarian Reform

To track peasant political struggles on the ground, I worked at the Agrarian Reform Archives in the cities of La Paz and Cochabamba. There, I reviewed about three hundred court cases (each of them could range from one hundred pages to several volumes) that contained the complaints, arguments, and strategies that peasants and landlords deployed in the conflict over land redistribution. These records became available after government intervention to reorganize the CNRA in 1993. The promulgation of a new agrarian reform law in 1996 further pushed the government to centralize the CNRA archives. Today, these archives—virtually untouched by scholars until now—are accessible at the Institute of Agrarian Reform (INRA) and offer an unprecedented view of decades of agrarian reform. Most trials comprised the history of a property for at least thirty years before the revolution, revealing the ownership and expansion of the large estates and the networks of landlord elites. They offer colonos' descriptions of their life on the hacienda before 1952, as well as descriptions of the landowner elites who have remained obscure behind the country's more visible mining elite. Every trial is also a powerful illustration of the contrast between state proposals and actual state attempts to enforce the laws. Every trial reflects state decisions from the local level to the national level and, thus, the history of what the state could and could not do.

In addition to the Agrarian Reform Archives, I drew on three valuable collections at the Archivo y Biblioteca Nacionales de Bolivia (ABNB), the Bolivian National Archive in Sucre. The Presidential Correspondence (PR) collection gathers letters and requests from all sectors of the society, including many from peasant leaders, indigenous communities, and landowners to the president. The letters offer insight into the proposals, demands, pledges, or political discussions that exceeded the frame of the political party debates or the voices of the recognized leaders. They depict ordinary people from rural and urban backgrounds and their concepts about the revolution, demands concerning land distribution, and views on what was considered fair or legal. Second, Walter Guevara Arze, one of the most important MNR leaders, donated his private documents to the national archive. His collection on the agrarian reform gathers private letters, official reports, and internal debates on land at the time of the revolution.[41] Finally, I used the collection of political pamphlets, political party programs, conference proceedings, and memoirs published throughout the 1940s by different political parties and actors. These offer a wonderful understanding of 1940s political debates, illustrating how each party understood agrarian reform. I completed my research with official correspondence at presidential, departmental, and local levels in the Archivo de La Paz (ALP), the Historical Archives of La Paz and Cochabamba, where I drew on the Prefectural Correspondence (PE) to review local official reports from the 1940s to the 1960s. Finally, at the Biblioteca y Archivo Histórico de la Asamblea Legislativa Plurinacional de Bolivia (BAHALP), the Library and Historical Archive at the Plurinational Legislative Assembly, in La Paz, I looked at laws, decrees, congressional debates, and newspapers. Overall, I used these sources to compare national debates and political party discussions with the everyday struggles at the rural level.

In this work I provide a comparative framework for three distinct and significant regions where the hacienda system was particularly strong: Germán Jordán, a temperate valley where large estates existed alongside expanding small mixed-race properties and where pioneering peasant trade unions grew increasingly influential; Omasuyos, a high plateau area with fertile irrigated land and strong Indian peasant organization; and Sud Yungas, a highland valley area profitable for coca-growing landlords where the peasants were less strong politically. Each province constitutes a window for understanding the hacienda system in a specific region—the valleys of Cochabamba, the semitropical valleys, and the highlands of La Paz. Despite the striking geographical differences and their distinct histories in terms of the expansion of the hacienda, the three regions make up the core of the latifundio (extensive estates) in the country prior to the revolution. Peasant political mobilization was also prominent in all the provinces before and after the revolution. First, President Paz Estenssoro decided to sign the Agrarian Reform Decree-Law in the historic village of Ucureña in the province of Germán Jordán. This decision was a recognition of the early organization of peasant unions in this region. Second, decades prior to the revolution, mobilized indigenous leaders organized rural schools all across

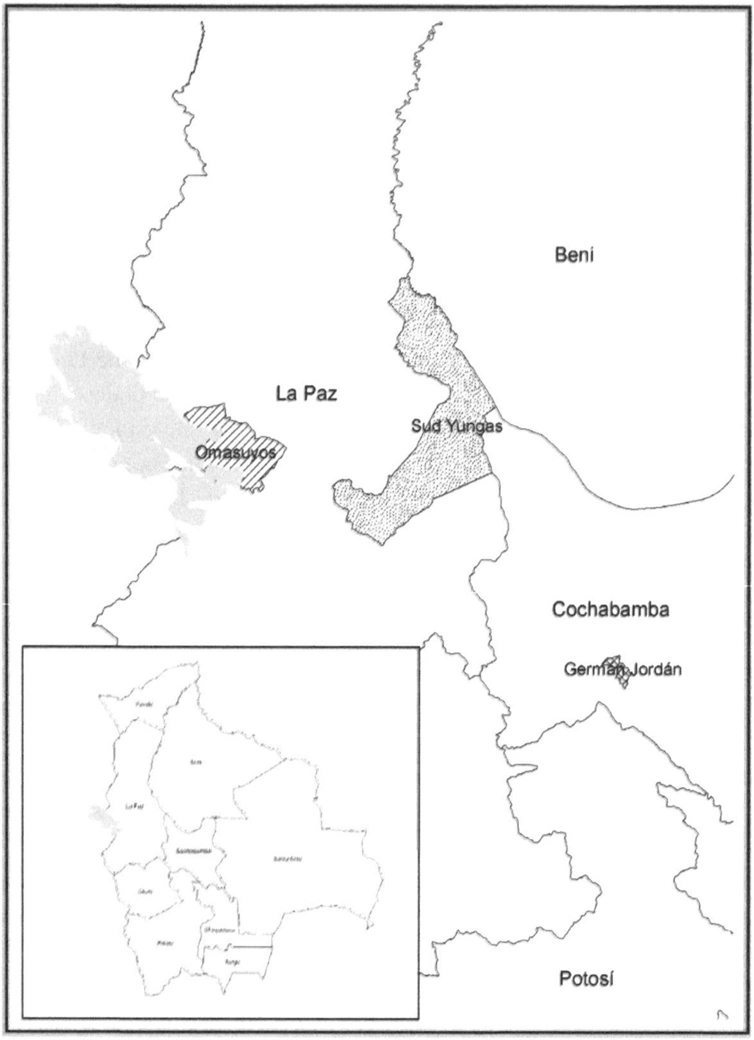

Map 1. Elaborated by José Octavio Orsag. The map indicates the three provinces described in this study: Omasuyos and Sud Yungas in La Paz and Germán Jordán in Cochabamba.

the altiplano, and the movement was particularly strong in Warisata in the province of Omasuyos. The most combative peasant union leaders after the revolution—such as Jorge Soliz, Luciano Quispe, and Toribio Salas—came from Ucureña (Germán Jordán) and Achacachi (Omasuyos). Third, several middle- and high-ranked leaders of the MNR came from the province of Sud Yungas. After the revolution, landowner Federico Álvarez Plata became not only one of the most prominent members of the MNR but also member to the Commission for Agrarian Reform.

My study of court cases in the three regions shows very similar tendencies: local judges tended to ratify local agreements, favoring the strongest voices in the region. For instance, in Omasuyos, where peasant unions held strong, local judges qualified several properties as latifundios, regardless of their investment. In Sud Yungas, where landlords preserved some power after 1952, judges granted almost all landlords at least 150 hectares, the maximum for a medium-sized property in the region according to law. The Ministerio de Asuntos Campesinos (MAC), the Ministry of Peasant Affairs and the president of the republic closely followed local verdicts. If applying any technical and legal criteria suggested by the CNRA meant sparking political conflict in the countryside, the president overlooked the law and changed the final verdict. For instance, large estates with demonstrated investment or medium-sized properties would be declared latifundios if this guaranteed that the strong peasants' unions in Germán Jordán and Omasuyos would be appeased. In other words, politics rather than legal or technical criteria shaped the course of the agrarian reform.

Remapping Bolivian Agrarian Reform

In this work I examine Bolivia's radical redefinition of property relations and power in the countryside beginning a decade before the revolution and continuing through to the 1960s, although some of the court cases lasted even up into the mid-1980s. In Chapter One, we analyze the central place of land in establishing, consolidating, and reifying the power of elites. In both buoyant times and downturns, miners, businessman, and politicians acquired land to secure their capital. We study a conservative program for land reform that emerged a decade prior to the revolution. This program saw landlords as the centerpiece of the economic change and development. In Chapter Two, we see debates over "agrarian reform" among left- and right-wing politicians prior to the revolution and examine how both the right- and left-wing parties' technical and avowedly scientific considerations of the agrarian question were deeply embedded in racial ideologies that saw indigenous communal landholding as incompatible with ideals of productivity and modernization. The focus in Chapter Three is on the first two years of the revolution, and on how expectations about "what the revolution could bring" changed for all political actors: the MNR's top leaders, civil servants, colonos, majordomos (hacienda administrators), and landlords, which reflects the fragmentary and complex politics of the revolution. We also track the failure of the MNR's moderate program of labor reform that preceded the agrarian reform. The nationalist party expected that turning colonos into waged workers would be sufficient to appease the turmoil in the countryside. But the program ultimately failed as colonos organized unions and militias that rejected attempts to limit reform to the renegotiation of labor contracts and instead forced the government to decree land redistribution.

In Chapters Four, Five, and Six we survey the politics behind land distribution. In Chapter Four, we look closely at the charged debates that followed the 1952 national revolution on agrarian reform. By tracing local petitions, intellectual proposals, and political party debates, I portray the challenges of running an expanded program of land reform that would expropriate hundreds of rural private properties. I also show the crucial role of Latin American intellectuals, especially those from Guatemala and Mexico, in nurturing Bolivian debates. Once the government enacted the law, we track the two most iconic cases of land distribution in Ucureña and Achacachi, both of which demonstrate the key role of peasant leaders in radicalizing the process from the start and from below. In Chapter Five, I engage with former members of indigenous communities' distinctive claims to land. Previously scholars have assumed that communal demands vanished with the MNR's enthusiastic embrace of a modernization plan focused on implementing a medium- to small-size individualized system of property. Instead, I show how ex-comunarios pressured the government to enact a decree for communal land restitution that challenged not only the properties of large established landlords but also, in some cases, lands more recently granted to other peasants. In Chapter Six, we see the effective transfer of ownership to the peasants. In this transfer, the government gradually stripped itself of the legal principles that the law had imposed to protect the owners of medium-sized properties or the landlords who had demonstrated investment by privileging distribution of land to peasants. We also see the leading role of peasants' unions in the land-allocation process. The multiplicity of shapes, sizes, and uses of land reflected on the new map of property that emerged after 1953 were rooted in the complex and contentious historic, social, and geographic practices of peasants rather than in the uniform vision of a successful state modernization project. In the final part of the chapter, we trace agrarian reform policies following MNR's overthrow in November 1964. Reviewing new demands concerning land distribution I show that military regimes were incapable of undoing the agrarian reform in the altiplano and valleys, but that landlords' old power continued to erode over the course of thirty years. It was over the 1960s, 1970s, and 1980s that peasants transformed the countryside into their own world.

CHAPTER ONE

THE LIBERAL PROJECT IN THE COUNTRYSIDE

> Unique opportunity for capitalists. On sale a magnificent hacienda, which has access to a valley and mountains. The hacienda is in Mecapaca, a one-hour drive from La Paz city. *Peonada* [peons, a term with derogatory connotations] are settled and obedient. The property has a modern house, electricity, and drinking water. Great Price. For more information call Salustio Lissón law firm.
>
> **Property sale advertised in *El Diario*, March 21, 1948**

In 1825, when Bolivia was born as a new republic, about 89 percent of the population lived in the countryside. The situation changed very little over the next one hundred years. In 1950, 76 percent of the population continued to live in the rural areas. Yet, during that century a dramatic transformation in land property took place. In the first half of the nineteenth century Indian communities controlled two-thirds of Bolivia's cultivable land, but by the 1950s they held only 26 percent.[1] Such a decrease in ownership reflected an assault on Indian collective property by the implementation of European liberalism in the countryside through the expansion of the hacienda system. Land privatization had not only stripped Indian communities of their former properties; it had also transformed a large number of their members into menial workers (see figure 1.1).

Although mining exports had connected the country to the world market for much of Bolivia's colonial and postcolonial history, landownership and access to free labor were central to the creation and accumulation of wealth. Land property was crucial to obtaining, sustaining, and generating economic capital as well as to gaining access to other forms of capital. Mineowners, industry owners, merchants, and politicians, eager to secure their capital against changes in economic and political fortune, all bought land. Land allowed the emergent middle class as well as the more successful elites, to maintain their place in high society. Regardless of the size of their capital, their social pedigrees, or their political connections, the work on most haciendas was based on unpaid labor. The prevalence of this

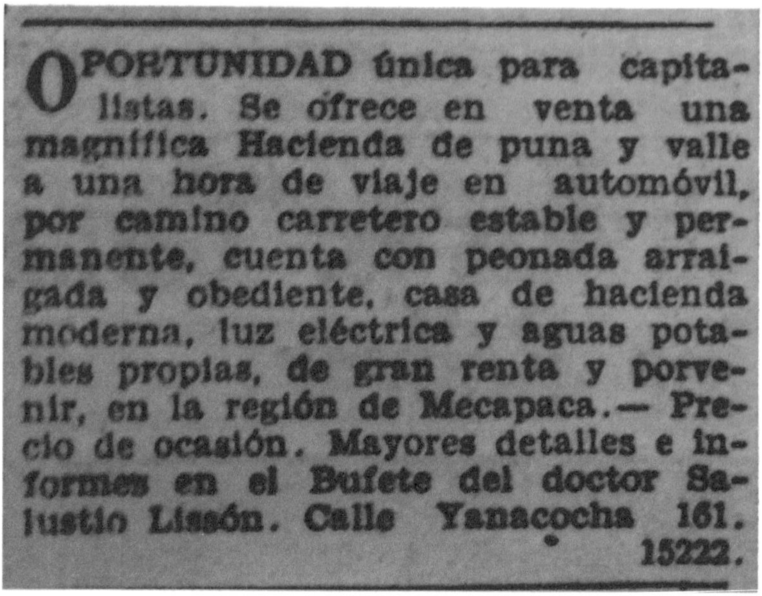

OPORTUNIDAD única para capitalistas. Se ofrece en venta una magnífica Hacienda de puna y valle a una hora de viaje en automóvil, por camino carretero estable y permanente, cuenta con peonada arraigada y obediente, casa de hacienda moderna, luz eléctrica y aguas potables propias, de gran renta y porvenir, en la región de Mecapaca.— Precio de ocasión. Mayores detalles e informes en el Bufete del doctor Salustio Lissón. Calle Yanacocha 161. 15222.

Figure 1.1. Property for sale, including colonos, from *El Diario*, March 21, 1948. Courtesy of Biblioteca y Archivo Histórico de la Asamblea Legislativa Plurinacional.

labor regime among large, medium-, and even small-sized property owners demonstrates how the seigniorial mentality and the practice of appropriation of labor went far beyond the small circle of the richest landlord elite. The hacienda system was hierarchical and racist, but it's allowance for some to aspire to social mobility helped the system persist for centuries. Elected colonos (working as majordomos for a year) might receive one-fifth of the harvest of the hacienda, and many colonos imagined they might someday buy their own plots with their own colonos. Such possibilities inspired many to invest in the success of the hacienda system, even if they weren't landlords themselves.

The historiography of the pre-1952 period has usually underlined the contrast between a dynamic mining economy and a stagnant traditional land production system.[2] These studies rightly drew attention to the servile conditions of work, the traditional means of production, and subsistence-oriented production.[3] The advertisement quoted above, one of dozens posted daily in local newspapers in the years before the revolution, illustrates the prevalence of a deeply hierarchical society in which subservient labor relations predominated. In this case, the "obedient peons" living and working in the hacienda were included in the sale. But, as the ad also suggests, the market for rural land was far from stagnant. Land was subject to constant transactions. On top of that, since the late 1930s, many landlords started investing in their properties by importing pure-bred livestock and installing modest industries producing dairy, jams, alcohol, or tiles for the local market or introducing services such as electricity or water. These economic investments were the outcome not solely of landlords' individual efforts but also of a larger state-run program that sought to modernize the countryside. A decade prior to the revolution, right-wing political elites started a conservative program for land reform that put landlords at the center of the economic change and development. The 1952 national revolution and the agrarian reform not only broke up manorial estates and abolished feudal-like servitude but also sidelined this conservative program of land reform that aimed to modernize the rural area by investing in rural properties based on unpaid Indian labor.

The Weight of the Rural Economy in Bolivia

Land tenure and the expansion of the hacienda in Bolivia were deeply linked to the country's mining economy. Since the early colonial period, mining structured and fueled the economy of the Andean Republic of Bolivia. Carlos Sempat Assadourian identifies the extended colonial economic circuit that flourished around the mining industry as an Andean economic space that spanned present-day Peru, Bolivia, Northern Argentina, and Chile.[4] Although some of these regional trade networks fell apart after independence and the creation of national borders, the agricultural production of the departments of Chuquisaca, La Paz, Oruro, Cochabamba, and Potosí in Bolivia continued to be tied to mining centers during the nineteenth century and much of the twentieth century.

The three provinces that are the subject of this study—Germán Jordán in the valleys of Cochabamba, Omasuyos in the highlands, and Sud Yungas in subtropical valleys of La Paz—exemplified well the deep connections between land tenure, agricultural production, and mining exploitation. In the valleys of Cochabamba and Yungas, latifundios (large estates) flourished during the colonial period as a direct result of the mining industry. Cochabamba's fertile valleys with their rich production of cereals and their proximity to the mines of Potosí turned the region into an early target for the expansion of the hacienda. Similarly, landlords were attracted to the substantial revenue earned from selling the coca leaves of the semitropical valleys of Yungas in cities and mining centers.[5] In the highlands of Omasuyos Province, indigenous communities' ability to retain their communal lands was also connected to the history of mining industry. The Aymara communities of the Bolivian highlands (an enormous tableland at extremely high altitude known in Bolivia as the altiplano) were able to maintain communal land for much of the colonial period because the Spanish Crown recognized it in exchange for corvée labor in the mines (mita) and the payment of tribute.

Economic fluctuation in the mining economy continued to shape political debates on land tenure after independence. Initial discussions on privatization of Indian communal land started immediately after the creation of the new republic. Simón Bolivar, the hero of the South American wars for independence and the country's first president, took the first step to dismantle Indians' corporate entities by creating a system of individual property. In 1824, Bolivar abolished the colonial tributes that Indian communities were required to pay, considering them one of the most repugnant signs of colonialism. However, his efforts were short-lived. Only two years later, unable to get revenues from the devastated mining industry, which had been destroyed in the independence wars, President José Antonio José de Sucre (1825–1828) restored the Indian tribute.[6] This tribute, renamed an "indigenous contribution" (*contribución indigenal*), represented the state's most important source of income until the 1860s.[7] Tristan Platt demonstrates that Indian communities were willing to pay the tribute as they had in the colonial period, as this guaranteed them state recognition of communal lands.[8] This fiscal pact between the state and the indigenous communities lasted about four decades.

The privatization of indigenous communal lands after independence started only in the second half of the nineteenth century. Once again, these policies were deeply connected to the economic fluctuations in the mining economy. Once mining exports replaced Indian tributes as the most important source of state revenue, emboldened local elites launched a more systematic assault against Indian communal property in the densely populated highlands of La Paz. President Mariano Melgarejo (1864–1871) launched one of the most brutal attacks on Indian communal lands in 1866. He abolished communal property and declared that Indians could only be individual owners of land parcels if they paid a fee within sixty days.[9] Unable to pay these fees, Indians lost their communal lands, which the government then sold at auctions to private bidders.[10] Laura Gotkowitz points out that "between 1866 and 1869, government auctioneers sold the land of 356 communities to private bidders." This took place primarily in La Paz, in the most densely populated provinces of Omasuyos, Pacajes, Ingavi, Sicasica, and Muñecas.[11]

Melgarejo's decree sparked a series of indigenous uprisings that briefly stopped the process of land privatization. After Melgarejo's overthrown in 1871, the National Assembly that met in Sucre in 1871 agreed to abrogate Melgarejo's decree. Yet, three years later President Tomas Frías (1874–1876) signed the Ley de Ex-vinculación, the Disentailment Law, a more refined attempt to abolish Indian communal property.[12] In contrast to Melgarejo's decree, Frías promised that the process of dividing individual plots among Indians would take place only with the consent of community members. Despite these safeguards the privatization policies that continued for much of the late nineteenth and early twentieth centuries severely curtailed indigenous communities' control over their lands. Elites championed the implementation of European liberalism in the Bolivian countryside and zealously defended private property at the expense of Indian collective property. And they did not hesitate to abuse their political influence so as to seize communal land. In the first decades of the twentieth century, prominent figures of the Liberal Party such as President Ismael Montes blatantly seized entire Indian communities and then turned them into personal haciendas.[13] The result of more than seven decades of land privatization were palpable in the first half of the twentieth century: Until the 1850s, the majority of the rural population continued to live in ayllus (Indian communities), which covered about two-thirds of cultivable land. But by 1950 Indian communities only held roughly one-third of cultivated property.[14]

Portrait of the Landed Elite in the Twentieth Century

How does this twentieth-century elite compare to the landlord elite of the colonial period? Herbert Klein's study on land tenure in colonial Yungas refers to a powerful rural elite who each held not one but several large estates. Klein notes the wealthy Tadeo Diez de Medina, who owned fifteen different properties in Yungas. Like their counterparts in the colonial period, many landlords in the nineteenth and twentieth centuries sought to accumulate multiple properties. For instance, the wealthiest landlord in Achacachi, Eulogio Franco, held seven large properties totaling six thousand hectares. In Sud Yungas, Héctor Lorini, held eight properties in three different provinces. Santa Clara Monastery owned the largest rural estate in Cliza, in Germán Jordán province, and smaller properties in the neighboring province of Quillacollo.[15]

Considering Bolivia's extremely diverse geography, it is difficult to compare the concentration of land in one region with that in another. The largest property in Germán Jordán was 800 hectares (Santa Clara), in Omasuyos (Casamaya) it was 19,332 hectares, and in Sud Yungas (Callisaya), 65,000 hectares. At the time of the revolution, when the government enacted the expropriation of the country's large estates, it instituted region-specific limits for the maximum size of a medium-sized property. For instance, in Germán Jordán, the maximum limit for a medium-sized property was 24 hectares (for the best cultivable); in Omasuyos and in Sud Yungas it was 150 hectares. The comparison of these parameters to those of the largest properties existing in each region prior to the revolution highlights the degree of land concentration. (See tables 1.1–1.3 in Appendix 1.1 to track the names and sizes of the largest haciendas of the three provinces.)

There was a close bond between landownership and other types of political and economic capital. The families of prestigious lawyers and politicians in La Paz city had ties to landlords in Omasuyos. The writer and diplomat Joaquín Aguirre Lavayén who lived in the city of Cochabamba owned a sizable property in Germán Jordán. Through these ties, landlords developed key urban and political alliances that helped them solidify their power and authority in the countryside.

Landlords also used family alliances to amass land. In Omasuyos, a network of families—Imaña, Monterrey, and Mollinedo—intermarried and consolidated a vast number of properties and political power in that region. Together, the group owned about ten properties and controlled 3,574 hectares. In Germán Jordán, the five Quiroga siblings owned five different properties. Their connections grew stronger when the women in the family married other landlords in the same province. Although many of these families lost their lands after the revolution, the links between political power and landholding continued. A number of influential MNR politicians, including Guevara and Arze in Cochabamba and Álvarez Plata and Lorini in La Paz, belonged to traditional landlord families.

Equally strong were the ties between mining capitals and rural property. The three wealthiest tin magnates in the country—Simón Patiño, Carlos Víctor Aramayo, and Mauricio Hochschild, who together controlled 80 percent of tin exports—had or developed investments in land. Patiño was considered to be one of the five richest men in the world in the 1940s. He controlled about half of the country's tin production.[16] He gained two hundred square leagues of land concessions (paying 10 cents per hectare) along the Chaparé, Chimoré, Mamoré, and Isiboro Rivers in exchange for building the railway between Cochabamba and Chimoré. In the same contract, the state granted Patiño forty hectares on each side of the railway for twenty-five years.[17] The father of Carlos Víctor Aramayo was the second of three generations of mining industrialists who diversified the family's wealth by acquiring the monopoly of the administration of the large territory of El Acre under the presidency of José Manuel Pando (1899–1904).[18] For his part, the wealthy mineowner Mauricio Hochschild created a company that imported Chilean fertilizers to the countryside in the 1940s.[19] This is not an exhaustive research into Patiño's, Aramayo's or Hochschild's rural investments. Rather, these examples show the astute ways in which Bolivia's wealthiest mineowners used their economic power to secure other concessions from the state and to position themselves for future economic possibilities. Finally, there was a flourishing relationship between land property and

Table 1.4. Properties in the Hands of Landlords and Communities

	Landlords with Colonos		Communities	
Size in Hectares	**Number of Properties**	**Percentage**	**Number of Properties**	**Percentage**
From 0 to 99	3,625	44.5	1,826	48.3
100 to 999.9	2,363	29.0	955	25.3
1,000 to 10,000	1,951	24.1	856	22.7
No information	198	2.4	142	3.7
TOTAL	8,137		3,779	

Source: Developed by the author based on Ministerio de Asuntos Campesinos y Agropecuarios, Instituto Nacional de Estadística, Organización de las Naciones Unidas para la Agricultura y la Alimentación *I Censo Agropecuario 1950*, 25–27.

industry. Factory owners in the nascent industry of La Paz also constituted a new landlord elite in Yungas. Domingo Soligno, owner of one of the most important textile industries in La Paz, held a large (six-thousand-hectare) and poorly cultivated property called Iquico-Totoral.[20]

Economic fluctuations in the mining or industrial sector had deep effects on the value of rural property and patterns of landownership. Erick Langer, who studied the hacienda regime in the southern region of Chuquisaca, explains that economic crises in the mining sector in the second half of the nineteenth century spurred investments in land. He shows that private owners acquired rural land to compensate for their economic losses in mining. Land, in contrast to mining, was a safe investment for riding out economic vicissitudes: "Once the silver magnates realized that land had become their financial mainstay, they poured a considerable amount of capital into their estates to improve their profitability."[21]

We find very similar patterns in Cochabamba after the 1929 economic crisis. Although several historians have shown that the fertile valleys of Cochabamba faced ongoing land fragmentation, often dating back to the end of the colonial period, analysis of agrarian court cases demonstrates that the 1929 economic recession led to a reconcentration of property.[22] One of the most significant examples of the reconcentration of land in the province of Germán Jordán was, once again, Simón Patiño. After the 1929 recession, and as a way to channel some of his investments from mining to land, Patiño bought two large properties in the province of Germán Jordán as gifts for two of his closest employees—the Quiroga and the Abasto families. Each property was three hundred hectares, making them two of the largest in the province.[23] Patiño's strategic decision was not unique. The crises in the mining sector in the late 1920s encouraged a number of other minor mineowners to invest in land.

Table 1.5. Structure of Property according to the 1950 Agricultural Census

	Hectares	%	Cultivated Hectares	%
Farmer	9,526,421	29.1	123,328	18.85
Farmer with colonos	12,701,076	38.8	290,165	44.35
Renters (*arrendatarios* y medieros)	2,365,879	7.2	49,673	7.59
Indigenous Communities	7,178,448	22	170,106	26
Other	978,023	2.9	20,986	3.21

Source: Ministerio de Asuntos Campesinos y Agropecuarios, *Censo Agropecuario 1950*, ii.

The concentration of land in few hands prior to the revolution was undeniable, yet previous scholars have overemphasized the extent of concentration of land in Bolivia. Several scholars indicate that 6 percent of the population held 92 percent of the cultivable land.[24] But in these considerations they wrongly assume that all properties of over one thousand hectares belonged to private landlords and ignore the fact that some Indian communities still had properties of more than a thousand hectares. In all, 1,951 private estates and 856 Indian communities held properties of more than one thousand hectares (see table 1.4).[25]

Bolivia's first national agricultural report published in 1950 shows that 1.78 percent of the population controlled about 44 percent of the cultivated rural property.[26] The fact that landlords held 44 percent (instead of 92 percent) of the cultivable land indicates that, prior to the revolution, property structure in Bolivia was much more diverse than was previously appreciated (see table 1.5). The census shows that landlords held about 12 million hectares (290,164 under cultivation) and communities held 7 million hectares (170,106 in crops) while 18.8 percent of properties were in the hands of so-called independent farmers. Haciendas and ayllus (Indian communities) continued to be the predominant system of property in the rural area. However, the balance of power favored landlords who controlled most of the cultivable land, had access to free labor, and were able to grow and strengthen their power through alliances with the emergent political, mining, and industrial elites.

There were remarkable economic and social differences among landlords. The term landlord elite (*elite terrateniente*), often used in Bolivian political debate to describe landowners in the countryside, tended to lump together groups that had highly diverse economic portfolios and capital funds.[27] Owners of one small hacienda each, with relatively few colonos, were grouped together with owners whose holdings spread over vast sections of the province.[28] Below this super wealthy elite, there was an extended group of second-tier landlords who each owned one medium-sized property. Although they did not have the political and economic connections of the wealthiest landowners, they had strong influence at the local political level. Beneath both groups, there was another group of minor landholders who increased the size of their properties one hectare at a time over many years. Additionally, in the three provinces there were large numbers of petty traders, craftsmen, and public functionaries working in the countryside who took advantage of their regional knowledge to acquire rural properties. Peasants and, in some cases, former colonos bought small pieces of land. Like the wealthiest landlords, these successful entrepreneurs relied on the servile work of colonos. In other words, holding both rural property and colonos was part of a broader strategy for accumulation not solely limited to a small established landlord class.

Another common feature of the three provinces was the vitality of the land market. Agrarian court cases show that the price of the properties typically increased during the first half of the twentieth century in spite of—or maybe precisely because of—the 1929 economic crisis. Land was a secure investment, and it proved to be a magnificent mechanism for accumulating wealth. For example, a study of the property transactions of one hacienda in Sud Yungas (Charvina Grande) reveals that the property had nine different owners over a period of thirty years. On average, each landlord owned the property for about three years. The price of the property fluctuated significantly over this time period, demonstrating the dynamism of the market. In 1919, Charvina was sold for twenty-six thousand bolivianos; it was sold again for ninety-five thousand bolivianos in 1935, and again in 1950 for roughly two million bolivianos.[29] This was not an exceptional case. An extended network of real-estate companies (as in the epigraph above) reveals the existence of a healthy land market before the revolution. The liberal project of the late nineteenth century opened up the market for land in the countryside and allowed the unlimited concentration of land.

Landlords' use of land varied considerably from one hacienda to the next. Analysis of five large estates in Omasuyos province reveals very distinct patterns. On the largest and most productive estate of Casamaya, the landlord used 86.9 percent of the property for breeding cattle. At the other extreme, the owner of Murumani cultivated only 0.3 percent of his property and allowed his colonos to use 1.8 percent of the cultivable land (see table 1.6 in Appendix 1.1 for specific examples in Omasuyos). Regardless, colonos' access to land within the hacienda was very restricted. In the best-case scenario, colonos used 30 percent of the property, whereas on other estates colonos' use of land barely reached 10 percent. Such data contradict the assumption of government officials in the 1940s who allegedly (based on technical studies) argued that landlords controlled only 19 percent of the land and, in practice, colonos generally cultivated 80.9 percent of any property for their own gain.[30] Regardless of the distribution of land among landlords and colonos, in general the productivity of most haciendas tended to be low. Despite their diverse economic portfolios, distinct social upbringings, and varied political connections, very few landlords introduced a salaried system on their properties. Until 1952 the overwhelming majority of landlords continued to use the colonato, a system of work that landlords defended zealously as part of their "uses and customs."[31]

"In Defense of Our Uses and Customs"

> We worked all day and every day in the countryside, except Sundays. Yet if the landlord got a sale contract we had to work on Sunday as well. In exchange he would give us 2 or 3 Bs for that day. At night, after untying the yokes, we started packaging and wrapping the corn until late at night. It was only after fulfilling our work in the countryside that we began our service as colonos. Insults were part of everyday treatment and sometimes he ordered the majordomo to beat us and to confine us in the house.
>
> **Report from colono Domingo Zurita, INRA-CBBA, Germán Jordán Province, box 4, file Liquinas.**

The predominant system of work in the haciendas was the colonato. The hacienda laborers worked on a landlord's property about five days a week without economic compensation. As part of their work, colonos were in charge of plowing, planting, harvesting, milking cows, working as house help, repairing stables, barns, fences, and roads, and taking the cattle out to graze. Colonos were also responsible for transporting and commercializing the hacienda's staples.[32] Although some colonos complained about the harshness of the work, many more complained that these tasks had to be accomplished at their own expense: they had to buy the rope to bundle the harvest, use their own animals for transportation, and provide their own tools for sowing and harvesting the landlord's land. In cases where landlords bought tractors, colonos often were responsible for paying for the fuel.[33] During periods of religious festivities, colonos were in charge of preparing the *chicha* (a beverage made of fermented corn), and many complained that they were expected to butcher their own animals for such celebrations as well. Colonos were often made to work as *pongos* and their wives as *mitanis* (a system that forced colonos and their wives to work as servants in landlords' houses), rotating between the countryside and the city. According to colonos' reports, the harshest work was in the city since colonos had to provide their own transportation, work twelve hours a day, and sleep out on the landlords' patio. The exploitation of an individual affected the condition of the entire family. As colonos had almost no time to cultivate their own plots, their wives, offspring, and poor relatives became crucial to the family's subsistence.[34]

Many landlords used contracts to force colonos to pay the taxes levied on their haciendas. A notebook, which was used to register the contracts between landlords and colonos in Canton Totora (in Germán Jordán Province in Cochabamba), serves as proof of this practice from 1888 onward.[35] In each contract, colonos who were mostly illiterate promised to pay the portion of the tax that corresponded to the plot of land they used within the hacienda. Tellingly, the contracts imposed no obligations on the landlord. Landlords used these mechanisms to guarantee colonos' payments and to make them accountable to local offices. Beginning in the 1930s, militants of the left-wing and nationalist parties would demand a contract between landlords and colonos to grant the latter some basic rights. Landlords roundly rejected all proposals that would limit their control over colonos' lives and their labor in the haciendas. The colonato system was so widely accepted in Bolivia that all private landlords, public institutions, and ecclesiastic institutions used it. Even state farms created in the 1940s and run by the Ministry of Agriculture, the army, and the university continued to rely on colonos' work.[36]

In exchange for their work on the hacienda, colonos had access to plots that they used to cultivate crops for subsistence and sometimes agricultural produce to sell at the market. Often they also had access to the pastures and woodlands for domestic use. Yet the utilization of these areas was not always free. In several haciendas, colonos had to pay with an animal or two each year. Agrarian court cases show that colonos' use of pastures and woodlands was at the heart of an ongoing conflict between them and the landlords. Colonos' reports from hacienda Alcoholería (in Germán Jordán) assert that the landlord, with a rifle in his hand, would fake the public execution of the offender in front other colonos to menace workers who dared to use the hacienda's pastures. In the first decades of the twentieth century, some congressmen made efforts to regulate this conflict. The most forceful policy on this matter was a decree enacted by President Villarroel in 1945 that guaranteed colonos free access to the hacienda pastures and woodlands for domestic use.[37]

On all the large estates, majordomos (hacienda administrators) managed the hacienda. They were often local mestizo residents who could follow up with work on the property. According to Donato Zurita, former colono of Liquinas in Cochabamba, "majordomos were harsher than landlords; they would report any minor mistake to the owners."[38] On the altiplano, some landlords used *hilacatas* (traditional Indian authorities) to supervise the work of colonos.[39] In exchange of their service, the hilacatas were given one-fifth of the hacienda's production.[40] On many haciendas, the landlord unilaterally designated one of his loyal colonos as a hilacata; in others, colonos could elect their hilacatas for one year, a practice reminiscent of the system by which authorities were elected in the ayllus. Landlords usually confirmed the selected hilacata. This demonstrates both the persistence of Andean practices within the structure of the hacienda and the astute ways in which landlords used them to administrate their estate.

To keep the colonato system in place, landlords and majordomos maintained strict control over the colonos' bodies. Physical punishment was widely used to enforce discipline; confiscation of goods or houses was another commonly used mechanism of punishment. At the time of the agrarian reform, hundreds of colonos complained about how landlords took their clothes, their harvest, or their animals to punish them for minor mistakes. Court cases after the agrarian reform are packed with colonos' vivid descriptions of their working conditions prior to the revolution. Esteban Mamani, former colono and leader of the union at the Tari hacienda, summarized the long list of abuses he and his fellow laborers suffered while working for landlord Irene Riveros de Oviedo:

> We also worked at her home in La Paz city. And we did not get a dime for it. She rented our labor to work with other landlords. For example, we were working for another landlord extracting sand. Señora Riveros got a lot of money for our work. We got nothing. If we refused to follow her orders, she threatened to evict us and seize our belongings. She even collected money from us to buy the roof of the church and if we did not pay, she ordered the removal of the roof from our houses. Miguel Mamani . . . Rufino Gutierrez, Tiburcio Mamani, Venancio Mamani, Alberto Nina, Marcelino Limachi, Calixto Mamani lost the roofs of their houses. She also fired some of the colonos from the hacienda, and when that happened, she seized the harvest of the evicted colonos for herself.[41]

This also reveals the landlords' broad use of the free labor of the colonos. Landlords often relocated colonos from their agricultural settings to work in the city, the mines, or other industries, even renting their labor to other landlords. All of this was allegedly permitted since the colonos had access to a plot of land.

Eviction was another means of punishment at the landlords' disposal. Landlords evicted a number of their workers to repress colonos' sit-down strikes in the early 1940s and their uprisings in the late 1940s.[42] Colonos accused many landlords of burning the homes of peasant leaders (called *cabecillas*) and ousting them from the property, which forced them to look for work in the mines.[43] Imprisonment was one of the last resources used for control. Although in most towns, landlords and their relatives occupied all civic and political positions, there was a great deal of rivalry among local landlords.[44] A landlord seeking to put a colono in jail required the compliance of several local authorities—the intendant, the police, the judge, and the *corregidor*. In the end, it was easier to exercise punishments within the hacienda where the landlord was the unquestionable master. Landlords were cautious about publicizing conflicts with their colonos. In contrast, the prefectural archives of Cochabamba and La Paz are filled with the recorded denunciations of landlords' mistreatment. Sometimes these complaints were directly raised by colonos, sometimes by local authorities, and at other times by rival landlords.[45]

Considering how little support colonos could find when appealing to state authorities, mobility was probably one of the few means available to them in seeking to escape the prevailing coercive work system. Many opted to find work on a different hacienda. The files on agrarian reform indicate that many colonos stated they had worked on the hacienda for five or six years before the revolution; few reported they had worked there for more than fifteen years.[46] This shows that the colonos moved relatively frequently from one hacienda to another. Dandler and Torrico, in their study of hacienda Yayani (in Ayopaya in Cochabamba), confirm this tendency. They explain that, after the rebellion in 1947, many fugitive colonos worked in different haciendas or in the mines. At the same time, these authors recognize that hacienda Yayani often recruited expelled colonos from other remote haciendas or from the valleys of Cochabamba.[47] This references a strong internal migration that we still need to study. We find similar rotational patterns in Yungas and the altiplano. When colonos migrated to other haciendas or to the mines they lost access to their plots of land and the improvements they had made in their parcels. Those improvements often included the construction of a house and their savings in crops from previous harvests—cereals (in Cochabamba), tubers (on the altiplano), and coca leaves (in Yungas). We know of these practices of eviction because of the countless reports that colonos presented before the local judge or the subprefect demanding the restitution of their capital.

Although power dynamics favored landlords over colonos, landlords' need for workers granted colonos few rights. The shortage of labor rather than any law or humanitarian consideration caused landlords to grant pastures to colonos or to restrict the violence they could exercise over them. In Yungas, where the shortage of manpower was more evident, landlords were willing to offer colonos symbolic wages in addition to their plots of land in order to attract workers from the altiplano (whether from Bolivia or Peru).[48] Some of these colonos turned into sharecroppers in Yungas. In contrast to colonos, sharecroppers were not subject to *pongueaje* (obligatory unpaid servitude); they usually had a clear contractual relationship with the landowner detailing the amount of time the tenant would remain on the property and the type of investment and revenue both landlord and tenant would receive from the harvest. However, the distinctions between colono and sharecropper were not clear-cut, and their roles varied considerably from one hacienda to another.

Landlords defended the colonato system as a fair exchange for the plot of land given to peasants on a private estate.[49] Some even claimed that colonos' work on the hacienda or at the landlord's home was the only contact Indians had with civilization.[50] Critics focused on landlords who treated their colonos badly but then neglected to challenge the system itself. For instance, landlord Macario Escobari in Achacachi argued that he treated his colonos well because he had created a school on the hacienda, hired a teacher for peasant children, and bought medicine for the colonos. His language, like that of critics, is framed in terms of paternalist generosity and kindness rather than in terms of workers' rights.[51] After the Chaco War, an increasing number of left-leaning and nationalist student and workers' organizations as well as political organizations raised their voices against the colonato system. Landlords defended their right to preserve their "uses and customs" against foreign and radical ideas.

Landlord and Colonos, Worlds Connected, Worlds Apart

The landlord-colono relationship was defined not only along the lines of property and class but also by strong ethnic differences. The members of the landlord elite were typically white or mestizo (mixed-race), and they used this distinction to justify the presumption that their presence in the countryside helped to enlighten the Indians. In his research on the altiplano at the time of the revolution, anthropologist William Carter describes a society that was highly stratified along the lines of education, geography, economic access, and political power:

> Ruling whites concentrated in the large cities; mestizo "petite bourgeoisie" divided their ranks between cities and towns; and subjugated Indians clung to time-honored traditions in ancient, rural communities. Whites attended high-school and university; mestizos took a few years of grade school; and the Indian was left illiterate. Whites traveled to other South American countries, to Europe, and to the United States; mestizos went to La Paz or, occasionally, to the Yungas and the Oriente (the north-east of the country); and the Indian traveled on foot to the local market, church, or, sometimes, to a contiguous region of the country. Whites made decisions of national importance; mestizos carried them out on the local scene; and the Indians obeyed.[52]

Although Carter's characterization is useful to help us grasp the most obvious features of Bolivian society, in the last decades a number of other works have analyzed the complexities of the social fabric prior to the revolution and the multiplicity of individual strategies to challenge those hierarchies. Alan Knight points out that in Indo-America, "ethnic categories were socio-cultural, rather than purely biological. They related to perceived characteristics—language, dress, income, food, literacy, domicile. Such characteristics, and the ethnic status they implied, were subjective and mutable."[53] Rossana Barragán highlights that migrating to the cities and dressing in mestizo attire were part of a long-term strategy used by the Indian population to attain social mobility and challenge those hierarchies. She also points out that Indians declared themselves mestizos in the census to avoid tributary obligations during the colonial period.[54] Xavier Albó and Olivia Harris in their study on the sociocultural relations between miners and peasants note that Indians or peasants returning to the countryside after working in the mines identified themselves as mestizos and highlighted their class identity over their ethnic identity so as to escape the stigma of being Indian or uncivilized.[55] After returning to the countryside, these peasants expected to buy a small plot of land to access owners' status. Focusing also on the history of the twentieth century, Jorge Dandler observes that writers noticed how narrow the divisions were that separated mestizos from Indians in the valleys of Cochabamba, especially in contrast to the highlands.[56] All these examples demonstrate different individual strategies to fight back against stigmatization and social and economic hierarchies.

In her study of the Bolivian elites Ximena Soruco, researching the nineteenth century, underscores the story of a number of politicians and wealthy merchants who came from mestizo or indigenous impoverished backgrounds. Soruco mentions the cases of President Gregorio Pacheco, who ended up being one of the richest men in Bolivia. He was a mestizo horse tamer who made his fortune in mining. She also mentions the case of the millionaire Juana Vidaurre de Arteche, a mestiza woman (*chola*) who made her fortune in mining. Soruco identifies three mechanisms for social mobility in the nineteenth century: either involvement in politics, activity in commerce, or entrance in the military (especially with the emergence of new caudillos).[57] All these show how difficult it was to establish clear ethnic markers between Indians and non-Indians. They also challenge the idea that the landed elite was a tight circle of white creoles as Carter discussed in the 1970s. Soruco adds that the fact the elites were so worried about the ethnic origin of every nouveau riche confirms that there was space for social mobility.

Agrarian court cases attest that owning rural property was in fact a key asset for social mobility, as in the case of traders and craftsmen in the valleys of Cochabamba who took the opportunity to buy land, which carried considerable social prestige.[58] Two such cases in Cliza are particularly noteworthy: Bernardino Quiroz and Severino Fuentes—whose colonos identified them as "Indian"—amassed medium-sized properties by buying one small plot after another.[59] We know of these two cases because their properties were expropriated in the 1950s, but a study of landownership of other small and medium-sized properties in the valleys of Cochabamba may reveal other cases.

Finally, despite the asymmetrical relations of economic and political power, historians Qayum, Barragán, and Soux underscore the cultural practices and religious beliefs shared by colonos and landlords that tended to lessen ethnic and class markers in the rural area. Colonos and landlords celebrated patronal festivals together. Some landlords were fluent in indigenous languages such as Aymara and Quechua.[60] Landlords cultivated clientelist and paternalist relationships with their colonos. Often, colonos named their landlords as godparents of their children so as to gain some leverage with them through fictive kinship, a common practice throughout Latin America used to cement ties across unequal social relationships.[61] There were also economic interests that strengthened the relationship between a landlord and their colonos. Legal petitions from the 1940s illustrate that there were fierce quarrels among landlords to secure the boundaries of their properties. In these cases, landlords did not fight each other directly but instead directed their colonos, especially landless peasants, to move the boundaries of the neighboring property. Of course, it was the colonos who paid the price for these quarrels, and many times with their lives. At the same time, these disputes solidified the alliances between landlords and colonos.[62]

The Order from Within

The hacienda was a world of social hierarchies and complexities on its own. The distribution of plots among colonos varied wildly. And these differences are key to understanding the outcome of the agrarian reform. On most haciendas, traditional Andean principles ruled land distribution among colonos. Aymara and Quechua societies traditionally recognized distinctive people's status within the community; the so-called *originarios* (the original member of a community) had different rights from the *agregados* or *forasteros* (migrants from other communities who received smaller parcels of lands).[63] In addition to these two groups, and depending on the region, other categories emerged that implied a different status within the community and therefore differentiated access to land. For instance, the *utawawas* (in Omasuyos) or *yanaperos* (in Yungas) were those who helped work the land of other colonos.[64] In Yungas, the *chiquiñeros*, who were usually migrants from the altiplano, had access to a small *cocal* (plot dedicated to the cultivation of coca leaves) and land for subsistence crops but no house in return for one day of labor per week performed by both the head of the household and the spouse.[65] These Andean categories not only survived the colonial

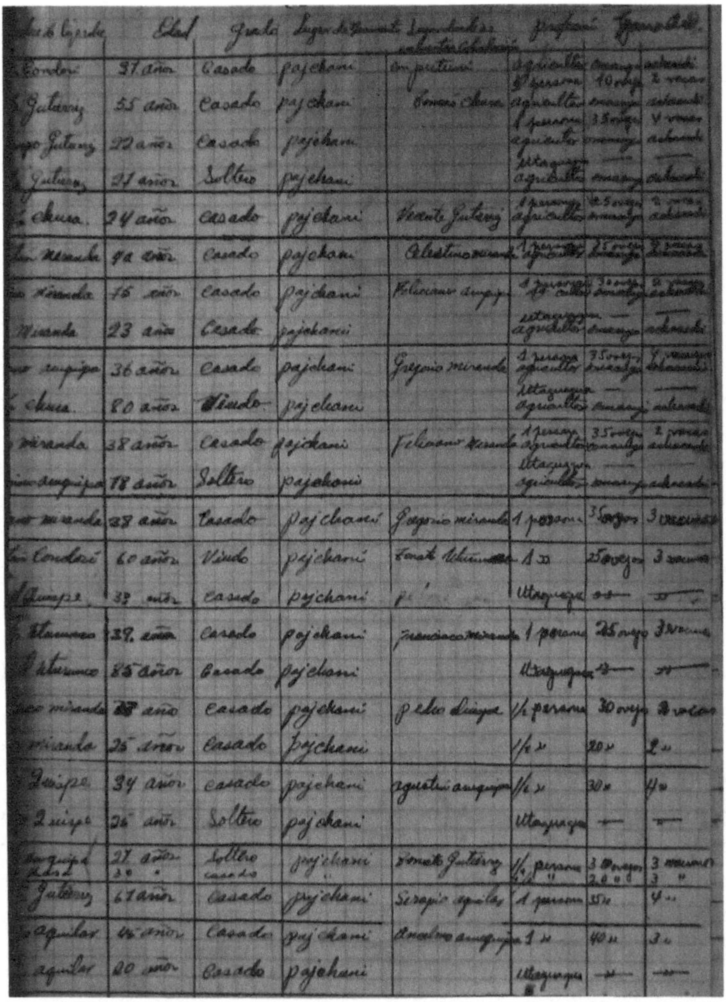

Apellido	Edad	Grado	Lugar	
Condori	37 años	Casado	pajchani	
Gutiérrez	55 años	Casado	pajchani	Tomás Chura
Gutiérrez	22 años	Casado	pajchani	
Gutiérrez	21 años	Soltero	pajchani	
Chura	24 años	Casado	pajchani	Vicente Gutiérrez
Miranda	[illegible] años	Casado	pajchani	Celestino Miranda
Miranda	45 años	Casado	pajchani	Feliciano Quispe
Miranda	23 años	Casado	pajchani	
Quispe	36 años	Casado	pajchani	Gregorio Miranda
Chura	80 años	Viudo	pajchani	
Miranda	38 años	Casado	pajchani	Feliciano Miranda
Quispe	18 años	Soltero	pajchani	
Miranda	38 años	Casado	pajchani	Gregorio Miranda
Condori	60 años	Viudo	pajchani	
Quispe	[illegible] años	Casado	pajchani	
[illegible]	39 años	Casado	pajchani	Francisco Miranda
[illegible]	85 años	Casado	pajchani	
Miranda	[illegible] año	Casado	pajchani	Pedro Quispe
Miranda	25 años	Casado	pajchani	
Quispe	34 años	Casado	pajchani	Agustín Quispe
Quispe	26 años	Soltero	pajchani	
Quispe	27 años / 30	Soltero / casado	pajchani	Donato Gutiérrez
Gutiérrez	61 años	Casado	pajchani	Serapio Aguilar
Aguilar	45 años	Casado	pajchani	Anselmo Quispe
Aguilar	20 años	Casado	pajchani	

Figure 1.2. Status of colonos within hacienda Pajchani (Omasuyos Province). It describes the name, age, marital status, status within the hacienda. From INRA–LP, Omasuyos Province, box 98, Pajchani file.

period but were also enforced by the Spanish Crown since originarios and agregados were subject to distinct tributary obligations.

These differences were not erased with the formation of the hacienda.[66] Colonos originarios and agregados were granted different types of access to land and working conditions. The originario received a plot of land in exchange for six days of work while the *arrimantes* or forasteros were given half of a plot in exchange for two or three days a week of work for the landlord.[67] Despite the seemingly rigid nature of these divisions, the status of a person could vary over time, whether they were living in an independent

Table 1.7. Characterization of the Population according to Occupation in 1950

Economic Sector	Percentage
Landlord	1.78
Employee	10.87
Day laborer	12.99
Colono	12.1
Comunario	10.3
Independent worker	11.04
Relative/assistant	40.28
No data	0.64

Source: Ministerio de Hacienda y Estadística, *Censo demográfico 1950*, 231.

indigenous community or on the hacienda. For example, if an originario died, the widow stayed on the hacienda but with a smaller portion of land, because of the assumption that a woman would not be able to handle the amount of work necessary for a full plot of land.[68] Forasteros with a large family could petition the landlord for a larger portion of land in exchange for more days of work. On the altiplano, originarios were considered one person (*persona*) and agregados were considered half of a person (*media persona*). The file of hacienda Pajchani (Omasuyos) details the status of each person within the hacienda and the relation of dependency between an originario and several utawawas (see figure 1.2).[69]

The status of a person within the community or the hacienda was not fixed. Many originarios or agregados (or members of their family) living in the highlands worked temporarily as *yanaperos* in Yungas. A colono originario or agregado on one hacienda could be working as a tenant or *piquero* on another hacienda. The following description of work conditions in the hacienda Monte Redondo in Cochabamba exemplify multiple and overlapping peasants' labor strategies: "Benedicto Orellana has worked 3 *arrobadas* for the last 14 years ago in Monte Redondo. He also has a *pegujal* on the property of Jorge Rivero. Agapito Delgadillo works 1 *arrobada* in Monte Redondo, he has a *pegujal* on the property of Ms. Balderrama. Jorge Terán works 1 *arrobada* in Monte Redondo and he also has a *pegujal* on the property of Ms. Balderrama. He also owns a small farm."[70] These examples illustrate the compound strategies that peasants developed for working in the face of an adverse and exploitative system. A large number of them looked for temporary work on neighboring haciendas, and many obtained seasonal work in the mines.[71] The differences between a *sayañero* and a colono in Yungas, between a piquero (owner of a small plot) and a peon in Cochabamba, or between one person and half of a person in Omasuyos indicates the latent economic differences in social status among peasants.

Figure 1.3. The caption reads: "National Tennis Champion Gastón Zamora is also an enthusiastic farmer who personally leads the coffee harvest on his property Cosullini, Nor Yungas." From "Cultivar la tierra es hacer patria," *Revista Campo* (Publicación Mensual del Banco Agrícola de Bolivia) 1, no. 3 (July 1947): 50. Photo courtesy of Centro de Información Fundación Flavio Machicado Viscarra.

The agrarian reform did not erase these differences. They outlasted the 1952 revolution and continued to shape different access to property.

There is no information available about the actual number of peasants working on the hacienda who did not hold a plot of land, as was the case for utawawas, chiquiñeros, and yanaperos. Yet, the 1950 census does shed some light on this question. It reveals that only 12 percent of the economically active population at that time worked as colonos. A similar percentage (10 percent) still lived in communities (see table 1.7).

The census identifies the majority of the economically active population (40 percent) as "relative/assistant." Although this does not specify where they worked, considering that the majority of the population lived in the countryside we can safely assume that the so-called relative/assistants lived in the countryside as well. I suggest that this category may have included at least three different subcategories. The first would be the mitanis, the wives of the colonos, who were subject to obligatory unpaid servitude in the haciendas. Although all women living on all haciendas were obligated to work as servants for the landlord, the census does not mention their work. The second subcategory is made up of the, colonos' male offspring, who were not considered "colonos" since they were not assigned a plot of land. The third subgroup consists of a large number of yanaperos, or utawawas without a plot of land. On many haciendas, these extra hands sometimes equaled the number of colonos. Some of those "assistants" also lived on ayllus, as these internal differences continued to be observed within the communities as well. Although this is a rough calculation, I suggest that at least half of the population classified as "relative/assistant" lived on haciendas. As a result, it is possible that 30 percent of the economically active population was subject to the colonato system, capturing the largest percentage of workers in the country. This data is important as it shows the number of people who would be demanding land after the agrarian reform.

"To Cultivate Is to Be Patriotic," 1935–1952

Until the first decades of the twentieth century, land in Bolivia served a variety of purposes: it was a valuable commodity, a supplier of free labor for the countryside and servants for domestic work at home, a sign of social prestige, and a source of secure revenue.[72] Yet few landlords contributed to its productivity. Not surprisingly, the leftist and nationalist literature, both prior to and after the revolution, described landlords as indolent rent seekers who spent most of their time in the cities of La Paz and Cochabamba and who regularly received the products of their haciendas.[73] However, from the late 1930s and especially in the 1940s, conservative and progressive governments alike launched a weighty reform to improve economic development. This program that sought to shake the archaic conditions of production in the countryside put landlords at the center of their program for rural development.

After the 1929 economic recession and the Chaco War in which Bolivia lost territory to Paraguay, conservative and progressive ruling politicians increasingly questioned the country's extremely dependent economy, which was based exclusively on the exporting of tin. In that context, political elites identified the altiplano, the valleys, and the vast lowlands as the most tangible sites for economic diversification. The most visible mark of this change (politicians turning their eyes to the countryside and the frontiers) was led by President Germán Busch who in 1938 created the department of Pando, signaling the government's efforts to consolidate the state's presence on the Bolivian northern frontier. President Germán Busch pressured landlords to increase the agricultural output of their properties, in order to fulfill the principles of the recently approved 1938 Constitution, which mandated that land should have a social function. In the same vein, President Carlos Quintanilla (1939–1940) encouraged landowners to submit a detailed report of their production to the Ministry of Agriculture. In return, the government promised machinery, fertilizers, and seeds.[74]

Conservative President Enrique Peñaranda (1940–1943) accomplished the most in terms of supporting landlords' productive role in the rural economy. He created the Agricultural Bank, which allotted twenty million pesos in loans to landlords so that they could improve their properties, build canals, and buy agricultural equipment, seed, and fertilizers. With the active support of the US State Department, Peñaranda created the Bolivian Corporation of Development.[75] Based on the recommendations of Plan Bohan, Peñaranda promoted the organization of experimental farms on the altiplano, Yungas, Villamontes, Sucre, Santa Cruz, Upper Amazon, and Beni.[76] Peñaranda recognized landlords as the government's main allies in the quest to boost rural development. He allowed them much influence in economic decision-making, and he decreed that two out of four representatives of the Agricultural Bank had to be members of the Bolivian Rural Society (SRB), the largest association of landlords in Bolivia.[77] In an effort to funnel public funding to the countryside, he allocated tax revenues from *chicha* (maize beer) and coca leaves to rural societies so that they could fund the construction of provincial roads. Peñaranda saw the rural societies as effective para-state agents capable of generating the country's urgently needed rural development.

In contrast, left-wing discussions had started to question the concentration of Bolivia's land in so few hands since the late 1920s, the conservative Peñaranda saw no need to attack the existing property ownership when he thought there was plenty of land in Bolivia.[78] Instead, he proposed to boost the settlement of the vast and underpopulated east and north of the country (a process that in Bolivia is called colonization). In fact, the lowlands were home to indigenous groups, many of them still nomadic. The elites considered the area to be effectively empty since, they thought that only *uncivilized* Indians lived there. In 1942, Peñaranda consequently launched one of the strongest initiatives to colonize the lowlands. The project involved transplanting peasants from the crowded valleys and highlands of Cochabamba to the Chapare region.

In 1943, the nationalist Gualberto Villarroel (1943–1946) overthrew Peñaranda. Although their policies differed greatly regarding relations with the elites, workers, and colonos, Villarroel continued Peñaranda's program of loans in the countryside. The Agricultural Bank's investments in La Paz and Cochabamba under both presidents clearly demonstrate the continuity of this policy, despite their fundamentally different political views (see table 1.8).

The impact of this investment in the countryside was uneven. Analysis of court cases prior to the revolution shows that the landlords of 30–40 percent of the haciendas in each province declared they had invested in their properties a decade prior to the revolution. In Yungas, many used

Table 1.8. Agricultural Bank Loans in La Paz and Cochabamba (in Thousands of Bolivianos)

Department	Investment under Peñaranda		Investment under Villarroel		
Year	1942	1943	1944	1945	1946
La Paz	23,699	10,584	11,454	21,802	15,138
Cochabamba	1,318	5,319	5,743	12,290	8,567

Source: Elaborated by the author based on *Revista Campo*, 1942–1946

the extensive forest at their disposal to build sawmills to extract, process, and export wood. On the altiplano, many invested in seeds and fertilizers and improved the breed of livestock. Others used Agricultural Bank credits to open small manufacturing facilities to produce alcohol, tiles, or dairy products. Macario Escobari, one of the most successful entrepreneurs of Omasuyos, reported receiving loans from the Agricultural Bank amounting to 805,000 bolivianos in six years (1941 to 1947). He used these loans to buy purebred cattle and a McCormick Deering tractor and to build a distillery "Industrias Omasuyos."[79] Landlords in Sud Yungas and Germán Jordán undertook similar initiatives that reflected the ongoing changes in the countryside in the 1940s.

Peñaranda developed one of the most significant programs to transform the countryside by investing capital to create experimental farms, to improve seeds and livestock, and to expand the colonization initiative. The MNR absorbed much of this agenda after 1952. However, it is striking that neither Peñaranda nor the US advisors who inspired much of this agenda questioned the system of labor exploitation that prevailed in the haciendas, almost all of which depended on unpaid servile Indian labor for their operations.

Until the 1940s, a number of upper-middle-class intellectuals, in the same vein as Peñaranda, supported the landlords' new economic ethos based on investment and productivity. For example, *Revista Bolivia*, edited by the intellectual and writer Gustavo Adolfo Otero, published an article praising the role of these modern and productive landlords. The article, "Una visita a la provincia Los Andes" (A visit to the province of Los Andes), exemplifies the mainstream political tone that reformists adopted in talking about the transformation underway in the countryside. Its message was that transformation, productivity, and social order were possible:

> A visit to the province of Los Andes cannot be complete without touring the Chirapaca and Karhuisa haciendas, both directed and organized by a radiant young man, in love with his country, who dedicates his work to increasing the

> production of his haciendas by applying the knowledge he attained at the best European universities. This man, Jorge del Solar, distanced himself from those idle landlords who only wanted to enjoy the rent from their haciendas and he led one of the most productive emporiums, without harming the lives of the colonos. . . .
>
> We have witnessed the respect and love that the colonos showed their landlord. "I tried to penetrate"—says del Solar—"into Indian psychology and I can assure you that the Indian is suitable for agricultural tasks, if we first educate him."[80]

The interview is interested in promoting landlord Jorge del Solar's entrepreneurial spirit and his alleged love for the Indians who, he claimed, could be made suitable for working the land. However, it exposes Solar's seigniorial and racist attitude that questioned the very humanity of the indigenous people. It also gives us a hint of how preposterous it may have sounded to men such as del Solar to hear the proposals of distributing land to peasants, as was the case just a few years later.

Conclusions

Prior to the revolution, the economic connections of the landed elite with the mining, industrial, and political sector were apparent as well as the role that land played in the generation and accumulation of wealth, in times of economic growth but even more in times of economic crisis. As important as it is to recognize that wealth and power were concentrated in the hands of a small number of people, it is also worth pointing out the economic and social differences among them. Some of these landlords possessed one single estate; others held numerous properties of thousands of hectares in multiple provinces. Whether their agricultural production was a subsistence crop or oriented toward the markets, whether their properties were large, medium, or small, whether they were private, public, or ecclesiastic, most landlords based their production on colonos' unpaid labor. The prevalence of this system of work demonstrates how the seigniorial mentality and the practice of appropriation of labor far exceeded the small circle of the richest landlord elite. About 30 percent of the active economic population was subject to this type of work. To keep this system of labor in place, landlords used multiple mechanisms of discipline and punishment, ranging from verbal violence to physical violence, to confiscation of property or eviction. In the practical absence of the state or any other mediator in the landlord-colono relationship, colonos' only options for escaping the authority of the landlords were migration to other haciendas or to the mines. Of course, this did not mean that the migrant colono was guaranteed better conditions of work or living on other haciendas or at the mines.

Although life for colonos changed little in the years up to the revolution, the countryside underwent significant changes from the 1930s onward. Without challenging the system of property and labor, political elites allied to the landlords sought to implement a program of land reform. This was one of the most serious attempts prior to the revolution to increase productivity and modernize the countryside. Measures were implemented to stimulate the rural economy, including the creation of the Agricultural Bank, which injected capital into the haciendas, and the levying of new taxes, which generated revenue that was channeled toward the SRB. The individual histories of each hacienda described thriving entrepreneurs who took advantage of the loans of the Agricultural Bank to buy purebred livestock and agricultural machinery and to open new roads. However, landlords in Bolivia, as their peers in Chile and Peru, demonstrated little interested in changing colonos' working conditions. In fact, several local reports reveal that work conditions on those modern large estates worsened for the colonos in the 1940s. They saw their tasks increase precisely because of the landlords' expanding role on the haciendas. Unlike the landlords who lived in the city and received crops from colonos without further involvement in the hacienda, these progressive landlords were present on the hacienda and placed additional demands on colonos. For instance, many of the local industries that landlords started in the 1940s used the existing labor force to work in these additional industries. The colonos saw their tasks multiplied in exchange for the usufruct of the same plot of land.[81]

Appendix 1.1

Table 1.1. The Ten Wealthiest Landlords in Germán Jordán Province (Cliza and Ucureña Cantons)

Landlord	Hacienda	Hectares	Colonos
Santa Clara Monastery	Santa Clara	779	765
Family Ocampo Quiroga	Liquinas del Rosario	104	8
	Lameo and Ayoma	76	20
	San Isidro	76	26
	Liquinas, El Rosario	66	12
	Liquinas . . . el Rosario	64	26
	Lultipata Lameo and Ayana	61	9
	Total	447	101
Agustín Villegas	Santa Lucía de Liquinas Pilicocha	399	46
	Chullpas Cuarto Suyo	36	8
	Total	435	54
Pacesa Sejas, widow of Arandia	Kehuinal San Antonio	434	19
Antonio and René Abasto	La Alcoholería	332	13
Harry Berger	Carcaje	286	0
Bernardina Ledesma	Laloma	156	32
Family Gandarillas	Toco Viejo	135	13
	Quinto Suyo	40	13
	Total	175	26
Roberto Angulo	Cucuntapa or San Rafael	113	5
Martha and Alicia Barrientos	Liquinas	112	23

Source: Agrarian reform court cases, INRA-Cochabamba, Germán Jordán Province.

Table 1.2. The Ten Wealthiest Landlords in Omasuyos Province (Achacachi Canton)

Landlord	Hacienda	Hectares	Colonos
Family Terrazas	Casamaya	19,332	78
	Ocorani	955	39
	Frasquia	1,231	70
	Total	21,518	187
Family Franco	Murumani	2,854	106
	Pacharía	1,386	
	Ckasina	1,377	82
	Cocani	590	25
	Chococopa Chica	830	29
	Tihipampa—Taramaya	216	
	Chocopata Grande	749	20
	Total	8,002	262
Family Mendoza	Merke Achacchi	2,107	35
	Cala Cala	817	
	Total	2,924	35
Macario Cusicanqui and Ubaldina Mollinedo	Challuyo	1,698	23
Macario Escobari Millán	Pajchani Grande	1,485	60
Ministry of Agriculture (state farm)	Experimental Farm Belén	1,468	45 workers, 239 colonos
José and Eduardo Imaña	Gualata Grande	1,287	130
Eduardo Imana Monterrey	Gualata Chico	802.8	122
Rosa Agramont de Cusicanqui	Umapusa	1,222	
Guillermo Sancristobal and Laura Sanjinez	Humacha	1,210	
	Sullulluni	1,210	113
	Total	2,420	113

Source: Agrarian reform court cases, INRA-LP, Omasuyos Province.

Table 1.3. The Ten Wealthiest Landlords in Sud Yungas Province (Chulumani, Irupana Cantons)

Large Estate	Landlord	Hectares	Colonos
Callisaya	Guillermo Velez	65,000	110
Iquico and Totoral	Domingo Soligno (son) Remo di Natale	6,093	57
Santa Barbara	Jose Segundo Cuevas	2,376	4
Santa Rosa	Hector Jemio	2,288	127
Totora Pampa	Propiedad Gutierrez Pinilla	1,907	43
Colompampa	Ventura Tamayo (Perez Saavera and Jaime Lorini)	1,774	26
Naranjani	Hector Lorini	1,281	80
San Isidro	Lugones Family	1,126	
Colimpampa	Humberto Gudino	905	28
Las Lomas		735	39

Source: Agrarian reform court cases, INRA-LP, Sud Yungas Province.

Table 1.6. Landlord and Colonos' Usufruct of Land in Five Haciendas in Omasuyos (in Hectares) before the Agrarian Reform

Hacienda	Cultivated by Landlord	%	Uncultivable	%	Cultivated by Colonos	%	Total
Casamaya[1]	16,807	86.9		0.0	2,525	13.06	19,332
Murumani[2]	10	0.3	2,475	86.7	52	1.8	2,853
Merke Achacchi[3]	10.3	0.48	1,625	77.12	35.15	1.6	2,107
Pajchani Grande[4]	56.65	3.8	172.5	11.6	508	34.0	1,485.1
Frasquia	528.12	42.9	641.48	52.1	61.4	5	1,231

Source: Elaborated by the author based on agrarian reform court cases, INRA-LP, Omasuyos Province: box 1, file Casamaya and file Frasquia; box 24, file Murumani; box 26, file Merke Achacachi; and box 11, file Pajchani Grande.

Notes: The table shows the significant variation in colonos' access to land from one hacienda to another.

[1] This property is entirely dedicated to grazing animals.

[2] There are 316 hectares that topographers identified as an area that could be potentially cultivated.

[3] There are 436.55 hectares that topographers identified as an area that could be potentially cultivated.

[4] The remaining 748.45 hectares that constituted about 50 percent of the property was an area dedicated to nurturing and grazing animals. Left for annual rotation it was used by landlord and colonos.

CHAPTER TWO

THE INDIAN PROBLEM AND THE AGRARIAN QUESTION UNDER DEBATE

> There is no agrarian problem in Bolivia. The density of population barely reaches a proportion of two and a half habitants per square kilometer.
>
> **Enrique Finot, 1940**

> Agrarian Reform does not imply implementing a socialist project, but rather a liberal one, because it tries to overcome a feudal stage that has been abolished in other countries. I do not propose to return land to its ancient owners but, rather, to give land to those who work it. . . . I do not intend to undermine the right of property owners but, rather, to protect the rights of the poor renters, which will improve the productivity of the countryside.
>
> **Congressman Víctor Paz Estenssoro, 1943**

Over the first half of the twentieth century, left-leaning and nationalist groups began questioning Bolivia's gross inequality in land distribution and the exploitative labor relations that colonos faced on the haciendas. Although these revolutionary demands were widely espoused among university students' federations, they remained marginal to the mainstream political debate. Yet, the 1929 economic recession and the devastating defeat of Bolivia in the Chaco War brought ideas that were previously considered radical to the center of the political debate. Some of these demands crystallized at the 1938 national constitutional convention. In terms of property, the new constitution ruled that all rural property should fulfill a social function limiting the absolute property rights that the liberal constitution of 1880 granted to rural owners. In the 1940s, two political parties—the moderate leftist-nationalist Revolutionary Nationalist Movement (MNR) and the Marxist-Leninist Partido de la Izquierda Revolucionaria (PIR), the Left Revolutionary Party—competed for the electorate and led political debates about the Indian problem in Congress. As much as these parties supported improving colonos' working conditions and guaranteeing their political organization, their proposals fell short of confronting the powerful Sociedad Rural Boliviana (SRB), the Bolivian Rural Society, that time and again blocked the MNR's and the PIR's projects, calling them radical, subversive, or communist.

Over the first half of the twentieth century, conservative and progressive political parties alike often used phrases such as "the Indian problem" and the "agrarian reform" to frame their proposals about the rural area. Yet, each group had something different in mind when they used such slogans. Progressive parties stressed the connection between the Indian problem and agrarian reform as two components of one essential problem. The conservatives argued that the two issues were very different in nature—they thought that the "Indian problem" required policies in terms of education and, ultimately, measures to achieve Indian civilization—and that "agrarian reform" referred to bank loans, technical modernization of haciendas, and at best, land concessions in the remote lowlands.[1] Thus, the term "agrarian reform," rather than a specific policy was a field for political struggle. Although the term appeared often in congressional debates, newspapers, and political parties' political programs, it meant different things for distinct segments of a deeply fractured society. While many of the most progressive voices—indigenistas, leftist, and nationalists—supported improving colonos' working conditions on the haciendas, they were reluctant to equate land reform to land distribution.[2] Despite their eloquent allegations against the landowning elite, many members of the young progressive elite shared the same prejudices as the conservative elite. They saw the surviving indigenous communities as symbolizing backwardness and agreed that the Indian population living on haciendas or in communities should be subject to an extended process of rehabilitation and civilization.

The Indian Problem from Academic Circles to the Palace

The land privatization policies that prompted the massive expropriation of indigenous communal lands in the altiplano from the late nineteenth century onward provoked a series of indigenous revolts. In 1899, and in the context of the Federal War in which liberals confronted conservatives, the indigenous leader Pablo Zárate Willka (1888–1889) commanded the largest Indian revolt of the nineteenth century. Indian communities joined the liberals demanding the restitution of their communal land. Yet, the liberals betrayed their old allies and accused the Indian leaders of engaging in a race war that caused widespread fear among the urban classes.[3] In the wake of this rebellion, and over the first two decades of the twentieth century, Indian communal leaders (called caciques apoderados) undertook a coordinated legal-based movement in the first decades of the twentieth century to demonstrate they were the legitimate owners of lands that had violently passed to private landlords.[4] This extended network of caciques apoderados demanded the restoration of communal territory via the call for a general inspection of land boundaries.[5] Parallel to their legal fight, caciques apoderados also led two widespread rebellions—the first in Jesus de Machaca (La Paz) in 1921 and the second in Chayanta (Potosí) in 1927.[6]

Parallel to the political mobilization that was taking place in the countryside, the Bolshevik revolution propelled the organization of radical political parties and student organizations in the cities.[7] Bolivian youth enthusiastically read the works of Karl Marx as well as those of the Peruvian Marxist José Carlos Mariátegui, such as *Siete ensayos de interpretación de la realidad peruana* (*Seven Interpretive Essays on Peruvian Reality*, 1927).[8] These intellectuals directly denounced *latifundismo*. Some also proposed the abolition of pongueaje (forced domestic labor) and the legal recognition of Indian communities. The most prominent and radical voice of this early movement was Tristán Marof, the leader of the Tupaj Amaru group.[9] He argued openly for a revolution that would begin by eliminating latifundia and rural feudal relations. Following Mariátegui, Marof insisted that "Indian liberation would only happen when the Indians recover the lands usurped by the whites and the creoles from the colonial period to the present."[10] In his book *La tragedia del altiplano* (The tragedy of the altiplano), Marof outlined a Marxist revolutionary program that would consist of agrarian reform, liquidation of the latifundio through the collectivization of land, socialization of the means of production, and finally, industrialization.[11]

In the early 1930s Alfredo Sanjinés published a lengthy study on agrarian reform that brought to Bolivia some of the principles discussed on agrarian reform in Mexico.[12] Sanjinés, who had served as ambassador to Mexico, believed that stagnation in agriculture was one of Bolivia's leading problems. To get out from this gridlock, he argued that the country should follow the latest trends in agrarian legislation in Europe and Latin America, where ownership of land was subject to the fulfillment of a "social function."[13] Sanjinés avoided referring directly to the debates that emerged after the Mexican revolution, but it is clear that his stay in Mexico and the contemporaneous debates over the Mexican Constitution—particularly Article 27, which granted the state property rights over land and water—influenced his approach. Klein stresses that these radical ideas were embraced only by a small group of intellectuals and had very limited impact among the mainstream political parties.[14] Both the Liberals, who ruled the country during the first decades of the century, and the Republicans, who took power in the 1920s, deemed education and military the mechanisms for solving the "Indian problem."[15]

The Chaco War that pitted Bolivia against Paraguay silenced much of this political upheaval. Under wartime conditions President Daniel Salamanca (1931–1934) suppressed labor unions, the left, and indigenous movements. Some prominent intellectuals, labor leaders, and radical politicians suffered exile or confinement, but political life resumed immediately after the devastating defeat in 1935. A large number of veterans, many of them indigenous people who had been forced to fight for the country, returned with extremely critical opinions not only of the leaders who led the disastrous military campaign but also of an economic and political model that had systematically excluded them. This was the context in which a number of anti-oligarchic political parties emerged—the Stalinist PIR, the nationalist MNR, and the Partido Obrero Revolucionario (POR), the Trotskyist Revolutionary Workers' Party.[16]

Some of the most strident criticisms against the traditional political party system came from the military officers who seized power in 1936. Unlike their predecessors, the self-proclaimed "military socialists" believed the state should have a more prominent role in the economy. President David Toro (1936–1937) nationalized oil concessions previously operated by Standard Oil.[17] He also launched the first policies to protect workers' rights, designated union leader Waldo Alvarez as minister of labor, and decreed the unionization of all workers.[18] Although the unionization decree primarily responded to the demands of workers in cities and in the mines, it had an immediate impact in the countryside. Shortly after the decree was passed in 1936, colonos on some ecclesiastical and municipal properties of Cochabamba organized unions and demanded the right to lease the properties where they worked.

Some of these disputes between colonos and owners captivated national media attention. For instance, in 1936 the colonos of Santa Clara, the largest hacienda in Germán Jordán Province (in Cochabamba), were well aware that the owners, the Clarisas nuns, had rented out the hacienda to different administrators for short periods. Often, such property transactions ended up making the colonos' work conditions worse.[19] Using President Toro's new decree, the colonos organized a union, and they asked the owners to lease the property to the union. By eliminating the mediation of the former tenant, the colonos hoped to avoid the abuses and arbitrary injustices to which they had been subjected.[20] Another group of colonos offered to buy some of the plots that the nuns of Santa Clara had put up for sale, but the nuns rejected both proposals. If the nuns sold plots of their property to colonos, this meant that Indians would become part of a very select group of landlords challenging the unwritten principles that ruled the land market in the countryside and that made class and ethnicity a crucial factor in economic transactions. Yet the colonos did not give up. With the support of Andrés Dávalos, a rural schoolteacher, Antonio Revuelta, the son of a landholder, and Doctor Cuellar, a local lawyer and a prominent intellectual of the leftist party, they asked the Ministry of Labor to help them rent some of the Santa Clara Monastery's plots.[21] The newspaper *La Calle*, which belonged to the recently created MNR, reported almost daily on the conflict between the colonos and the nuns, demonstrating the national significance this local conflict reached in the late 1930s. The new union federations used this media platform to criticize the practices of landowners, calling for the abolition of peonage.[22]

The lobbying of the minister of labor Waldo Alvarez by left-wing intellectuals and the widespread media attention the case received in the newspapers prompted President David Toro to respond favorably to colonos' demands.[23] Toro enacted two crucial decrees that sought to regulate the rents and sales of all religious and municipal rural properties. The first, signed in 1937, ordered religious and municipal landowners to prioritize colonos in their leasing contracts, because, as he explained, "it is the duty of the Military-Socialist government to encourage the colonos' rehabilitation as well as their use of cooperative systems to work the land; giving the indigenous people the chance to prove their ability to manage agricultural labor. . . . The government decreed that all municipal and religious entities that hold rural properties that are managed by lessees should instead rent their properties to the same colonos working on those estates organized in unions."[24] It is noticeable that the president spoke of "colonos' rehabilitation" in referring to the decree that guaranteed few rights to colonos living in ecclesiastic and municipal haciendas. Both the conservatives and the self-proclaimed military socialists referred to the Indian population as second-tier people unable to manage and administer their own labor. These prejudices had deep roots in the colonial caste system and in the social Darwinism of the late nineteenth century.[25]

President Toro's second decree ordered that if, the Santa Clara nuns decided to sell their property, the sale must be made exclusively to the colonos.[26] Both decrees offended not only the nuns but also all landlords, who carefully protected property as a sign of their social prestige. Antezana and Romero described the landholders' public reaction to the decree: "the Cochabamba Rural Society accused the government of implementing an experiment for land collectivization that would end up threatening the principles of private property."[27] Trying to minimize the scale of the dispute and the effects of the decree, Luis Añez, the minister of agriculture, stated: "There is no need to be alarmed. This is only a lessee contract replacing the last one the Monastery had."[28] Overall, President Toro's decrees did not affect the majority of rural property held in private hands, but these measures were a decisive sign of the new era.

In 1937 President Germán Busch replaced President Toro. Busch, who also subscribed to the principles of military socialism, called a national convention that revised the liberal constitution under which the country had been governed since 1880.[29] Rossana Barragán argues that one of the most important outcomes of the convention was the granting of a major economic role to the state. The agrarian question was the subject of fierce debate. Representatives Gregorio Balcázar, Eguino Zaballa, Víctor Paz Estenssoro, and Walter Guevara Arze were the first to propose that the constitution should require that landed property fulfill a "social function." This principle, which followed the example of Mexico's social constitutionalism, challenged the liberal constitution that Bolivia had approved in 1880. Article 13 considered individual property rights to be absolute, whereas the new proposal held that the state could expropriate property that was not used for economic production. After an intense debate, the proposal was approved, dealing a sharp blow to rural landholders.[30]

Guevara Arze and Alfredo Arratia insisted that the Indian problem was not one of education but of access to land. Landownership was the only way, they said, to solve the problem of two and a half million landless Indians, the majority of the Bolivian population. Two proposals were up for debate. On the one hand, Paz Estenssoro proposed that latifundia should be expropriated and divided among peasants; on the other hand, Guevara Arze argued that latifundia should be turned back into communities so as to protect the collectivization of agriculture.[31] Both proposals were roundly rejected. Representatives from the departments in the east of the country (Santa Cruz, Beni, and Pando) emphatically denied that Bolivia's problem was a lack of land: "there is plenty of land in Bolivia, we do not have the resources to colonize the vast lowlands and make them suitable for agriculture."[32] Constituent Bilbao Llano provided the harshest criticism, arguing that private properties on the altiplano were under constant threat. "Our courts are packed," he said, "with cases of conflicts between private owners and comunarios regarding limits because the latter are constantly menacing the borders of private property."[33] Bilbao Llano, appealing to the familiar dichotomy between civilization and barbarism, insisted that landlords represented modernization in the countryside and were under continuous Indian threat.

To counter the many voices that described his project as communist, Guevara Arze claimed that it actually embraced the principles of liberalism: "Our liberal republic has been unable to fulfill the goals of liberalism. Liberalism did not eliminate colonial latifundia." Prophetically, he warned: "It is advisable that the country introduce some changes by law now, or else they will be introduced by force in the future."[34] Although Guevara Arze's final speech was met with applause, the assembly did not approve the project and it failed 36 to 49 votes.[35]

Nonetheless, the 1938 constitution included some significant changes. It recognized the legal existence of indigenous communities, defying both the liberal principles of the 1874 Disentailment Law and the 1880 constitution. The new constitution also approved the principle of land expropriation for public use in exchange for indemnification even if the convention also expressed the political limits of the age. Leftist intellectuals criticized the landlords' unproductive possession of land, but they remained skeptical about redistributing it to Indians whom they considered both culturally and economically backward. Presidents Toro and Busch, along with many progressive politicians, spoke of the need for the "rehabilitation" and "civilization" of indigenous people.[36] Antezana and Romero noted that even Toribio Claure, the director of the Vacas indigenous school, spoke of the "ethnic cultural problem of the indigenous peoples, instead of an economic and social problem."[37]

The preparation of the indigenista congress gave intellectuals another opportunity to discuss the Indian problem. Still under the Busch administration, a team of Bolivian academics and artists began organizing the First Inter-American Conference on Indian Life, which initially was to be held in La Paz in 1940.[38] The congress proceedings summarized the interpretation of the "Indian problem" among self-identified indianistas. Elizardo Pérez, director of Indigenous and Peasant Education (an office under the Ministry of Education), led the debate.[39] In his speech, Pérez highlighted "the important work of redemption of the Indian" that was taking place in Bolivia. He represented himself as "the voice of the indianista educators of Bolivia," who had built twelve indigenous education centers. Different themes constituted the agenda of the congress, and the headings already distilled the indigenista interpretation of the Indian problem: "Peasants' biology, anthropology, and psychology. Regimes of work and of agrarian property in America. Does the Indian exist? Is indigenous legislation necessary?."[40] These topics contrasted sharply with the debates led by left-wing and nationalist intellectuals at the 1938 convention. There, deputies attacked latifundia and demanded the state's recognition of Indian communities, whereas the indianista congress debates focused instead on elements of indigenous *culture*. While the 1938 convention demanded the recognition of indigenous communities, the 1939 document posed the question, "Does the Indian exist?"

The first indigenista congress took place in Patzcuaro, Mexico, in April 1940.[41] Of all the intellectuals who were part of the commission in Bolivia, right-wing President Carlos Quintanilla sent Enrique Finot, one of the most conservative voices on Bolivia's political spectrum. Finot highlighted the work that the country was accomplishing in terms of Indian education, which allowed them "to acquire the habits of a civilized life." When addressing the question of agrarian reform, Finot asserted: "There is no agrarian problem in Bolivia. The density of population barely reaches a proportion of two and a half habitants per square kilometer."[42] This view was far from exceptional. Many believed that the solution to the "Indian problem" lay in educating, which meant "civilizing" the Indian. They denounced the abuse and exploitation of Indians, but they presumed that liberation would come through education and cultural and moral improvement. They spoke of Indians' redemption but questioned their juridical and political capacity. Gotkowitz rightly points out that the term "indigenista" was not univocal; it incorporated an array of political proposals that ranged from the most conservative to the more radical positions. She argues that "the most influential indigenistas sidestepped the questions of land and instead centered their attention on education and the law.[43]

Colonos' Working Conditions at the Center of the Political Debate

In August 1939 President Germán Busch, unable to manage political pressures, committed suicide. His death marked the rise of two conservative presidents, Carlos Quintanilla and Enrique Peñaranda, who strove to dismantle the rights presidents Toro and Busch had approved in favor of the colonos. This conservative wave fell apart when the nationalist president Gualberto Villarroel was in power between 1943 and 1946. During those years there were major debates, regulations, and counterregulations on the Indian problem. Political debate and legislative focus moved away from previous cultural approaches and moved to the Indian question, which had centered on education, military conscription, and *civilization*. Instead, the political battle concentrated on colonos' working conditions on the haciendas and their rights to unionize.

Only a month after he took power, President Quintanilla nullified the decree obligating the Santa Clara Monastery to sell its parcels exclusively for the benefit of the colonos. Later, he prohibited colonos' unionization in the countryside.[44] This decree, followed by a wave of fierce political repression against indigenous and peasant leaders, stopped the growing demands for unionization among peasants in the countryside. The immediacy of this decree demonstrates not only Quintanilla's close relationship with the recently created Bolivian Rural Society (SRB) but also how imperative it was for landlords to prevent the political mobilization of colonos.[45]

Quintanilla's successor, Enrique Peñaranda, did not believe that Bolivia's land problem was the concentration of land in few hands. Instead he believed the problem was the state's very limited efforts to expand the agricultural frontier. To implement his program, Peñaranda launched a program of peasant colonization—transplanting colonos from the valleys and highlands of Cochabamba to the Chapare region in 1942. Peñaranda desig-

Figure 2.1. This is one of the few surviving hacienda houses from prior to 1952. Notoriously, Freddy Revuelta was the son of an hacendado who supported Loreiro defending colonos' right to organize a union. The house is in the town of Cliza (Germán Jordán Province). Photo by Carmen Soliz.

nated Eduardo Arze Loureiro, a PIR member, to lead the project. Loureiro promoted the migration of colonos from the community of Ana Rancho (which was where colonos organized the first union in 1936) in Germán Jordán Province to the east of the department of Cochabamba. The area for colonization received the name "Aroma Cooperative."[46]

Loureiro had worked before with the colonos of Cliza. He was one of the intellectuals who supported the organization of the first rural unions under Toro's administration. Loureiro's role in the Toro and Peñaranda administrations suggests a left that was more practical than ideological. Loureiro adapted his activity to the agenda of the national government and looked for ways to give land to peasants. Instead of confronting the powerful SRB and the existing property structure, Loureiro, under President Toro, encouraged colonos to lease land from landlords. Under Peñaranda, he supported the program for colonization of the lowlands benefiting colonos in the populated province of Germán Jordán.

Despite Quintanilla's and Peñaranda's attempts to stop colono unionization in the countryside and to suppress peasant political activism, landlords across the countryside reported generalized sit-down strikes in the early 1940s. Those in Oruro complained that colonos sabotaged production by refusing to fulfill their obligations. Colonos were protesting the excessive duties to which they were subject on the haciendas and were demanding that local authorities enforce the new laws passed in favor of the peasantry.[47] As in 1936, the national press gave wide coverage to the conflicts between landlords and colonos. As the intensity of the conflict grew in the countryside, the University Federation of Oruro volunteered to organize a forum so that "landholders and colonos would discuss their differences." The SRB refused to take part in any debate, declaring that members would discuss the problem with the government instead.[48] On his part, President Peñaranda sent peasants leaders "who were inflaming the '*indiada*'" (a derogatory, condescending term used to refer to the indigenous population) into exile in the recently created penal colonies of Coati (La Paz) and Ichilo (Santa Cruz).[49]

Colono strikes sparked a new wave of congressional debates focused on working conditions on the haciendas. Representative Eguino Rodas proposed the abolition of the personal service (pongueaje) that colonos were forced to provide in landlords' houses (in both the countryside and in the city). Since President Peñaranda controlled Congress, the project was rejected. Senator Hugo Salmón defended the institution of pongueaje in unqualified terms: "The system of pongueaje is now the only thing that binds [our society] with the Indian. Suppressing this system would sever the last connection and the Indian would remain isolated. We have to keep in mind that the Indian who serves as a pongo [a servant in a landlord's house] in the city, he hears the radio, walks the street, becomes interested in the news, and is well fed."[50] The newspaper *La Calle* responded ironically to Salmón's proposal: "It turns out that pongueaje is the best way to civilize the Indian."[51]

The state's conciliatory politics toward the rural elite and its repression of colono activists changed drastically after Colonel Gualberto Villarroel's coup d'état in December 1943. Villarroel instituted one of the most significant setbacks for the rural elite as soon as he assumed power. He reviewed the country's policies on rural taxes. The few landholders who paid taxes did so on the basis of an antiquated registry. Villarroel ordered the registers to be updated, causing alarm among the rural property owners.[52] The increase in taxes created such turmoil among landlords that, unsurprisingly, the conservative president Enrique Hertzog eliminated Villarroel's program immediately upon assuming power in July 1946.[53]

The SRB's opposition to the regime grew stronger when two MNR congressmen, Paz Estenssoro and Guevara Arze, aligned with Villarroel in support of a new proposal to change the agrarian regime. The project was based on the principles approved in 1938, and it proposed the following: first, the right of the peasants, especially colonos, to unionize (a political right that had been tacitly approved with the constitution of 1938 but that the government of Quintanilla banned in 1940); second, an end to the arbitrary eviction of colonos without fair notice and compensation, especially if they had worked there longer than three years; and, third, the formation of cooperatives among indigenous communities.[54]

As in 1938, many congressmen opposed the project. For instance, deputy Franz Tamayo, a recognized lawyer, journalist, and writer, declared that the project would be "the first step in the dissolution of the Bolivian nation."[55] He argued that Paz Estenssoro and Guevara Arze's proposal wrongly copied the foreign policies of the Mexican revolution and foreign ideologies from the Peruvian Aprista Party (APRA). According to Tamayo: "The Indian is profoundly bound to the land, but he lacks any notion of property." As such, any attempt to turn indigenous communities into cooperatives would only end in failure.[56] For his part, SRB president Raúl López Videla warned that a law that did not guarantee landlords' judicial security over their properties would be harmful to the economy. Hacienda production would immediately fall, compromising food provision to cities. Videla added: "If a law limits landlords' rights to evict their colonos, we would be tacitly granting colonos co-ownership of the hacienda. . . . if the state recognizes communal property, Bolivia will reverse decades of consolidation of individual property in the countryside."[57] Videla believed that unionizing the peasants, a practice copied from abroad, would not work with illiterate masses.[58]

Paz Estenssoro insisted that the proposal did not question landlords' rights to private property and that he was simply suggesting mechanisms to regulate colonos' work. He suggested that Tamayo and Videla were exaggerating the scope of the decree. Paz Estenssoro defended his proposal by referring to examples from the Roman Empire in an attempt to separate it from Peruvian and Mexican influences: "Agrarian Reform does not imply implementing a socialist project, but rather a liberal one, because it tries to overcome a feudal stage that has been abolished in other countries. I do not propose to return land to its ancient owners (as Tamayo has accused us of doing) but, rather, to give land to those who work it. I do not intend to undermine the right of the property owners, but, rather, to protect the rights of the poor renters, which will improve countryside productivity."[59] Paz Estenssoro and Guevara Arze's program aimed to stabilize relations between colonos and proprietors, to defend the rights of the colonos by guaranteeing trade unions in the countryside, and to limit landlords' arbitrary evictions. The proposals questioned neither the structure of property nor the unpaid system of work on the haciendas. Yet despite the proposal's moderate tone, it did not get the votes to pass as a law at the national convention.

Although Paz Estenssoro and Guevara's project failed to reach the national level, President Villarroel enacted an agrarian law for the Department of Tarija in December 1944.[60] Tarija, which was Paz Estenssoro's place of birth, was without doubt an ideal place to launch such a pilot program. It was an economically peripheral region with little demographic pressure in comparison to La Paz or Cochabamba. The agrarian law contained the protections that Paz Estenssoro and Guevara wanted. It obligated landlords to sign written contracts with their colonos guaranteeing the colonos' right to a plot of land and free use of pastures and woodlands for the subsistence of their families in exchange for their agricultural work on the hacienda. It prohibited landlords from renting colonos out to work on other properties, and it protected colonos against landlords' arbitrary eviction. Although scholarly literature has not seen the MNR as a party primarily concerned in attending to peasant demands, Paz Estenssoro and Guevara Arze's work in the parliament petitioning labor protections for colonos as well as the enactment of the agrarian reform law for Tarija proves we need to temper that statement. Although the MNR was neither concerned with the Indian communities' demand for land restitution nor invested in participating in the indigenista congress, they offered concrete policies in terms of working protections within the haciendas.[61] Incapable of passing a law that protected colonos' rights at the national level, President Villarroel and his MNR supporters decided to take the political debate on the Indian question from the national convention to the streets, assembling the largest indigenous congress in 1945.

From the Palace to the Streets

In May 1945 President Villarroel convened twelve hundred indigenous representatives from across the country for the first national indigenous congress. Previously, the indigenista congresses had brought together a number of intellectuals to debate the "Indian problem" and had gained momentum in many countries in Latin America, However, the Bolivian indigenous congress was significant because it brought together indigenous peoples to debate and to formulate their own demands.[62] Organizing a national congress was not an alien idea in Bolivia nor to indigenous leaders. Forrest Hylton revealed that a few caciques apoderados already participated in the third national congress of the Workers' Federation sponsored by the anarcho-syndicalists in 1927.[63] A number of similar meetings took place both before and after the Chaco War and under the thrust of the military-socialist governments that had encouraged workers' unionization. Teachers, mine workers, and artisans organized regional and nationwide congresses to debate their demands.[64] Prior to the 1939 indigenista congress in Mexico, directors for indigenous schools in Bolivia had organized a first national congress in 1936. This event, which was attended by teachers from the rural areas, publicized the work of the indigenous schools at the national level and attempted to "counteract landlords' malicious campaigns of provocation and defamation against their work."[65] This 1936 congress had considerable impact in the areas where these schools were operating. It seems likely that several years later, indigenous leaders looked to the indigenous schools congress as a model for their own. It is also worth stressing that the 1936 congress took place in a moment when deputies were trying out a new approach to politics. A new generation of politicians was eager to take politics beyond the walls of Parliament and to engage with ordinary people. For example, members of the MNR started to read their congressional interventions directly in the capital of provincial towns. This was true of Congressman Germán Monroy Block who submitted his annual report as a member of Parliament in the town of Viacha in 1941.[66] Conservative deputies questioned the MNR's practices, accusing them of organizing protests with the "illiterate, ragged, and malnourished Indians" for their own political interests.[67]

The indigenous congress had more immediate antecedents in the—scarcely studied—indigenous Quechua congresses held in the city of Sucre in 1942 and 1943. The newspaper *Tierra* noted that the event featured community (ayllu) leaders from the Quechua area. The first congress presented twenty-one demands, the most significant of which included:

> Review court cases ruling on the dispossession and fraudulent purchases of indigenous land; conduct investigation on land rights [*revisita de tierras*, which would establish the legality of the lands possessed by landholders]; abolish the system of personal services on the haciendas and sanction those who infringe on this law; endow the communities with a sufficient number of schools; organize juridical offices to protect indigenous rights with the intervention of departmental trade unions; extend the services of the Office of Agriculture Development to indigenous communities; allow free transportation for muleteers and llama herders; grant maternity leave to indigenous women for one month prior to birth; offer irrigation works that reach all communities; and request a study of a Bolivian Code of Agriculture.[68]

The organization of the congress demonstrated that the network of caciques apoderados, which had coordinated a powerful movement for the restitution of their lands in the first decades of the twentieth century, was still active in the 1940s. The congress combined the demands of leaders of the indigenous communities, who wanted a new *revisita de tierras* that would expose fraudulent sales of communal lands, with those of colonos, who petitioned for the elimination of pongueaje. It is worth noting here that colonos questioned pongueaje (the system of personal servitude at the landlords' houses) but not the system of colonato itself, which allowed estate laborers access to a plot of land in exchange for working a parcel for the landlords. Other demands reflected indigenous leaders' awareness of the latest executive and legislative changes in the country. Comunarios asked that the advances made during the administrations of David Toro, Germán Busch, and Enrique Peñaranda—such as schools, juridical offices, maternity leave, and agricultural development—also be extended to indigenous communities.[69] The set of demands presented in the congress of 1942 reveals how indigenous leaders selectively rescued proposals and political projects enacted by recent administrations. These were articulated alongside long-standing demands such as those created by the conflicts over the dispossession of community lands.

In 1943 the second indigenous Quechua congress took place in Chuquisaca with the support of the Department Workers' Federation. As with the first meeting, the event garnered little coverage in newspapers. The nationalist MNR *La Calle* declared that, although the reporters did not know the conclusions of the congress: "It does not require a stretch of the imagination to learn that they want rights similar to those granted by the laws of the Republic to the rest of the citizens."[70] *La Calle* compressed the multiple demands of the indigenous peoples into an undifferentiated package, and the editors ignored, for example, demands for a new *revisita de tierras* that were specific to comunarios. The newspaper oversimplified the indigenous demands and stripped them out of its complex and diverse political content.

The regional Quechua congresses, the 1939 indigenista congress, and the rural teachers' congresses that began in 1936, all served as models for the congress held in 1945. In contrast to the regional indigenous congresses, the 1945 congress was promoted by the government as a nationwide experience that would include not only Quechua but also Aymara and Guaraní leaders (the Guaranís constituted the largest indigenous groups of the lowlands). The official call invited two leaders per province to participate—one from the haciendas and one from the communities. In contrast to previous indigenous congresses, the conference themes were predetermined by the government and included the suppression of unpaid services, indigenous education, organization of agricultural cooperatives and farms, rural police, and the regulation of peasant work.[71]

The speeches and papers presented during the conference reflected the government's priorities. The congress focused on the working conditions of colonos on haciendas. The goal of the government, in the short term, was to force landholders to pay the laborers for their services and, in the long term, to develop an agrarian labor code (mirroring the labor code that President Busch approved in 1939) that would regulate the relationship between landowners and workers. The government's agenda paid little attention to the insistence from the indigenous community members that it reexamine the legality of landlords' property, which they claimed had been illegally usurped over the last decades. When the government referred to indigenous communities, it described their situation as one marked by backwardness, and it discussed mechanisms such as the creation of collective farms to put them on the so-called road to development. Villarroel's reluctance to include comunario demands for the revision of fraudulent sales is even more striking when we consider that caciques apoderados were denouncing the dispossession of their lands in national newspapers at the same time as the 1945 indigenous congress was taking place. During the months of preparation before the congress, caciques apoderados from Omasuyos (La Paz) paid for advertisements in *La Calle*, denouncing a recently arrived citizen, Juan Roberts, who intended to strip them of their land.[72] Villarroel's aversion to addressing such demands shows the limits of the government's agenda and the unwillingness of the regime to challenge the structure of property itself.

Gotkowitz suggests that government willingness to include grassroots demands shrank over time. When the government first agreed to launch the congress, it relied on a nongovernmental entity known as the Comité Indigenal Boliviano, the Bolivian Indigenous Committee, that prepared a list of twenty-seven demands starting and ending with the slogan, "land belongs to the Indians that it be returned to the community."[73] The driving force behind this platform was Luis Ramos Quevedo, a labor organizer who belonged to the Federación Obrera Sindical in Oruro and had developed contacts with caciques apoderados since the 1920s. Gotkowitz argues that in the face of continued landlord accusations against Ramos Quevedo for subversive activity in the countryside, the government put him in jail and launched a more moderate political platform. She also notes that most of the items listed in the twenty-seven-point agenda did not appear in the official program or government decrees.[74]

Despite the restrained political agenda, the very presence of twelve hundred indigenous leaders in the political capital of the republic had an enormous impact on Bolivian society and was seen as a serious blow to the SBR. The politically moderate paper *Revista Bolivia* described the political atmosphere in the aftermath of the 1945 congress:

> The first National Indigenous Congress took place in La Paz . . . despite the enormous anxiety of those who thrive at the expense of the natives. They thought it was nonsense to call a meeting of the indigenous peoples because this would only light the fire of rebellion. . . . They know that the Indians had become conscious of their situation and that now they know well they are irremediable victims of oppression . . . but the congress surprised most people and, later, it gathered genuine support for their demands. . . . They ask to be considered as human beings and not as slaves. . . . They ask for schools, agrarian institutions, and a labor regime that would prevent them from doing vile non-paid work.[75]

Although this description captures the feelings produced by the political momentum of the 1945 congress, it overlooks the long-term political fights waged by comunarios and colonos to protect their rights, from the early political and legal struggles of the caciques apoderados to the 1920s rebellions to colono sit-down strikes and the early efforts at unionization. The magazine inaccurately suggested that Indian political consciousness and awareness had started with the congress—a political narrative that suited Villarroel's desire to portray the regime as the only engine for social change.

At the conclusion of the indigenous congress, the government signed four decrees that recapitulated Villarroel's agenda on the Indian question. In an interview in the monthly publication *Revista Bolivia*, Francisco Chipana Ramos, the indigenous leader who presided over the congress, described the decrees as a watershed moment in the transition from indigenous slavery to citizenship and as a challenge to the principles of hierarchy and authority that characterized everyday relations between landlords and colonos and comunarios. Considering how difficult it has been for historians to locate Chipana Ramos's views in his own words, it is worth transcribing this text to its full extent:

> Q: Are you pleased with the Congress over which you presided?
>
> A: I am happy with the four decrees signed by the President of the Republic. . . . We can now work peacefully and without harassment. But even more so, they have restored our confidence that we will now be free. They have ended our condition as slaves. The four decrees satisfy our claims. Before the decrees . . . we suffered and we were treated as animals. There were no laws for us, no guarantees. . . .
>
> Q: What is the content of the decrees?
>
> A: The first states that there will be a Code of Agrarian Work. The Ministries of Labor, Health, Social Provision, Agriculture, Farming, and Colonization are in charge of writing it. We will not be assigned obligatory work for more than four days a week. We will not be forced to work for free or on other haciendas. When the *patrón* [landlord] wishes to have extra work done, he will have to pay wages. This law regulating agrarian labor will be ready by the end of 1945. The second law protects our rights within the estates. We will willingly work for the hacienda because we can control our own crops and dispose of them as we see fit. It will no longer be obligatory to grant to the landholders our lambs, wool, poultry, and other things for free. The other law says that we will have schools, principally where there are agricultural businesses, estates, or haciendas. And the last and most important law refers to the end of the system of personal

> servitude. That is to say that we will no longer work for weeks or months in the house of a *patrón* as pongos [colonos] for no pay. . . . From now on, our services will be paid as with any other job.[76]

The decrees regulating work on the haciendas represented a serious state intervention into customs in the countryside. Gotkowitz notes that, although the official program and the presidential decrees suppressed discussions concerning land and property, both President Villarroel and Hernán Siles, a prominent member of the MNR, made statements in favor of land reform. In a final speech to the indigenous congress, Siles declared that "land should belong to those who work it."[77]

The indigenous congress and its decrees were met with numerous criticisms from conservative and left-wing parties alike. Members of the PIR, the MNR's most important political rival, viewed the congress with skepticism. José Antonio Arze, leader of the PIR, criticized the event in a pamphlet titled *Bolivia bajo el terrorismo nazifacista* (Bolivia under Nazi Fascist terrorism) accusing Villarroel of having persecuted the opposition, including the worker leaders whose support he claimed to have. Arze considered the congress a joke, a "laughable comedy," a parody that would not alleviate "the feudal misery of the Indians."[78] Arze criticized the MNR's duplicitous actions of encouraging the representatives of the Comité Indigenal and later repressing them. "A few weeks ago, the government promoted the meeting of a so-called indigenista congress that was the most laughable comedy. When a few Indians, taking seriously the agrarian stirrings of the government, began to develop actions against the large hacendados, the police arrested them as communists, as agents of pirismo [members of PIR], and Villarroel himself, in a closing speech at this congress, specified to the Indians that the government was not willing to help them, but that their obligation was to continue to be obedient to their *patrones*."[79]

From Santiago de Chile, Ricardo Anaya, another prominent PIR leader, published a document titled *Unidos venceremos. PIR, mensaje al pueblo boliviano* (Together we will win: PIR message to the Bolivian people). Anaya believed that the congress was not a serious effort to understand the "peasant problem" but rather a mechanism to prevent a peasant revolt: "In the face of a peasant uprising, the government hastened to stop it by immediately convening an indigenous congress. . . . But before calling for the congress . . . the Ministers of Government, Agriculture, and Labor, accompanied by a large number of civil servants made trips to the provinces of La Paz, Oruro, Cochabamba, Potosi, Sucre, and Tarija as appeasers of the peasant rebellion. In every place they visited, they left armed police pickets to hold off the peasants and submit them to the authority of the hacendados."[80]

Both leaders criticized Villarroel's top-down reformist program, which curbed grassroots' agendas by jailing and sending local community leaders into exile. Anaya attacked Villarroel's duplicitous language. "Right after Villarroel spoke about the Indians' redemption, his government assured landlords that his administration would protect private property. In fact, before the beginning of the congress, Minister Carlos Morales Guillén, stated: it is false that the government intends to carry out the so-called reversion of lands to the Indian; the government will comply with legal obligations and property rights and will warn indigenous people to peacefully and quietly return to their labors with the mark of respect owed to the authorities and to private property."[81]

Anaya argued that Villarroel's decrees did not challenge property relations and that the conclusions of the congress amounted to "the dismissal of peasant aspirations, since the 1,200 Indian delegates . . . remained zealously guarded by police authorities for the entire duration of the congress." The congress's minutes addressed "the abolition of peonage, or unpaid personal service; the creation of rural schools in haciendas and communities; the definition of patrons' obligations and duties toward Indians; and other questions of lesser importance." However, they neglected one fundamental issue—the distribution of land—an element that, as Anaya suggested, "the government had eliminated and suppressed from discussion beforehand."[82]

Although the formal agenda of Villarroel's government silenced the indigenous demands for land, Gotkowitz argues that the mere calling of the congress allowed indigenous leaders to articulate their interests and claims to the land.[83] She suggests that the language of "Indians rights" promoted by the government and officially sanctioned by central authorities was a powerful mobilizer for the more than twelve hundred indigenous leaders who returned to their communities to confront the abuses of landholders and local authorities in the name of the law.

President Villarroel and the members of the MNR who supported his regime incorporated Indian exclusion as a key element of their political agenda. This was demonstrated in both their initial proposals to Congress and the final congressional declarations. However, they were cautious and evasive when it came to proposing a redefinition of property rights. As Anaya pointed out, Minister Carlos Morales Guillen insisted that the government would protect private property. Did the members of the PIR have a better-formulated proposal for the expropriation of the latifundio? Anaya details his party's proposal for what he considered a real agrarian policy in 1945:

> Our agriculture demands a major transformation encompassing from the big to the small farmer who needs the help and the orientation of the State. The

> problem of the Indian, as we have said ten thousand times, is a problem of land, *and the problem of agrarian reform is a question of overcoming feudalism through vast irrigation and modernization that benefits everyone who possesses land, great or small,* so, in this period of bourgeois democratic revolution, the first task consists in putting the fields in a state which will be conducive to producing enough to feed our population; *it consists of enabling the individual property owners as well as the indigenous communities to use machines and apply scientific knowledge, in organizing collective farms, in granting to the small peasants facilities to exploit the land more efficiently.* When the communities, the collective farms, the productive cooperatives, with the help of the elements that give us progress, begin to produce on a large scale, intensify cultivation, and lower the costs of production, the *latifundistas* themselves will be overwhelmed by this formidable process and will have to adopt the rhythm of civilization. (emphasis added)[84]

Because of the difficulty of challenging the predominant economic and political voice of the SRB and its representatives in Congress prior to 1945, the PIR seemed reluctant to openly challenge existing systems of property. Anaya's proposal mentioned irrigation and modernization, which the PIR hoped would transform Bolivia from a feudal economy into a modern economy. PIR members issued slogans for agrarian reform, but they did not clearly advocate for the expropriation and redistribution of lands. Nevertheless, such cautious behavior did nothing to prevent multiple accusations that members of the left were instigating subversion in the countryside.[85]

On July 21, 1946, a popular revolt led by teachers and university students produced a general strike that culminated in the violent death of the president in the main plaza of the presidential palace in La Paz. Villarroel's murder buried the agenda of protecting colonos' work in the countryside. The PIR, suppressed during the government of Villarroel, formed a peculiar alliance with the most conservative forces in the country in what was called the Frente Democrático Antifascista (FDA), the Antifascist Democratic Front.[86] This alliance brought together notable PIR figures such as Ricardo Anaya and José Antonio Arze with reactionary former government minister Pedro Zilveti, one of the harshest persecutors of left-leaning politicians during the Peñaranda administration.

Circumventing the Question of Land Reform

The assassination of the nationalist Villarroel started a six-year period of conservative presidents known in Bolivia as the *sexenio.* President Enrique Hertzog (1947–1949) persecuted, jailed, and exiled most of Villarroel's followers, primarily members of the MNR. Despite governmental attempts to suppress Indian and peasant leaders demanding the fulfilment of Villarroel's decrees, the government was not able to control the wave of urban and rural revolts and uprisings.[87] Soon after Villarroel's death, Indian uprisings occurred in many important areas including Pucarani, Topohoco, Aygachi, Tacanaca (La Paz), Norte de Potosí, Yayani, Tirita, Morochata (Cochabamba), and Chuiriga (Chuquisaca). The official reports from local authorities included rumors of uprisings, attacks on landowners, riots, and even cases of murders of hacendados or majordomos.[88]

The wave of rural unrest put the PIR in an increasingly difficult position. While the PIR had supported peasant demands since the early 1940s, the party had to adapt its rhetoric to function in its new alliance with the conservative government. According to Anaya: "It is true that during the uprisings some Indians participated in bloodthirsty acts; this happened because of the centuries of suffering of the Indian people."[89] His rhetoric resembles the one used by the liberals and republicans that described the uprisings as ruthless acts. Anaya reinforced the negative stereotype of the "barbaric Indian" circulated by their conservative allies. Rather than disputing the characterization of the Indians as barbarians, the PIR explained that the uprisings were the result of indigenous peoples' living conditions. In essence, there was little difference between the racist ideologies of the PIR and those of the right-wing political elites that justified and naturalized Indians' subordinated place in the society.

Responding to the growing violence in the countryside and in an attempt to distance their agenda from the one promoted by Villarroel and the MNR, the PIR presented its own reform proposal to Congress. The proposal outlined the creation of an institute of agrarian reform that would manage production scientifically and would have the capacity and authority to expropriate large unproductive estates based on strict technical criteria. After the 1938 national convention, this was the most significant attempt to reposition the debate on land reform in Congress by shifting the focus from labor rights to property rights. Since the nineteenth century, Bolivian legislation had allowed the expropriation of properties for public use.[90] This principle was applied numerous times to both urban and rural properties. For example, the government expropriated several rural properties in Cliza (Germán Jordán Province) in 1941, 1947, and 1948 for the construction of a dam on the Angostura Strait. In each case, the state compensated the property owners. The novelty of the PIR proposal was to apply that principle broadly to unproductive large estates and give them to the peasants who worked them. In an attempt to be conciliatory, the PIR publicly recognized that some rural properties were productive, and it proposed the creation of an independent agrarian institute that would be in charge of classifying which properties should face expropriation. According to José Antonio Arze, leader of the party: "We think that in the initial period . . . *we should only apply the expropriation to properties that fall under one of the following criteria:* (a) *those that are voluntarily offered by their owners*, (b) those that are unproductive and mismanaged by their owners. We would like to see large properties worked scientifically and intensively. Only this process will lead to an anti-feudal revolution" (emphasis added).[91] The PIR acknowledged that their proposal challenged fundamental principles of private property, and because of that, they strove to temper their project:

> We know *there are progressive landholders* who were not able to introduce agricultural machinery to their properties, because they don't have enough capital to do it individually. . . . *The backwardness of agriculture cannot be blamed on the landlords but, rather, on the stagnation from which the countryside suffers.* . . . I say that the State should interest itself in the plight of progressive landowners . . . help them to escape from feudal forms of production in which they are trapped even against their own will, and impose . . . the agenda of improvement and transformation of living conditions and production in the countryside. (emphasis added)[92]

The PIR did not propose a process of general expropriation—as had happened after the revolution of 1952—but, rather, a measured and gradual redistribution that only targeted unproductive lands. The language of the proposal sought to reconcile increasing grassroots demands for agrarian reform with the consolidated property rights of rural owners and the inflexible standpoints of the SRB. The PIR attempted to appear sympathetic to landlords' needs by claiming that rural owners were not responsible for the backwardness of agriculture since most of them were eager to get the loans and machinery necessary to manage production scientifically. They effectively used technical assessments as the means to pull Bolivia's countryside out of the feudal stage. They believed that growing peasant demands could be met with a controlled and limited program of land redistribution combined with a plan for the colonization of the Eastern Lowlands.[93]

The PIR attempted to create a middle-ground project for land reform that could promote rural development, placate the demands of the peasants, and protect the property rights of those labeled as progressive property owners. The Federación Rural de Cochabmaba (FRC), Rural Federation of Cochabamba, one of the most powerful landlord organizations in the country, angrily attacked the project. The tone of the arguments of Eduardo del Granado, the FRC's legal representative, demonstrates once again the narrow limits within which progressive political parties sought to effect change. In a document titled, "El presente estudio crítico del Dr. Eduardo del Granado ha sido aprobado por la federación rural de Cochabamba como expresión de la defensa de los derechos del agricultor contra el comunismo" (Communist attack of the PIR on democracy and agriculture), del

Granado argued: "Our liberty is attacked by communism. Inspired by the liberty bequeathed by our forbearers, we take up the pen to defend it. The Rural Federation, breaking the silence and indifference, stands up to say that it is time to defend the tutelary institutions of democracy and the vital interests of agriculture [threatened] by the PIR project."[94]

According to del Granado, the project for creating the Institute of Agrarian Reform did not represent rural property owners. He asked: "Why do they try to silence the voices of those who are best prepared and most knowledgeable? It is simply because communism intends to control agrarian planning through this institute, endangering in this way the right to private property."[95] On the question of expropriation of unproductive estates, del Granado commented: "The result of expropriation will be to give to the colono the lands of his employer, for which the state would have to spend countless sums to establish collective farms, badly managed by the fiscal functionaries." He also remarked on the indigenous communities by reminding his readers of another common trope—indigenous communities as a symbol of backwardness. He stated:

> The indigenous communal system, instead of being a force of progress, is a hindrance, due to the lack of divisions which creates all sorts of problems. . . . *We were not aware that giving the land to the peasants was a method for augmenting food production, increasing the raw material of plant origin, and providing welfare to the farmworkers.* Experience demonstrates the opposite. Indigenous communities have never been factors of progress because their mentality is full of prejudices. As a result, we do not see dikes on communal lands, or irrigation works, roads, new forms of cultivation, experimental studies, or the use of machinery. All of this is done at the initiative of the *patrón* who is, according to the communists, an exploiter who should be attacked without quarter, stripping him of all of his rights and burdening him with taxes. (emphasis added).[96]

In a passionate defense of the system of peonage, del Granado argued: "The authority of the employer over his colonos responds to the imperative need for discipline and organization in agricultural work. . . . Should we suppress these services to follow some non-sense schedule or due to an aversion to peonage? In the frame of our current legislation, property owners and their colonos display traditional customs by which the indigenous willingly abide."[97] As to the longings of the leftists for the "acculturation of the Indian," del Granado proposes that, in a superior environment, the Indian and even a savage could acquire the civilized life.[98]

Against such a shattering critique of the project for the Institute of Agrarian Reform, Mario Rolón Anaya, another member of the PIR, declared that the FRC was determined to stop all discussion by alarming the public with the specter of communism and assuming that any project for reform was an attack on private property. Rolón Anaya believed that the transformation of agriculture was a national necessity and should not be halted in the name of what the FRC called traditional customs. Rolón Anaya asserted: "After more than a century in which traditional customs prevailed unaltered, we can see that they require a substantive and radical transformation, not only because Indian slavery under the ominous institution of peonage is an act contrary to civilization and the dignity of our people but also because in more than a century of feudal domination of agriculture."[99] He argued that the project was simply giving life to principles already approved in the 1938 constitution: "The project only speaks of expropriation with indemnification of large estates that fail to fulfill the principle of social function. . . . Expropriation is not viewed as a method to be applied generally."[100]

Congress rejected the PIR's project in 1947. However, many of the ideas introduced in this proposal were later included in the 1953 decree of agrarian reform—the classification of land according to size and region, the creation of the Institute of Agrarian Reform, the indemnification of the affected large estates, and colonization as a response to peasants' increasing pressure for land of their own. The multiple proposals presented in Congress during the 1940s illustrated the numerous ways in which the rather cautious and moderate nationalist and left parties tried to change the structure of power in the Bolivian countryside before the revolution. Those proposals ranged from regulating colono working conditions to taxing rural properties to considering the expropriation of uncultivable land. The notably careful language regarding regulation and the emphasis on absolute respect for landlords' private property bore no fruit whatsoever. The Bolivian Rural Society and their representatives in Parliament defeated all congressional attempts at change.

Conclusions

Rafael Reyeros was a prominent Bolivian writer whose political thinking combined Hispanism, anticlericalism, and Marxism. Concerned with the ways in which the Bolivian state should deal with the "Indian problem," he fought against the organization of the indigenous schools, arguing that they locked the Indian into their ayllu instead of promoting their incorporation into the nation. In 1937, he published a work titled *Caquiaviri. Escuelas para los indígenas bolivianos* (Caquiaviri: Schools for indigenous Bolivians) in which he argued for incorporating natives into the nation through education and saving them from the vices of alcoholism and coca-leaf addiction (coquismo). A decade later, Reyeros published *El Pongueaje* (Peonage) in which he denounced the conditions of exploitation to which the Indians were subjected on the haciendas.[101] This intellectual trajectory is characteristic of the broader transition of a generation of intellectuals over the first half of the twentieth century. Despite a few marginal voices that, in the 1920s, targeted the question of land as the essence of the "Indian problem," most intellectuals, including many who considered themselves indigenistas, thought that the "Indian problem" and "his incorporation into national life" would be resolved through education. In the 1940s, Bolivia witnessed an agitated political debate over colono living conditions on the haciendas, the system of peonage, and peasants' access to land. But this transformation did not mean that the views of these intellectuals, including the most progressive, were free of profound contradictions and racism. When Reyeros was writing *Peonage*, as director of the Department of Indigenous Affairs, he created a questionnaire of 650 questions intended for the local state functionaries (subprefects, *corregidores*) so that he could be informed about the living conditions of Indians on haciendas and communities. Rather than an exploration into indigenous living conditions, the questionnaire was a confirmation of most of the prejudices that the middle and upper classes in Bolivia held concerning indigenous peoples. Some of the questions included in the pamphlet were: "What vices are predominant in the community? Do they drink out of spite, over setbacks? Do they drink at every opportunity and to excess until getting drunk and passing out? Is degeneration owing to alcohol abuse notable among them? Do they treat their women and children badly? Do they have a notion of private property? Are they inclined to robbery or theft? Do fathers and sons sleep in promiscuity? Do they join with the mestizos, do they separate from or repudiate them?"[102]

The indigenistas, the military socialists, and later, the nationalist and leftist parties dramatically expanded the political debate over the Indian question in the first half of the twentieth century. All these actors brought an arsenal of new ideas into the national political arena focusing on protection of the colonos' working conditions against the landlords' defense of rural traditions. Nationalist and leftist questioned the tenancy of large unproductive lands, yet both were also careful not to offend the vociferous SRB that asserted that landlords were essential for the modernization and development of the countryside. Although the conservative parties and the SRB blocked the changes proposed by the nationalist and leftist parties, progressive intellectuals' own views of the Indians as backward prevented them from recognizing indigenous political actions and agendas in their own right. Both the leftist and the nationalist parties overlooked the long-term petitions coming from traditional indigenous authorities. Communities continued to fight against ongoing dispossession by landlords, but the PIR and the MNR only referred to indigenous communities when discussing how to overcome their backwardness and how to drag them onto the path of modernization and development.

CHAPTER THREE

REVOLUTION COMES TO THE COUNTRYSIDE

In 1946 a coalition of right- and left-wing political parties overthrew nationalist president Gualberto Villarroel and held power for six years. Although the conservative presidents that ruled between 1946 and 1952 did not dare repeal Villarroel's decrees of 1945, they crushed the peasant leaders' attempts to implement the decrees in the countryside.[1] Despite the blatant political repression, President Mamerto Urrolagoitia (1949–1951) sought to maintain a façade of democracy in the country by calling for elections in 1951. Most of the leaders of the MNR were in exile. Yet, the party won the election. Unwilling to confer power to the political party that had so closely worked with President Villarroel in the 1940s, President Urrolagoitia granted power to the army. The rule of that military junta ended abruptly in April 1952 when a mass upheaval overthrew the regime headed by General Hugo Ballivián in a three-day popular insurrection. Militia workers, party activists, townspeople, and miners defeated the army in an extraordinary step to quell counter-revolutionary forces. Víctor Paz Estenssoro, the leader of the MNR who was exiled in Buenos Aires, returned to Bolivia as the leader of the revolution.[2]

In August 1953 after sixteen months in power, in the village of Ucureña in front of thousands of peasants, Paz Estenssoro signed the Agrarian Reform Decree-Law. The historical decree abolished personal labor services and implemented one of the most extensive programs of land redistribution among peasants in Latin America.[3] As part of his political capital, President Paz Estenssoro and his party have usually proclaimed that the successful process of land distribution that started in 1953 was already part of MNR's initial agenda.[4] However, the government was in fact reluctant to begin a generalized program of land redistribution and instead attempted to introduce a wage system on the haciendas.

To understand the transformation of the MNR's agrarian program, it is important to consider two critical political processes that occurred immediately after the revolution: a profound democratization of the state apparatus and the erosion of landlords' formal and informal means of power. These processes were the result of parallel and intricate events unleashed after the revolution. When the MNR came to power, they believed that regulating labor relations rather than property relations would be sufficient to appease the conflict between landlords and colonos in the countryside.[5] To implement this plan, the government sent hundreds of local officials to haciendas throughout the countryside to establish labor contracts between landlords and colonos. At the same time, the government rescinded the law that prohibited peasants from organizing unions in the countryside. According to the government's plan, the secretary of each union would be responsible for signing the contract for each hacienda.

However, the peasant unions not only disputed the working conditions on the haciendas (as the MNR expected), they also challenged landlords' long-standing control over selecting local authorities. Initially, the peasant unions constituted the most efficient mechanism to restrain the discretionary power that local authorities had over colonos and comunarios. Later, with the support of agents of the Ministry of Peasant Affairs, peasant unions gained the power to name these authorities themselves. When the existing network of local political authority began to crumble, both the landlords and the national government found it increasingly difficult to impose labor contracts on the haciendas. In most provinces, the plan to transform colonos into waged workers only lasted between one and two years. To pressure the government to order the expropriation of the lands they worked, the peasants declined to sign new agreements with the landlords or refused to share the harvest with them.

Fulfilling President Villarroel's 1945 Agenda

During the first months of the revolution, the political goal for both MNR leaders and peasants was to implement the decrees that President Villarroel enacted in 1945. After six years of ruthless political oppression, colonos and comunarios viewed the MNR's victory as a major opportunity to petition for the liberation of their leaders. President Paz Estenssoro received many letters from the provinces of La Paz, Oruro, Cochabamba, and Chuquisaca demanding freedom for their leaders who had been jailed and confined since the 1947 uprisings.[6] According to many petitioners, they had been incarcerated for simply demanding the implementation of the 1945 Villarroel decrees. In July 1952, in response to these multiple petitions, the president decreed the freedom of all workers, miners, and peasants who had been jailed because of the political mobilization over the last six years.[7]

Despite this important concession to peasant demands, many members of the government were uneasy with the idea of openly siding with the peasants against the landlords. For instance, when the government freed the peasant leaders who led a revolt in Cochabamba in 1947 (Yayani), and the still powerful Cochabamba FRC made an outcry in the newspaper: "The assassins of Yayani will be freed," the Minister of Agriculture Germán Vera Tapia who signed the order liberating the peasants was careful not to look as if he was on the peasants' side. Rather than proclaiming their freedom, he admonished them by saying, "I hope you learned from the experience. . . . I hope you will use your freedom to work for the nation."[8]

The peasants' initial petitions and their expectations of the revolution were rooted in the ongoing political struggles of the 1940s. They covered a broad range of subjects that included ending landlords' abuses, establishing rural schools, accessing pastures, and abolishing pongueaje.[9] The document that best exemplifies this is the pact signed by Paz Estenssoro, then leader of the MNR, with Antonio Álvarez Mamani, the leader of the Peasant Agrarian Federation a year prior to the revolution. This "secret pact" (as the newspaper called it) was published by the newspaper *El Diario* in January 1953 as a way to expose MNR's alliances with peasants before the revolution.[10] In exchange of peasant support, the MNR agreed to encourage cooperation from the Agricultural Bank for agricultural support for community members; to grant fellowships for Indian peasants to go to universities; to create a radio and a newspaper oriented to the nurturing of the Indian race in Aymara and Quechua languages; to create cooperatives for Indian people; to permit citizenship for all indigenous men and women; to recognize peasant unions as well as the Agrarian Peasant Federation; and to eliminate pongueaje and all nonpaid work as was established by President Gualberto Villarroel.[11] The pact reveals an ambitious and elaborate platform that included Villarroel's 1945 decrees on behalf of Indians and other crucial demands for political participation, education (sometimes expressed as a "civilizing" endeavor), and loans to community members for agricultural production. Yet, the detailed agreement did not include a single word about land expropriation. Rather than exposing the inflammatory politics of the MNR and the peasants agrarian federation, the pact demonstrates that 1945 Villarroel decrees provided "a language of contention" (as Gotkowitz points out) that continued to be strong and valid after the revolution.[12]

Considering the importance of the agenda President Villarroel initiated in 1945, it is not surprising that, in May 1952, President Paz Estenssoro reenacted the decrees and publicized them throughout the media. The enactment of the decrees granted Paz Estenssoro immediate peasant political support. The decrees established that colonos could not be forced to undertake any work other than agricultural tasks unless landlords and colonos had previously discussed fair economic compensation. They abolished all unpaid personal services including pongueaje, *mitinaje*, delivering goods to the city, spinning, selling products in the market, and *mukeo* (chewing corn to prepare *chicha*). The decrees also gave colonos the right to keep their harvest. They could use it or sell it at their discretion. Additionally, landlords could not force colonos to pay property taxes, nor could they use physical violence against colonos. Finally, the decrees mandated that landlords must provide schooling for their workers' children on their properties.[13]

The decrees also prescribed serious punishment for peasants involved in subversive activity. The ratified Decree 318 (May 15, 1945) prohibited peasant leaders from collecting economic contributions from their followers to campaign against landlords within the hacienda. It stated that those involved in subversive political activities (*agitación política*) would be removed from the hacienda and lose access to their plots. They could also be "relocated" to one of the colonies that the Ministry of Agriculture had established in the lowlands. This relocation effectively amounted to confinement.[14]

Initially, the government expected that the release of political prisoners and the enactment of labor contracts would bring political stability to the countryside, but by the end of the year political conflict in the countryside had only increased. At the same time that the MNR was actively operating in the countryside, militants of the POR, the Trotskyist Party, were promoting a more radical agenda in these areas. The POR proclaimed that the government should carry out an agrarian revolution instead of an agrarian reform. Government and media reports reveal that Cochabamba's valleys were at the heart of POR political action.[15]

At the end of 1952, the MNR aggressively discouraged POR's demands and announced that the government would not launch such a program for land redistribution. In a public rally in December 1952, the Minister of Peasant Affairs Ñuflo Chavez Ortiz joined the Minister of Mines Juan Lechín Oquendo (one of the most radical voices within Paz Estenssoro's cabinet) to declare that by promoting labor contracts and creating peasant labor courts (*juzgados de trabajo campesino*) the government was already leading an "agrarian revolution," directly borrowing POR's political terminology.[16] Vicente Echenique Falcon, who was in charge of the Office of Peasant Affairs in Cochabamba, declared: "Peasants now realized that there will not be land distribution."[17]

The president hoped that a prompt intervention of state agents in the countryside would also pacify landlords' concerns about disorder, turmoil, and uprisings. In order to implement labor contracts on the haciendas, the government created the Ministerio de Asuntos Campesinos (MAC), the Ministry of Peasant Affairs, in May 1952. This was the first time that an entire ministry was dedicated to "peasant affairs," which had previously been the purview of a simple administrative department. It was also the first time that issues such as agriculture, labor, and peasants' petitions were to be considered jointly by the same bureau. One of MAC's first initiatives was to send commissioners to the rural provinces to establish work contracts in the haciendas from the end of 1952 to 1953.

By reinstating Villarroel's decrees, the party claimed that the revolution would protect colonos' working conditions on the haciendas without challenging the core structure of property in the countryside.[18] Although, discursively, the MNR assured the contracts were designed to protect colonos against the landlords' arbitrary decisions, in reality, many of these contracts underscored colonos' obligations more than their rights. One contract signed on hacienda Merke Achacachi (Omasuyos) in July 1954 illustrates the rigorous work conditions even after the revolution:

> The peasants of Merke Achacachi estate will work on all tasks related to agriculture. They will retain 60 percent of the production for their own use and grant 40 percent of the production to the landholder. In exchange, the owner will provide seeds to the peasants. The owner will not pay any kind of salary, seeds, or tools to the colonos. Each herder will be responsible for the death or illness or any neglect of the cattle. The peasants' general secretary will be responsible for not letting the colonos use pastureland belonging to the large estate. We peasants declare our full compliance.[19]

The government was unable to establish one standard contract across the countryside. Rather than proving the government's authority, the contracts largely adopted ongoing local practices. In Sud Yungas, several haciendas had implemented labor contracts before the agrarian reform; these included specifications as to some kind of wage. Therefore, when the MAC officials arrived, they encouraged landlords and colonos to continue signing wage contracts. The contracts signed with the mediation of the MAC's commissioners drastically increased the colonos' salaries from five bolivianos to two hundred or even three hundred per week.[20]

The contracts also disclosed the striking differences in salary between men and women. Prior to the revolution, women's labor on the hacienda counted for only one-half or two-thirds of men's. The new labor contracts consolidated these gender disparities instead of challenging them. Before the agrarian reform, women's pay was about one-third less than that of men. In some cases, women worked more days per week than men. After the revolution, women's wages also rose, but wages were still at least one-third less than those of their male counterparts. The revolution did not alter the widespread belief that women's labor could not be compared to men's work. Landowners, mayordomos (hacienda administrators), MNR leaders, civil servants, and peasants all shared these convictions. (See Appendix 3.1 for some examples of women's wages.)

However, the contracts did not last long. Although many state officers at the local level convinced landlords and colonos to sign contracts for the

Figure 3.1. A revolutionary political cartoon from 1953 describes the situation of the Indian before and after the revolution, according to the MNR. "Admired initiative from the government," *La Nación*, April 22, 1953. Photo courtesy of Biblioteca y Archivo Histórico de la Asamblea Legislativa Plurinacional.

years 1952 and 1953, the colonos refused to sign another agreement in 1954. Some of the factors that led to their failure to sign were the rapid decline of landlords' political power at the local and national levels, the destabilizing political activities of a number of colonos, and comunarios' petitioning for control of the political power at the local level, and the subversive role of the POR as well as of some of the state agents working for MAC who spread the word about land distribution (instead of promoting the labor contracts).

Rural Political Power under Fire

From the start of the revolution, colono and comunario leaders demanded that the national government curb the abuses they continued to suffer at the hands of local state officials. Both groups complained that local authorities illegally forced them to perform random tasks, such as repairing public buildings or even their own houses with no compensation at all. Some protested that corregidores (the executive heads each of one subsection of a province), policemen, and local judges imposed arbitrary taxes. In essence, peasants demanded that the state be transformed from one focused on the surveillance of peasants to one that guaranteed their rights.

Denunciations of this type were not new. Neither were the letters or admonishments from higher-ranked authorities ordering their subordinates to halt their abuses. What had changed, however, was the national government's strict scrutiny through the ministry. Gotkowitz states that, from the late 1930s through the 1940s, indigenous and peasant leaders used the language of "rights" to bolster their demands. Although this language may not sound particularly revolutionary, in a rural world where powerful landlords and merchants were used to controlling political and economic power, the simple demand of protection from the state deeply shook the traditional hierarchies.[21] A cartoon published a year after the revolution vividly depicts the new situation (see figure 3.1). The cartoon suggests that whereas before the revolution the army repressed Indians and peasants, after the revolution the army would persecute the "local state officers" and landlords because of their abuses against peasants. Landlords, as well as a sizable portion of the state bureaucracy, were now under suspicion.

The MNR had strong tactical reasons to create a solid pact with the peasantry against local officials. The party had learned firsthand during Villarroel's presidency that seizing the presidency was not enough to retain political power. They now understood that the subprefects and corregidores represented entrenched cliques allied to local landlords, and that government authority would be constantly threatened if it did not have full control over the countryside. When Villarroel was in office, he was unable to break the ties between landlords and provincial officials. As a result, the landlords easily reversed his policies only months after his death. The MNR realized that only a powerful alliance with the peasantry could protect the government, especially the head of state.[22]

In order to limit the power wielded in the countryside by subprefects, corregidores, and intendants (authorities that depended on the Ministry of Government), the president ordered that agents from the MAC (agrarian inspectors) would now deal directly with the demands of colonos and Indian community members. This turned the countryside into a battleground for denunciations and counterdenunciations between MAC inspectors and other local state officials. Although the new appointments did not replace the old bureaucracy, long-serving local authorities soon complained that the new functionaries from La Paz city were eroding their power and creating disorder. The police intendant of Los Andes province complained: "How could a simple MAC functionary arrogate to themselves the power to name local authorities in Los Andes [province] in complete defiance of the competences of the Minister of Government?"[23]

Similar complaints from different rural provinces accused MAC inspectors of seizing new powers in the countryside and ignoring the authority of the existing functionaries. In response, MAC agents argued that their interventions sought to end routine abuses against peasants, and they criticized local officers for viewing all peasant meetings and union organizing as acts of subversion. It is difficult to grasp the actual political situation in the countryside in the midst of this long list of charges and countercharges. When news about general subversion would reach La Paz from one source, another state source would claim that activities perceived as subversion were actually leading up to a rally in support of the government. For example, in April and May 1953, two official reports were filed from Capinota Province in Cochabamba with distinctly different interpretations of the same scene. On the one hand, an agent of the MAC informed the head of the ministry of the successful organization of a peasant regiment. Mario Montenegro declared that he had organized a union with eight thousand members with the support of Sinforoso Rivas, the executive secretary of Cochabamba Peasant Federation. They are ready, he said, to fight for the revolution. He also complained about landlords' continuing abuses against colonos: "We want to denounce the corregidor and carabineros' continued abuse of peasants, they want peasants to continue working without fair retribution and no salary at all."[24]

Two weeks later, a subcommander from Capinota reported to the Ministry of Defense that there had been a violent assault of properties by peasants who were allegedly led by Mario Montenegro:

> Extreme agitation reigns in this region. Attacks on properties and landlords are common. I can tell that peasant leaders are inciting Indians to assault properties, to seize harvests, and to beat landlords. The other day the father of Captain Vidal Ayala Mercado, who serves in this command, had been jailed and beaten by the Indians when he was trying to return to his property Airampu [Totora in Carrasco Province]. Additionally, Colonel Nestor Valenzuela heard that a peasant leader, Mario Montenegro, a former member of the Office of Peasant Affairs [dependent of MAC], ordered Indians to seize lands because they think landlords no longer have rights from now on.[25]

It is difficult to assess the real situation in Capinota in 1952, since each of the informants had close ties to the local actors. As seen above, Montenegro had a close relationship with Sinforoso Rivas, the main leader of Federación de Campesinos de Cochabamba, the Cochabamba's Peasant Federation. On the other hand, the letter sent by the subcommander illustrates the close links between his informants and the local landlords. The conflict against these two branches of the state in Capinota also demonstrates that violence was a key political tool for delegitimizing the opponent. At least until the beginning of 1953, national authorities carefully avoid choosing sides, when the balance of power began to shift.

Attacking Landlords' Political Power from above and below

In addition to the newly created Ministry of Peasant Affairs (MAC), whose agents worked to destabilize local power networks, the MNR undertook key steps to undermine landlords' power at the national, regional, and local levels. At the national level the MNR seized landlords' most important regional organizations; at the local level the party promoted peasant political organization. Comunarios and colonos seized the opportunity to organize thousands of unions, comandos, and peasant regiments all across the countryside. The unions became the de facto political organization in charge of nominating political authorities in the countryside. This political implosion from below sealed a pact between peasants and government that outlived the overthrow of the MNR in 1964.

In February 1953 Paz Estenssoro struck a blow to landholders' political power on the national stage. He ordered the seizure of the assets and an audit of the Landlord Rural Society in Yungas (SPY), and he directed the arrest of many members of the rural societies of Cochabamba and Sucre, the most potent advocates of landlord interests in the country. SRB had successfully curbed PIR and MNR proposals for agrarian reform in the 1940s. Despite being private organizations, these institutions had access to public funding and loans. In many provinces, rural societies were in charge of administering public funds and even obtaining credit to build roads and infrastructure that would contribute to the development of the countryside.[26] All these characteristics made rural societies powerful political and economic organizations. In April 1953, responding, according to the MNR, to small landholders' accusations of corruption, nepotism, and inefficiency, the MNR seized control of the SPY in Yungas and then closed it down, suppressing one of the landlords' most important political voices.[27] While other rural societies continued to operate, and many maintained a voice in the media after the revolution, their power eroded as many of their members were jailed on the grounds of suspected participation in plots against the government.[28] The MNR specifically targeted members of the right-wing Falange Socialista Boliviana (FSB), the Bolivian Socialist Falange organized in 1937 and inspired by Spanish Falangism, which had many landowners among its militants. The government imprisoned a number of Falangistas in February 1953. They disbanded another plot in late March, just as the MNR was preparing for the first anniversary of the revolution, and in late June they halted another plot by the FSB to stop the agrarian reform.[29]

The MNR also promoted the organization of unions and party comandos to represent every canton (a section of a province) in the countryside. Unions and comandos undermined landlords' control of public offices in the countryside. Prior to the revolution, the rural councils comprised of local landlords and merchants suggested three names for every local state position (subprefect, corregidor, and intendant). The national authorities usually selected the person for the position from this list. After the revolution, the MNR transferred this responsibility for the nomination of candidates to the peasant unions. These mechanisms significantly eroded the traditional networks of power in the countryside. This was a radical transformation in terms of the state's role in boosting democratization, and it was arguably one of the most important results of the 1952 national revolution.

Although unionization was at the core of the MNR's agenda and was strongly encouraged from above, comunarios and colonos were able to organize unions throughout the countryside at an exceptional speed by using the very territorial limits of the former haciendas and indigenous communities. To keep up with the lexicon of the national revolution and link their political demands to the MNR's nationalist program, dozens of indigenous communities simply added the word "union" to the name of their community. (Appendix 3.2 lists the names of indigenous communities that organized a union only between January and July of 1953.)

Previous scholarship has criticized the post-1952 MNR politics of peasant unionization for its controlling and corporatist top-down nature. In particular, scholars questioned MNR's vertical agenda, which undermined local indigenous systems of authority.[30] Yet, these critiques often attribute much more power and control in the countryside to the MNR than it actually possessed, and they overlook the peasants' and Indians' own aspirations in joining the MNR and supporting the revolution.[31] The initial moves toward peasant unionization had started in the late 1930s when President Germán Busch approved the first labor code in 1938.[32] However, President Peñaranda soon put a stop to these initial impulses by prohibiting peasant unionization in 1943.[33] In 1952, the MNR dropped the prohibition. Yet, without this active participation from below, the MNR would not have been able to create such an extended network of unions and comandos in only one year.

Figure 3.2. Representatives of Carlos Montenegro Peasant Regiment. The caption reads: Group of leaders of the Peasant Union of Cochabamba with the leaders of the Carlos Montenegro Peasant Regiment, which now has ten thousand posts. From *La Nación*, April 1, 1953. Courtesy of Biblioteca y Archivo Histórico de la Asamblea Legislativa Plurinacional.

José Gordillo argues that the formation of unions in the countryside was far from being a univocal project. He shows that the unions reflected the multiple political tendencies both from above and from below that shaped the political rural scene after the revolution. Within the MNR, right-wing and left-wing leaders competed to control the unions. The right wing, usually positioned in the prefecture, and the left, often stationed in the MAC, fought to strengthen their influence in the countryside by each naming as ally as the general secretary of various unions. Both sides invoked the principles of the revolution to defend their interests, and although the right accused the left of being Trotskyists and extremists, the left accused their opponents of being rosco-falangistas (the term *rosco* meant "belonging to the *rosca*," the old mining landlord elite).[34] The peasantry of Cochabamba was divided along ideological lines between the left wing of the MNR and the Trotskyist POR.[35] Soon after the revolution, the Catholic Church began to promote the organization of Catholic conservative peasant unions to contain Trotskyist influence.

Anthropologist Maria Lagos assert that many townspeople succeeded in taking political control of the peasant unions and that peasants ended up under the control of these new elites.[36] It is true that new power relationships surfaced in the countryside, but the fact that peasants could nominate their local political authorities and had a strong representation in the Confederación Nacional de Trabajadores Campesinos de Bolivia (CNTCB), National Confederation of Peasant Workers of Bolivia, gave them a political influence that had been the exclusive privilege of rural councils before the revolution. In addition to the organization of peasant unions starting in late March 1953, the government also supported the organization of peasant militia regiments. These units were expected to demonstrate power and peasant support for the government, especially since the government feared that landlords and the Falangistas were preparing another plot.[37] In April 1953, peasants in Cochabamba reported the organization of the first Carlos Montenegro Regiment, named after one of the founders and leading thinkers of the MNR. The regiment was the largest one in Bolivia with ten thousand members (see figure 3.2).[38]

Several other regiments were established on the altiplano: the Germán Busch First Cavalry Regiment in Patamanta, the Tahuantinsuyo Second Infantry Regiment in Omasuyos, the Eduardo Avaroa First Artillery Regiment in Camacho, the Pedro Domingo Murillo First Cavalry Regiment in Los Andes, the Gualberto Villarroel First Infantry Regiment in Aroma Province, the 9 de Abril Regiment in Collantaca, Los Andes, and the Jose Fellman Velarde Regiment in Taraco Province.[39] Most of these names refer to national heroes and MNR ideologues. Peasants who had fought in the Chaco War were the primary organizers. This was part of the impact of the Chaco War among peasants that still needs to be studied in further detail. In the face of the constant threat of coups, the government widely disseminated pictures of the regiments with the message that, in essence, said "they fully support Paz Estenssoro and they are ready to fight for the revolution."

By promoting the organization of unions and by replacing the old local authorities with members aligned with the MNR, the government hoped to create an extended network that could prevent future landlord plots against the government, a process that involved a major restructuring of the state apparatus. However, a handful of internal official reports reveal that peasants used these units to gain political control independently of the direction of the state.[40] The national government soon recognized that peasants had begun to take direct action against established local authorities and, in some cases, had bypassed the supervision of the state. The subprefect of Camacho province detailed the situation early in 1953:

> I personally traveled to the Cantons of Escoma and Carabuco to get a sense of the actual situation in the countryside. I realized that indigenous communities have refused to present their communal authorities (*mandones*) to the corregidores. I also realized that in Escoma, the peasants themselves have selected the

> new subprefect, intendants, and corregidores, and that they did so when they were all drunk. They simply shouted the names of the new authorities while they vociferated against the townspeople. Then, I went to Carabuco and all along the way, I found groups of peasants who claimed that they would stand there until they could talk to the Minister of Peasant Affairs. I also learned how peasant leaders continue to collect money (*ramas*) only to get drunk with that money for many, many days. And when I questioned their actions they argued that they were organizing in the name of and with the support of MNR comandos.[41]

The examples of Escoma and Carabuco were not unique. Many unions were dropping the MNR's initial plan of collaborating with landlords to establish better working conditions, and unions were pushing landlords out instead.[42]

Of all the simultaneous, subversive political activities taking place in the countryside, the MNR worried the most about the POR militants in the countryside. After the nationalization of the mines in October 1952, POR leaders traveled to the countryside to promote what they called the "agrarian revolution," which would consist of an immediate distribution of lands.[43] According to the MNR, the POR units encouraged peasants to seize land, to murder landlords, and to sabotage what it called the constructive work of the government.[44] Much of the POR activism took place in the rather remote cantons of Colomi and Pojo, where the MNR had less immediate control.[45] In January 1953, however, the POR struck a strong political blow when it seized the leadership of the Federación Departmental de Campesinos de Cochabamba (FDCC), Peasant Federation of Cochabamba's Department. Afraid of the political control that the POR was gaining in the countryside, the MNR did not hesitate to question the revolutionary goals of the new leaders of this regional peasant organization: "these false revolutionaries pretend to precipitate the peasant masses into violent situations so that they won't work the land, sabotaging the constructive work of the government which wants to encourage mining and agricultural production."[46]

A private report from Ñuflo Chavez Ortiz, the minister of peasant affairs, shows how concerned the government was about the role of the POR in the countryside and the scope of rural crises in early 1953. He denounced a series of uprisings, kidnappings, and assaults against majordomos and claimed that POR leaders were threatening peasants in Sacabamba, Ucureña, Colomi, and Totora with repression if they did not follow their orders. To control the situation, Chavez Ortiz ordered the detention of local Trotskyist leaders Modesto Sejas and Juvenal Vargas, arguing that the movement would be unstoppable unless the president ordered the exile of all POR leaders and militants. The individuals under arrest in Cochabamba, he added, were merely followers: "the government needs to take more radical measures against the party itself that so far enjoys guarantees and privileges." In a parting shot, he threatened to resign if the president did not imprison the POR leaders.[47] The MNR jailed the recently elected Peasant Federation of Cochabamba's Department FDCC leaders and imposed new leadership. In response to this resolution, hundreds of peasants from the town of Ucureña, the center of POR influence, entered the city of Cochabamba en masse to demand the liberation of their leaders.[48] Although many of their weapons were agricultural tools or old rifles, the city dwellers panicked. Three ministers were immediately dispatched from La Paz to Cochabamba to negotiate with the Ucureña peasants. The MNR carefully monitored the movements of POR activists in the countryside and jailed many of them. Yet Ucureña continued to be one of the most important centers of independent peasant resistance.[49]Although the POR was without a doubt the MNR's most important ideological and political competitor in the countryside, it was not the only one. Official reports in Yungas showed that members of the Bolivian Workers Federation (COB) were urging peasants to seize lands and harvests and to murder landlords if necessary.

In the midst of this growing mobilization, the government became increasingly worried about the decline in food production and the provision of food to the urban areas. The government feared that the food shortages associated with mobilization in the countryside would create a reaction against the government among urban sectors, undermining the government's stability. For this reason MAC agents continued to enforce landlord-colono labor contracts, with considerable effects on the political convulsion within the haciendas and the deterioration of the work contracts that landlords and colonos signed in 1952 and 1953.

The Decline of the Labor Contracts, 1953–1954

Throughout the 1940s, the SRB's answer to political and union demands for change in the countryside was to threaten that any change in land tenure would create immediate food shortages in Bolivia's mines and cities.[50] These claims persisted throughout the first two years of the revolution. In November 1952, the SRB warned that the country would meet "only 50 percent of its agricultural production." In April 1953, it announced the "ruin of agriculture."[51] The government responded to this threat from the onset of the revolution by launching a major program to boost agricultural production.[52] Although Paz Estenssoro called for the organization of a commission on agrarian reform to study the question of land in January 1953, his government continued to encourage the implementation of labor contracts on the haciendas. Moreover, it was now the landlords rather than the colonos who were more interested in signing labor contracts, showing a readiness to adapt to new regulations if this guaranteed that the government would protect the rural private property.

The private correspondence between a landlord and her majordomo in Omasuyos provides a telling illustration of the changes taking place in the countryside. In Tari, one of the most productive haciendas in the province, the colonato system was still in place almost a year after the revolution. It was only in March 1953 that Moisés Castro, the majordomo of the hacienda noticed that peasants were beginning to mobilize: "The colonos of Tari, almost certainly following the orders of some saboteurs, insisted on setting up a school here, and they want to install Fermín Rojas, a rebellious Indian [*indio sublevado*] who does not recognize any master [*que no conoce patrón*], as a teacher. He used to work for Nestor Paredes Mendoza [another landholder of Omasuyos] and I am certain that he is trying to emancipate the Indians here too. . . . I will remain expectant of your orders."[53]

Peasants had already organized unions on many haciendas and communities, and colonos on other haciendas in Omasuyos were demanding that schools be set up. Considering the euphoria of the postrevolutionary political period, this demand was rather moderate. The valleys of Cochabamba and the altiplano of La Paz were certainly the most politically dynamic regions after 1952.[54] Castro's letter also illustrates that the political mobilization in the countryside varied considerably from one hacienda to another.

As soon as Irene Riveros, the owner of the Tari hacienda, heard from her majordomo, she wrote to the MAC asking for their mediation so that she could sign a contract with her former colonos. The agreement between the landlord and the colonos in Tari continued to be in force until September 1954, that is, for a year after the government signed the Agrarian Reform Decree-Law. There was no official breach of contract nor an epic seizure of the hacienda; instead, the colonos just stopped sharing the harvest with the landlord. This is how Moisés Castro reported on the harvest in September 1954:

> The Indians of Tari won't give you the three truckloads of barley they harvested this year. They say they can't give you anything because you do not have the order of the Ministry. The quinoa was rotten and it won't be useful even to feed it to the pigs. They took all the muraya, the caya (two types of tubers), and the beans, and redistributed it all amongst themselves. Later, the colonos picked the worst part of the production for you. They say they won't give you anything unless you pay them back for all the things you took from them. They also said they would use all the barley collards to feed the cattle. . . . Everything is going from bad to worse in Tari. They are up to their old tricks and the worst of them is Donato Mamani. I would strongly suggest that you do something

> because they said they won't let us into the estate anymore. They also say they are looking for potential buyers for your cattle so you can pay them back what you owe them.[55]

In October 1954 Cornelio Chávez, technician of the National Council of Agrarian Reform (CNRA), filed a report on ten haciendas in the same province where he noted increasing acts of violence by colonos. As in the case of Tari, Chávez observed that peasants were not fulfilling the contracts despite landholders' willingness to continue with them. He reported that peasants were withholding all production, keeping harvests for themselves, confiscating machinery, and arming themselves. If anything, they granted a very small portion of the harvest to the owners: "the owner of Taramaya told me that he is not receiving even a tenth of the production that he usually received."[56]

According to Chávez, landlords continued to complain that peasants were responsible for the disappearance of their cattle. In the case of hacienda Pajchani Molino, he recounts how the colonos had used the landlords' cattle to offer feasts to state authorities arriving from the city: "One hundred and sixty-three cows are missing in Pajchani Molino. I asked the shepherds about the cattle and then asked the members of the peasant unions. They said all had died of illnesses. But it turns out that that was false because I realized that the peasant union leaders had used the cows to prepare a feast for the state authorities coming from the city. I energetically admonished the peasants' leaders that they would receive sanctions if they continued to act like this." In the case of hacienda Chijipina Chico: "There are about eight hundred cows missing and the Indians don't know how to explain this. One of the colonos secretly told me that at least two hundred were sold and that Juan Huanca, the leader of the 'Gualberto Villarroel' peasant regiment, is holding the money. Juan Huanca has absolute power over the colonos." Chávez also reported that the few industries that had once functioned in Omasuyos were being dismantled. Macario Escobari, owner of the Putuni alcohol plant, complained that he could barely produce anything "because of the continued sabotage of the Indians." When the plant manager wanted to take the machinery to the city, the colonos told him they wouldn't let him take anything from the factory, and they would use violence if necessary.[57]

The landowners protested that the amount of the harvest reserved for them after the signing of the contracts did not resemble the amount they had received before the reform. By September 1954 most landholders were complaining that they were unable to agree to a deal of any kind. According to Chávez, "Peasants preferred to go ahead with the demand for land expropriation that they presented to the agrarian courts."[58] In Sud Yungas, the local CNRA office in charge of receiving peasants' demands for land expropriation under the Agrarian Reform Decree-Law reported that the colonos on the large estates of seven haciendas refused to sign any type of contract.[59] Ironically, the reform office's president, Isaac Tamayo, condemned what he called the nonrevolutionary attitude of the "peasant comrades [*compañeros campesinos*]." He claimed that colono resistance would encourage chaos and uncertainty in the countryside, adding that "the landholders were willing to sign contracts and, therefore, they were not the ones to blame."[60]

We find similar conflicts in Cochabamba. In August 1954 in Arque province, Nataniel Aspiazu, owner of the hacienda Chillachirca, made a formal complaint that the former colonos of his property refused to work despite the fact that he paid them the wage they had established in a contract.[61] On Tari, Majordomo Moisés Castro warned Irene Riveros in the last sentence of his last letter to her that, "If you don't do anything, I don't think you are going to be able to go back on the estate." Yet the situation on the Tari hacienda only deteriorated. The colonos refused to sign another agreement, demanding that the property be expropriated. Castro now opted for a new strategy. In December 1954 he resigned from his job as majordomo to become secretary of the recently formed rural council, a new state office organized to attend land expropriation demands.[62]

This testimony reveals how ordinary people's expectations of the revolution and their roles in the new order changed. In 1953, Moisés Castro evidently believed that the effects of the 1952 revolution would be short-lived in the countryside, as had been the case with other uprisings so common before the revolution. Up until 1954, he probably believed that the powerful Irene Riveros would be able to negotiate a new deal with the colonos, as she had often done in the past. The fact that the colonos were still working under contract even two years after the revolution shows that the peasants were equally uncertain about the course of the process.

In the vivid descriptions of the increasing difficulties that Castro experienced in running the estate, his letters also show that landholders did not lose complete power over their estates immediately after the revolution. Despite rumors of violence, several landlords found a way to maintain some control over their former properties for at least two or three years after 1952. The letters also show the gradual process through which the demands of the peasants of Tari became increasingly radical. A year after the revolution, the colonos' first claim was to have the right to set up a school. Two years after the revolution, not even a labor contract with the mediation of the MAC was enough to appease their demands.

The political agenda of 1945 continued to prevail in the political imagination of 1953. Even after the government signed the iconic Agrarian Reform Decree-Law that enabled the expropriation of hundreds of estates in Bolivia, many colonos continued to believe that the new decree would primarily ensure labor conditions on the haciendas. In October 1953, two months after the government signed the Agrarian Reform Decree-Law, peasants from hacienda Chillamani, Coripata Nor Yungas, denounced the majordomos of the hacienda for insisting on paying them only one hundred bolivianos per day when the government had established a wage of two hundred bolivianos.[63] Although the Agrarian Reform Decree-Law did not address this question, during the August 2 ceremony at which it was formally enacted, Minister of Foreign Affairs Walter Guevara Arze declared in his speech: "Colonos' servitude to landowners is over. If the owners want people to work for them, they have to pay 200 bolivianos a day."[64] It is likely that these words had a stronger impact than those of Paz Estenssoro about ending oppression among peasants, not just because Guevara was from Cochabamba and spoke Quechua but also because waged labor had been the hallmark of the MNR's rural policy since the beginning of the revolution.

This particular interpretation of the decree was not unique to Yungas. In September 1953, the unionized peasants of Socamani, Huañapasto Grande, Huañapasto Chico, Cala-Cala, Vinto, and Iquilla haciendas in the La Paz department expressed their contentment with the Agrarian Reform Decree-Law, which they understood would mainly regulate peasant labor and salaries:

> We heard about the Agrarian Reform Decree [Decree–Law] that specifically regulates the day's wage [*jornal de trabajo*] and the salary per day that we have the right to receive. We want to report that in this area landowners seemed resistant to the government's decree and they still force us to work without any type of compensation. We want to ask you to order them to enforce the law and we will defend the government. We also want to ask you to give us weapons. We are 285 organized peasants and the haciendas are only five kilometers from Oruro, so we could be ready to defend the government.[65]

This letter illustrates some of the complexities of the political moment. On the one hand, it shows the degree of peasant mobilization, but at the same time it also reveals that, even after the government signed the Agrarian Reform Decree-Law, many colonos were unsure about the scope of the reform and continued to use the political paradigm set by Villarroel to petition for their rights, focusing on labor relations rather than property structure. News of the revolution's progress filtered through to the countryside unevenly.

Previous studies have relied heavily on news accounts that reported violence in the countryside following the 1952 revolution, including accounts of peasants seizing haciendas. As a result, scholars have often assumed that the MNR was forced to start a program for land distribution from the outset of the revolution. However, it is clear that the MNR's initial policy was to run a general program focused on the transformation of labor conditions in the countryside by improving peasants' labor conditions and turning them into wageworkers. Nonetheless, the strengthening of the peasant unions at the local level, the decline of landlords' power at the local and national levels, the political battle within the state, and the activism of the POR and the COB consolidated the agenda for land expropriation, a political agenda that was still budding by April 1952.

Violence, Political Conflict, and Discourse in Revolutionary Times

The various news reports from the countryside were often contradictory, making it difficult to measure the precise scale of the violence after 1952. If there was news about peasants organizing unions, the subprefect, the intendant, or the corregidor would most likely report on these events, portraying the activities of peasants as organizing general turmoil (*agitación indigenista*). By contrast, agents from the MAC depicted euphoric rural support of the government, and if they referred to violence they highlighted landlords' and local state authorities' acts against peasants.

The term "violence," which was widely used in the newspapers, described a range of activities: colonos organizing a union, peasants demanding their right to name a local political authority, colonos abandoning their agricultural tasks, colonos seizing the production of the hacienda, peasants searching for arms at landlords' property, peasants blocking the streets, or the actual looting and burning of landlords' houses. The antigovernment press such as *Los Tiempos* and *El Diario* referred to all those incidents as "the emergence of rampant violence in the countryside." On the other hand, the government often tried to minimize the magnitude of the news claiming that these were isolated events or simple misunderstandings. In order to calm rumors of violence, the official newspaper *La Nación* occasionally published headlines such as: "Peace and Tranquility Reign in the Countryside"; "There Is No Violence in . . . Santiago de Huata, Achacachi, Carabuco, Los Andes, etc."; or (the MNR's favorite) "Peasants Stated to the President That They Are Committed to Production." *La Nación* countered the alarming news of violence with interviews of local officials or MAC commissioners who said they had personally witnessed the situation and who argued that confused informers mistook a peasant meeting to organize a union for an uprising.[66]

Contrary to the MNR's efforts, newspapers opposed to the government such as *El Diario*, *Los Tiempos*, and *Ultima Hora* tended to magnify any event that resembled an uprising or suggested violence. Two stories published in *Los Tiempos* of Cochabamba show the flagrant exaggeration of the press. The first story reports on peasant leaders who arrived in the city of

Cochabamba on May 1, 1953, to deny that there had been a peasant siege in the town of Tacopaya as had been reported in the newspaper the previous day. According to the Tacopaya delegates, the coordinator of peasant affairs had called a meeting to explain the scope of the new laws in favor of the peasants. They had duly attended the meeting in Tacopaya, but they certainly had not besieged the town or threatened it.[67]

The second story relates to the alleged death of a landlord in Anzaldo. The newspaper reported that colonos had whipped Eduardo Ferrufino, owner of hacienda Cuchira, to death.[68] Another article claimed that the anguished relatives could not recover the dismembered body, dumped in the middle of the street, because they were afraid of the fury of the Indians. On May 13, 1953, a government commission traveled to Anzaldo to investigate the events and found Ferrufino walking around, completely unaware of the news that had circulated about him in the panicked city of Cochabamba.[69]

Of course, there were political motives behind this exaggerated portrayal of the situation in the countryside. Both the landlords and the media wanted to discredit the government's capacity to rule the countryside and increase police control. For its part, the MNR hoped to show that moderate reform could bring about rural peace. In light of these overlapping and contradictory reports, is it possible to capture the actual situation in the countryside after 1952? The media accounts and the official reports constitute an invaluable window through which to explore the political situation in the countryside, but it is worth remembering that they were often far from objective and they corresponded to political motives. Additionally, it is difficult to generalize about the situation of a region as a whole. Internal reports about haciendas varied greatly not only from one region to another but also from one hacienda to another. Several peasant regiments demanded weapons, in itself evidence of strong political mobilization, but there were also reports such as that of the majordomo of Tari that colonos' most radical action was simply ceasing to share the harvest with the landlord.

Conclusions

The 1952 national revolution sparked a rapid escalation of peasant political goals. Starting in April 1952, colonos and comunarios called for the government to put a stop to the abuses of the landlords and the local authorities. Colonos demanded the full implementation of the rights they had been granted under President Villarroel in 1945. As Gotkowitz points out, these demands did not emerge only in 1952 but had been made for decades.[70] One of the most significant changes in the countryside after the revolution was the major democratization of the state apparatus. Although ambivalent in their policies, the MNR unleashed a political explosion by promoting peasant unions across the countryside. These newly formed peasants' unions were able to select rural authorities and became a major player within local political affairs, gaining a type of representation that, prior to the revolution, was the privilege of the small circle of citizens organized in rural councils. The elimination of these neighbors' councils for electing representatives offered colonos and comunarios new and unprecedented access to local political power.

The role of the peasant unions after 1952 has been the subject of major debates in Bolivian historiography. Some scholars argue that peasant unions encouraged by those outside and above became a vehicle for the MNR to gain political control in the countryside.[71] Although this perspective certainly highlights the revolutionary state's attempts to control the peasant movement from 1952 onward, it fails to explain why comunarios and colonos organized unions during the first year of the revolution. Considering the fragility of the Bolivian state, it is hard to imagine that the MNR could have organized hundreds of unions solely on the basis of a decree. Unionization was also a demand from below. Peasants had embraced the idea of organizing unions since the late 1930s. Peasant unions grew from existing organizations. Colonos and comunarios built unions that maintained the previous territorial limits of the haciendas and the indigenous communities. In other words, unions were not an artificial creation; they solidified and gave visibility to economic, social, and political units that had formed and operated before the revolution. Unions did not simply follow the MNR's political agenda. Political action from below forced the government to give up on its initial agenda, which focused exclusively on labor reform.

Both the government and the peasant movement were subject to internal and external contradictions. Gordillo argues that in the valleys of Cochabamba the state was broken from within, into two opposite wings—the left wing usually linked to the MAC and the right wing whose members occupied seats in the Prefecturas and the Ministry of Government. At the same time, other political parties and organizations, such as the POR and COB, sought to expand their political influence in the countryside by organizing unions. On the altiplano, ex-comunarios who supported the revolutionary nationalist government organized unions in pursuit of an independent agenda: they demanded that the government carry out a new land survey to determine landlords' legal possession over their rural properties. In contrast to the colonos, who demanded "land for those who work it," the ex-comunarios demanded "land for its original owners." Rather than a unified ideology, the revolution unleashed these different interest groups, all struggling to impose their varying, locally specific agendas.

Table 3.1. Labor Contracts in Sud Yungas before and after the Agrarian Reform

Property	Number of Workers	Before the Agrarian Reform	After the Agrarian Reform
Chica	26 workers and 6 colonos	2 days of work a week for men and 4 days a week for women.	200 Bs for men and 100 Bs for women (weekly).
Coca Yapu	20 colonos	3 days of work a week for men and women. Men received 3 Bs and women received 2 Bs per day.	2 days of work a week for men and women. 280 Bs for men and 150s Bs for women (weekly).
El Calvario	14 colonos, 4 *arrimantes*	No payment.	280 Bs for men and 200 Bs for women (weekly).
Guayrapata	10 colonos	3 days of work a week for men and women. All kinds of work without payment.	1,500 Bs for men and 1,200 Bs for women (monthly).
La Plazuela y Otros	55 workers	There were contracts. No information about the conditions.	They continued with the same labor contracts after the revolution.
Machaca-marca	14 colonos, 12 arrimantes	4 days of work a week for men and 5 days a week for women. Men received 0.50 cents Bs and women received 0.25 cents Bs per day.	2 days of work a week for men and women. 200 Bs for men and 100 Bs for women (weekly).
Quiaconi el rancho	39 colonos	2 days of work a week for men and women. Men received 5 Bs and women 3 Bs per day.	280 Bs for men and 200 Bs for women (weekly).

Source: Elaborated by the author based on INRA-LP, Sud Yungas Province: box 7, file Chica; box 4, file Coca Yapu; box 7, file El Calvario; box 5, file Guayrapata; box 8, file La Plazuela y otros; box 3, file Machacamarca; box 3, file Quiaconi El Rancho.

Appendix 3.1: Conditions of Work and Labor Contracts in Sud Yungas

In Sud Yungas, incipient labor contracts were in place on several haciendas before the agrarian reform. After the revolution, the commissioners were not able to establish a standard system of wages. Instead they negotiated a particular contract for every estate. Many contracts were signed in late 1952, and as the implementation of land expropriation did not fully begin until the second half of 1954, several contracts were still signed in 1953 and 1954.

In Yungas, I found seven haciendas for which the Ministry of Peasant Affairs successfully drew up labor contracts. The chart below contrasts colonos' labor conditions before the revolution and after they signed the contracts (see table 3.1).

I found seven other properties where peasants refused to sign contracts (see table 3.2). Interestingly, in most of these cases there was some kind of

Table 3.2. Properties Where Colonos Refused to Sign Contracts after 1952

Property	Number of Workers	Before the Agrarian Reform	After the Agrarian Reform
Colonia San Pedro	52 colonos	6 days of work a week for men and women.	No contract
Colimpampa	13 arrenderos	There was an established labor contract already before the revolution.	No contract
Misquimayo	6 peasants	2 days of work a week for men and women. Paid labor.	No contract
Poxi	18 arrenderos and 64 yanaperos	2 days work a week.	No contract
San Martín y San Martín Chico	14 colonos	3 days of work a week for men and women. Paid. Although they gave extra free labor.	No contract
San Isidro	35 colonos	3 days of work a week for men and women. Unpaid labor.	No contract
San José de Chaui	5 colonos	Unpaid labor.	Peasants signed contracts but they refused to work. There was no production on the property.

Source: Elaborated by the author based on INRA-LP, Sud Yungas Province: box 2, file Colonia San Pedro; box 6, file Colimpampa; box 10, file Misquimayo; box 5, file Poxi; box 10, file San Martín y San Martín Chico.

wage system before the revolution. The last two cases listed are instances where there were contracts, but landowners reported they refused to work.

Appendix 3.2: Indian Communities Enthusiastically Organized Unions in the First Years of the Revolution.

The following list shows the indigenous communities that organized a union or an MNR command only between January and July 1953 and whose constitution was noted in the newspaper. The official newspaper *La Nación*, interested in highlighting peasant support for the government, paid close attention to these events. Of course, many other unions were organized in the following months and years that are not part of this list. The length of this list of unions organized in only six months shows how appealing the formation of unions was to the indigenous communities and contradicts the assumption (at least at the very beginning of the revolution) that the process of unionization was only a political process enforced from above. Often, *La Nación* only gave the name of the region and did not specify whether the members of the new union were comunarios or colonos. The list below corresponds to all the cases in which the newspaper specifically referred to indigenous communities. It is noteworthy that these newspapers used headlines that could mislead the reader as they give very little information about the role of the comunarios in the revolution, and most of the time they underlined peasant support for the government, as in, for example, "Peasants of Amacari Expressed Their Support for the Government."

Union of community Amacari (Manco Kapac Province, La Paz), *La Nación*, January 30, 1953.
Union Gualberto Villarroel of Curahuara, Sajama Province, *La Nación*, January 30, 1953.
Communities Machu, Collana, Sullcahuta, Collana o Chipana, Taipi, Collana Sullca, Tunca, Sullcahuta, Manasaya, Jilahuta, Choque Marca, Taipihuta, Coquemarca formed the union Gualberto Villarroel, Sajama Province, Oruro, *La Nación*, January 29, 1953.
Peasant Command of Sulcatiti, Jesus de Machaca Province (Ingavi Province), *La Nación*, February 1, 1953.
Communities Calacala, Chambi, Achuta, Higuaqui Grande, Higuaqui Chico organized Peasant Union Ingavi, *La Nación*, February 1, 1953.
Union of Ex-community Kollantaca Laja Canton, *La Nación*, February 7, 1953.
Union of Community Taracollo-Condorica, *La Nación*, March 6, 1953.
MNR Command of former community Chojacive (canton Aygachi), *La Nación*, March 9, 1953.
Union of Ayllu Thunupa in Salinas de Garci Mendoza Province Ladislao Cabrera (Oruro), *La Nación*, March 24, 1953.
Union of Communities Taraco, Desaguadero, San Andrés, Jesús de Machaca, *La Nación*, March 24, 1953.
Union of community Hacha-Hila in San Pedro de Buena Vista in Potosi, *La Nación*, April 14, 1953.
MNR Command Caquiaviri (Pacajes Province), *La Nación*, April 23, 1953.
MNR Command of Caquiaviri composed by colonos from twenty-two haciendas and comunarios from fifteen ayllus, *La Nación*, May 12, 1953.
Union of Panacachi formed by communities Panacachi, Copana, Chucarasi, Quisi quisi, Calacala, Coajata, Pacara, and Quilla-quilla (Bustillo Province, Potosi), *La Nación*, May 17, 1953.
Union of Communities Bella Vista, Belen, Muyllapucara, Huaylluma, Lupecunda de Chuquichambi, Quillacas y Huayllamarca in Carangas, *La Nación*, May 17, 1953.
Union of Chivo (Taraco, Ingavi Province, La Paz) *La Nación*, July 31, 1953.

CHAPTER FOUR

REDISTRIBUTE LAND SOON

A full year after the revolution of April 1952, the MNR were still reluctant to address the question of land distribution. In April 1953, the Minister of Agriculture Germán Vera Tapia told a massive peasant meeting in the provincial town of Arani: "The agrarian reform won't attack anyone's property. . . . The goal of the agrarian reform is to increase production and consumption." This cautious approach was endorsed by the official newspaper *La Nación*: "As these are the words of such a highly ranked functionary, this means the citizens should feel confident about this process."[1]

Yet, unable to ignore the increasingly agitated political situation at the end of 1952, Paz Estenssoro announced the organization of a commission to study a project for agrarian reform in January 1953. The commission drafted a decree in about eight months and held debates in relative secrecy. Official publications such as *La Nación* and *Gaceta Campesina* announced the names of the members of the commission and the frequency of the meetings; however, government officials were cautious about sharing the content of the discussions. The newspapers published a number of proposals from independent intellectuals and representatives of institutions who were supposedly experts on agrarian reform; they included the director of indigenous schools and the director of the Society of Agronomists who voluntarily submitted their propositions on this issue. Many of the proposals reflected the blatant racism that prevailed among Bolivian intellectuals when discussing peasants and Indians. These proposals show how vague were the discussions on agrarian reform. These experts along with prominent members of the MNR continued to use terms such as "Indian redemption," "Indian rehabilitation," and "economic development" to refer to the content of the agrarian reform decree, clouding their commitment to the question of land distribution. The still influential landlord rural societies in Cochabamba, Oruro, and Sucre also sent their proposals to the commission on agrarian reform. Eager to participate in the political debate, they continued to emphasize that productivity rather than unequal distribution of land was the source of Bolivia's agrarian problem. The few proposals that addressed land expropriation showed their ambivalence and uncertainty regarding the mechanisms for economic compensation to landlords. With the exception of the POR, who insisted on the expropriation of all large and medium landholdings without economic compensation, most political groups were careful not to challenge the almost sacred principles that protected private property. They argued that colonos should buy the plots they were working or receive land located in Bolivia's remote lowlands areas that had been designated for settlement; this process of settlement is known as colonization in Bolivia.

When these debates were taking place at the national level, Mexican and Guatemalan advisors arrived to the country to help drafting the decree. Paz Estenssoro's admiration for the process of agrarian reform that President Jacobo Arbenz was leading in Guatemala played a crucial part in framing the Bolivian agrarian agenda. Mexican and Guatemalan advisors who worked for their governments, along with Food and Agricultural Organization (FAO) consultants (many of them also Mexican), helped the Bolivian government transform its broad goals for land reform into actual public policy. The Bolivian revolution and the Agrarian Reform Decree-Law also generated discussion among intellectuals in Latin America. The three initiatives that the MNR launched for the countryside in the first two years of the revolution—universal suffrage, peasant unionization, and land distribution—represented a call for change in other predominantly rural societies and constituted a vital contribution to the uncertain process of democratization across Latin America during the Cold War.

Yet, a study of two cases of land expropriation in two of the most belligerent provinces of the country—Ucureña (in Germán Jordán) and Achacachi (in Omasuyos)—exposes the contrast between the set of procedures that were set to lead the process of land distribution according to law and the actual politics of land distribution.[2] While the MNR, as well as the network of Latin American intellectuals that supported the Bolivian agrarian reform from abroad, continued to focus on the multiple legal and technical steps that would determine the expropriation of a property, the events in Ucureña and Achacachi demonstrate the political character of the expropriations under the leading role of the peasant unions. The peasant unions carried out de facto expropriation of the properties without waiting for due process. Their actions challenged the MNR's depiction of the agrarian reform as relatively moderate in nature.

The Bolivian Commission of Agrarian Reform

No other postrevolutionary reform provoked as much debate in Bolivian society as the agrarian reform. The MNR's decrees regarding universal suffrage and education received far less attention than did its proposals on land. The so-called Indian problem and the question of land inspired generalized discussions in which many sectors of Bolivian society claimed their right to be heard, because of their technical expertise or their detailed knowledge of the "Indian problem." However, many were reluctant to turn the agrarian reform into a general assault on rural property. Nationalist and left-leaning intellectuals as well as technocrats and self-proclaimed specialists on agrarian issues were reluctant to put land in the hands of what they called ignorant peasants, and all proposals feared that changes in land tenure would undoubtedly incite more violence.

In January 1953, the MNR reprinted its 1942 proposal on agrarian reform, which focused on granting land to indigenous men and women in designated areas for new settlement (colonization) in the remote lowlands: "We petition that the policies of colonization make all men and women owners of the land. We look for Indian redemption, economic freedom, and Bolivian sovereignty."[3] The proposal confirms that the MNR believed land redistribution should follow the principle that claimed land for those who tilled it. The extent of the party's commitment to land reform was nevertheless limited, and it ultimately viewed *colonization* as the principal mechanism to grant land to peasants. The slogan "Indian redemption" was rather vague in that it circumvented the issue of land redistribution. Both proposals and their actions during the first year of the revolution indicate the limited scope of the reform the MNR hoped to implement.

However, the widespread political mobilization in the countryside and reports that peasants were increasingly ignoring the MNR's exclusive focus on labor reform pushed the president to call for a multi-party and multi-sector commission to analyze and draft a law for agrarian reform.[4] Paz extended this invitation to leaders from the PIR and POR, representatives from COB, and a representative of small and medium-sized rural properties.[5] Several members of the PIR—including Arturo Urquidi, José Flores Moncayo, Eduardo Arce Loureiro, and Raimundo Grigoriú—and Ayala Mercado from the POR joined the commission.[6] Oscar Alborta represented the landowners of small and medium-sized properties, and Zenón Barrientos Mamani, the only peasant leader on the commission, represented the Agricultural Bank.[7] Although the commission included Hugo López Avila on behalf of COB, the Workers' Federation, it is quite astonishing that Federico Álvarez Plata, a senior leader of the MNR from a landlord family in Yungas was the representative of the peasant federations.[8] This reflects the MNR's paternalist attitude toward peasant representatives. The MNR created a great deal of rhetoric about peasants' rights, but it certainly didn't deem them capable of drafting the new law.[9] One of the most explicit expressions of this patronizing behavior occurred in February 1953 before the MNR's first convention after the revolution. Peasant leaders discovered that they could not register as delegates at the convention but only as observers. In reference to this news, Minister of Peasant Affairs Ñuflo Chávez Ortiz contended that the party made this decision because "the majority of the rural population was ignorant."[10]

Ironically, during this twelve-day convention, MNR leaders began to discuss the possibility of launching a program of land distribution. Several speakers, in a tone that combined bewilderment and resignation, declared that the party should carry out some form of land expropriation. Others voiced concerns about the colonos' ability to be independent landholders. Álvarez Plata, who was acting as executive secretary of the MNR at this venue, stated: "The agrarian reform can have no other resolution than to grant the land to those who work it. . . . However, we know that granting land to peasants will not solve the entire problem, we need to include modern techniques of cultivation." Álvarez Plata represented that sector of the landowning elite that had been formally calling for agrarian reform since the 1940s. However, this call focused only on technological modernization in the countryside and was based on the understanding that the Indian problem hinged on the "backwardness" of indigenous communities. Admitting that the government should implement some measures for land redistribution, he added, "Nothing will change if those who get the land continue to live in ignorance and to work without any knowledge of modern techniques." The reform would eventually redistribute many large cultivated farms and many medium-sized properties to hundreds of peasants individually. But at this early stage, Álvarez Plata contradicted the very idea of that type of distribution: "The agrarian reform will benefit all Bolivians but it will not—as rumors on the street are saying—fall into redistributing land individually. Instead the government will enforce a cooperative system of production. We are going to institute an agrarian reform that goes against unproductive large estates and protects small and medium-sized property."[11]

Similarly, Vice President Hernán Siles Zuazo, who was preparing the public for the upcoming policy on land redistribution, sought to alleviate the anxiety of owners of small and medium-sized properties: "There is an exaggerated fear about the agrarian reform. That fear is senseless and baseless for all small and medium-sized landowners. . . . In fact, aside from the peasants, it is the small and medium-sized owners who are going to obtain the most benefit. . . . They are going to be on the crest of the new wave of progress in which Bolivia is now entering."[12]

José Salmón attempted to gain landlord support by stressing the benefits that land redistribution would bring to them. A program for land reform would appease the countryside and guarantee social peace: "If landowners thought about their own convenience, they would contribute to solving the current situation. There are some landowners—whom I know personally—who have for a long time been facing a series of strikes and passive resistance from their colonos, and that situation can only affect their estates' profit, so it is appropriate to look for an alternative."[13] It was at this national convention that many MNR leaders realized they could no longer avoid the demand for land distribution. This was a late response to the growing political mobilization in the countryside that was unleashed in November 1952.

As the closed-door discussions in the Commission of Agrarian Reform were taking place, the Cochabamba FRC launched a public debate on this issue in September 1952. The FRC, dedicated to the defense of the interests of powerful landowners, staged a march in favor of the agrarian reform that included tractors and plenty of banners. The banners read: "For a technical and social agrarian reform," "More irrigation, less bureaucracy," "More machinery, more production," and "To seed is to build nation."[14]

After the march, *Los Tiempos*, which energetically promoted the interests of the FRC, published an op-ed on the topic on an almost daily basis. All of these focused on the same argument—that it was important to undertake a reform in the countryside, but land redistribution was not the solution. Some editorials defended the sacred right to private property.[15] Others exposed the disastrous outcomes of other radical agrarian reforms such as those of China and Yugoslavia.[16] Some articles even argued that it was useless to give land to colonos since they already enjoyed a comfortable tranquil life that placed them among the members of the middle class in Bolivia.[17] Others referred to Indians' precivilized status, which made them unable to live independently of their landlords, who, it was argued, offered them security and protection.[18] *Los Tiempos* also argued that in some departments, as in Oruro, the land was already in the hands of the indigenous communities who paid little or no taxes. The challenge in those regions was to make the lands productive.[19] Dozens of articles charged that government intervention in matters of private property would bring disgrace to the countryside and hunger and ruin to the cities.[20] A core argument, often repeated as a mantra, was that the state was the true large landowner in Bolivia, so the government should focus on a distribution of state lands rather than private properties.[21]

Aside from the rural societies, many who considered themselves experts on agrarian reform held conferences or published opinion pieces in newspapers on how to draft the new law. Such proposals highlighted the difficulties of imagining a widespread program for land expropriation. Hugo Balderrama, who had been the director of the indigenous school centers (*núcleos indigenales*) for twenty-six years, developed a proposal supposedly based on consultations with colonos on haciendas in Cochabamba. Balderrama argued that colonos should have the right to buy the plots they were working on: "As a rural teacher, I have heard colono complaints about the insecurity they felt about improving the plots they are working on. They felt afraid of being ousted from these plots. I know that peasants were more than willing to pay for plots they were already working."[22] Balderrama's proposal expanded President Toro's 1937 decree that obliged religiously owned and public haciendas to rent or sell their plots to their colonos. Instead of expropriation, Balderrama proposed a controlled process in which the colonos would have the opportunity to buy plots if they were already working on them. Aware of the difficulties in paying for their plots, Balderrama suggested a credit system to guarantee that peasants could afford their purchases.

Also, in January 1953, the Sociedad de Ingenieros Agrónomos de Bolivia, the Bolivian Society of Agronomists invited engineer Augusto Valdivia to give a speech on agrarian reform. His talk equated agrarian reform to modernization and economic development, as did the proposals of the 1940s. Valdivia argued: "The agrarian reform does not consist in redistributing the land to Indians. If we do that, nothing is going to actually change. We need mechanization because the real problem is that the land is poor and eroded."[23] Valdivia did not even mention the colonos' demand for land in his speech. Alberto Mendoza López, a specialist in colonization and agriculture, argued that the state should focus on expropriating land concessions that it had granted in the north and east of the country. His argument effectively suggested that the state should not touch the extended haciendas of the altiplano and the valleys, which were the focus of colono and comunario political demands.[24]

Oscar Herrera, another self-proclaimed expert on the agrarian question, called for a general program on land redistribution following the Mexican and Guatemalan models. He argued that, since neither the state nor the peasants have the funds to pay any economic compensation to the landlords, Bolivia should emulate the bond funds system used in both countries. Herrera might have had a viable proposal for indemnification, but he argued that land should be allocated only to dynamic and capable peasants who had a "spirit of progress," failing to explain exactly who would identify the presence of such a spirit and evaluate whether it was up to an imaginary standard. "Within the peasantry, land should be given to those people with a spirit of progress and to those willing to accept the leadership of the technical entities that have to direct the production of the economy."[25]

These various proposals illustrate the complexities involved in developing a program for land redistribution. Those who did advocate for redistribution conspicuously failed to explain how the reform would operate. Herrera's ambiguous and capricious proposition for granting the land to peasants "with a spirit of progress" reveals how reformers foundered when they tried to envision the agrarian reform in concrete terms. Even after the revolution, many held back from turning the agrarian reform into a general confiscation of land that would undermine even small and medium-sized properties.

Meanwhile, the Trotskyist left offered a much more radical program. Edwin Moller, representing the COB, argued that agrarian reform had to be considered primarily as a political challenge and only secondarily as a technical or economic problem. He argued that the people should learn from the experience of the nationalization of the mines in which technical commissions, supposedly representing the distinct social classes, ended up favoring the bourgeoisie and the landlords. The POR voted for general expropriation and did not contemplate any compensation at all. From their perspective, neither the state nor the peasants should have to pay compensation to the landlord elite. In terms of redistribution, they argued that, rather than grant land to individual peasants, the state should create collective farms that it would administer. Finally, the POR disagreed that medium-sized properties should be protected from expropriation, supporting the protection of small properties only. Although the other proposals still envisioned a rural world in which landlords and peasants coexisted, the POR proposed turning colonos and Indian communities into proletarians under the management of the state.[26] The MNR feared the Trotskyist challenge and claimed that the POR's radical proposals and discourse would only incite more violence in the countryside.[27]

Overall, advocates of an agrarian reform that would include land redistribution faced serious trouble defining three crucial questions: (1) the scope of land expropriation, (2) the mechanisms of compensation, (3) and the procedures for land distribution among colonos. Considering Bolivia's marked geographical differences, proponents encountered problems in defining the maximum limit of a medium-sized property versus a large estate. They were also troubled about how to reconcile the issue of size with other criteria such as investment, quality of soil and yield, and accessibility. Time and again, the proponents of reform insisted that expropriation would only affect unproductive estates. But the mere attempt to impose such so-called technical criteria on each property would cause endless fights among landlords, colonos, and state functionaries.

Most reformers agreed that any process of land expropriation had to include some economic compensation, especially if the owners demonstrated that they were the legal owners of the property. However, as the debates unfolded, most proposals declined to address expropriation because of the inability of the Bolivian state to compensate landowners and the peasants' even more meager resources. The question of indemnification was crucial for the MNR since economic compensation marked the difference between outright seizure and legal expropriation. Questions about the procedures for land redistribution among peasants were equally challenging. Endless discussions broke down over which criteria would be used to distribute land among beneficiaries and the amount of land that would be assigned to each beneficiary. It was problematic to find common ground in a country that had striking geographical differences and diverse working and living conditions among the colonos within the haciendas.

"Redistribute Land Soon"

In May 1953, Brazil hosted a conference of the UN's Food and Agricultural Organization (FAO). The conference convened delegates from all over Latin America to discuss questions of land tenure in the region. In that meeting, the Mexican delegate began his speech by stating, "I only want to say a few words to the Bolivian delegates: Redistribute land soon."[28]

In the midst of Bolivia's political debate on agrarian reform, the MNR demonstrated increasing interest in the experiences of Mexico and Guatemala. The government invited Mexican and Guatemalan advisors to work with the Bolivian Commission of Agrarian Reform. Discussions of agrarian reform and land distribution had long been a feature of sociopolitical debate in Latin America, especially among leftist circles. As in the Bolivian case, these debates covered a wide range of perspectives ranging from technological reform to land redistribution.[29] But beyond these general discussions, only Mexico and Guatemala had implemented concrete programs for land redistribution among peasants. Seeking to translate broad notions of agrarian reform into practical public policy, the MNR invited Edmundo Flores, a Mexican economist working at the FAO, to participate as an advisor to the Commission of Agrarian Reform in Bolivia.[30] Reflecting on his role in the commission, Edmundo Flores stated in a conference in 1965: "Land reform is a revolutionary measure which transfers power, property, and status from one group of the community to another . . . to be effective it must take place rapidly and massively, it has to involve the taking of productive land . . . productive land must be taken without immediate compensation."[31]

The MNR took a special interest in the radical agrarian reform that democratically elected President Jacobo Arbenz had implemented in Guatemala from 1952 onward, by confronting the United Fruit Company, Guatemala's largest landholder. The MNR invited a number of Guatemalan leaders to participate in a dialogue on agrarian matters and, more broadly, on Latin American countries' relationships with US imperialism. One of these figures was the president of the Guatemalan Congress, Julio Estrada de la Hoz, who was invited by the government to La Paz in 1953 to talk about agrarian reform in his country.[32] Commenting on Estrada de la Hoz's speech, the official newspaper *La Nación* said: "Guatemala and Bolivia are struggling with a very similar situation, and our country has identified Guatemala as one of our best friends."[33] Estrada de la Hoz's speech, closely followed by many newspapers in Bolivia, caused panic in Cochabamba, where *Los Tiempos* asked: "Will Bolivia's land reform be a copy of the one in Guatemala?" The author first dismissed Estrada de la Hoz's conference by stating, "We learnt nothing new." Later the article asserted it was preposterous to compare Bolivia's situation with that of the Central American country: "Guatemala has 29 habitants per km2 and Bolivia 0.4 habitants per Km2. Guatemala has land shortage; Bolivia has plenty of land."[34]

That same month, Adolfo García Montenegro, the Guatemalan ambassador to El Salvador, referred to the Bolivian government when he said, "You have been walking alone for a long time, but you are not alone anymore. Now Latin America resonates together in unison."[35] In April, Marco Antonio Villamar, a former student leader and member of the Agrarian Reform Commission in Guatemala, gave a talk at the Universidad Mayor de San Andrés in La Paz. The MNR invited Villamar to stay in Bolivia and become an advisor to the Agrarian Reform Commission. Both Estrada de la Hoz and Villamar helped to shape Bolivia's new Agrarian Reform Decree-Law. Estrada highlighted the purely technical issues underlying the Guatemalan agrarian reform and explained how they were decisive in rebutting the allegations of the landlord elites who denounced agrarian reform as a land grab. He reported that the Guatemalan government recognized at least two types of property and that under this classification, only large and unproductive land faced expropriation.

The MNR also followed Mexico's strategy closely when Mexicans were drafting their policies on how to compensate landlords for the expropriation of their properties. This was crucial for the government as it demonstrated that its program was not an assault on property.[36] During his visit to Bolivia, José López Bermudez, general secretary of the Mexican Agrarian Department, published his views on the question of indemnification. López Bermudez wrote: "One of the most important risks of implementing agrarian reform is the threat of spurring violent reactions from the affected sectors. Therefore, the government should declare its interest in compensating those affected by the expropriation." Then he added: "Agrarian reform . . . does not mean confiscation." López Bermudez also addressed the problems that the country would face in paying indemnification to landlords: "The compensation should be made in such a way that the amount and the conditions of payment do not annihilate the Bolivian Agrarian Reform." Mexico, he explained, "decreed a one-year time limit for landowners' demands for compensation and a twenty-five-year time limit for that compensation to be paid to them." López Bermudez, watchful of the national and international risks that could ensue from a failure or refusal to pay indemnification, stated: "The agrarian reform is an act of sovereignty, not a communist attack. Some leaders of the extreme Left had been suggesting a complete confiscation of the land, without compensation. You should carefully avoid falling into excesses or exaggeration, even in the vocabulary you use. Use words that fit into Bolivian reality and are inspired in Bolivian rural needs."[37]

In addition to offering important legal and political advice, López Bermudez's article aimed to ease US suspicions that Bolivia's revolution might turn communist. The piece appeared on July 24, 1953, just a week prior to the enactment of the Agrarian Reform Decree-Law. The Mexican strategy allowed the MNR simultaneously to claim that the decree respected private property and to guarantee that the question of indemnification would not become an immediate obstacle for peasants who were the intended beneficiaries of the land.[38] Following the Mexican example, the Bolivian decree for agrarian reform required that those who had received land (called "beneficiaries" in Bolivia) pay that compensation within twenty-five years through bonds issued by the Agricultural Bank.[39]

The Bolivian Decree-Law on Agrarian Reform

After days of intense work, the Commission for Agrarian Reform delivered a final project to the president on July 29, 1953. Newspapers offer little information about the work or the discussion undertaken by the commission. In his memoir of Paz Estenssoro, Guillermo Bedregal, a high-ranking member of the MNR, stated that the commission worked behind closed doors because it preferred to keep the two irreconcilable positions within the commission private. One of these positions was championed by the PIR leader Arturo Urquidi, who defended "land for those who work it," a political position that included landowners of small and medium-sized properties and allowed former landlords of large estates to retain ownership of medium-sized properties. The other position fought for "land for peasants," thereby excluding all former landlords. According to Bedregal (who had an undoubtedly partisan perspective), President Paz Estenssoro reluctantly accepted the first proposal, although he and his cabinet preferred the later version.[40]

The president and his cabinet approved the project on July 31 and rushed to sign the decree on August 2, in time for the Bolivian commemoration of the Day of the Indian. The government selected the village of Ucureña in Cochabamba as the place in which to stage the public signing of the historic document, in order to honor the village where colonos had organized the first peasant union in 1936.[41] The selection of Ucureña also reflects the strong voice of the PIR in the Commission for Agrarian Reform, since the original union was closely linked to the work of PIR militants. Ac-

Figure 4.1. President Paz Estenssoro in Ucureña, August 2, 1953. He is wearing the traditional Andean hat called *Lluchu* while giving his speech in Ucureña enacting the Agrarian Reform Dedcree-Law. *La Nación*, August 3, 1953. Photo courtesy of Biblioteca y Archivo Histórico de la Asamblea Legislativa Plurinacional.

cording to *La Nación*, the event in Ucureña (see figure 4.1) was attended by between one hundred and two hundred thousand peasants. It was a formal ceremony that gathered dignitaries from many Latin American countries and effectively sealed the political alliance between peasants and the government. Although less sumptuous, similar rallies were held in Santiago de Huata and Copacabana in La Paz and Camiri in Santa Cruz to celebrate the signing of the Agrarian Reform Decree-Law.[42]

Figure 4.2. The monument memorializes the place where President Victor Paz Estenssoro signed the Agrarian Reform Decree-Law in August 1953. Photo by Carmen Soliz.

The Agrarian Reform Decree-Law was a lengthy document with 16 sections outlining 177 articles.[43] In its preamble, the decree is set up as a major attempt to rectify four hundred years of marginalization of the majority Indian population, a process that started with Spanish colonialism and continued during the republican period. The emphasis is on how both Spanish colonizers and, after them, local creole elites maintained the same system of dispossession, servitude, and political oppression against the majority of the Indian population. The six fundamental objectives of the Agrarian Reform Decree-Law were: "To allot cultivable land to the peasants who did not have any or had very little; to expropriate lands which *latifundistas* have in excess; to restore to indigenous communities the lands usurped by landlords after 1900; to free campesino workers from their condition as serfs; to stimulate the production and commercialization of the agricultural industry; to preserve the country's natural resources; and, to promote internal migration . . . excessively concentrated in the inter-Andean zone."[44]

In the decree were specified the types of property that the state would henceforth legally recognize. These were the residential plot (*solar campesino*), the indigenous community, the small or medium-sized landholding, the agrarian cooperative, and the agricultural enterprise. The maximum size of a small and medium-sized estate was carefully defined for highlands, valleys, subtropical, and tropical regions. Because of Bolivia's striking geographical diversity, these definitions varied considerably; the maximum size of a small estate in the wine-growing areas was set at three hectares, but in the dry area of the Chaco (closer to the border with Paraguay) it was eighty hectares. Most importantly, latifundia were declared illegal and thus subject to expropriation, defining a latifundio as a large, unproductive, and inefficient estate. As in the Mexican and Guatemalan laws on agrarian reform, in the Bolivian decree beneficiaries were ordered to pay economic compensation for the received land. To do so, the government would help peasants pay the amount of the indemnification with bonds from the Agricultural Bank, which the beneficiaries were given twenty-five years to repay.[45]

Regarding labor arrangements, in the decree the colonato and all other forms of servitude were eliminated, and landowners were obligated to pay wages as compensation for any type of work.[46] One of the premises on which the decree was rooted was that Bolivia had vast, uncultivated, and uninhabited territories in the north and east of the country. Based on this premise: "all Bolivians over the age of 18, regardless of their sex, who dedicated themselves to agricultural pursuits, or who wished to do so, would after due process of law, be allocated land."[47] The decree consequently established that former colonos who, after the expropriation of a large estate, did not have access to sufficient land would be compensated with land located in areas designated for colonization.

The iconic Agrarian Reform Decree-Law was only the first regulation on agrarian reform to be implemented. Over the following years, the government enacted a series of new decrees that redefined the contours of the process of agrarian reform. In a variety of ways, many of these new rulings would obscure, if not contradict, the initial spirit of the law. Such was the case of the ruling that explicitly challenged the scope of the expropriation by declaring that latifundia of the north and east of the country were not subject to expropriation. The decree of 1955 stated that landlords could instead simply sell the portion of their properties that exceeded the maximum limit of the medium-sized landholding.[48] While it passed virtually unnoticed at the time, this measure drastically restricted the impact of the Agrarian Reform Decree-Law to the Andes and the valleys.

After signing the initial decree, the government took nearly a year to create the bureaucratic architecture that would support Bolivia's first national agrarian reform program. Government officials established rural councils and agrarian courts at the provincial level and the CNRA at the national level. It was only in 1954, after the creation of these new offices, that the colonos of each hacienda, represented by their union leaders, were able to present their demands for land expropriation.

According to the decree, each demand for land expropriation had to go through at least four stages and face three verdicts. First, peasants presented a petition for land expropriation to a local rural council, an office in charge of collecting all relevant information about the case including the owner's name, the property's name and size, the extent of the investment, the numbers of workers, and the conditions of work. Based on this crucial information (size, productivity, investment, and the system of work), a local judge on agrarian matters would hand down the first verdict. Then, in La Paz, the president of the CNRA provided a second verdict based on a further technical evaluation. Finally, the minister of peasant affairs—with the signature of the president—issued a third and final verdict either endorsing or reversing the previous decisions. At each legal stage, claimants and defendants could present objections and new evidence that the agrarian authorities could consider in their successive verdicts. This thorough procedure guaranteed that each demand received careful consideration from both local and national authorities. However, the procedure soon caused a severe bottleneck, halting hundreds of land demands for years and, in some cases, for decades.[49] Each demand for expropriation of a large estate or for the reassignment (called "consolidation" in Bolivia) of a small property took an average of seven years.

The Effect of the Bolivian Agrarian Reform across Latin America

Political debates and programs for land reform in other Latin American countries strongly shaped the formulation of the Agrarian Reform Decree-Law in Bolivia. Conversely, the enactment of Bolivian agrarian reform had a major impact in other countries. Two former Mexican presidents, Lázaro Cardenas and Emilio Portes Gil, praised the enactment of the Bolivian agrarian reform.[50] Intellectuals throughout the region observed that Bolivia's achievement generated a sense of urgency for the implementation of similar changes in other rural economies. A cartoon published in the nationalist newspaper *El Combate* in Quito, Ecuador, in August 1953, a few days after the Bolivian government enacted its Agrarian Reform Decree-Law, illustrates this influence (see figure 4.3).

The same newspaper highlighted how Bolivia was capable of implementing a well-organized process of land redistribution, which was different from usurpation: "Hundreds of thousands of peasants who did not have access to land will now have it. This is not usurpation, as the enemies of any economic and social change may think. This is about the leadership of a government that has acted with the well-being of most of its people in mind. The Bolivian decree clearly established which properties were going to be subject to expropriation."[51]

According to Edmundo Flores, the Mexican advisor to the agrarian reform in Bolivia, the Peruvian government was "terribly upset by the [Boliv-

Figure 4.3. Political cartoon that compares the situation of the Indian in Bolivia and in Ecuador. The caption reads: "Our Indians are waiting for Agrarian Reform like in Bolivia." Originally published in *El Combate*, August 6, 1953; reprinted in *La Nación*, August 25, 1953. Courtesy of Biblioteca y Archivo Histórico de la Asamblea Legislativa Plurinacional.

ian] reform and its effects on the Peruvian Indians and we [Bolivian government and advisors] were afraid of an invasion from Peru." The Mexican journalist and political analyst Francisco Martínez de la Vega underlined what he saw as the anti-imperialist political role that Guatemala and Bolivia played: "Bolivia and Guatemala are the conscience of Latin America. . . . On our map, two shiny points traced a path for solidarity: Bolivia and Guatemala are not only fighting for legitimate national demands, they are also testing the destiny of America. Bolivia and Guatemala are leading our fight against imperialism."[52]

The Peruvian writer and politician Luis Alberto Sánchez was in Bolivia when the government enacted the decree. He disregarded the charges that an agrarian reform would encourage violence in the countryside:

> When I was in Bolivia, several men who were close to the government were afraid of the consequences that the enactment of the agrarian reform law could bring. . . . A few months before the decree was enacted, peasants in Cochabamba began taking over land de facto. . . . This news seemed to announce that Bolivia would rise up and that it was going to be shaken by a major battle between Indians and landlords. . . . But once the law was enacted, most of the news about disturbances simply disappeared. The Agrarian Reform Decree-Law protects the small estates and the law only targets unproductive large estates. At the same time, all those whose land had been expropriated would have the right to receive/demand an indemnification.[53]

Alberto Sánchez's report on Bolivia reinforced the perception that it was possible to implement changes in the countryside through gradual and rational mechanisms. This was particularly useful to the MNR, enabling it to celebrate its achievements at the national and international level. In fact, the MNR controlled much of the information coming from the countryside and argued that most rumors of uprisings were isolated and sporadic. The Bolivian example became popular for Latin American activists and intellectuals who had argued that change without violence was viable. Their emphasis on Bolivia's technical and legal approach rather than the reform's revolutionary character served a political purpose in protecting Bolivia from any US intervention. Mexican advisers highlighted how careful the MNR needed to be in the language that it used. Making the legal facets of the process explicit became a key strategy in the face of US suspicions.[54]

Alejandro Quezada, a Mexican engineer working for the FAO, argued that one of the most valuable outcomes of the agrarian reform was the integration of Indians into the capitalist economy. Quezada stressed that "turning the Indian into a better producer would turn him into a better consumer, and this was the basis for the country's development."[55] Both Alberto Sánchez and Alejandro Quezada portrayed Bolivian agrarian reform as a rational and technical process. The Bolivian case became an international symbol for a practical type of reform that could be aligned with moderate change and development. The Bolivian and Guatemalan agrarian reform decrees were very similar—both agreed to protect small and medium-sized estates, as well as productive large estates; both agreed to pay economic compensation to expropriated owners; and both were accelerated by the local demands of peasants. However, only Bolivia succeeded in promoting its model as a non-extremist program.[56] In 1954, however, a CIA-backed coup halted Guatemala's ten-year political opening and reversed the agrarian reform.

The Bolivian agrarian reform was in fact far more radical and politically charged than the government, other Latin American intellectuals, or the CIA acknowledged. Moreover, the MNR had limited control over the process of expropriation. Peasants forced the government to respond to demands challenging the criteria that had initially been developed in the decree to target expropriation. It is worth recognizing the MNR's success in portraying Bolivia's reform as moderate, technical, and legal to international audiences. This is especially noteworthy given the dire consequences for the MNR's Guatemalan advisors who failed to achieve the same in their own country.

The First Expropriation, in Santa Clara

While discussing and drafting a new law on agrarian reform, the MNR decided to directly intervene and solve the long-standing confrontation between the Clarisas nuns, owners of Santa Clara monastery, and their colonos. Santa Clara first became nationally famous in 1937 when President Toro signed a decree that obligated the monastery to sell or rent their property only to colonos. The socialist military regime sided openly with colonos and challenged the landlords' control in the countryside. However, the monastery disregarded Toro's decree and continued selling plots of the property to many private owners. In 1939, conservative President Quintanilla overturned Toro's decree and declared that the sales completed prior to the decree were legal, thus allowing the monastery to sell or rent its property "to whomever the monastery found more convenient."[57]

The dispute over Santa Clara was a political priority for the MNR. The institution was the largest estate in the region, and the conflict had been the top story in local newspapers in the past. The MNR's decision on this issue was a crucial test for the government. Four months before enacting the agrarian reform in April 1953, Paz Estenssoro declared that only sales from the monastery to the colonos were considered legal.[58] It was a controversial decision, as this ruling overturned about a decade of property transactions between the monastery and various landholders.[59] On the basis of this decree, Jorge Soliz, the general secretary of the peasant union, demanded the expropriation of Santa Clara. His demand not only covered the 281 hectares held by the monastery in 1953 but also the 799 hectares it had owned in 1937.[60]

The church sent a furious letter to the government. The abbess of the Santa Clara monastery and her trustee, Antonio Cabrerizo, declared: "It is true that the government at that time [1937] ordered the monastery to sell the property to colonos; but the monastery disagreed with that decree and we communicated our disagreement to the government. The monastery considered those sales as consolidated. Therefore, we recommend to Jorge Soliz (the leader of the peasant union) that he initiate a claim against the respective owners of the other properties. . . . The monastery sold those properties years ago."[61]

The response eloquently reveals the history of the relationship between the monastery (and the church) and the government. The nuns, owners of the monastery, had interpreted Toro's decree as an opinion rather than as law. Despite this decree, the nuns continued to sell their property to non-colonos, confident that no government would challenge the religious institution's power. The monastery expected that a letter explaining its point of view would suffice to stop the government's decision, as it had before 1953.

But 1953 was not 1939. In response to the monastery, the union seized the property and stopped sharing the harvest with the nuns. The abbess sent a new letter describing the situation and demanding that the government stop the peasant union: "The colonos took our entire property including the houses and the barns. The union leader ordered [the colonos] to take the entire harvest and give nothing to the monastery. The peasants occupied the house in Cliza. . . . As far as we understand, the agrarian reform should not be able to affect urban property." The abbess finally realized that the colonos would not leave the property, so she changed her strategy and asked for an indemnity for Santa Clara—not for the actual value as was established in the Agrarian Reform Decree-Law but for six times the value of the estate. The abbess claimed this price was fair because, "Before the revolution, the monastery had to pay taxes based on the six-fold value of the property."[62]

The dispute with the monastery gave the government one more political enemy to add to the list of those it had created in 1952 after the nationalization of the mines. In addition to the United States and the tin barons, the entire Catholic Church now opposed the government because of the Santa Clara case. The head of the church in Bolivia sent several letters to the president accusing peasants of acts of violence. The government did not answer the church until 1955, when the expropriation of Santa Clara was consolidated. Minister of Foreign Affairs Walter Guevara Arze sent a conciliatory letter to the Bolivian bishop suggesting that the seizure of Santa Clara's property in fact followed the guiding principles of Fray Bartolomé de las Casas, the sixteenth-century bishop who had declared himself protector of the Indians. "Illustrious Bishop[,] . . . I apologize for this delayed answer, but the very urgent matters of the government have not allowed me the time to answer you properly." The three pages that followed sought to show how the MNR's policies shared a common vision with the Catholic Church: "The MNR shares the same principles that guided Bartolomé de Las Casas and the Church's Encyclicals."[63]

As expected, the peasant union leading the case against the Clarisas nuns faced dozens of additional judicial petitions. The landholders of small and medium-sized properties who had bought plots from the monastery in the late 1930s and 1940s were going to lose their property because of the union's demand. Many of these landholders were small traders, dressmakers, cobblers, and even former colonos who had bought a small plot from another landholder. Although Paz Estenssoro's decree declared that all those sales had been illegal, in practice, the leader of the union, Jorge Soliz, played a crucial role in defining whose properties were going to be expropriated. Soliz denied property rights to the landholders of large or medium-sized properties, but he tended to recognize the rights of landholders of small properties. He also valued landholders' ties with the union. For example, in two similar cases where the landholders were dressmakers who had each bought about four hectares from the monastery, Soliz responded to the first appellant: "As Nélida Aráoz holds a small property 'in strict observance of the law,' the peasant union will be respectful of her property and goods." But to the second one, he responded: "as Eloina Lobo illegally bought land from the monastery, thus, 'in strict observance of the law' her property should be expropriated and she should submit a claim to the monastery to get her money back."[64] Soliz played a critical role in orchestrating the very complex expropriation of the Santa Clara property by defining which demands were legal or fair.

Only three months after Soliz presented the case against the monastery, the local judge signed a verdict ordering the expropriation of hacienda Santa Clara from the monastery. The verdict redistributed 799 hectares among 765 former and evicted colonos and small landholders in a complex reorganization that detailed the amount of land that every beneficiary would receive individually. Some sections were also distributed collectively, and in most cases, the colonos opted for that solution since the plots were too small to be divided individually.

Not all was lost for the nuns. First, the judge granted them fifty hectares in the nearby province of Quillacollo. Second, he ordered peasants to return to the nuns the house they owned in the town of Cliza. And, third, the judge required the colonos to pay an indemnification (as had been established by the law) according to the size of the plot they received and based on the registered value of the property.[65]

The expropriation of the monastery proved a radical turning point for notions of rural property in the country. It defined the MNR's political position in the long-term battle between the monastery and the colonos, which of course had broader repercussions for the rest of the countryside. The decision challenged the church, one of the most powerful institutions in the country, and challenged the property of some landholders of medium-sized properties. The expropriation became a powerful precedent for how far the government was willing to go to enact land reform. Santa Clara became a significant precedent for hundreds of cases of expropriation. After the national newspapers reported the final verdict on Santa Clara, unions across the country began to demand the expropriation of the haciendas where they worked. The old principle of "land to the tiller," enacted in the 1938 constitution, finally became true in practice as well as in law.

Achacachi, Embodying the Law

On a par with the case of the Monastery of Santa Clara, Achacachi became the symbolic locus of the radicalization of the agrarian reform. These drastic actions took place under the leadership of Luciano Quispe, the president of the local rural council. If in Germán Jordán, the leader of the peasant union became the central figure of the process of expropriation, in Omasuyos, Quispe, the president of the rural council and a public functionary, became the leading figure by accelerating the redistribution of properties in the region.

Quispe was already a strong and well-known local leader before the revolution. In the 1940s, despite landlord opposition, he opened a rural school in Belen (Omasuyos Province), a former hacienda close to Warisata, which became the country's first indigenous teachers' school.[66] Throughout the 1930s, landowners had complained about Warisata's role in stirring conflicts between the landowners and their colonos. President Villarroel played a key role in this battle when, in 1945, he ordered all landowners to open schools for peasant children on their haciendas.[67] Although most landholders ignored Villarroel's decrees, indigenous communities used their own means to open dozens of rural schools. Luciano Quispe was part of this political movement.

When running the rural council, Quispe not only accepted demands for expropriation, as had been established by the law, he also declared the expropriation of the property without waiting for the judge's verdict. Quispe thus assumed the role of the judge and directly decided the fate of the haciendas. But even more interesting was the manner in which Quispe led the public hearings he convened to address these demands. He not only summoned peasants from the estate in question but also called forth peasant representatives from the neighboring estates. More than a public hearing, Quispe instituted a sort of popular assembly with a large indigenous presence in such a way that no landholder dared to attend these public events, which were legitimized by the presence of the subprefect.[68] At the public hearing of hacienda Ckasina, Quispe pointed out: "The session of the rural council for Agrarian Reform of Omasuyos will now commence, led by comrade Luciano Quispe, with the presence of comrade Subprefect Virgilio Arona; comrade Natalio Colque from the Provincial Agrarian Federation; Paulino Quispe representing comrades from hacienda Ckasina; as secretary of the rural commission, comrade Carlos Augusto Rojas . . . ; comrade Basilio Chipana, representing hacienda Pajchani Grande; comrade Manuel

Figure 4.4. Political cartoon that shows the reaction of the elite to the agrarian reform. *La Nación*, August 25, 1953. The caption reads: "What do you think about this agrarian reform thing?" "No idea, Toty. But my husband—who used to have several large estates—is now looking for jobs in Peru." Courtesy of Biblioteca y Archivo Histórico de la Asamblea Legislativa Plurinacional.

Quispe from hacienda Tola-tola; and Colque from Hacienda Pacharía. . . . The hearing is going to take place in spite of the landowner's absence."[69]

At the public hearings, Quispe declared the expropriation of the property and all of the assets on it, including houses, machinery, and cattle. However, Quispe did not claim to act beyond the law; instead, in every decision, he quoted from specific articles of the Agrarian Reform Decree-Law. For example, when he ordered the redistribution of hacienda Cala-Cala, Quispe stated that the expropriation would include the house, the agricultural tools, and the cattle based on Article 105 of Decree-Law 3471.[70] In fact, Article 105 did refer to cattle and machinery, but in the exact opposite sense—the article prevented peasants from seizing the cattle or the machinery of large estates. The article also allowed landholders to sell the cattle in cases in which the state authorities had decided on expropriation, but Quispe interpreted the language as authorizing terms of expropriation that were favorable to the peasants.[71]

It is difficult to tell whether Quispe challenged the law on purpose or whether he misunderstood it. Either way, the result was that this initial decision allowed peasants to immediately seize the estates in the name of the law. In all likelihood, the illegal appropriations of land that made Achacachi famous were rooted, at least partly, in the application of the Agrarian Reform Decree-Law. The newspapers portrayed these actions as illegal seizures of land by peasants, but from the perspective of the plaintiffs, these were legal acts made after a public hearing with the consent of an officially appointed state authority.

In response, landholders from Omasuyos denounced Quispe's procedures as illegal. They took their complaints to the press and to the national authorities (see figure 4.4). One of the most powerful landowners of the region, Consuelo Millan, protested to the CNRA: "Quispe illegally ordered the expropriation of my land plus the seizure of the agricultural machinery and the cattle, ignoring the principles of the Agrarian Reform Decree-Law."[72] The Terrazas brothers, owners of hacienda Casamaya who claimed to have sixty-five hundred sheep and one hundred head of purebred cattle, demanded that the MAC stop Quispe's public hearings: "Peasants of hacienda Casamaya followed through with the legal papers for the expropriation of our estate despite the technical reports and the order of the Ministry of Peasants Affairs to stop the public hearing. The peasants mistakenly think that, right after the public hearing, there will be expropriation and that the landowners will no longer have access to the hacienda."[73]

Quispe's actions went against the very institutional structure that the MNR had designed and that allowed the government to represent agrarian reform as a legitimate legal and technical procedure. The government feared that appointed state authorities would begin to act independently, as Quispe had, ultimately challenging the state's structure of power from the countryside. To remedy this situation, national authorities sent Cornelio Chávez, a technician from the CNRA, to report on the functions of the rural council and the situation on ten haciendas in Omasuyos.[74] According to Chávez, landowners were unable to enter their estates or be present during the public hearings. All of the owners interviewed in the report claimed that Luciano Quispe was responsible for their situation, and they accused Quispe of organizing his own headquarters in Omasuyos. As one owner quoted in the report stated, "The colonos of Ckasina, Masaya, Pacharia are the most rebellious. These are actually the headquarters of the president of the rural council, Luciano Quispe. He does not allow anyone to get close to these large estates."[75]

For his part, Chávez seemed to give more credence to the remarks of the owners than to those of the colonos or peasants working on the haciendas.

He portrayed the peasants as extremists, and he described landholders as rational and understanding actors:

> I have talked to the owners of the estates and they all agree with the principles of the Agrarian Reform Decree-Law. They agree on giving to the former colonos the plots they were already working on. I explained to the peasants that the Agrarian Reform Decree-Law won't take away their cattle, their agricultural machinery, or their houses. But the colonos don't seem to understand. They told me they would continue waiting for the agrarian judge's decision because they keep thinking—wrongly—that the expropriation would be for free and would include the entire property and all the equipment on it.[76]

Cornelio Chávez's report had an immediate impact on the national authorities. The government decided to fire the radical Luciano Quispe and designate Toribio Salas instead. Historians know very little about the dispute between Luciano Quispe and Toribio Salas, though Albó, in one of the few studies that discuss these two local leaders, suggests that the two men were rivals and that their conflict ended with Salas defeating Quispe.[77]

Agrarian court records reveal that this was more than a personal rivalry. Quispe's downfall implied the defeat of a more radical approach to land reform. His methods included immediate redistribution, both unfavorable to landholders and threatening to the jurisdictional authority of national leaders. Toribio Salas, by contrast, was more careful with the procedures, and his role as the new president of the rural council allowed the government to claim it had regained control over the region. Imposing Salas in the place of Quispe enabled the MNR to prove to national and international audiences that it was committed to following the strict legal procedures written in the Agrarian Reform Decree-Law.

The transition from one authority to the other was far from simple. The difficulties in replacing Quispe show the power he held in Omasuyos, and they may also indicate that he was indeed following his own path. Cornelio Chávez reported the events that followed his dismissal: "Doctor Jiménez Vega, officer of Peasant Justice, came from La Paz to arrest Luciano Quispe. When Dr. Jiménez went into Achacachi, Quispe's henchmen were waiting for him at the city hall building, hidden in the corner of the windows and doors. Dr. Jimenez could barely escape. When he finally captured Quispe, his followers threatened that they would assault the city of Achacachi if he did not free Luciano in 48 hours. Later, Luciano Quispe's people rose up again; they besieged Achacachi, cutting off all communication with La Paz. . . . Fortunately, after a little skirmish, Luciano Quispe's supporters disbanded."[78]

Luciano Quispe's history represents the difficulties the MNR faced in controlling the countryside. In implementing the agrarian reform, it not only had to manage the pressures and demands of peasants and landlords but also those of its own functionaries. His story demonstrates the fragile equilibrium of factors involved in the implementation of the agrarian reform. Achacachi illustrates the challenges of any attempt at portraying the political scene in the countryside in binary terms, as either violent and uncontrollable or quiet and manageable. Instead, these experiences are filled with paradoxes; in the midst of what seemed like one of the most uncontrollable situations in Omasuyos, landowners' complaints were successful and informed the national government's decision to dismiss the radical Luciano Quispe. In appointing Salas, national authorities could actually claim that the government had regained control of the region. However, neither Cornelio Chávez nor Toribio Salas was able to stop the peasants from acquiring landowners' estates. The MNR could claim that the process of expropriation was carried out in accordance with the law, but in practice, the MNR did not reverse peasants' control of the haciendas.

As the MNR sought to show that it had regained control of the region, the government ordered Toribio Salas to annul all public hearings led by Luciano Quispe. This delayed peasants' demands, and they had to start the process from scratch again. In order to make the legal ritual even more visible, Toribio Salas led the public hearings in the presence of two MAC inspectors who visited from La Paz. This adherence to following laws and procedures was the government's answer to the newspapers' denunciations of the revolutionary arbitrariness and the illegal confiscation of lands. This became even more crucial for the Bolivian government in the international context of 1954, when the United States overthrew Guatemalan President Jacobo Arbenz through a CIA covert operation while he was leading an agrarian reform. Paz Estenssoro was aware of the importance of maintaining a legal facade so that his government would not risk being overthrown.

Although Toribio Salas was politically more moderate than Luciano Quispe, landholders still complained about his tactics. Adett Saravia, a landlord in Achacachi, accused the president of the rural council of using deceiving tactics that caused her to miss the hearing: "There is no legality in this process. According to what criteria did Toribio Salas describe my property as a large estate when it is clear that my property is a medium-sized property? How could the president of the rural council classify my property as a large estate if only half of my estate is cultivable? I am willing to make an agreement with the former colonos. I am only claiming the correct application of the Agrarian Reform Decree-Law."[79]

Other landlords accused Salas of using their absence from public hearings "as evidence of their lack of interest." When leading the public hearing on Tari, Toribio Salas pushed for the expropriation of the property based on the following arguments: "As the landlord has not demonstrated any interest in his property, as she has not attended the public hearings and has not sent an attorney for this trial. As he used a feudal system of work on the hacienda, the Rural Council classified this property a *latifundio*."[80] Landholders often alleged that it was not due to a lack of interest but out of fear for their lives that they did not attend the public hearings. But as Toribio Salas's decisions were only preliminary classifications and not a final verdict, the government validated the public hearings and allowed the legal process to continue at the level of the CNRA.[81]

Cornelio Chávez's and Luciano Quispe's stories highlight the coexistence of at least two marked tendencies within the state. The perspective that limited land redistribution to very specific cases of large unproductive estates was supported by Minister of Agriculture Germán Vera Tapia and the CNRA technocrat Cornelio Chávez. The latter, when talking about his visit to Omasuyos, explicitly stated his perspective on what the scope of the agrarian reform should be: "I explained to the colonos that Jahuira Lacka, a medium-sized property, won't be expropriated. The owner of Jahuira Lacka, as evidence of his good will, agreed to distribute and give the colonos the legal property of the plots they were already working on. However, the colonos told me that they prefer to wait for the judge's decision, because they knew they would get the distribution of the entire property for free. Unsuccessfully I tried to explain to them that the Agrarian Reform Decree is not about that. But they did not want to listen to me."[82] This position contrasted with that of Luciano Quispe and Toribio Salas, also state functionaries, who had a more radical notion of the process of land redistribution. They thought that if there were colonos on a property, land should be redistributed whether it was a large, medium, or small estate and whether it was productive or not. The tension among state officials did not stem exclusively from the biases of those who wanted to favor peasants versus those who wanted to favor landlords. The division also found its origins in two broader conceptions of what the goals of the agrarian reform should be—those who supported redistribution versus those who privileged agricultural production and economic growth. The Agrarian Reform Decree-Law embraced both principles and the government promoted both. Although officials in the government publications strived to demonstrate that the agrarian reform did not hurt output, in courts the local judges and CNRA authorities often faced the dilemma of privileging agricultural yield or redistribution.

Conclusions

When the government called for the organization of a commission whose work would focus on agrarian reform in January 1953, it was evident that the government was going to encourage a program for land expropriation.

Yet, the multiple proposals show the extent to which these intellectuals agonized over the scope and the mechanisms of land expropriation. Until the very end, many argued that Bolivia was neither Mexico nor Guatemala, they defended the idea that the country had wide potential for colonization, and it was not really necessary to challenge property relations in regions where haciendas were well established. The decree that the government enacted in August 1953 protected those properties where landlords were able to demonstrate market-oriented production, investment, and personal involvement.

After the decree's signing, intellectuals who were interested in the success of this process, in Latin America and the United States, highlighted its technical and legal facets rather than the revolutionary character of the reform. Reacting to US intervention in Guatemala in 1954, their speeches and writings attempted to protect Bolivia from another CIA covert operation or another right-wing outburst.[83] In his memoir of the Bolivian agrarian reform, former FAO advisor Edmundo Flores wrote: "I happened to believe the Bolivian Land Reform was a much more drastic step than that of Guatemala, and yet the Bolivians didn't get into trouble at all, while the Guatemalans did. The phraseology used in the two cases accounts for much of the difference."[84] But, from the beginning, colonos, local leaders, and state authorities sped up the pace of the process and expanded the initial objectives for land expropriation. In Germán Jordán, the Santa Clara nuns were forced to accept the process of land expropriation once they learned the colonos had already seized the property, the harvest, and the house. In Omasuyos, the president of the rural council bypassed legal procedures by declaring that all properties were latifundia and authorizing the immediate occupation of the plots and the seizure of the agricultural machinery and the cattle. In both cases, authorities at the national level tried to tame peasant political forces: in Germán Jordán, colonos were required to return the house and agreed to pay economic compensation; in Omasuyos, the government appointed a new president for the rural council who reset the judicial processes for agrarian reform. In both cases, however, the government did not dare to challenge colonos' land occupations. The MNR struggled to maintain a legal and technical portrayal of the reform, but in practice, it did not reverse peasants' control of the haciendas.

CHAPTER FIVE

LAND TO ITS ORIGINAL OWNERS

In October 1952, six months after President Víctor Paz Estenssoro took office, he received a letter from Indian community representatives of seven of the country's nine departments:

> The principal caciques [*caciques principales*] of the republic—representing all the Indian race—come to greet you, Your Excellency, and to put ourselves unconditionally at your service. . . . Mister President . . . the Indian race has been fighting for the restitution of our lands since [President Mariano] Melgarejo [1864–1871], and later President Ismael Montes [1904–1909, 1913–1917] took 12 indigenous communities to consolidate his personal hacienda. . . . We know that with the April 9 Revolution the time for our vindication has arrived. We now ask you for a new land survey [*comisión revisitadora de tierras de origen*] so that the usurpers are forced to present their legal titles or give back the land to the original owners.[1]

This letter was one of many that Paz Estenssoro received from comunario leaders during the first two years of the revolution. After 1952, they expressed their commitment to the national revolution not as "Bolivians" or "citizens," but as members of the "Indian race." They staked claims for land but did not follow the established nationalist and left principle embraced by the revolution: "land for those who work for it." Instead, they upheld their own principle of "land for its original owners."

Students of the Bolivian agrarian reform have primarily focused on its impact on colonos, who were the great beneficiaries of the reform. The scholarly literature has shed very little light on the role of comunarios at the time of the revolution. However, since the 1980s, some researchers, increasingly critical of the MNR, have examined the state's relation with the indigenous communities. In this, they criticize the MNR for having promoted a land tenure system based on small and medium-sized private properties, and they argue that this system dismantled indigenous communities' collective forms of organization as well as their traditional systems of authority.[2]

In the most recent work exploring the relation between the state and the indigenous communities at the time of the revolution, Waskar Ari argues that the 1952 revolution was one of the most consolidated efforts by local elites to modernize and westernize Bolivia's Indian population. For Ari, the MNR-sponsored unions—controlled by the mestizo provincial elite—became a tool to bring about racial assimilation in the countryside: "As integration became official state policy, indigenous communities had to shift, at least in legal terms, from being Indians to being peasants and accept a process of domestication that the new elite had designed from the top down."[3]

Although it is true that MNR discourse tended to suppress ethnic distinctions and advocated "bringing the Indians into the nation" in order to consolidate a single homogenous country, in its day-to-day practices, the MNR constantly had to readjust its policies and accept, at least partially and behind its rhetoric, long-standing indigenous community claims to land. For their part, indigenous communities sought to link their demands to the revolutionary nationalist project and push the new government to restore the lands they had lost, particularly during the late nineteenth and early twentieth centuries. Comunario leaders enthusiastically supported the revolution, but with an approach that was very different from those of other peasant groups.

To explore the political role of the ex-comunarios during the revolution and their strategies for securing land after the revolution, in this chapter we analyze both the petitions for land restitution and the attempts to regain their lands through the courts at the National Council of Agrarian Reform (CNRA). These sources show that the MNR could not simply ignore ex-comunarios' petitions. The lobbying, petitioning, and even seizure of lands by ex-comunarios after the revolution obliged the government to respond, and during its first year it began to incorporate ex-comunario denunciations into its political discourse. However, the president himself conceded in public only those demands that supported the MNR's agenda, ignoring any that might disrupt the party's nationalist narrative. Reluctant to challenge decades of rural property transactions, Paz Estenssoro only addressed the assaults on communal land that took place after 1900, even though many petitions demanded the restitution of lands taken in the nineteenth century. This allowed him to claim that the MNR was rectifying the misdeeds of the early twentieth-century liberal regimes but without having to fully embrace calls to revisit centuries of land titles.

Despite Paz Estenssoro's selective embrace of ex-comunario demands, the 1953 Agrarian Reform Decree-Law included a clause on land restitution, and this was further buttressed by a 1954 decree for the restitution of communal land.[4] This 1954 decree was a major deviation from the MNR's initial policies, and it provoked objections not only from landlords but also from leftist leaders and colonos, whom historians have considered the major drivers and beneficiaries of the revolution itself. Prominent leaders of the left thought the restitution of communal properties an obstacle to Bolivia's modernization, while the colonos feared that the ex-comunario principle of "land to the original owners" would threaten their own rights to land under the MNR principle of "land for those who work it."

Indian Communities and the National Revolution

After the MNR took power, President Paz Estenssoro received numerous letters from ex-comunario leaders demanding the restitution of their lands. Although most came on behalf of individual communities, some claimed to represent several villages across multiple provinces and departments, suggesting the persistence of a network of community-elected indigenous representatives, the caciques apoderados, since the early twentieth century. One claim came from a network of caciques from Achocalla, Achacachi, Caquiaviri, Ayllu Belén, Ayllu Pocuni-uyo, Ayllu Pallareti, Callapa, and Guancollo.[5] Even more surprising is a petition signed by cacique principal Santos Cornejo claiming to represent an "Indian Republic" that spanned seven of the country's nine departments.[6] This set of indigenous leaders independently orchestrated community action in ways that paralleled the efforts of political parties and workers' organizations encouraging colonos to form unions. However, unlike those groups, the caciques embraced the political goal of the restitution of their communal lands rather than the expropriation and redistribution of the latifundios.[7] The comunario petitions in 1953 suggest that the cacique apoderado movement continued after the revolution. Most of the petitions came from Indian communities within the department of La Paz, where scholars such as Silvia Rivera Cusicanqui, Roberto Choque Canqui, Vitaliano Soria, Esteban Ticona Alejo, and Laura Gotkowitz have documented struggles over land dating back to the late nineteenth century.[8] However, Paz Estenssoro also received some petitions from departments such as Cochabamba, Oruro, and Potosí, which shows that indigenous communities throughout Bolivia saw the revolution as an opportunity to push for land restitution.[9]

We register ex-comunario petitions by province and department, with the first five petitions listed from the network of caciques apoderados (see table 5.1). It is hard to tell if the 1952 network of caciques apoderados led by Santos Cornejo was a continuation of the broad-based legal movement of caciques that emerged in the late 1910s and early 1920s. Several studies have argued that this latter movement declined in the early 1930s because the Chaco War had triggered fierce political persecution of peasants, workers, and left-leaning activists.[10] After the war, indigenous communities' campaigns in defense of communal land rights lost strength and visibility,

Table 5.1. Ex-comunario Petitions to President Víctor Paz Estenssoro and the Ministry of Peasant Affairs, 1952–1953

Ex- comunario Petitioners	Province	Department
"Principales caciques of the Republic representing the Indian race"	NA	La Paz, Oruro, Potosí, Cochabamba, Chuquisaca, Santa Cruz, Tarija
Community Chivita, Haciendas Camiraya, Arache, Sancalacala	Murillo	La Paz
Achocalla	Murillo	La Paz
Achocalla, Achacachi, Caquiaviri, and alcaldes mayores of Ayllu Belén, Ayllu Pocuni-uyo, Ayllu Pallareti, Callapa, and Guancollo	Omasuyos, Pacajes, Murillo	La Paz
Tihuanacu, Achaca, Huánuco Kasa Achuta, Achuta Grande, Huacullani, Kiruni, Rosa Pata, Huma Marca	Ingavi	La Paz
Chillilaya	Los Andes	La Paz
Ex-communities Huarina	Omasuyos	La Paz
Guaqui	Ingavi	La Paz
Ex-community Pituta, Guaqui	Ingavi	La Paz
Irpa Chico	Ingavi	La Paz
Ponama-Ambaná	Camacho	La Paz
Tamampaya	Camacho	La Paz
Ex-community Collantaca	Los Andes	La Paz
Thirteen communities in Huarina	Omasuyos	La Paz
Huarina, Chua Santiago de Huata	Omasuyos	La Paz
Ayllus Ichoca, Sacaca, Curaguazi, Colquiri	Inquisivi	La Paz
Sindicato Agrario Karazani	Muñecas	La Paz
Quena-Chivita, Mocomoco	Camacho	La Paz
Guyahuani y Utavi	Omasuyos	La Paz
Tujuyu	Los Andes	La Paz
Timusi and Cohoni	Muñecas	La Paz
Chijcha	Ingavi	La Paz
Sora	Pantaleón Dalence	Oruro
Humahuarajta	Cercado	Oruro
Viluyo, Cancha Pata	Sud Lípez	Potosí

Source: ABNB-PR, files 765 (1952), 803 (1953), 836 (1954).

Note: The first five petitions listed come from the network of caciques apoderados.

and political parties began to focus on the living conditions of the colonos working on the haciendas rather than on the fate of the remaining indigenous communities. In other words, political debate shifted away from indigenous communal property rights to labor rights.

It is also possible that the network of caciques apoderados petitioning in 1952 had revived after the regional Quechua Congresses of 1942 and 1943 and the first National Indigenous Congress of 1945. Although the resolutions adopted on the latter focused only on the situation of the hacienda colonos, six hundred of the fifteen hundred delegates came from independent Indian communities. Gotkowitz has shown how, despite President Villarroel's attempts to control the congress agenda, local leaders used the congress to boost their own objectives, which included calls for land redistribution. Perhaps this provided the political space where the network of caciques and their older political struggles could reactivate demands for the restitution of communal lands.[11]

Numerous letters from the 1950s reveal a keen connection between indigenous demands and the MNR's nationalist political ideology. For instance, Santos Cornejo embraced the MNR's general defense of social justice to petition protection for the Indian race: "Now, Señor President, that you claim that we are in a new era in the defense of the rights for the majority [*para la mayorías*], now that you claim to govern with social justice for all the nation, we ask you to look out for the well-being of the Indian race. . . . We demand that you enact the agrarian reform, meaning a new revisita de tierras, so that the government shall order all landholders to present the legal titles of their properties and if they don't have them, the land may revert to the true owners."[12] Here the *cacique principal* expresses his support for the national revolution, but rather than the "land to the tiller" slogan used by leftist and nationalist parties since the late 1930s, he invoked the promise of the contemporary revolutionary moment to legitimize or reinstate indigenous property claims based on titles before the republican period. The term "agrarian reform" is employed in a request for a survey of legal property so that Indian communities could prove that the landlords had illegally expanded onto their lands. Santos Cornejo effectively combined two political traditions, usually presented as mutually exclusive, as part of one political project. He asserted the right of indigenous groups to be heard as active members of the nation, but he asked for recognition of their land rights as members of a specific group.

Many of the indigenous petitions centered on a detailed reading of history that rooted indigenous land claims in the colonial period, when the Spanish Crown ratified communal titles in exchange for indigenous tribute and work in the mines. The caciques apoderados from the Ichoca, Sacaca, Curaguazi, and Colquiri ayllus in Inquisivi province wrote of "our titles dated from 1500, 1600, [and] 1700, when they were registered and delimited by ayllu, as was ordered by Viceroy Toledo [in 1574]. . . . as recognition for our work in the mines."[13] Several letters traced a direct line of indigenous communal property ownership from the colonial period to the second half of the nineteenth century, when President Mariano Melgarejo enacted the first decrees allowing the transfer of Indian communal property to private owners, with many petitioners identifying his presidency as one of the worst moments of dispossession.[14] As the caciques apoderados of Inquisivi province explained, "We have been fighting for the restitution of our former lands since President Melgarejo, who was the first one who assaulted our lands."[15] The indigenous representatives from seven departments specifically traced the history of their struggle to the nineteenth century, under Presidents Melgarejo and Montes: "We have been fighting [to recover] our land since President Melgarejo began taking over community land; he was the first oppressor of the indigenous race. Later, it was President Ismael Montes who seized 12 communities from Taraco. Now, all these 12 communities are turned into one large estate and all comunarios are subjected to servitude, with neither protection nor guarantee in the face of poverty and dispersion."[16]

Several petitioning communities described successive waves of land seizures under liberal governments, mostly in the extensive provinces of Ingavi and Omasuyos. Communities in Taraco asserted that President Montes had taken advantage of his political power to turn the municipality into his personal hacienda in 1907, in violation of colonial titles. They claimed that Benedicto Goitia, a leading liberal, and his son-in-law General Julio Sanjinés usurped more indigenous land between 1920 and 1922, and that Sanjinés, then commander of the regiment at Guaqui, used the army to kill hundreds of men and women in order to evict indigenous people from their lands, hiring *mayordomos* and *hilacatas* (Indian authorities who managed colono work at haciendas) from other regions.[17] The petitions also illustrate how indigenous communities lost their lands through illegal sales made possible by local authorities, forced incarcerations, and violent conflicts with the army or armed landlords.[18] In some petitions, ex-comunarios complained that caciques apoderados sold communal property when bribed, or they demanded money from comunarios to recover their property. For example, in Chrungalla ex-comunarios accused Manuel Poma, a cacique apoderado, of extorting three million bolivianos from them after claiming that he was going to fight for the restitution of their land.[19]

Various petitioners denounced new assaults by landlords on Indian property on the eve of the revolution. Most of these conflicts were in Eliodoro Camacho and Muñecas provinces in La Paz, where the incursion of the hacienda estates onto indigenous and peasant property had started in the decade prior to the revolution. Ex-comunarios from Timusi and Cohoni in Muñecas denounced a landlord who had appropriated their lands in the late 1940s during the conservative governments of Enrique Hertzog and Mamerto Urriolagoitía (1949–1951). Members of the former community of Tamampaya, in Eliodoro Camacho, denounced Socrates Rea, owner of hacienda Cariquina, for usurping their property in 1952.[20] These examples show how landlord expansion into peasant lands did not end in the 1910s, when the liberals were in power, but continued up to the revolution.[21]

Ex-comunarios linked their own demands to disputes at the national level, openly embracing left and nationalist discourses that framed Bolivian history as a contest between the people, or "the nation," and the oligarchy, or "anti-nation."[22] They identified nationalist presidents Germán Busch (1937–1939) and Gualberto Villarroel as protectors of the Indian cause, "martyrs who fought for our redemption and were murdered by the elite." In several petitions indigenous leaders proclaimed themselves MNRistas, representatives of the ex-communities of Huánuco Kasa Achuta, Achaca, and Tihuanacu declaring that "we deeply adhere to the principles of the April 9 Revolution. We are your soldiers. We know that it is time to fight for our social demands."[23] We also find petitions that attempted to combine their class and ethnic identities. Some, such as Santos Cornejo, affirmed links to their traditional organizations, presenting themselves as hilacatas or caciques. Others adhered to the MNR's new unionist language, identifying themselves as secretaries general, the standard name for the leaders of the peasant unions being promoted by the government. However, this newly adopted language did not surrender their Indian identity. In one case the petitioners identified themselves as "the union of former comunarios whose land was usurped."[24] Such "language of contention" shows ex-comunarios embracing the modernizing revolutionary lexicon without forsaking their traditional political identity and long-standing set of material demands.[25]

Along with land restitution, some communities demanded the other benefits of modernization that were being widely promoted by the government. Santos Cornejo, the Indian republic's cacique principal, requested schools "for every ayllu, every community, every village," asking Paz Estenssoro "to make a revolution by giving literacy to Indians."[26] A letter from Mariano Mayta, the leader of the communities of Huarina (Omasuyos, La Paz), asked the president to include the Indians in economic development: "We, the Indians . . . want to be part of the development as well . . . want you to increase trade, bank loans, and construction of homes so that Indians can also live in houses with electricity and comfort." Mayta embraced the MNR's nationalist agenda, but instead of referring to its beneficiaries as citizens, Bolivians, or the people, Mayta made his demands on behalf of "we, the Indians."[27]

Petitions for the expansion of government programs to include the Indian population were not new. Vitaliano Soria Choque has documented how Indian leaders were inspired by the liberal education reforms in the late nineteenth century to launch their own autonomous movement for Indian rural schools. Gotkowitz has shown how Indian and peasant leaders strategically couched their demands within the language of the late 1930s' military socialist laws and the constitutional guarantees against pongueaje approved in the 1940s.[28] Alliances between Indian leaders and urban political organizations were also not new. One of the most striking was that between the Indian leader Zárate Willka and the liberal president José Manuel Pando during the 1899 civil war. Lehm A. and Rivera Cusicanqui have documented Indian leaders' alliances with the anarchist movement and the FOL in the first decades of the twentieth century.[29]

Waskar Ari and Gabrielle Kuenzli present two distinct readings of these alliances. Ari argues that Indian leaders saw these alliances as instrumental, for they were in reality fighting for an autonomous Indian political project. Kuenzli, who focuses on Willka's 1899 rebellion, argues that his alliance was not merely instrumental. She points out that the idea the 1899 insurrection was an autonomous Indian project was based on the testimonies of imprisoned Indian leaders who were forced to declare they were persecuting a race war. Portraying Willka's uprising as a race war was part of the Liberal Party's strategy to detach their own project from the Indian insurrection.[30] Kuenzli's argument reminds us to pay attention to the political circumstances in which memory and political discourses emerge, and in approaching comunario petitions it is important to acknowledge the political context not only of the 1950s but also of the 1980s, when many organizations—including the emergent think tanks of Aymara intellectuals—sought to separate themselves from the MNR's political legacy. Both were moments when the question of Indian participation in the revolution was politically potent. The question became even more charged after 1985, when Paz Estenssoro, once again in power, led the country's transition to neoliberalism. Over the last three decades, the tendency to downplay the Indian connection to the MNR's program has grown as the country has witnessed the emergence of strong indigenous political movements campaigning for the construction of a multiethnic society—a direct challenge to the MNR's old ideal of building one homogeneous nation. The heated nature of contemporary debates about the revolution in Bolivia has led James Dunkerley to remark that "the Bolivian Revolution did not 'become historical' until quite recently."[31]

Whether genuine or pragmatic, ex-comunario campaigns pursued in the revolution were relevant because of their success in reshaping the MNR's agrarian program. Despite its modernizing rhetoric, the MNR government was not able to fully implement a uniform individual property regime on the former large estates. Instead, because of ex-comunario pressure, government officials had to acknowledge communal property rights and returned some community lands "to the original owners."

Reshaping the MNR's Nationalist Discourse

In addition to the petitions sent to the president from September 1952 onward, numerous indigenous delegations traveled to La Paz city to talk with the president and representatives from the MAC. Media coverage of these developments shows how the MNR's reluctant incorporation of comunario demands into the new revolutionary program led to changes in its agrarian agenda.[32] When Paz Estenssoro came to power, he was familiar with Bolivian agrarian conflict but largely unconcerned with specific comunario demands. In his early speeches he mostly addressed the clash between what he called "the nation," the "peasants, workers, and small bourgeoisie," and the "anti-nation," the local oligarchs more allied with foreign economic interests than with Bolivia's people.[33] During the first year of the revolution, Paz Estenssoro encouraged local courts to attend to what he thought the most urgent matters in the countryside: the arbitrary dismissal of colonos from the haciendas. Like other nationalist and leftist intellectuals, Paz Estenssoro preferred the term "peasant" (*campesino*) to "Indian," stressing that the rural workers' problems were class- rather than race-based. The generic term "peasant" disregarded the differences between colono and ex-comunarios demands.[34]

In his first speech to the nation in January 1953, Paz Estenssoro was vague about his program for the countryside: "We need to overcome feudalism in the countryside."[35] The policy of breaking up the haciendas but not returning land to the indigenous communities reflected the ideas of the specialists and advisers, such as the socialist Félix Eguino Zaballa, the appointed head of the new Bolivian Indigenista Institute in May 1952.[36] Eguino Zaballa's program, outlined in the first issue of *Gaceta Campesina*, in August 1952, entailed ending the concentration of property and modernizing the communities, which he described as "archaic economic entities, survivals from Inca and pre-Inca times."[37] This completely ignored ex-comunario petitions for land restitution. Instead, Eguino Zaballa believed that the government had to eliminate the anachronistic communities by turning them into modern cooperatives; he was clearly a politician enthusiastic for modernization and civilization of the type criticized by Rivera Cusicanqui and Ari.[38]

However, when Paz Estenssoro began organizing the agrarian reform commission in January 1953, as hundreds of peasant delegations began arriving in La Paz city amid news and rumors of violence in the countryside, *La Nación* made its first public reference to specifically ex-comunario struggles, noting how liberals at the beginning of the twentieth century had used their political power to usurp indigenous lands.[39] The newspaper published the ex-comunario petition from Taraco, which was used to reinforce the MNR's image as the defender of Bolivia's national destiny against the corrupt elites who had run the country in the past. *La Nación* then ran interviews with ex-comunarios from Taraco who denounced the Montes, Mantilla, and Ordoñez families for forcing Indians to sell their properties for almost nothing, quoting the ex-comunario Domingo Quispe, who said he had refused to sell his property and was forced to flee from the region when President Montes hired henchmen to kill anyone who resisted doing so. The new landowners, according to Quispe, then offered to let those who sold their property to stay on and work as colonos.[40]

Confident in their rights, the heirs of President Montes responded to Paz Estenssoro's similar charges in the media, claiming that Taraco was not communal land when they bought the property from other private landholders. They insisted that their father had bought individual plots from some Indians from Taraco, without exerting any kind of pressure: "Other ex-comunarios sold their properties to other people such as Benita de Daza and Manuela Carrión. Both ladies were not part of the government, and yet both were able to buy land. This is evidence that Indians freely sold their land to anyone they wanted." The Montes family emphasized their large investment, "several millions of bolivianos in mechanized irrigation, tree planting, and cattle with high genetic value." They argued that their family had actively improved the living conditions of the colonos, "as we put in schools for Indian kids' education."[41]

The government published a half-page response by Hugo López, an expert on indigenous legislation, who listed all the laws from the colonial and republican periods that protected communal property. López insisted that it was illegal for private persons to buy indigenous property without state permission, a rule that the Montes family had clearly disregarded, and he argued that the claim of Taraco's former ex-comunarios against the Montes family was both fair and legal. López also drew attention to what would be a crucial point of debate among members of the government: "Assuming these sales were illegal, how far back in the past is the government able to go in terms of allowing community land restitution?"[42]

The pro-government newspaper *La Nación* reproduced several petitions from individual communities but carefully excluded those from the caciques apoderados network; no letter from Santos Cornejo ever appeared in the media. *La Nación* portrayed indigenous people as victims and published petitions that emphasized landlord brutality, omitting those recounting the long tradition of ex-comunario political struggles. *La Nación*'s reporting of the January 1953 visit of indigenous leaders from twelve communities to La Paz city and the newspaper's offices is typically patronizing: "We are already used to receiving the visit of our colorful peasant comrades, who come far from the countryside to bring their revolutionary spirit. Yesterday we received the visit of hilacatas from 12 communities from Jesús de Machaca, Jilatiti, Sullkatiti, Chama, Parina, Achuma, Kalla, Yaurini, Kanko, Titicani, Amoaque and Pueblo. They came with apoderado Tito Morales, provincial governor Alfredo Claves Ramos, and MNR provincial leader Patricio Chabilla. They came to visit the president and to thank him for the creation of the commission that is going to study the agrarian reform."[43] There was no mention of the fact that the precise purpose of their visit to La Paz was that the government would approve a new law protecting the right to give land to those who work it (the Agrarian Reform Decree-Law), which would end their longtime struggle to return land to its original owners. *La Nación* noted the presence of these communal leaders, but by listing cacique apoderado Morales alongside the provincial governor and an MNR party leader, the paper suggested that the ex-comunarios were aligned with the MNR's position. Headlines such as "Yesterday, 5,000 Expressed Their Unconditional Support to the Government" or "Indian Delegates Return to Their Communities" show how *La Nación* reported the comunarios' presence but ignored the substance of their complaints.[44]

Although biased, this coverage probably encouraged ex-comunario leaders from the town of Guaqui to ask the president to sign the Agrarian Reform Decree-Law in nearby Taraco, because "Taraco was the region where Indians suffered the most landlord expansion and usurpation of communal land. We know that after the nationalization of the mines, the second most important policy of [the Bolivian Revolution] is agrarian reform. Taraco was the place where the elites like Goitia, Montes, [Benita] Daza, and [Jorge] Zalles took more land with the help of henchmen who burned, stole, and plundered our communities."[45] In Ucureña, where, as we have seen, the decree was signed, indigenous communities had broken down long before, back in the colonial period.[46]

Similar tactics were used with respect to *La Nación*'s coverage of the agrarian reform commission. The newspaper frequently published the commission's findings but hardly ever their debates over comunario petitions. Only one article, entitled "Before His Trip, the Head of the Agrarian Reform Commission Presented Several Suggestions," mentions these debates, noting among the topics to be addressed by the proposed Agrarian Reform Decree-Law "the revision of past unlawful appropriation of land."[47] This silence in the media and the commission regarding comunario demands underlines how contentious their political program was for the government.

Nonetheless, comunario mobilization did yield some tangible results. Article 42 of the 1953 reform established that "land usurped after 1900 would be restored to the indigenous communities."[48] This was a major departure from the modernization program outlined by Eguino Zaballa one year before. In May 1954, Paz Estenssoro passed a new decree establishing that all indigenous community property that had been transformed into large private estates after 1900 would be returned to the communities. Its preamble declared: "considering that the revolutionary government and the Agrarian Reform Decree-Law aim to repair the injustice and the violence committed against the Indian ex-comunarios, returning to them their land or paying them an indemnification for the damages and losses they suffered . . . all communal land turned into individual property after January 1, 1900, will be subject to restitution, without economic compensation."[49]

The 1954 land restitution decree generated biting critiques from several intellectuals, including even prominent members of the government. In June 1954, Arturo Urquidi, the leader of the by-then-defunct PIR who had headed the agrarian reform commission, sent a private letter to Paz Estenssoro questioning the restitution of all communal lands converted into private property after 1900.[50] Urquidi's criticisms equated the indigenous communities with the haciendas and latifundios as obsolete and unproductive institutions: "It has been proved that the large estate and the indigenous community are two typical forms of agricultural backwardness; this is why both have to be eliminated, to free the productive forces and allow the country to enter the stage of capitalism. If we restore to the indigenous community plots that have already been granted individually, it would be only a sentimental project to please and satisfy idealists. However, the primitive collectivism that we can still find in some Indian practices may be used only if they enable us to carry out agricultural development." He also argued that Indians would not assimilate the "modern mechanisms of faming" pursued by the small and medium-sized landholders who currently owned the former communal lands. Urquidi charged that the project had "a racist character," breaching the "absolute respect for the small and medium properties" that were foundational to proper agrarian reform for "an exaggerated and senseless Indiophilia."[51] Notwithstanding the public rhetoric depicting Indians and peasants as comrades, the letter shows how difficult it was for the leaders of the national revolution to integrate indigenous demands into their program.[52]

The 1954 decree provoked such criticism from leading government supporters such as Urquidi that the MNR seems almost to have covered up its existence. While the Agrarian Reform Decree-Law was signed by the president in front of two hundred thousand peasants in Ucureña, the 1954 decree for land restitution elicited no public meetings or speeches whatsoever. Hundreds of commissioners traveled to the countryside to spread the word about the 1953 decree, but no emissaries or provincial MNR leaders promoted the communal land restitution decree. The lack of publicity is not surprising, since ex-comunario demands for communal land defied the MNR's original political agenda of creating a small and medium-sized property system. However, party leaders also feared that the new law could cause clashes between ex-comunarios and colonos, and a few days after the decree on land restitution, *La Nación* published a number of articles making it clear that the government favored the colonos working former communal lands over the ex-comunarios who had once owned them.[53]

Disputes over Land Restitution on the Ground

Were indigenous communities able to recover lands through the state-sponsored process of restitution? Comunarios employed various strategies in the courts to recover their lands. These tactics show not only that ex-comunarios embraced the MNR's nationalist agenda on their own terms during the revolution but also that their political and legal organizing continued to shape the legacy of the revolution through the courts for decades afterward.

Immediately after Paz Estenssoro signed the 1954 decree, ex-comunarios began petitioning in local agrarian courts for the restitution of communal lands. In most cases, these petitions took at least a decade to be resolved, and there were a number that were still being fought into the 1970s. Analysis of these court cases shows the persistent and long-range scope of ex-comunario battles for land restitution and the critical role played by state authorities who favored these claims over those of landlords, even when some ex-comunarios claimed lands usurped before 1900. Court files also reveal that conflicts between ex-comunarios and colonos flared up when the demands for restitution threatened the interests of those currently working the lands.[54]

To understand these challenges, it is necessary to clarify the differences between cases for expropriation, usually presented by former colonos against landlords, and cases for restitution, presented by ex-comunarios against landlords. It was easier for colonos to win the former cases than for comunarios to win the latter. To receive expropriated plots, colonos had to demonstrate that they suffered unacceptable working conditions on the haciendas. In the majority of these cases, colono testimony about lack of wages and daily mistreatment was sufficient proof of labor exploitation and therefore justified expropriation. By contrast, it was not enough for ex-comunarios to simply testify that they had lost their lands; they had to prove they were the property's legal owners. Ex-comunarios brought forth colonial and nineteenth-century titles or presented judicial claims that they had made prior to the revolution to get their lands back.[55] Another crucial

Table 5.2. Judicial Process on Agrarian Reform from August 2, 1954, to February 28, 1955

Department	Endowment	Expropriation	Restitution	Consolidation	TOTAL
La Paz	832	254	803	11	1,900
Chuquisaca	229	240	37	39	545
Cochabamba	29	526	53	62	670
Oruro	13	50	110	28	201
Potosi	429	381	511	20	1,341
Tarija		16		1	17
Santa Cruz	296	99		10	405
Beni	16				16
Pando	1,844	1,566	1,514	171	5,095

Source: Ayala Mercado, *Qué sucede*, 14.

difference concerned the size of the plots under dispute. Usually, colonos were petitioning for the expropriation of the plot of land they were currently working, while ex-comunarios were demanding the restitution of all land they had lost, which was much larger than one plot assigned to a colono. Finally, in expropriation cases landlords were able to submit claims for economic compensation from the colonos, while in restitution cases communities were able to recover their lands without paying any compensation to the landlords.[56]

It is difficult to tell how many agrarian reform cases involved expropriation and how many demanded restitution. Most national agrarian statistics in Bolivia simply signaled the number of hectares under dispute and the number of people who had received them, usually referred to as "beneficiaries." Based on the national agrarian statistics, it is impossible to tell if the beneficiary had received land as a result of the expropriation of an uncultivated large estate, the restitution of a former latifundio, or simply from the allocation of a medium-sized property. However, there are two atypical reports that do offer information about land restitution cases. The first comes from a report filed by Ernesto Ayala Mercado, a POR militant who was serving as functionary for the CNRA in 1955 (see table 5.2).[57] This shows that number of the cases of expropriation (1,566) was almost the same as for those involving restitution (1,514) in the first year of implementation of the agrarian reform, which clearly reflects the impact this measure had among ex-comunarios. Unsurprisingly, the vast majority of cases involve La Paz and Potosí, although the table also reports some cases in Oruro, Cochabamba, and Chuquisaca:

The second report, published by CNRA in 1964, states that between 1960 and 1964 there were 64 cases of land restitution (4 in Cochabamba,

Table 5.3. Land Restitution Cases in Achacachi, Omasuyos, La Paz

Court Case	Landholder	Plaintiffs	Hectares
Challuyo	Jorge Cusicanqui and Ubaldina Mollinedo	23 comunarios, 67 colonos	1,698.6
Granja experimental Belén	The state	220 comunarios and colonos	1,468
Pacharía	Eulogio Franco	53 comunarios	1,386.1
Pongon Huyo	Carmelo Mollinedo	71 colonos, 54 comunarios	674.1
Suntía Grande	Carmela Riveros de Pabón	13 comunarios, 49 colonos	365.3
Cojata	Carlos Meave	n.d.	173
Warisata	Julia Ayala v de Viscarra	17 comunarios	120.7
Pantini y adyacentes	Esteban Casablanca	8 comunarios and colonos	84.5
Pallareti	Samuel Vilela	1 comunario and 16 colonos	73.91
Quinquipa	Julia viuda de Arismendi	9 comunarios and colonos	58
Pongon Huyo	Juana, Sofia, and Margarita Zamorano	10 colonos	55.5
Pongon Huyo Circapata	Juan Villarroel and Rosa viuda de Villarroel	3 comunarios	28.1
Patanui Cuchu	Victoria viuda de Saravia	1 comunario	10
Warisata	Francisco Rivas and Norverta Cuentas	1 comunaria	8.5
Sancajahuira	Guillermo Meave	1 comunario	8.4

Source: Agrarian reform court cases, Omasuyos province, INRA-LP.

8 in Potosí, and 52 in La Paz) compared to 755 cases of land expropriation during the same period.[58] Although we do not have any information for the years from 1956 to 1960, the second report shows that both the number of demands for land restitution and expropriation declined. The demands for land restitution fell during the second presidency of Victor Paz Estenssoro.

Here we can undertake the first analysis of land restitution cases in Achacachi, one of two municipal sections of Omasuyos province in the 1950s, when there were sixteen demands for land restitution and twenty-eight for land expropriation (see table 5.3). We detail the restitution demands, though some of the properties mentioned there faced an expropriation case as well. Petitions in Achacachi included some claims for restituting a community and some for individual plots.

In Achacachi, most ex-comunarios who presented cases were able to successfully reassert their forefathers' property rights via restitution claims. Out of the sixteen cases, only one set of landlords, Juan Villarroel and Rosa viuda de Villarroel, retained their land. Using Article 32 of the 1953 Agrarian Reform Decree-Law as a shield, they alleged that their medium-sized property should not be subject to any kind of confiscation.[59] This result is surprising when we consider that even smaller properties, such as Patanui Cuchu, Warisata, and Sancajahuira, were restituted to their legitimate owners.

In several cases, both ex-comunarios and landlords presented legal titles that went back to the colonial period, which made it hard for state officials to identify the real owners of the disputed lands. For example, Carmela Riveros de Pabón claimed to be the owner of the Suntía Grande estate, whilst the comunario claimants presented legal titles from the last revisita de tierras in Omasuyos in 1882. Riveros de Pabón responded by presenting titles dating from the colonial period to demonstrate that her family had owned the plots for over a century. After a string of claims and counterclaims, the ex-comunarios were able to demonstrate that, although Riveros de Pabón was the legal owner of only one plot, she had illegally exceeded the limits of her property over time, a very common strategy among landlords.[60] Jorge Cusicanqui and Ubaldina Mollinedo similarly demonstrated that they owned particular individual plots before 1900, but the comunarios successfully argued that the Challuyo estate had dramatically expanded after 1900. The judge ordered the entire property to be expropriated and redistributed between both comunarios and its current colonos.[61]

Land restitution cases did receive significant support from state authorities. Although many landlords tried to use the 1900 time limit to block ex-comunario demands, in most of the cases, state authorities willingly accepted ex-comunario evidence as valid even when it predated 1900.[62] In Achacachi, most ex-comunarios demanded land restitution based on the titles they had received from the state in 1882, during the last revisita de tierras in Omasuyos province. This revisita followed the principles of the Disentailment Law of 1874, which applied liberal ideology to the agrarian sector, legally nullified Indian communities, and gave former community members the opportunity to purchase a title to individualized parcels. Lands not purchased by former ex-comunarios could then be sold off by the revenue-hungry state to other private buyers looking to expand their landholdings. The result was that those ex-comunarios who did not lose their lands ended up with individual rather than communal titles. After 1954, ex-comunarios played a double game in the courts: they presented cases for the restitution of their lands collectively, but their evidence consisted of individual legal titles received in the late nineteenth century. It is worth noting the persistence of their collective ties, since in many of the cases ex-comunarios combined their individual demands into one communal claim under the leadership of one cacique apoderado and one lawyer. It is, then, something of an irony that the individual titles from the late nineteenth-century revisita de tierras that opened the door for private owners to break up and seize communal land constituted the most solid evidence for Achacachi ex-comunarios to show the legality of their communal claims in the 1950s.

State officials also supported ex-comunario demands either by expanding the time frame set by the decree for land restitution or by converting a case of restitution into one of expropriation. National authorities did not challenge these decisions. There was one case in which the ex-comunarios failed to demonstrate past ownership of a large property, but the local judge ordered the redistribution of the landlord's entire property anyway on the grounds that "because of the size and conditions of work" the property was a latifundio and subject to expropriation under the Agrarian Reform Decree-Law. The judge expropriated the property—which included the grassland and the landlord's house—in order to "reconstitute the old boundaries of the community."[63] To date, scholarly interpretations have tended to present an intrinsic opposition between the MNR's model for agrarian reform, based on small and medium-sized individual properties, and the Aymara communal property systems. However, these examples show that, notwithstanding public rhetoric and media coverage to the contrary, the MNR state was rather supportive of local petitions and property designs.

In many cases, land restitution disputes did not end when the president officially granted ex-comunarios the right to occupy the land. Such cases continued because the ex-comunarios also had to deal with the colonos living on the former estate. In the case of ex-hacienda Challuyo, the judge, following the principle of the 1954 Land Restitution Decree, allowed the colonos to hold onto the plots that they were already working in exchange for economic compensation to the legitimate owners, the comunarios. Once the trial was over, the heirs of ex-comunario Juana Cruz received half of her former sayaña (parcel of land). The judge had granted the other half to the three colonos currently working the sayaña, but each had to pay an indemnification to the Cruz family in proportion to the size of the plot received.[64] The judge granted the heirs of Florentino Aruquipa a major portion (61.5 hectares) of his former sayaña and divided the remaining 23 hectares among the colonos already working those plots.[65] Such cases also show significant differences in the size of the plots received by ex-comunarios and by colonos. On average in Omasuyos, colonos received between 5 and 10 hectares per head of family, compared to the 60 hectares received by the Aruquipa family in restitution. The differences in the plot size granted by the courts was a crucial reason that the heirs of ex-comunarios presented demands for land restitution rather than land expropriation.

The distinct and diverging property agendas of the ex-comunarios and colonos had larger political implications. While ex-comunarios defended their traditional organization and authorities as a way to actively assert and protect their communal rights, colonos tended to align with the MNR's rural unions, which gave political support to colono claims to land, mostly against landlords but sometimes against rival comunario petitioners. One of the harshest disputes between a landlord, ex-comunarios, and colonos involved the former community of Pongon Huyo. In this legal dispute, the ex-comunarios opposed not only the landlord, Carmelo Mollinedo, but also the colonos. They claimed that Mollinedo had brought in outside peasants to steal and settle old community plots: "Those thugs are now the colonos of Mollinedo and with the agrarian reform they sought to become the owners of our *sayañas*."[66] Fabian Condori, whom the ex-comunarios called the "leader of the thugs," responded by defending the right of the colonos to obtain their plots:

> I never took a sayaña . . . of the Pongon Huyo community. I am a simple peasant; I am a simple colono at Mollinedo's property, and I would never dispossess my own comrades. Working as a colono, I have a plot and according to the Agrarian Reform Decree, we—the colonos—have the right to obtain those plots because we have been exploited and we have been suffering even more than the comunarios the humiliations of the oligarchy. I have been working for more than seventeen years on these plots. However, for the sake of harmony and good relations with my comrades, I will grant a portion of my sayaña to the comunarios, but I demand economic compensation.[67]

This case was not at all exceptional and resulted in some unexpected agreements. To avoid the ex-comunarios' demands, Mollinedo presented a parallel demand for the "allocation of his medium-sized property." He made an agreement with his former colonos to present a collective demand, so that the landlord and each of the colonos could obtain the legal title to the plots that they were holding before the agrarian reform. The agreement would allow the colonos to receive their properties without any type of indemnification to the landlord. Mollinedo then illegally brought the case to a different agrarian court. During the public hearing, all the colonos described Mollinedo as a good landowner personally involved in agricultural production. The local judge granted the property to Mollinedo, whom he classified as a progressive medium-sized property owner. The judge said nothing about the ex-comunarios' demands for land restitution.[68]

The ex-comunarios appealed this decision to the CNRA and the MAC. The colonos defended Mollinedo's property rights and argued that, because they had been working his land for some sixteen years, they deserved to receive a plot. The colonos also accused the ex-comunarios of having already received plots on other large estates where they had worked as colonos. It is impossible to know how this case was resolved because it disappeared from the legal file in 1959, but it is telling that the ultimate decision did not halt conflict between colonos and ex-comunarios, who continued to fight in the courts through the 1970s, with both sides accusing their opponents of using firearms to intimidate them.[69]

As with Pongon Huyo, other land restitution cases in Achachachi provoked dispute that the judges seemed unable to mediate. In several cases, despite a judge's decision colonos simply refused to give back land to ex-comunarios. After a decade of court struggle in which comunario Diego Rojas proved that he was the legal owner of a plot on the former estate of Warisata, the colonos working the plot still refused to leave, arguing that Rojas had already received plots from the expropriation of another hacienda in the 1950s. The dispute did not end until 1991, when the colonos reported that the Rojas family had migrated to the city and that no land remained in their hands.[70]

The cases for land restitution also revived old conflicts over the boundaries between communities and large estates. Prior to the revolution, those few indigenous communities that had kept their lands often complained that neighboring estates were continuously enlarging their property at the communities' expense. After 1953, these communities petitioned the state for legal recognition of their historical boundaries. However, the colonos on the estates defended the old limits of the hacienda and justified landholders' expansion before the revolution. Valentín Chuca, the hilacata of community Pallareti, in a dispute with the colonos of the neighboring hacienda accused union leader Bruno Choca, a former colono, of defending landlord expansion into communal land in order to protect colonos' rights: "We, the community members, have been evicted from our plots, the ones that we legally inherited from our parents. These plots are now occupied by union leaders such as Bruno Choca who redistributed our land among peasants who came from other regions. Landlords Vilela and Véliz Portugal took our sayañas, and they construct their haciendas on our plots and brought other colonos. This happened with the support of peasants like Bruno Choca."[71]

As this statement suggests, the legal contests between colonos and comunarios had major political implications that transcended the disputes over land. On the one hand, the colonos embraced the unions; on the other, the ex-comunarios reinforced ties to their traditional organizations (ayllus) and authorities (hilacatas). The colonos saw in the unions a powerful instrument for linking their local demands to regional and national politics. Especially on the altiplano, the unions helped colonos organize against community claims. Ex-comunarios, by contrast, embraced their old communal identity not only because of a strong collective memory but also because it allowed them to challenge the demands of both landlords and colonos.

Despite the MNR's nationalist and assimilationist discourse proclaiming the end of ethnic differences in Bolivia, the land restitution decree played a crucial role in the revalidation of traditional indigenous organizations and authorities. Each case for restitution encouraged the heirs of comunarios to recall their collective territory and history. The MNR heavily promoted Indian integration, if not assimilation, as a crucial feature for building the nation, but in practice the MNR's agrarian reform policies ended up protecting ex-comunarios' demands even when they did not fit well into the party's original political program. Although the 1953 decree clearly strengthened colonos' rights by proclaiming that land was for those who worked for it, the 1954 decree promoted comunario demands by implicitly granting land back to its original owners. As a result of active pressure from below, both political principles found validation in the national revolution, and the political agendas of both smallholding peasants and indigenous communities grew stronger in these concrete historical circumstances.[72]

Conclusions

Initial appraisals of the national revolution's effects in the Bolivian highlands championed the MNR's leadership in changing the land system. Several works since the late 1950s have challenged that top-down understanding of the revolution. Focused on the role of the unions and colonos, these revisionist interpretations emphasized how the Agrarian Reform Decree-Law and the fast pace of land redistribution were the outcome of peasants' political pressure from below. However, when analyzing the role of the comunarios during the revolution, these same scholars, especially those associated with indigenismo, highlighted how the MNR's assimilationist and modernizing agenda eroded traditional indigenous claims to communal lands. Focused on the party's political discourse, in this perspective the MNR's ability to implement their policies in the countryside is taken for granted, overlooking the success of the comunarios in changing not only the pace of land redistribution but also the character of the agrarian reform.

The network of caciques apoderados initiated a major campaign for the restitution of comunario lands, with the revolution and its nationalist discourse being a rich opportunity for their campaign. Comunarios took up the revolutionary discourse because it asserted the rights of the lowly and dispossessed against the oligarchy. However, ex-comunarios objected to the MNR's promotion of agrarian reform if it was limited to land redistribution among the colonos already working on haciendas. Over its first year in power, the MNR increasingly realized the difficulty of silencing ex-comunarios' demands. As a result, government officials played a double game, becoming more flexible in their practices and resolutions while keeping the public presentation of the agrarian reform's primary goals and mechanics unchanged.

The intricate way in which ex-comunarios and the revolutionary party took up each other's projects demands that we rethink how Bolivian nationalism has been understood. Luis H. Antezana urges us to think of revolutionary nationalism not as a fixed ideology but as a concept that functions as a container in which different actors can place different agendas, "such as socialism, nationalism, indigenismo, anti-imperialism, fascism, and leftism."[73] Like other competing interests, indigenous communities found a way to include their own political demands within revolutionary nationalism's broader agenda.

Ex-comunarios' conflicts with the colonos also force us to confront the complexity and heterogeneity of the peasantry in Bolivia. The official revolutionary narrative reproduced the MNR's original schema of a clash between the nation and the anti-nation. This binary does little, however, to explain the different projects contained within the nationalist project. When these distinct interests proclaimed agrarian reform, they did so with different meanings in mind. For ex-comunarios, agrarian reform meant a comprehensive review of all existing legal titles. For colonos, it meant the redistribution of hacienda property to its resident labor force. For nationalist and left intellectuals, it meant industrialization, mechanization, and modernization. The broader outcome of the national revolution was the complex and contradictory convergence of these three fundamentally different, if rhetorically related, projects.

CHAPTER SIX

LAND FOR THOSE WHO WORK IT

Samuel Vilela was the owner of a property of seventy hectares called Pallareti in the province of Omasuyos. In November 1958, he expressed a grievance with the office of the CNRA: "If we continue going in this direction, the government will end up transferring all properties to peasants no matter if they are large, medium, or small."[1] Vilela's words reflect the alarm that gripped the landlord class after the agrarian reform. Immediately after taking power, the MNR issued reassurances that the government would protect private property and that expropriation would target only large unproductive estates. The letter of the law formally guaranteed the continued ownership of landlords who held small or medium-sized properties as long they could prove investment, personal involvement, and that their production was oriented toward the market. In sum, the law protected the ownership of those whose properties showed signs of agricultural "improvement."[2]

Despite the apparent protections for landlords, peasants demanded the expropriation of the properties where they served as colonos, whether or not these properties fit within the parameters allowed by the 1953 Agrarian Reform Decree-Law.[3] Since unremunerated servile labor was banned by the decree, peasants urged the government to grant them all the property—even if it was a small or medium-sized productive estate actively managed by its owners—as a form of reparation for past labor abuses. This made claims about abusive working conditions and the absence of pay pivotal points in challenging the landlords in court. Nonresident and landless peasants (agregados, forasteros, sitiajeros, yanaperos, and the colonos' offspring) also gained land after the agrarian reform. While landlords initially tried to restrict land distribution to colonos who already worked a plot of land, landless peasants also asserted their right to hold a plot, which enlarged the process of land distribution.

For their part, landlords had lost most of their political influence after the revolution and saw the courts as their last opportunity to retain at least a portion of their former properties by using—and stretching—the parameters of size and investment inscribed in the law. Both the colonos and the landlords who petitioned the government to "enforce the law," drew upon different legal and technical criteria established in the Agrarian Reform Decree-Law. In other words, the law was not a rigidly enforced set of principles. Rather, in the hands of different actors, the law became an effective instrument with which to pressure state officials and to shape decisions in a variety of directions. Yet, despite the contentious and chaotic nature of the implementation of the agrarian reform, a tendency emerged: when state officers were forced to decide whether they should protect investment (an argument usually raised by landlords) or whether they should privilege distribution (an argument raised by colonos and landless peasants), these officers ultimately chose the latter, and property for all became the most important guiding principle of Bolivia's land reform.

Land distribution entailed significant differences in the amount of land each beneficiary received. The process of land distribution within the hacienda cemented the differences between originarios, agregados, arrimantes, *sitiajeros*, and utawawas that existed on haciendas before the reform. Ex-comunarios also obtained larger properties than colonos. The final outcome of the process of land redistribution created a map comprised of both individually and collectively owned plots in a variety of different shapes, sizes, and uses. State verdicts mostly formalized local arrangements rooted in these long-standing historical practices. The very chaotic and uneven character of this map reveals the strength of bottom-up decisions over top-down governmental planning.

Some disputes over land continued decades after the downfall of the MNR. In November 1964, General René Barrientos overthrew President Paz Estenssoro. This started a cycle of military regimes that continued until 1982. When the conservative Barrientos took power, a number of former landlords who lost property in the 1950s, asked the president to review past cases of land expropriation. However, neither the conservative Barrientos nor the more reactionary government of Hugo Bánzer challenged peasant ownership. Archival evidence shows that under the military regime peasants continued to expand the boundaries of their properties into former landlords' properties with the silent acquiescence of these governments. Conscious of how crucial peasant support was for their own political stability, military regimes did not venture to question the peasant's land conquests in the altiplano, the valleys, and Yungas.

Investment versus Conditions of Labor

Landlord political power waned during the first year of the revolution. The government took control of the two most powerful rural societies in Bolivia, those of Cochabamba (FRC) and Yungas (SPY). Deprived of their traditional political connections, landlords went to court to seek the legal protection. Many presented proofs of their investments to justify their right to keep ownership of at least a portion of their properties. But peasants contested these arguments by denouncing the deplorable conditions of their work on the haciendas. They asserted that the dreadful working conditions were sufficient evidence to demonstrate that the property should be qualified as a latifundio. Exposed to political pressure and demand from both groups, agrarian judges, members of the CNRA, and the minister of peasant affairs (MAC) issued very different verdicts on the same property even though they were allegedly based on the same technical and legal criteria.

One case that illuminates the dilemma was the dispute between the landowner Agustín Villegas and his former colonos for the expropriation of Santa Lucía de Liquinas, in Germán Jordán province, Cochabamba. This was a large and very productive property of nearly four hundred hectares. The owner was an agronomist who had been trained in Belgium; he had invested a great deal of capital in his property and ran the hacienda personally. Although Villegas insisted that the property was a "modern agricultural enterprise" and claimed that his investments in tools plus machinery exceeded twenty-five thousand US dollars, the forty-six colonos on the estate initiated a legal case for the expropriation of what they called a latifundio, based on the large size of the hacienda and, especially, the harsh and exploitative conditions of work.[4]

Villegas was not a man prepared to make concessions. He was convinced that his investment—and the agrarian reform law's very principles—meant that his property rights were secure. But the peasants were not prepared to cede ground. The colonos claimed that before the agrarian reform not only had they been obliged to cultivate hacienda lands but they had been subject to domestic service at the landlord's house (pongueaje and mitanaje). In their statement, colonos described working under the orders "of vicious overseers," the mayordomos. They maintained that the owner only came to the hacienda during planting and harvest to supervise their work and, the rest of the time, he worshiped "Morpheus . . . the god of dreams."[5]

In response, Villegas maintained that the labor regime prevalent in his hacienda was consistent with the practices established under the Gualberto Villarroel government in 1945, which permitted the use of peasant labor for agricultural tasks, canal building, and the construction of roads. He insist-

Figure 6.1. During my research, I wanted to visited some of the old haciendas in Germán Jordán and Omasuyos. In most cases, as in this picture, I found the remaining of the old houses. In other cases, the peasant union reused the house as the basis for a school or for the seat of the peasant union. Photo by Carmen Soliz

ed that he ran a productive estate before the revolution and that productivity had only dropped in the hands of the peasants afterward. He asked: "If the owner . . . only worshipped Morpheus, . . . then why is it that not one of the numerous machines left work now? Why has production slumped and the hacienda's infrastructure fallen apart?"[6]

The conflict became sharper still when three new actors became involved in the case: forty landless peasants (called arrimantes) who claimed their right to have a plot despite their being temporary workers; five former miners who had been settled via decree on the hacienda by the Ministry of Mining; and ninety displaced peasants who were also settled on the hacienda via decree by the Minister of Agriculture.[7] In the first verdict, the local judge deemed Santa Lucía to be an "agricultural enterprise," primarily "due to the significant investment the owner made in the property, bringing advanced agricultural technology to the country, and due to his entrepreneurial spirit, personal involvement, and academic training in agronomy in Belgium."[8] Based on these criteria, the judge ordered that only the forty-six colonos and five former miners would receive the plots of land on which they were already working. The rest of the land would be granted on behalf of the owner. Also, according the judge, the beneficiaries were supposed to pay Villegas a compensation of 6,822,195 bolivianos.[9]

But the forty landless peasants and ninety displaced peasants appealed the judge's verdict, filing the appeal first with the CNRA and then with the MAC. In the last stage of the case, the president of the republic and the MAC reconsidered the difficulties and the political cost of expelling the peasants who had been settled for about six years on the property.[10] They overturned the classification of Santa Lucía de Liquinas as an agricultural enterprise and declared it a medium-sized property instead, authorizing the government to assume the cost of the indemnification. To understand how peculiar this last verdict was, we must bear in mind that a medium-sized property in this area was supposed to be a maximum of fifty hectares and Villegas's property measured four hundred hectares. This reclassification allowed the colonos, arrimantes, former miners, and displaced peasants to all win access to the land and entitled Villegas to a direct indemnification from the state. This final decision did not adhere to the ostensible features of the law, but it effectively responded to the different contending groups in question (see figure 6.1).

There were other cases in which landlords demanded their right to keep their properties based on former investments and the productivity of their property, but it was precisely on such productive estates that colonos experienced the worst labor conditions. As landlords were trying to make the leap to modern agricultural production, they incorporated new agricultural technology but maintained traditional patterns of work and forced new obligations upon their workers: on top of farming and working as servants in the haciendas, they had to work on road construction, build and repairs barns, fences, and stables, and transport and sell products to the city at their own cost. After the enactment of the agrarian reform, these cases turned into major battles in which both colonos and landlords demanded the state attend to their demands in the name of the new law.

The definition of concepts such as investment, productivity, and relationship with the market were central to the implementation of the law, yet they were subject to wide interpretation.[11] During the agrarian reform trials, many landlords complained that state authorities equaled investment to the number of tractors each property had while overlooking other types of investments that addressed different climatological and environmental factors.[12] Landlords complained that the state authorities' limited capacity to evaluate the scale of different types of investments led to uneven and unfair verdicts. For example, a landlord who claimed to have built fences received more land than one who had bought machinery, purebred cattle, and water pipes. While some landowners' chances of holding on to their property may have been lowered by the authorities' narrow definitions of "investment," the court cases also show that many landlords stretched this concept as much as possible.

Other owners denounced the technical and legal reports for having uncaringly ignored the current political situation in the countryside. Some argued they were unable to provide proof of their investment since many of their assets had been destroyed or had disappeared in attacks on their property after the revolution. For Samuel Vilela, from Omasuyos, the issue was simple: "How can I prove my investment now if I can barely get onto my property?"[13] Others claimed that their former homes had been looted and burned time and again after the revolution. In Omasuyos, Macario Escobari reported the loss of his small alcohol factory in Putuni.[14] Another former landlord, Ismael Arguedas, maintained that after the revolution his small-scale tile machinery was ruined.[15] Most landlords claimed that the peasants ate, sold, or simply made off with the cattle they used to own.[16] Landowners in Cochabamba declared that the tractors they used to own were ruined after the agrarian reform.[17]

Although state authorities' verdicts on each property varied greatly, it is possible to establish some trends. The first verdict, the one signed by an agrarian judge at the provincial level, often reflected the interests of the stronger political voices in the region. In Omasuyos, where the local judge had close ties to the peasant union, he unfailingly declared all properties latifundia and thus subject to expropriation. In Sud Yungas, judges were more inclined to grant the landowner a portion of his or her former hacienda as a medium-sized property. However, the influence of the unions declined when the court case arrived in the CNRA offices in La Paz for its second verdict. The CNRA functionaries, many of them lawyers and geographers, tended to pay less attention to the local political struggles and gave more consideration to arguments about investment, agricultural expertise, or connection of produce to the market. Such considerations often favored the landowners.

This was the case for hacienda Tari in Omasuyos, where the landlord succeeded in changing the initial local verdict of expropriation. In 1955, the local judge declared Tari a latifundio: "because of the size of the property, the obsolete system of work, the cruel exploitation of the peasants, and the absence of any agricultural machinery. This judge orders the expropriation of the entire property."[18] The owner, Irene Riveros, appealed the decision to the CNRA. She claimed she had not had a chance to defend herself in the local court. She argued that the judge ignored her major investment in livestock and the money she spent sending her son to Argentina to study agronomy with the sole purpose of introducing technical knowledge on the estate. After listening to Riveros's arguments, the topographer of the CNRA sent a very positive report about the owner. The purchase of livestock and the issue of professionalization resonated powerfully among the middle-class officials working at the CNRA, especially in a context in which it was still rare to hold a bachelor's degree, even more so a foreign degree. The topographer's report described in great detail the landlord's investment, information that had been absent from the local judge's verdict: "The local judge had not considered the purebred livestock existing on the property. He said nothing about how one of the owners is an agronomist who used fertilizers to encourage production. Authorities should also consider that the owners built drinking troughs for the animals plus fenced lots. The value of the investment might be about 20,000,000 bolivianos."[19]

In his vivid defense of the landlord's right to keep the property, the topographer reminded higher-ranking authorities of the true spirit of the agrarian reform: to increase the country's agricultural production and to "overcome Bolivia's rural backwardness." He hoped that wording his report in this way, he would appeal to high-ranking officials, who usually talked about the achievements of the agrarian reform in those terms:

> I think that the National Council is supposed to rectify the mistakes of lower-rank officials. I think that the law of agrarian reform was made for all Bolivian people who want to work the land. From a technical perspective, it is going to be very fruitful for the process of agrarian reform if it is directed and controlled by technicians. In this case, we have a technician who cannot even get onto his property. This would be very beneficial, especially for the peasants.[20]

As intended, the report had a strong effect on the CNRA council. It reversed the local judge's verdict and granted 220 hectares (out of a total of 933 hectares) of pasture to the owner, recognizing her investment in cattle and the construction of the barns. Although the topographer's intervention did not stop the expropriation of Tari altogether, it did help Irene Riveros hold on to a considerable amount of her property.

The cases of Santa Lucía de Liquinas in Cochabamba and Tari in La Paz illustrate how colonos and landlords battled over the definition of what constituted a latifundio and that these battles ended differently in different courts. At the highly productive Santa Lucía de Liquinas hacienda, occupied by former colonos, arrimantes, and displaced peasants, the former owner, Agustín Villegas, was unable to hold on to any land. On the other hand, Irene Riveros's connection with some technicians of the CNRA was crucial to the categorization of her Tari as a livestock enterprise instead of a latifundio, allowing her to keep some of her land.

Analysis of the court cases shows that there was little correlation between investment and the landlord's consolidation of property. Despite having proved they had invested in their estates, some landholders saw their property declared a latifundio and subject to expropriation regardless. Yet, there were significant regional differences. When landlords in Yungas made the case for their right to property based on their past investment, this

Table 6.1. Number of Hectares that Landlords Retained after Agrarian Reform and the Co-relation (or not) to Investment in the Province of Germán Jordán for Properties above Fifty Hectares

Property	Owner	Other Properties	Investment	Hectares Remaining in Land-lord's Hands	TOTAL
Santa Clara acumulado	Monasterio	Yes	No	0	779.3
Kehuinal San Antonio	Pacesa Sejas viuda de Arandia	No	No	0	434.0
Santa Lucia de liquinas Pilicocha	Agustin Villegas	Yes	Yes	0	393.0
Liquinas del Rosario	Familia Quiroga	Multiple houses	Yes	189	386.3
Carcaje	Harry Berger	No	Yes	286	286.0
La Alcoholería	Antonio y Rene Abasto	No	No	0	267.9
Laloma	Bernardina Ledesma	Yes	Almost none	0	156.0
Toco Viejo	Herederos Gandarilla	Yes	Some	10	135.0
Cucuntapa o San Rafael	Roberto Angulo	The wife owned another property	Some	10	113.0
Liquinas[1]	Martha Barrientos	No	No	47.1	112.1
Liquinas	Aguirre-Lavayén	No	Yes	43.7	104.7
Monte Redondo	Andrade Delgadillo	Yes	Almost none	76.7	92.8
Toco Molino	Co-owners Pardo, Zurita y Prado	Yes	Yes	21.5	76.7
San Isidro	Concepcion Ocam-po (Quiroga family)	Yes	No	13.5	76.0
Calcontho lote 13	Manuel Flores	The wife owned other property	No	20	61.4
Huallpero 2222	Herederos de Alber-to Pareja	The extended family	No	26.9	56.3
Chullpa 5to suyo	Ambrosio Tapia (hijos)	No	No	48.2	53.5

Source: Agrarian reform court cases, INRA-CBBA, Germán Jordán Province: box 1, file Calcontho lote 13, file Laloma; box 2, file Chullpa 5to suyo; box 3, file Huallpero 2222; box 4, file Liquinas; box 5, file Liquinas del Rosario, file Liquinas, file Monte Redondo, file Toco Molino; box 6, file Kehuinal San Antonio, file Carcaje, file Cucuntupa o San Rafael; box 7, file Santa Lucia de liquinas Pilicocha; box 8, file San Isidro; box 9, file La Alcoholería, file Toco Viejo; box 12, file Santa Clara acumulado.

Notes: Carcaje was the only case in which the landowner was able to held the entire property. The owner demonstrated the investment he had made in the property and that a salary-based system had long been established on his estate.

[1] Several haciendas in Cochabamba have the same name, which could lead to confusion. That was the case of Monte Redondo, Liquinas, Huallpero.

Table 6.2. Large, Medium, and Small-Sized Properties that Faced a Demand for Land Expropriation

Rural Properties	Number of Cases	Hectares	%
Germán Jordán			
Latifundia	16	3,725.8	82.1
Small and medium-sized properties	58	814.4	18.0
Omasuyos			
Latifundia	29	34,029.0	95.4
Small and medium-sized properties	20	1,625.5	4.5
Sud Yungas			
Latifundia	33	9,2350.3	99.2
Small and medium-sized properties	21	703.1	0.75

Source: Developed by the author based on Agrarian reform court cases, INRA-LP, Omasuyos, Sud Yungas, and INRA-CBBA, Germán Jordán Province.

was met with a more positive response among state authorities. Landlords in Omasuyos were less successful at convincing state authorities that their property was an agricultural enterprise rather than a latifundio, and it was there that landlords complained most frequently that their investments had been stolen, broken, or burned.

The percentage of land that landlords were able to retain in their hands at the end of each verdict varied considerably (see table 6.1). Some owners held more than 80 percent of their former property, as in the case of Monte Redondo, whereas others received less than 10 percent, as in the case of the Toco Viejo or Cucuntupa properties. As in the cases of Santa Lucía de Liquinas and Tari, the outcome of these cases depended less on the owners' capacity to demonstrate investment and more on their connections to local, regional, national authorities, or in their capacity to seal an agreement with their former colonos based on their previous paternalistic relations with them.[21]

Redefining the Meaning of Latifundio

Despite the government's initial claims that the agrarian reform would protect small and medium-sized properties at any cost, a number of peasant unions in Omasuyos, Sud Yungas, and Germán Jordán demanded the expropriation of these properties.[22] As the work of Charles Erasmus shows, peasant unions also demanded the expropriation of small and medium-sized properties in Tarija and Chuquisaca.[23] Archival review shows that this practice was stronger in Germán Jordán, where pressure over land was severe even before the revolution. For example, in Germán Jordán, 76 percent of the expropriation claims—that is, fifty-eight of seventy-six cases—were directed at small and medium-sized properties. In Omasuyos twenty out of forty-nine cases and in Yungas twenty-one out of fifty-four cases focused on small and medium-sized properties. Colonos won these cases by strategically arguing that working conditions and not size should be the guiding principle for defining a latifundio. In all three regions, however, such estates accounted for a very small proportion of the total amount of land under dispute: 18 percent in Germán Jordán, less than 5 percent in Omasuyos, and less than 1 percent in Sud Yungas (see table 6.2).

Although it is not surprising to learn that colonos petitioned for the expropriation of small and medium-sized properties, it is surprising that state authorities did not object to peasant demands. This was the case of hacienda Monte Redondo (plot 1046) in Germán Jordán Province, where the limit of a medium-sized property in this region was fifty hectares. The owner, Antonio Rivera, assumed that his forty-seven-hectare property was not subject to expropriation. However, in their demand for expropriation, the colonos argued that the size of the estate was irrelevant because of the disgraceful conditions of work they experienced as colonos and pongos, forced not only to farm but also to clean the landlord's house in the town of Toco. Moreover, they claimed that the owner had not made investments in agricultural machinery or cattle. Initially, the local judge accepted both sides' arguments, granting ten hectares to Antonio Rivera and thirty-seven hectares in total to the thirty-seven colonos and the arrimantes.[24] Rivera then complained that the judge was biased and asked the CNRA to reconsider the case. The CNRA, and later the president, declared Monte Redondo a latifundio and ordered the expropriation of the entire property. The final verdict indicated that a property would be classified as a medium-sized holding only when owners were able to demonstrate investment, which Rivera could not prove. This ruling contrasted with several rulings (especially in Sud Yungas) in which large landholders were able to keep substantial portions of their land despite the lack of investment.

During the trials, owners of small and medium-sized properties argued that bureaucrats' notions of investment were better suited to owners of large properties. Samuel Vilela, owner of a medium-sized property, argued that it was not disinterest but his limited capital that had prevented him from obtaining more machinery. Vilela's complaint suggests that the implementation of agrarian reform was not punishing disinterest so much as lack of capital.

Among the judicial cases we find some cases of owners of medium-sized properties who identified as Indian or mestizo. In court they highlighted their Indian background in the hope this would help them preserve their former property. Although it was rare, before the revolution a few Indian or mixed-race peasants had succeeded at becoming medium-sized landholders by acquiring multiple plots of land. They became entrepreneurs who controlled productive and mercantile circuits linked to the town of Cliza. These landholders made their enterprises productive by imposing exploitative labor conditions on other peasants. After the decree, the colonos working on their estates demanded the expropriation of these properties. In the court proceedings the colonos tried to highlight the harsh conditions in which they were obligated to work, but the owners of these medium-sized properties stressed their ethnic backgrounds and their industrious spirit, two characteristics that were supposed to match the MNR's political program.[25]

Severino Fuentes was the owner of a property of forty-two hectares called Monte Redondo. In identifying as a campesino (peasant) landholder, Fuentes sought to highlight that he did not belong to the creole elite. Although his property came within the definition of a medium-sized estate, the twelve colonos and nineteen landless peasants who previously worked for Fuentes demanded the expropriation of what they deemed to be a latifundio. They argued that Monte Redondo was a latifundio because Fuentes owned houses in the towns of Punata and Cochabamba city and because of the cruel conditions he imposed on those who worked on the estate. Fermín Ayala, a leader of the peasants' union, declared: "Severino Fuentes despite his class [by which they meant a peasant with indigenous origins] was an archetypal exploiter. He subjected peasants to the most degrading servitude." After hearing testimony from the colonos, the local judge ordered the expropriation of the property declaring Monte Redondo a latifundio."[26]

Severino Fuentes appealed the judge's decision to the CNRA, claiming his right to "at least defend himself in the courts without pressure." He stated that he was not a *latifundista* but the "owner of a medium-sized property with investment in water pumps, a tractor, and agricultural tools." He presented dozens of receipts proving that the corn produced on his property had been sold in the markets of Cochabamba city. He said he represented the MNR's ideal of a productive landholder of a medium-sized property and did not want to live off rent, as he was personally involved in the farming and marketing of his products. The CNRA's second verdict protected Fuentes's property rights: "considering that Monte Redondo was a medium-sized property, that the owner has demonstrated investment and personal involvement, considering that Señor Severino Fuentes effectively produced corn in Punata and Germán Jordán and carried it to the markets in Cochabamba, the property should only be partially expropriated."[27]

The CNRA decided to grant twenty hectares to the owner and ten hectares to the twelve former colonos. Its decision made no mention of the nineteen arrimantes who were part of the demand. The arrimantes appealed the decision and refused to leave the plots on which they were already working. The presidential final verdict arrived a full three years later, by which time it was understood that Severino Fuentes had little chance of recovering control of property that was now being worked on individually by the former colonos and the arrimantes. Thus, the president's verdict legalized the de facto situation: "Because of the harsh conditions of work that the landowner imposed on the colonos, . . . the property was a latifundio." On this basis, the president ordered the expropriation of the entire property in favor of both the twelve colonos and the nineteen arrimantes peasants.[28]

Severino Fuentes's case challenged a polarized view of rural reality: powerful white landowners on the one hand and poor indigenous peasants on the other. This taxonomy had little or no space for Fuentes, a prosperous, empowered, and exploitative Indian peasant. Fuentes was, in any case, more representative of Cochabamba, where, as Brooke Larson has shown, peasants had played a noteworthy role in the local economy since the late eighteenth century.[29] Although there were not many Indian landowners, this case crystalizes the challenges of implementing the law as the final decision did not involve a transfer from nonproductive landholders to productive small peasants but, rather, the decline and fragmentation of a dynamic small business.

Land for All and Distribution of Land for Landless Peasants

After 1954, when demands for land expropriation were at a peak, landlords seemed almost willing to give up their ownership of the plots on which colonos had been working before the revolution. Yet, they still hoped that the state would grant them the property that used to belong exclusively to the hacienda and which had the best land. Over time, their hopes faded as landless peasants (yanaperos, sitiajeros, and utawawas) started to occupy those lands and state authorities legalized these claims in order to appease political conflict in the countryside. When facing a demand for land expropriation, the landlord of hacienda Naranjani in Sud Yungas, Hector Lorini, complained that seventy-eight peasants illegally had asked for the expropriation of his property. Lorini alleged that fifty colonos used to work for his property, the rest were yanaperos who had come to the property to work for the colonos. Lorini protested: "It was the colonos who decided to bring people to work on their own plots. Why should my property benefit people who have never worked for me?"[30] Although, in the first verdict, the local judge sided with the landlord, the CNRA and later the president sided with the yanaperos' petition. The final decision of these high-ranking authorities was far from unusual. Their verdicts, more than any technical or legal considerations, were intended to avoid the political cost of evicting peasants who were already settled and cultivating the land. They granted the property to the seventy-eight appellants, demonstrating that property for all became the most important guiding principle of Bolivia's land reform.

Landlords in all provinces often complained about the growing number of people included in the list of beneficiaries for the expropriation of their properties. In a dispute over the Cocani estate in Omasuyos, the landlord Mercedes Franco protested that her property was going to be distributed among ninety-eight people when only twenty colonos had worked on her estate before the revolution. According to Franco, the other beneficiaries were "merchants of alcohol, coca leaf, and tocuyo [homespun] who used to trade around the large Cocani estate."[31] Despite landlords' complains, it is worth underscoring that changes in the list of beneficiaries were only made with the approval of the peasant unions of each hacienda. In other words, landlords and state authorities had little control over the number of beneficiaries. In fact, unions carefully regulated the number of beneficiaries against newcomers as they sought to preserve cultivable land, collective lands, and pasturelands for future use. Over time, these decisions would empower peasant unions at the expense of national authorities.

The question of access to land for both permanent and nonpermanent resident peasants is crucial to understanding the scope of the Bolivian agrarian reform. This matter is especially important when comparing Bolivia to other experiences in Latin America. In Chile as Peter Winn and Cristobal Kay have shown, the Christian Democrat government (1964–1970) restricted land redistribution to the permanent resident labor force of the old estates *(inquilinos)* and left out their sons (*voluntarios*) and the nonresident workers (*afuerinos*). The result was the creation of a privileged stratum of peasants that turned around and hired laborers for minimum wages as the previous landlords had done.[32] After 1970, despite President Salvador Allende's attempts to protect the rights of the *voluntarios* and *afuerinos*, political opposition used the existing divisions among peasants to undermine Allende's legitimacy in the countryside.

In the case of Peru, Linda Seligmann similarly encounters severe disputes between permanent and temporary laborers, showing that the government favored the former over the latter: 75 percent of the rural population "was excluded from the reform and received no, or only indirect, benefits because they did not qualify for membership in [cooperatives or agrarian societies]."[33] Likewise, Enrique Mayer observes that the creation of the cooperatives left out temporary workers, thus exacerbating the conflict between cooperative members and others.[34] In Bolivia, as soon as landowners abandoned their properties, landless peasants seized plots that were reserved for landlords' production. These nonresident peasants became key actors whose demands were crucial in expanding the limits of the agrarian reform beyond the MNR's initial design.

Landlords Looking for a Way Out

Aware of the power they had lost as a social and political class and the endless hurdles they faced in the judicial arena, landlords opted to use informal mechanisms of arrangement with peasants or with state officials. Many felt that informal negotiations on the ground could help them recover some land or part of their former capital more effectively than a judicial appeal. Some appealed to their allegedly previous "good relations" with their colonos to seal an agreement; others forced the colonos to buy a plot or turned them into sharecroppers as soon as they heard the government was about to enact the Agrarian Reform Decree-Law. Some appealed to their political connections with people within the MNR or the government, hoping to change the president's final verdict; some hoped to delay the judicial process as long as possible, waiting for a political regime more favorable to their interests to come to power. None of these strategies was a recipe for success, but many landlords were partly able to curb the expropriation of their properties.

A testament to the ability of landowners to negotiate a favorable agreement for their interests was the case of the Quiroga family who owned an extensive property in the Cochabamba valleys. The property was next to haciendas Santa Clara and Santa Lucía de Liquinas, which were seized by the colonos in 1953 and 1954 respectively.[35] The five siblings who owned the property were aware that the peasants had begun to seize the land in the neighboring haciendas. They knew that a rapid agreement with their colonos would prevent other peasants from settling on their property. As soon as the government enacted the Agrarian Reform Decree-Law, the siblings offered the colonos to recognize the legal property of the plots they had worked without economic compensation. In exchange, the colonos were expected to recognize the former limits of what used to belong to the owners. The Quirogas' lawyer convinced the colonos that this agreement would benefit them, as it would prevent them from being indebted to the owners for the next twenty-five years.[36] Although the principle of indemnification was certainly included in the decree, in reality the government did not enforce the payment and we know that very few colonos actually paid the economic compensation prescribed in the Agrarian Reform Decree-Law. The Quirogas' attorney used this article of the law as a strategy to avoid further lawsuits. The colonos accepted the proposal, which guaranteed two hectares to each originario and one hectare to each arrimante.[37] In contrast to what happened to the hacienda of Agustín Villegas (the owner of Santa Lucía) and the Monastery of Santa Clara, the Quirogas confined the negotiation with their former workers to the size of the land that the colonos and the arrimantes would receive individually, taking out of the equation the most productive parcels, which were left in the hands of the family.

The Quirogas sealed the agreement with the approval of the agrarian judge. In the court, the Quirogas' lawyer argued that the case at hand concerned not one large hacienda held in common but, rather, five medium-sized properties that belonged to each of the five siblings.[38] Once the judge accepted that statement, the colonos lost their chance to demonstrate that the property was a latifundio. Also, although only one of the brothers bought agricultural machinery for the hacienda, the other brothers presented the same machinery as proof of their investment, a claim that contradicted the argument that there were five properties instead of one. Surprisingly, neither the colonos nor the state officers challenged the argument. Disregarding the fact that prior to the agrarian reform colonos of Liquinas were subject to the pongueaje, the state officials ratified the agreements between the Quirogas and the colonos. In contrast to the peasant unions of the neighboring haciendas, the colonos of this property only consolidated the legal rights to the plots they had held before the agrarian reform. The Quiroga family held on to the best cultivable land, and the early arrangement prevented landless peasants from making incursions onto the property.

The agreement was possible because of what landlords and colonos called "good relations" with their colonos. In practical terms, those "good relations" amounted to a more flexible labor relation, which allowed colonos more control over their own time. Such arrangements predominated on estates in which landlords had kept a distant relation to their property, living off the rent of the property rather than actively managing agricultural production. In his study of the haciendas in Chuquisaca (Bolivia) at the turn of the twentieth century, Erick Langer appeals to James Scott's concept of moral economy to explain the continuity of the hacienda system over centuries. Langer points out that "accommodation and reciprocity between landlord and peon appear to have played a much greater role than we had thought." In Cochabamba conflicts between landlords and peasants became critical after the 1929 economic crises when several mineowners decided to increase production by investing in agricultural equipment and increasing colonos' unrewarded workload. In the courts, the colonos spoke of the conditions on these modern estates, claiming that in addition to farming they were forced to build fences, open roads for the tractors, take products to the markets, among other burdens.[39]

These good relations were nevertheless built on paternalist patron-colono relationships, centered on kindness and gifts rather than pay. When Yolanda, one of the five Quiroga siblings, signed a written agreement with her former colonos, they asked if she could expand the size of the plots by a small margin: "As our plots vary in size, we ask Señora Quiroga to expand each of our plots to two hectares so that there won't be quarrels among us.

Table 6.3. Results of Land Expropriation of Large Estates in Omasuyos, Germán Jordán, and Sud Yungas

Provinces (Cantons)	Landlords (%)	Peasants (%)	Shared (%)	Hectares	Number of Properties Included in This Study
Germán Jordán (Cliza and Toco)	13.2	73.3	8.8	3,241.0	51
Omasuyos (Achacachi)	5.4	84.9	9.7	29,606.0	42
Sud Yungas (Chulumani and Irupana)	7.3	14.5	7.9	94,177.3	60

Source: Elaborated by the author based on cases in files of land expropriation in Omasuyos, Germán Jordán, and Sud Yungas. In the cantons of Irupana and Chulumani (Sud Yungas) 71.8 percent of the land was redefined as state land and was reserved for future endowments.

If there is sufficient space, we ask for one hectare per person for the landless peasants. If she agrees to our proposal, 'the lady' would receive our gratitude and support for anything she would need."[40] The hesitant and careful language used by the peasants to make their demand is striking. They do not seem to be claiming their plots as a right, but rather to "request" them almost as a gift, illustrating continued relations of subordination among landlords and peasants even after the revolution and the agrarian reform. Both violence and political euphoria went hand in hand with landlord-colonos' negotiations and arrangements.[41]

Some astute landlords sold their property to their colonos in the short period between when the revolution broke out (April 1952) and the signing of the 1953 decree. Following his intuition, Macario Escobari, owner of the hacienda Taramaya Grande in Omasuyos, did this. After the government enacted the Agrarian Reform Decree-Law, he asked the agrarian council to legalize the sales. The council was obliged to approve those transactions because they had been made before the signing of the decree. Although he kept 175 hectares of his old property (out of the 839 hectares he previously owned), in 1957 he granted the colonos these last 175 hectares for an indemnification of 2.5 million bolivianos.[42] Escobari constituted another case of a landlords who kept "good relations" with his former colonos, which had been instrumental in sealing his agreements in 1953 and 1957. Although he later stated that the 2.5 million bolivianos barely represented the value of the hacienda and his investment, he did well compared to his neighbor Roberto Terrazas, the owner of hacienda Ocorani, who was awarded 800,000 bolivianos for the expropriation of his 955 hectares, "an amount that barely covered the price of a cow," according to Terrazas.[43]

Distribution and Inequality

A quantitative comparison of the process of land distribution of the large estates in the provinces of Omasuyos, Germán Jordán, and Sud Yungas confirms that there was a far-reaching transfer of property from landlords to peasants in these regions (see table 6.3).[44] In all, about 90 percent of the latifundios in Omasuyos and about 70 percent of those in Germán Jordán were transferred to peasants.[45] In Sud Yungas, although 14 percent of land was assigned to peasants, only 7 percent of land remained in landlords' hands, as the state designated the remaining 70 percent for future endowments.[46] These numbers reveal the strength of the peasants unions in consolidating the initial moderate program for land reform that the MNR launched in 1953 based upon vague claims on Indian redemption.[47]

The Bolivian agrarian reform addressed a long history of concentration of land and turned hundreds of thousands of peasants into landowners; however, land distribution among the various beneficiaries was far from even. On average, former landlords were able to hold on to properties that were five to ten times larger—depending on the region—than those of the newly benefited peasants. Not surprisingly, peasants and landlords received more land in the large provinces of Sud Yungas (subtropical mountain) and Omasuyos (altiplano) than they did in the smaller province of Germán Jordán where demographic pressure over land was already strong before the revolution. On average, peasants in Germán Jordán received 1.7 hectares and landholders held onto 13 hectares; in Omasuyos, peasants acquired 10 hectares per head of family and landholders retained 40 hectares; and in Sud Yungas, peasants gained 12 hectares per head of family (comparable to their counterparts in the dry province of Omasuyos) and landholders held on to 150 hectares per family. In Sud Yungas, authorities were more willing to consider the petitions of former landlords, most of whom held the maximum quantity of land allowable for a medium-sized property in the region. This was not the case in Omasuyos, where there was stronger pressure from the peasant unions, and local judges were therefore less willing to listen to the former landlords' demands. Furthermore, former landlords usually retained the most fertile plots, the areas closest to the road (a key factor in the impenetrable area of Sud Yungas), and the land with the best access to water in the arid region of Omasuyos.

To illustrate the transformation in terms of property ownership, it is worth scrutinizing the case of the landlord Franco, one of the most powerful owners in Omasuyos. His family owned seven properties totaling almost eight thousand hectares—in a region where the revolutionary government declared the maximum size of a medium property was fifty hectares. As a result of the Agrarian Reform Decree-Law, the Francos' properties were di-

Table 6.4. Land Redistribution of the Franco Family Property

Property	Landlord	Peasants	Shared Land	Compensation	Future Endowments	TOTAL
Murumani	0	2,854		Yes		2,854
Pacharía	0	1,377				1,377
Ckasina	0	625	589.53	Yes	162.3	1,376.83
Chococopa Chica	3.3	45.68	781.4			830.38
Chocopata Grande	33	273	446			752
Cocani	0	222.09	368.03			590.12
Tihipampa—Taramaya	0	216.4		Yes		216.4
	36.3	5,613.17	2,184.96		162.3	7,996.73

Source: Elaborated by the author based on files of land expropriation of Agrarian Reform Court Cases, INRA-LP, Omasuyos Province.

vided among 571 peasants. However, the family did not lose all. They held onto 36 hectares of cultivable land plus 2,184 hectares of grasslands to be shared with the peasants. Additionally, they received economic compensation for three of their eight properties (for information on the distribution of the Francos' former properties, see table 6.4).

The expropriation of the Francos reveals the essential role that the colonos played in the legal and technical implementation of the agrarian reform in many cases. As the CNRA did not have data on rural property, it was nearly impossible for the state officers to know if a landlord held other properties, especially if these were in different provinces. Yet, colonos were well aware of the number of properties their landlord held. When the Francos petitioned the president to declare one of their properties (Murumani) an agricultural enterprise because of the investment they made in the property, the colonos counterattacked by claiming that Franco was the owner not only of an agricultural enterprise but of six other unproductive haciendas. Because of that final report, President Paz Estenssoro ordered the expropriation of Murumani.[48]

The analysis of presidential verdicts also shows that President Paz Estenssoro in his second term (1960–1964) guarded colonos'access to property more than his predecessor Siles Zuazo had done (in his first term, 1956–1960). Siles Zuazo tended to ratify CNRA verdicts, and in some cases, he returned sections of land to former landlords or granted grasslands for the collective use of colonos and landlords. In contrast, Paz Estenssoro's verdicts sided with colonos over landlords or handed the use of the grasslands exclusively to peasants. The agrarian trials reveal that many landlords asked

Table 6.5. Distribution of Chiquero Hacienda in Sud Yungas

Number of Hectares	Beneficiaries
Up to 2	9
From 2.1 to 4	20
From 4.1 to 6	25
From 6.1 to 8	10
From 8.1 to 10	5

Source: INRA-LP, Sud Yungas Province, box 2, file Chiquero.

the president to grant them a larger piece of land arguing, that they had to distribute the property among numerous siblings. Siles Zuazo was more receptive to those arguments, but Paz Estenssoro declared the expropriation of the entire property in favor of the peasants.[49] (To review in further detail the decisions on land distribution of Siles Zuazo and Paz Estenssoro, see Appendix 6.1.)

Paz Estenssoro's final verdicts could indicate that he was more committed than his predecessor to the peasants' cause, but they could also reveal Paz Estenssoro's attempts to strengthen his alliance with the peasants. The MNR-peasant pact became increasingly important for the sitting president when the government lost the support of the influential mining unions. His verdicts could also reflect the growing importance of the peasants' unions at the local level, to the detriment of landlords' political influence. Over time, local judges' verdicts gradually became indifferent to landlords' attempts to retain land based on prior investment and more sympathetic to peasants' demands for land for those who were occupying it and working it.

Although the role of state authorities was decisive in the process of expropriation (that is, in the dispute between landlords and colonos), peasant unions played a pivotal role in the process of land distribution among the beneficiaries. The peasant union of each ex-hacienda defined who got land and how much land each person would receive. The state relied on local organizations, union leaders, and communal authorities to implement the long, tedious, and less politically profitable process of land distribution among peasants. The state failed to develop a single homogenous project in terms of land distribution and, instead, accommodated ongoing local arrangements rooted in both recent and long-standing practices.

Analysis of court cases on land distribution illustrates how local arrangements, rooted in pre-agrarian reform practices, guided the distribution of land among beneficiaries. Land distribution cemented the differences between originarios, agregados, arrimantes, sitiajeros, and utawawas that existed on haciendas before the reform. As soon as the process of land expropriation of a hacienda took off, every peasant union cautiously detailed how

Table 6.6. Land Distribution in Hacienda Pajchani Grande, Omasuyos Province, after the Agrarian Reform, Based on Land Usufruct before the Agrarian Reform

Distribution	Hectares
Plots for the school	18.7
Individual plots for the ex-colonos	508.25
Landowner plots	56.65
Aynocas (shared landlord and ex-colonos)	117.2
Ahijaderos (shared landlord and ex-colonos)	602.2
Lake (shared)	9.6
Uncultivable	172.5
Total	1,485.1

Source: INRA-LP, Omasuyos Province, box11, file Pajchani Grande.

many people would gain access to that land, the status of that person within the hacienda, and the amount of land they should receive according to their status. In general, arrimantes, sitiajeros, utawawas received accessed land, yet these groups never received properties equal to those of an originario. Surprisingly, state authorities rarely challenged these decisions. There were many cases in which the agrarian judge or the topographers of the CNRA would recommend the expansion of individual plots or land granted for collective use to agregados, utawawas, or arrimantes. Yet neither the judge nor the president of the CNRA would grant the same amount of property to all. This is evidenced, for example, when we study the distribution of hacienda Chiquero (Sud Yungas) among sixty-nine beneficiaries (see table 6.5). The majority of peasants received between two and eight hectares, five peasants received more than eight hectares, and nine peasants received less than two hectares. This schema of land redistribution—where most of the beneficiaries were in the middle, and few on the extremes—confirms Enrique Mayer's view that the social structure in Andean communities resembles a rhombus rather than a pyramid.[50]

In the process of land distribution, colonos urged the state authorities to acknowledge geographic and climatic differences within the hacienda. Prior to the agrarian reform, some landlords and colonos reserved specific sections of the hacienda for use by individuals (for cultivation) and others for collective use (pastures and woodland areas).[51] After the agrarian reform, colonos continued to petition for the recognition of both individual and collective properties. An example is the distribution of hacienda Pajchani Grande in Omasuyos. A map of the hacienda (see figure 6.2) shows the land allocation prior to the agrarian reform. The landlord controlled the plots on the upper center of the map; the plots reserved for the eighty-six

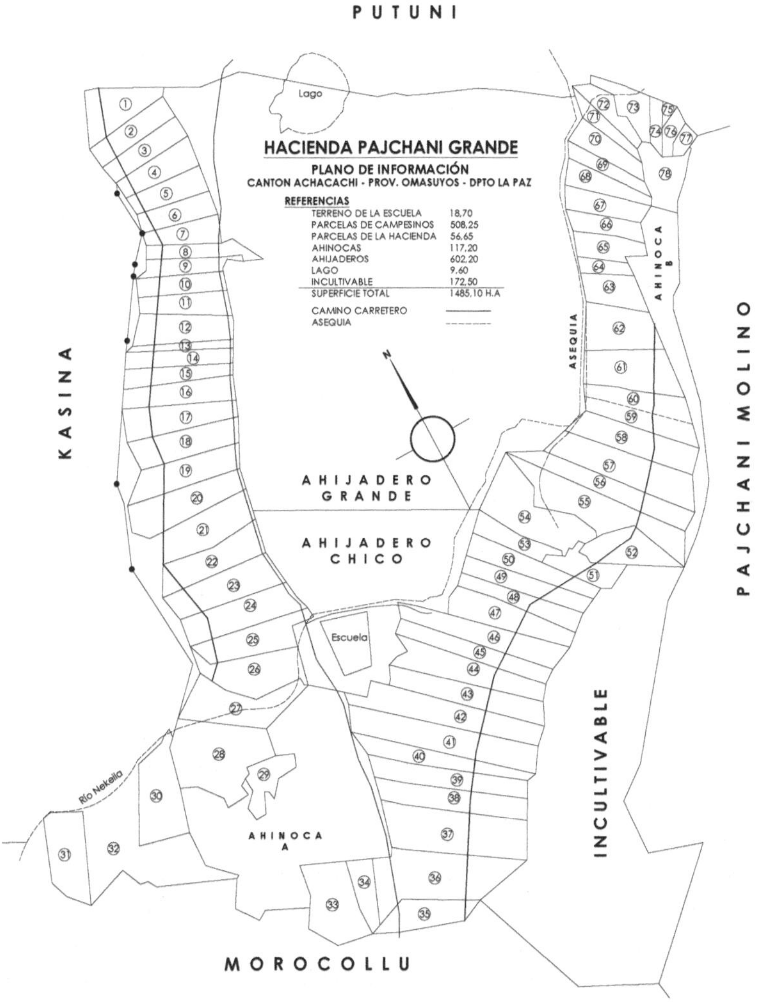

Figure 6.2. Land distribution in hacienda Pajchani Grande, Omasuyos Province, after the agrarian reform based on land usufruct before the agrarian reform. From INRA-LP, Omasuyos Province, box11, file Pajchani Grande.

colonos are marked individually around the landlord's main plot. The map also indicates the areas designed for livestock breeding and farming, called *ahijaderos*, and collective lands, called *aynocas*. The final verdict maintained the distribution of land that had been in place prior to the agrarian reform. The landlord held fifty-six hectares from expropriation, which was the same amount of land under his control before the reform. The rest of the property was divided among the 132 former colonos, all heads of families. State authorities reserved ahijaderos and aynocas for the collective use of all of the owners (see table 6.6).

Table 6.7. Distribution of Land in Favor of Eugenio Condori, Chiquero Hacienda

Hectares	Type of Section
0.6	Corn section (maizal)
0.82	Banana section
1.18	Banana section
0.48	Coca section (cocal)
0.38	Coca section
0.34	Coca section
0.1	Coca section
1.28	Coca section
2.1	Coca section
1.78	Coca section
0.32	Huerta
9.38	TOTAL

Source: INRA-LP, Sud Yungas Province, box 2, file Chiquero.

Each property constituted a world of its own, and the distribution of land varied drastically from one hacienda to another depending on the geographic and climatic characteristics of the property. In some cases, and based on the demands of the colonos, each person received four or five different plots within the hacienda, so each person could access different types of terrain. For example, in the redistribution of the former hacienda Chiquero in Sud Yungas, the president ruled that 363 hectares of the former property be granted to sixty-nine peasants. Instead of petitioning for one consolidated plot of property, the new beneficiaries demanded multiple small plots of land, so that all of them could have access to land suitable for coca leaf cultivation, banana cultivation, and corn cultivation. According to this plan, each of the beneficiaries would receive an average of about seven or eight plots of land. Eugenio Condori, one of the beneficiaries of the former hacienda Chiquero, received almost ten hectares in total, which were divided in eleven small sections (see table 6.7).

The diversity of these local arrangements explains why it took topographers from five to ten years or more to allocate the land titles after the president signed his final verdicts. During this long period of consolidation of individual and collective property, change naturally occurred. People died and their heirs had to initiate a claim for succession, and people got divorced, engendering new disputes in terms of access to property. Such individual issues usually delayed the process of allocating land titles to the other members of the union.

The post-1953 property map reflects the historical patterns of each region. For example, in Omasuyos Province, where hacienda expansion took

Table 6.8. Number of Hectares that Were Declared Individual or Collective, Based on 152 Haciendas

Provinces	Distribution between Peasants		Percentage
Germán Jordán	Individually	1,636.02	68.8
	Collectively	740.9	31.2
Omasuyos	Individually	11,040.2	43.9
	Collectively	14,085.6	56.1
Sud Yungas	Individually	7,447.3	54.6
	Collectively	6,192.2	45.4

Source: Developed by the author based on Agrarian reform court cases, INRA-LP and INRA-CBBA.

place primarily at the end of the nineteenth century, collective traditions remained strong. In this province, approximately 56 percent of the land was declared collective during the implementation of the agrarian reform (see table 6.8). In contrast, in Germán Jordán Province, a region where communities had been weakening since the colonial period and had undergone an intense process of property fragmentation, only 30 percent of the land was designated for collective use. In subtropical Sud Yungas, 56 percent of the forest was designated for collective use.

The agrarian process privileged the property rights of men, considered to be heads of family. Women only appeared as landowners in the list of beneficiaries if they were widows. When they were accorded land, they received smaller portions compared to other owners. Neither the state authorities nor the peasants disputed this new regime of rights. Peasants and state authorities affirmed, sometimes tacitly, sometimes explicitly, that women were unable to work the land as efficiently as men. For example, several court cases show that colonos used gender-based arguments to legitimize the expropriation of a property when the landlord was a woman. They alleged they should get the land because a woman would not be able to work the hacienda. Neither lawyers nor state authorities challenged these deeply patriarchal arguments. Although over the years, few peasant women received access to land, there was no clear state policy that protected women's property rights with respect to land until 1996 when the government enacted a new law for agrarian reform. Of course, this was not specific to Bolivia. Scholars Carmen Diana Deere and Magdalena León argue that women were excluded as beneficiaries in the majority of the countries that undertook significant reforms agrarian reforms (the exceptions were Cuba and Nicaragua).[52]

Overall, the process of land distribution among beneficiaries reveals that the state relied on peasant unions to shape the new configuration of property in the countryside. In the absence of maps or census data and having very little knowledge of Bolivia's geography, official authorities used the peasant union as a mechanism to distribute land to all the members at once, instead of dealing with hundreds of individual petitions. In practical terms, this meant that if someone individually petitioned the state to delimit their property, local authorities usually prompted this claimant to present their petition through the union. Such a system reinforced the vitality of the union, encouraged peasants toward collective action, and urged them to elect representatives whose jurisdiction was defined by the limits of the old hacienda, which in the altiplano especially were also the boundaries of the former communities that had been dispossessed in the late nineteenth century. Thus, the state reinvigorated a collective peasant identity linked to a particular territory and reinvigorated peasants' communal ties as a means to secure their property and to negotiate with the state. Rather than imposing an individualized experience of citizenship (as revisionist scholars have argued), this practice reinforced a collective relation with the state.

The agrarian trials registered tense negotiations between peasants and technicians who were seeking to assign individual plots when peasants were petitioning for a collective or mixed (individual and collective) allocation of land. These conflicts are described in petitions in the agrarian files, which include complaints that state authorities distributed land without regard for peasants' local practices. When these complaints reached the presidential office, presidents in general favored the distribution of land according to the peasants' demands, especially when this guaranteed less conflict in the countryside.[53]

Neither Paz Estenssoro nor Siles was as invested as Peru's President Velasco Alvarado, for example, in implementing a single model of land redistribution based on state-managed cooperatives.[54] There were a few attempts to implement cooperatives in the countryside, but these projects quickly fell apart.[55] Instead, because of the scarce political gain that a president could win from ruling the distribution among each group of beneficiaries, the meager budgetary allocation to run the program on land reform, and the enormous volume of peasant demands for expropriation and endowment of public lands, the state readily ceded the implementation of the process of land distribution within the former haciendas to the unions.[56]

Unions not only ruled much of the process of land distribution, they also became guarantors of the beneficiaries' property rights. The final verdict on a case of expropriation arrived years after peasants had initiated their demands. In the meantime, the former colonos occupied and cultivated those lands. In this legally chaotic setting, one could expect that outsiders and landless peasants would invade the former haciendas and fuel a new wave of violence and conflict among peasants.[57] Instead, years of relative peace emerged after the agrarian reform.[58] There were low-intensity conflicts (endless disputes over limits, succession, or divorces), but the strong social ties that united community members rather than state power prevented the emergence of high-intensity conflicts. In the two decades of implementation of the agrarian reform, the list of new beneficiaries in each hacienda grew, but the inclusion of these new names had to be recognized by the union.

The Military-Peasant Pact

In November 1964, General René Barrientos overthrew President Paz Estenssoro, ending twelve years of MNR rule. Barrientos's coup d'état launched a sequence of military regimes that lasted until 1982 when the country returned to democracy. Revisionist scholarship argues that the peasants' subordinate relationship to the government deepened under the military.[59] According to Albó, under Barrientos, "the peasantry was largely pacified and transformed into a veritable conservative battering ram, available for periodic deployment against the rebellious miners."[60] Yet this view that highlights peasant subordination to the interest of the military overlooks one of the peasants' most important achievements—neither General Barrientos nor the more conservative and authoritarian Colonel Hugo Bánzer challenged the peasants' right to land. In contrast to the cases of Guatemala, Peru, or Chile, these military leaders insisted they were continuing the principles of the nationalist revolution by protecting the achievements won through the agrarian reform. Furthermore, analysis of court cases of the late 1960s and 1970s in the highlands shows that peasants continued to challenge the limits of medium-sized properties that were granted to former landlords with the silent acquiescence of the military governments.

When General René Barrientos took power in 1964, some landlords saw a new opportunity to revisit the agrarian reform. In August 1965, landowners from Cochabamba requested that he reconsider the process.[61] They claimed that the reform "implemented during a general revolutionary euphoria had created only anarchy, poverty, and hunger in the countryside." Former landlords presented six key demands: the government guarantee of private property; the rectification of mistakes made and anomalies created over the course of the implementation of the agrarian reform; the compensation of landowners whose properties had been expropriated; the marginalization of unscrupulous leaders from the unions, whom they called "traffickers"; the confiscation of weapons that were still in peasant hands; and the reconsideration of any verdicts the president had signed because of illegal pressures and impositions. Finally, they reassured Barrientos: "We are committed to forging progress for the countryside, without hatred, without resentments, as it should be in a civilized and cultured country."[62]

Despite the demands of the landlords, however, Barrientos, who was eager to legitimize his government and to portray himself as a continuator of revolutionary nationalism, immediately enacted legislation guaranteeing the alliance between the military and the peasantry. Decree-Law 7033 of 1965 stated: "Considering that the agrarian reform constitutes the most important conquest of the revolution, the Army must keep that conquest effective." Through this decree, Barrientos linked his presidency not only to the principles of the 1952 revolution but also to the military nationalist traditions of General Germán Busch and Gualberto Villarroel dating back to the 1930s and 1940s. The decree ordered the army to create a special commission to protect the agrarian reform.[63] Two years later, Barrientos enacted a new constitution that ratified the principles of the 1952 national revolution. The text endorsed the main principles of the Agrarian Reform Decree-Law by declaring latifundios illegal and by stating that land should have a social function.[64] The even more conservative and authoritarian Colonel Hugo Bánzer also ratified his alliance with the peasants. Symbolically, he ended peasants' economic obligations to landlords.[65] During his regime, Bánzer did not hesitate to proclaim that his government followed the "philosophy of President Villarroel."[66] During his administration, the CNRA published retrospectives that highlighted "25 years of agrarian reform," which—at least discursively—served as proof that Bánzer's regime continued the policies that the MNR had started in 1953.[67]

The Barrientos and Bánzer policies were merely symbolic and had little effect on the peasants' economic conditions. However, as it gradually became clear that neither Barrientos nor Bánzer would revisit previous verdicts, a number of former landlords who consolidated a medium-sized property under the administrations of Siles Zuazo and Paz Estenssoro began selling these lands to their former colonos. Many did so alleging disputes over property boundaries with their neighbors, the former colonos. This demonstrates that the landlords recognized they would find no allies in the conservative regimes of Barrientos or Bánzer if this meant questioning the control of the peasant unions in the altiplano, valleys, and yungas.

Over the course of the 1960s and 1970s, there was a new transfer of rural property from landlords to former colonos in the countryside. The landowners who had not sold their estates found it increasingly difficult to keep their property, as illustrated by a court case initiated in the late 1970s. In Omasuyos, Carlos Terrazas, who consolidated 58 of the 955 hectares he owned before the agrarian reform, insisted that peasants who had never worked for him were illegally seizing plots. Terrazas claimed that it would be illegal to redistribute this land again, as it had already been subject to expropriation after 1953.[68] In response, the leader of the peasant union declared that those lands had been abandoned for fifteen years. The peasants argued that, following the principles of the reform, the government should grant the land to those who worked on it.[69] The dispute lasted almost ten years in the courts, ending only when President Paz Estenssoro (who returned to power in 1985) ordered the expropriation, as the peasants had demanded.[70] The case against Carlos Terrazas reveals the difficulties experienced by altiplano landholders in attempting to keep their properties after the agrarian reform, as they faced new union petitions for expropriation of the properties that the state had granted them in the 1950s or 1960s.

Agrarian conflicts in Omasuyos in the 1980s also revealed the increasing tension and rivalry between the peasant union and the state decisions. Some peasants appealed to the state to guarantee their property rights, but the peasant union in the highlands tied property to community obligations, adhering to Andean principles of the use of land. As previous scholarship on the state-peasant relation has argued, the state's understanding of property seemed to clash with that of the Andean communities. However, the agrarian court cases showed that different views about property rights created not only friction between the state and the peasant communities but also frictions within the communities themselves. The increasing political power of the communal/union authorities shows that over time they acted as more than mediators between state and individual, imposing specific sets of rules that dictated people's access to property, such as contributing to the construction of the school, irrigation canals, or participating in patronal festivities.

Court cases in Omasuyos, Germán Jordán, and in Sud Yungas in the 1970s and 1980s also attested to the strength of the peasant union in guaranteeing property rights. For instance, people petitioning for the sale or succession of a property usually legitimated their claim by presenting the certification or agreement from the union. The union certified, for example, that the person was indeed working on that plot, that the requested limits of the property were correct, and that the person was indeed the legitimate heir of the previous owner. Again, in the absence of state rural registries, the union became the prime guarantor of individuals' rights. Anthropologist Caroline Conzelman who studied the role of the unions in the 2000s corroborates the strength of the unions in Yungas. She argues that the "*sindicato agrario* [peasant union] is today also responsible for ensuring distribution of land, providing water and other public resources, addressing internal conflicts, and representing the interest of the community." She asserts that unions worked directly with school and hospital boards and other neighborhood associations.[71] All of these cases highlight the strength of the peasant unions in the countryside; their role expanded from creation of petitions related to land expropriation to involvement in health, education, and disputes among members.

Conclusions

The 1953 Agrarian Reform redrew Bolivia's political landscape. After 1953, no actors could make any request to the state without claiming that they supported the proper implementation of the Agrarian Reform Decree-Law. However, each actor selectively highlighted in his or her request different principles of the law. Landlords embraced some of the legal criteria established in the law that curbed the expropriation of their properties; peasants highlighted the principle about their former labor conditions, to prompt the government to order the expropriation.

Considering how much verdicts changed from one stage to the next, it was difficult for the appellants to predict the final outcome of each legal process. In multiple cases, the property that a judge declared an agricultural enterprise or a medium-sized property the president then declared a latifundio. Despite this seemingly disorganized process, a clear pattern was set in place: peasants continuously forced land redistribution well beyond the agenda initially set by the MNR, arguing that they had been subjected to servile labor conditions. Peasants repeatedly asserted the principle that "the land is for those who work it," so as to force redistribution. Although the individual histories and even the outcome of individual cases could vary widely, the peasant unions' political participation was key in all those experiences of land expropriation. Peasant unions played a key role in representing all their members in the demands for land expropriation, and they were significantly instrumental in the internal redistribution of that land. The union, rather than the state, defined who would be the beneficiary and the amount of land to which each person gained access after the government decreed expropriation.[72]

The new map of land property that emerged after the agrarian reform illustrates the role that peasants had in the process of land redistribution. The multiplicity of shapes, sizes, and uses of land reflected on this map were rooted in the complex and contentious historic, social, and geographic practices of peasants rather than in the uniform vision of a successful state modernization project. In the creation of this new map, many factors including Andean social distinctions between originarios, agregados, yanaperos, and utawawas, distinctions between private versus communal property, access to different ecosystems, and gender were critical to the peasants' process of defining access to property.

The process of land distribution did not reverse the process of community fragmentation that started with the expansion of the hacienda during the colonial period in the valleys of Cochabamba and in the late nineteenth century in the highlands. However, presidential verdicts cemented much of the communal ties that were in place and did not dare to implement a standardized system of private property across the countryside. The process of land redistribution—the results of which are still in place in Bolivia today—was relatively peaceful, controlled, and extremely redistributive, precisely because of the participation of these networks.

Even the most conservative military regimes of the 1960s and the 1970s did not venture to challenge the peasants' recently attained property ownership in the valleys, altiplano, and yungas. Under the military-peasant pact, peasants consolidated their territorial control of the highlands and the valleys at the expense of former landlords, who withdrew to the cities and the lowlands. After 1952, peasant unions not only became the most important mediators between peasants and the state, but they also developed into the premier institution to resolve internal conflicts, demonstrating the precarious position of the state in the countryside.

While peasants consolidated the land in the valleys, Yungas, and highlands that had been at the heart of the political struggle since the late nineteenth century, military governments expanded the country's agricultural frontier in the lowlands, the north, and the eastern region of Bolivia. General Bánzer, and later Luis García Meza, recklessly granted hundreds of hectares to people affiliated with their regimes at the expense of the indigenous groups of the lowlands creating a new process for the concentration of land.

Peasants in the highlands and valleys received little more than a land title in the countryside. Most of the investment in education, health care, and job creation was concentrated in the cities, and bank loans stimulated agribusiness in the lowlands.[73] Yet, the agrarian reform and its implementation granted peasant unions a large degree of autonomy that grew stronger in the second half of the twentieth century. Neither the military regime of the 1970s nor the neoliberal governments of the late 1980s and 1990s eroded their power. In fact, in the 1990s and 2000s, the peasantry became one of the most powerful actors in Bolivia, challenging and helping to remove the neoliberal regime.

Appendix 6.1: Verdicts on Land Distribution during the Presidencies of Hernando Siles Zuazo and Víctor Paz Estenssoro

The percentage of land that local judges, the CNRA, and the president granted to peasants and former landlords in each of the three provinces studied here, from 1956 to 1964, differed according to the president. The verdicts of the CNRA and the president used local judges' decisions as a template to make their own decision (see tables 6.9, 6.10). Between 1956 and 1960 local judges decided that 49 percent of the land should remain in the hands of landlords. President Siles Zuazo reversed that process and maintained that 57 percent of the land should remain in landlords' hands.

In Sud Yungas, local judges granted 23 percent of the land to former landlords; President Siles granted them 30 percent. Only in Omasuyos, it seems, did President Siles push further land distribution in favor of peasants. In contrast, Paz Estenssoro's final verdicts reveal that he tended to boost expropriation in peasants' favor one step further from what local judges and the CNRA had previously decided.

Table 6.9. Verdicts on Land Distribution during Hernando Siles's Presidency (1956–1960)

	Germán Jordán			Omasuyos			Sud Yungas		
Verdict	L	P	S	L	P	S	L	P	S
Local Judge	49.6	50.0	0.4	14.0	74.6	11.4	23.8	70.8	5.4
CNRA	59.1	39.3	1.6	8.1	86.3	5.6	28.3	66.1	5.6
President	57.9	41.6	0.5	8.3	76.1	15.6	30.1	63.1	6.8

Source: Developed by the author based on agrarian reform court cases. INRA-LP and INRA-CBBA.

Notes: In each case, Column L is the allocation of land in favor of the landlord; Column P is the allocation of land in favor of the peasants; Column S is the allocation of land for both landlord and peasants.

Table 6.10. Verdicts on Land Distribution during Víctor Paz Estenssoro's Presidency (1960–1964)

	Germán Jordán			Omasuyos			Sud Yungas		
Verdict	L	P	S	L	P	S	L	P	S
Local Judge	22.2	77.5	0.3	5.5	72.3	22.2	40.0	52.1	7.9
CNRA	19.4	77.5	3.1	3.4	95.8	0.8	15.6	46.8	37.6
President	11.0	84.5	4.5	2.0	97.6	0.4	9.1	44.3	46.6

Source: Elaborated by the author based on agrarian reform court cases, INRA-LP and INRA-CBBA.

Notes: In each case, Column L is the allocation of land in favor of the landlords; Column P is the allocation of land in favor of the peasants; Column S is the allocation of land for both landlord and peasants.

EPILOGUE

EVERYDAY FORMS OF REVOLUTION

> October 29, 1965
> The year of Marshal Andrés de Santa Cruz
> To the Minister of Peasant Affairs:
>
> We are writing to salute you in the name of all of the community members and legitimate heirs of community Antarani [Pacajes Province]. We ask for your help so we can finally consolidate the legal title of our communal property that we hold from the time of our ancestors. We are in the last stage of the judicial procedure—which has followed the principles of the agrarian reform decree—and we are waiting for the presidential signature. We ask you for the possession of our lands.
>
> For the unity of peasants,
> [Signed] Mariano Ramos, representative of the Antarani Community; comunario Policarpio Ramos, comunario Eleuterio Ramos, and Samuel Alejandro Cabrera, manager of the cooperative of the peasant rural council and coordinator for the national agricultural fair.

The letter of the leaders of community Antarani to the minister of peasant affairs was one of hundreds that peasant unions and Indian communities sent to government authorities petitioning for the legal titles to their lands in the aftermath of Bolivia's 1953 agrarian reform.[1] In terms of its format, the letter followed the language that the military regime imposed in the country after 1964. General René Barrientos, in order to legitimize his regime and assert his nationalistic credentials, gave the name of a national military hero to each of the years of his presidency. The leaders of the community Antarani, attentive to this change, started the letter commemorating the nineteenth-century national military hero Marshal Andrés de Santa Cruz. Yet, the letter's content reasserted the community members' long-standing demands—the restitution of Indian communal property.

In the letter the community officials stress the central arguments I have presented in this book. They show how important it is to consider the long historical arc of the agrarian reform process, which effectively started in August 1953 and continued for decades after the revolution. This letter is a testimony to the long and tenacious legal struggle of peasants to obtain legal land rights even during the dictatorship. It reveals the peasants' enduring efforts to secure communal property rights, despite the MNR's initial program for redistributing land on an individual basis.

Appraisals of the Bolivian revolution have swung dramatically over the last seven decades. Scholars' initial enthusiasm about the achievements of the revolution and the agrarian reform have dissipated. One of the most pugnacious critiques of the revolution was raised in 2003 by the historian Herbert Klein who downplayed the centrality of the national revolution. He argues that the structural changes that took place in Bolivia in the second half of the twentieth century, such as improvements in literacy, life expectancy, and child mortality, were more likely attributable to continent-wide developments rather than the economic policies unleashed by the revolution. Focusing on schooling, Klein argues that the expansion of educational opportunities to all social classes did not start in 1952 but, rather, was part of a longer-term process that began at the turn of the twentieth century.[2] Klein's analysis adds to a robust literature that in previous decades had questioned the shortcomings of the national revolution's promises of economic growth, diversification, and the elimination of ethnic and class inequalities.

However, this perspective that highlights the "uncompleted," "betrayed," "defeated," "vanquished" aspects of the revolution overlook the success of hundreds of colonos and comunarios in securing land.[3] It ignores the power that the landlord elite continued to hold even after the revolution and minimizes the fact that conservative military regimes were unable to reverse the radical process of land distribution, unlike many other examples in Latin America. The MNR dismantled landlords' official and unofficial mechanisms of power. Peasants' day-to-day battles inside and outside the courts were crucial to the practical implementation of an agrarian reform that had such profoundly transformative dimensions. The agrarian reform emerged as the result of a history of peasant mobilization and insurgency prior to 1953, what Laura Gotkowitz has called a "revolution before the revolution."[4] But it also continued through campaigns after 1953, which could be considered a "revolution after the revolution." The Bolivian case shows that the peasant "wars" of the twentieth century, in Eric Wolf's phrase, were not just limited to dramatic military mobilizations. They also included campaigns waged in quotidian and often invisible ways in remote rural settings and in dingy courthouses, arguing over plots of land that may seem modest in size or market value, but which were fought for tenaciously.

Despite the chaotic administrative and legal process of agrarian reform, a clear pattern was set in place: peasants continuously forced land redistribution well beyond the agenda initially set by the MNR, arguing that they had long been subject to servile labor conditions.[5] Because of peasant pressure, authorities expropriated productive large, medium-, and even small-sized properties. Prior to the revolution, few political parties (such as the Trotskyist POR) insisted on carrying out a reform that would entail expropriation without economic compensation to previous landlords. Although most parties (including the moderate MNR and the PIR) rejected such a principle, in practice peasants conquered land without indemnification. Yet, in contrast to what the POR proposed, the state had little control over those expropriated farms. Peasant unions took control of the process of land distribution. The diversity in the design of rural property that emerged after the revolution exposed how historic, social, and geographic practices shaped the final outcome of the agrarian reform and challenged the state's modernizing project.

The revolution wiped away traditional structures of power, opened new mechanisms for political representation, and reshaped the role of peasants who made up the majority of the population within Bolivian society. Soon after the revolution, the newly organized peasant unions began to appoint the rural authorities and became a major voice within local political affairs, gaining a type of representation that, prior to the revolution, was the exclusive privilege of the small circle of citizens organized in neighbors' councils. The elimination of these neighbors' councils and of their ability to elect representatives to positions of power offered colonos and comunarios unprecedented access to local political power. The feverish organization of hundreds of unions across the countryside in the first two years of the revolution does not point to the strength of the MNR in the countryside but, rather, to the power of the peasants. Given the historical fragility of the government and the state in Bolivia, it is hard to imagine that the MNR could have organized hundreds of unions solely on the basis of a decree. Peasant unions grew from existing organizations; colonos and comunarios organized unions based on the contours of haciendas and indigenous communities, maintaining previous territorial boundaries. The peasant unions elected their representatives following the Andean system of rotation of authorities: union leaders were selected for one year and their positions alternated among all union members. All of these factors reflect the strength of indigenous forms of political representation rather than the separate strength of the state or of the MNR. In other words, syndicates were not an artificial creation from the top; instead, these territorialized unions solidified and gave visibility to economic, social, and political units that had formed and operated before the revolution.

Considering the success of peasant unions in consolidating land for their members and in shaping policy at the local level, it is worth reconsidering the assumptions about cooptation and corruption in peasant unions. This criticism has been a common theme in Bolivian literature for the past three decades. It has its origins in the persistent attempt by the MNR and the military to manipulate the peasantry through their unions.[6] Yet, agrarian court cases also show that landlords often used these charges as a political weapon against their opponents. To docilely accept those claims could imply, as Gilbert Joseph warns, that we are playing the dominant classes' game.[7] By leaving unquestioned these assumptions about peasant union leaders' cooptation and the manipulation of their bases, we also reify another trope—that is, peasants' lack of political agency. Concerns about the corruption and cooptation of the process of agrarian reform misses a critical point—the success of peasant unions in consolidating the land.

The study of the agrarian reform in Bolivia is an opportunity to reexamine more broadly the relationship between the state and the peasants. Merilee Grindle has shown that land reforms gave states an opportunity to assert their presence in the countryside. She argues that, once landlords' economic and political power in the countryside weakened, the state became the new mediator of local conflicts.[8] This was the case in the paradigmatic reforms of Mexico, Peru, and Cuba where radical policies undermined rural elites and extended state control in the countryside. In Bolivia, when the power of the elites fell apart, however, it was not the state but the peasant unions and the Indian communities that won increased power. Once landlords fled the countryside, peasant unions became conflict mediators in other political conflicts. After the reform was instituted, the state had little ability to regulate the numerous disputes among peasants—over territorial boundaries, or the rights to pasturelands or water, or even family and personal affairs such as inheritance or theft. In the new political scenario, the unions as well as traditional community authorities performed a critical political and legal role.

Today, the altiplano and the valleys in Bolivia continue predominantly in the hands of Aymara and Quechua peasants organized in unions and indigenous communities. These organizations continue to have a leading role in issues concerning land property as well as schooling, water access, and political organizing. Implicit rather than written rules encourage property owners to be involved in the union in order to secure their access to land and be recognized as part of the community. Participation in the union demands families' labor, monetary contributions, and involvement in local festivities. These changes demonstrate that a profound transformation in understanding rural property has taken place in Bolivia since 1952. Land indeed has a social function, as many constitutions in Latin America have declared. In Bolivia, however, peasant unions have seized on that principle and taken control of it. In Bolivia, access to land is linked to the contribution and participation of owners in the community.

In this book I outline the intricate ways in which subaltern groups embraced a political project from above, as Marisol de la Cadena's writings do in Peru and Charles Hale's do in Guatemala.[9] Despite the elitist and racialized character of the MNR's nationalism, colonos, and comunarios used concrete mechanisms to take account of and adapt the 1952 revolution to their own objectives.[10] This requires reconsidering the almost essentialist approach that many times authors have used to describe the relationship between state and peasantry in Bolivia. Instead of envisioning the relationship as a binary one structured through such fixed dichotomies as modernity versus tradition or private property versus communal property, in fact each shaped the other. The presidential final verdicts on cases of agrarian reform mostly confirmed decisions made at the local level. This reflects the powerful impact of community decisions at the national level, and it reveals the strength of peasants to shape the agrarian reform from below. The agrarian trials show the close relationship between the members of the union and the state authorities at the local level. Often, we find the same names exercising roles as the general secretary of the union, representatives of the rural council, or the corregidor or the subprefecto of the province.

The Disguise and the Politics behind the Numbers

From the 1950s onward, the CNRA has published annual reports outlining the implementation of land reform in Bolivia. On August 2 of every year since 1953, all newspapers celebrate the signing of the agrarian reform decree by publishing photographs, articles, and statistics highlighting the yearly achievements of this policy. Printed under the vigilant eye of the government, all this information details the progress of the land distribution. Since the 1970s, several scholars, most notably Xavier Albó in his well-known analysis *Requiem para una reforma agraria*, have concluded that it was difficult to evaluate the reform based on those statistics because the official data was inconsistent and contradictory.[11] In 2003, when commemorating the fiftieth anniversary of the agrarian reform, Miguel Urioste states that Bolivia's reform had been the object of intense ideological debate with very little empirical evidence.[12]

We seem to be facing a contradiction. On the one hand, the effort each government made to monitor the policy on agrarian reform and inform the public about it is evident. On the other hand, the reports are almost useless, since one report contradicts another. How contradictory are they? Studies from three scholars based on CNRA statistics reveal just how inconsistent the results may be. James Clark reports that the government distributed twelve million hectares between 1953 and 1959.[13] Alfonso García, the president of the CNRA, reports that up until 1964 the government had distributed four million hectares (eight million less).[14] James Wilkie states that ten million hectares were distributed between 1953 and 1969.[15]

Some scholars such as Robert Turovsky argue that the CNRA's poor data and inconsistent information were the result, at least in part, of the meager budgets that the central government assigned to the agency. Turovsky accuses the Bolivian government of a double discourse that exploited "the rhetoric of agrarian reform without actually dedicating enough desire or money to enable the program to attain the goals set forth in its original legislation."[16] But the budget shortage only partially explains the problem.

I argue that the CNRA reports were primarily a tool of political propaganda. The CNRA reports constituted one of the MNR's most refined political instruments to both assert its leadership in the revolution and publicize its most important, if not unique, achievements. Publicizing the progress of the agrarian reform became increasingly important for the party, because all the other promises of the national revolution—on mines nationalization, industrialization, and the diversification of the economy—had failed. After the mid-1950s, workers in the mines and in the cities had grown exasperated with the economic recession, inflation, food shortages, wage freezes, and MNR's submissive compliance with US economic and political pressures.[17] In this context, Paz Estenssoro in his first term (1952–1956) and Siles Zuazo used the data on agrarian reform as part of a political strategy to highlight the most progressive facets of the revolution.[18]

In his second presidency, from 1960 to 1964, Paz Estenssoro also resorted to the results of the agrarian reform to secure economic support from the United States by connecting his political agenda to President John F. Kennedy's program for Latin America's development called the Alliance for Progress. This was the most prominent US nonmilitary response to the Cuban revolution.[19] In the context of increasingly tense relations between the United States and Cuba, Paz Estenssoro positioned Bolivia's agrarian reform as a moderate reformist program that could serve as a model to other countries in Latin America. Paz Estenssoro was able to build such a narrative because Bolivia's agrarian reform appeared to be far less threatening to US interests. Unlike the reforms of Guatemala and Cuba, Bolivia's agrarian reform had not affected the properties of North American companies.[20] Paz Estenssoro promoted the Bolivian agrarian reform as a moderated policy based on technical and legal policies, as was proudly stated in a CNRA report in 1962: "The Bolivian experiment, that in the past provoked attacks from the conservative and reactionary sectors of Latin America, has proven to be a guide to other nations currently discussing the implementation of the agrarian reform within the framework of the Alliance of Progress."[21]

MNR leaders also used the results of the agrarian reform to legitimize their government against their political rivals. For example, the CNRA's reports published at the end of Paz Estenssoro's second administration show that he granted more property titles in the last three years of his administration (542,334 titles) than Siles Zuazo conferred during the last four years (201,676 titles). Paz highlighted the successes of his administration over the accomplishments of Siles Zuazo who led the country between 1956 and 1960. Yet, the data does not reflect the long and tedious process that was required to petition for the expropriation of property, which started under Siles Zuazo's government.[22]

The military dictators that ruled the country following the overthrow of the MNR also used the results of the agrarian reform as proof that they continued the hardcore principles of the national revolution.[23] In 1975, Hugo Bánzer, the right-wing dictator, widely distributed a booklet entitled, "25 años de reforma agraria en Bolivia" (Twenty-five years of agrarian reform in Bolivia). The report linked Bánzer's policies in the countryside to policies instituted in 1953, as a mechanism to assert his own legitimacy. These reports emphasized the leading role of the government and its institutions (the CNRA and the Ministry of Peasant Affairs) in the process of agrarian reform, and again ignored the role of the peasant unions. Strategically, the CNRA's statistics often used the terms "beneficiaries" or "hectares distributed," neutral language that concealed how much land actually remained in the hands of former landlords and how much passed to former colonos and comunarios. Most CNRA reports displayed information that was only organized by department (or state). Presenting the information in this way was particularly deceptive in the case of the departments of La Paz and Cochabamba (both subjects in this study).

Both these departments were the target of two different initiatives. The highlands of La Paz and the valleys in Cochabamba were subject to the expropriation of large, medium-, and small-sized estates, whereas the subtropical north of La Paz and the east of Cochabamba were designated for colonization (settlement).[24] By combining the results of both processes under the category of "distributed hectares," CNRA statistics gave the impression that expropriation was far more ambitious and radical than it actually was.

In celebration of the ten-year anniversary of the agrarian reform, in 1963 the CNRA published a graph that visually guides readers' conclusions (see figure 7.1). The image uses the icon of an Andean peasant to represent all beneficiaries. The graph leads the reader to think of the progress of the reform as a uniform (homogenous) project. The image obscures comunarios, colonos originarios, and colonos agregados in their individual access to land and conceals the many contentious debates over land rights and visions of property that I have discussed in this book. Anyone viewing the graph might wonder what happened to the property of the "progressive landlords" (most of them criollos or mestizos) that the MNR claimed to defend in 1953.[25] The graph obscures geographical differences and the dis-

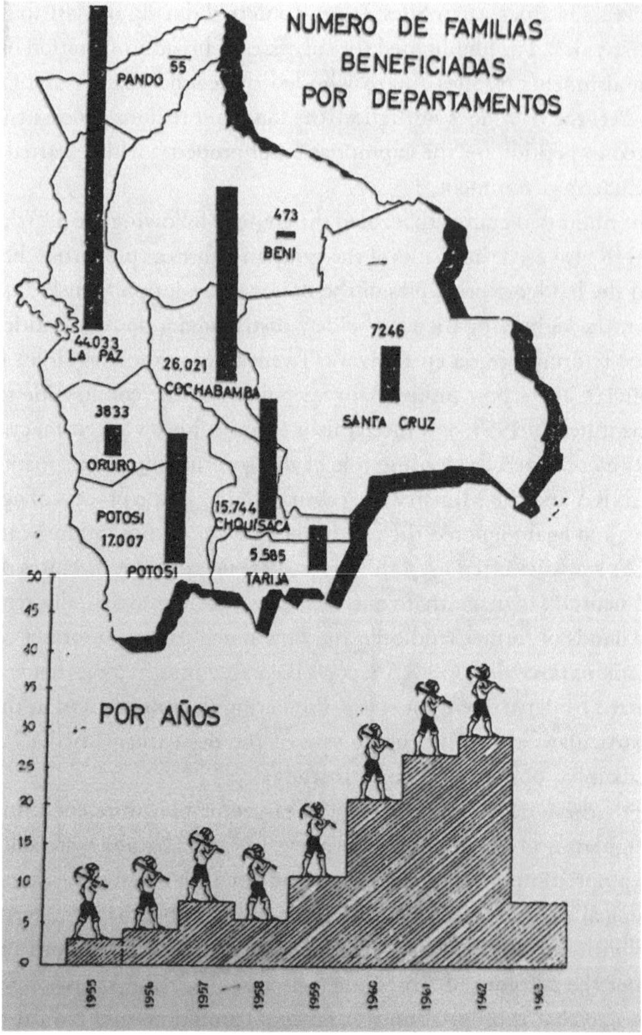

Figure 7.1. The beneficiaries of the agrarian reform. From García, *Diez años*, 109.

tinct historical practices played in the process of land expropriation and the distribution of land among beneficiaries.

The Continued Salience of the Agrarian Reform

Struggles over land remain at the center of politics in Bolivia and Latin America today. It is remarkable how much of the current discussion still focuses on narrow legal and technical aspects, tending to overlook the broader political dynamics of conflict. Until the 1970s, most judicial and extrajudicial struggles over land in Bolivia focused on the implementation or consolidation of the 1950s agrarian reform in the highlands and the valleys of Bolivia. After the 1970s, the character of land struggle began to change. Some provinces on the high plateau but especially those in the valleys faced extreme fragmentation of property. Yet the most significant land problem in Bolivia shifted from the highlands to the lowlands (the eastern plains and the Amazonian region) when military governments granted vast and often illegal land concessions to landlords and private companies for cattle ranching and logging to pay back political favors. Anthropologist Nancy Postero argues that General Bánzer awarded almost ten million hectares of large land concessions in Santa Cruz alone to individuals and agribusiness.[26]

These new landholders usurped the territories of lowland indigenous peoples, many of them still nomadic. In the late 1980s, it was clear that Bolivia faced a new process of land concentration (neo-latifundio) in these areas. In response, lowland indigenous peoples who previously had little political visibility emerged as strong political actors, denouncing their violent expulsion from their lands. These indigenous groups organized a confederation named Confederación Indígena del Oriente Boliviano (CIDOB), the Indigenous Federation of Eastern Bolivia, in 1982. Initially, the CIDOB encountered very little acceptance for their demands at the national level. However, in 1990 they organized the First March for Territory and Dignity in which they walked from the city of Trinidad to La Paz over thirty-two days. The march had a powerful impact on national politics. It turned the indigenous peoples of the lowlands—and the CIDOB—into major political actors at the national level. It forced President Jaime Paz Zamora (1989–1993) to sign three decrees guaranteeing indigenous peoples the right to hold territories.[27] As anthropologists Ricardo Calla and Ramiro Molina have argued, the march challenged the monocultural foundations of the state. Indigenous groups claimed recognition of a distinct ethnic identity rather than solely a class identity and collective rights rather than individual rights.[28]

Indigenous demands emerged in Bolivia at a time of profound institutional crisis for the CNRA. News about corruption in the process of land titling and the illegal appropriation of land filled the local newspapers. In 1992, Congressman Miguel Urioste, the director of Fundación Tierra, an NGO that specialized in land and rural development, denounced the minister of education for using his political power to grant himself a large property in Santa Cruz.[29] In response to these charges of corruption and the ongoing political mobilization from indigenous peoples of the lowlands, President Paz Zamora seized the offices of the CNRA, banned all land titling to stop any further land allocations, and called for the drafting of a new agrarian law.[30]

The 1992 closure of the CNRA marked the end of the 1950s agrarian reform. In 1996, the neoliberal president Gonzalo Sánchez de Lozada enacted a new agrarian law, called the Instituto Nacional de la Reforma Agraria (INRA) law. The INRA law was not only a response to Bolivia's internal crises but also part of a more generalized process of reform promoted by the World Bank in many countries in Africa and Latin America. As part of the neoliberal privatization of the economy during the 1990s, World Bank officials encouraged new programs for agrarian reform that would open up land to markets, considering the organization and clarification of landholders' legal property to be crucial for establishing a healthy land market. These international lawmakers argued that state-led agrarian reforms did not succeed because they were costly and unwieldy. Instead, market-led agrarian reform, they argued, would create a much more efficient, lower-priced redistribution of land.[31] World Bank analysts did not explain that many of the 1950s, 1960s, and 1970s reforms failed in Latin America because of the emergence of conservative military dictators who reversed much of the process of land distribution.

Such discourse, which dominated land reform programs in the 1990s, did not consider the deep political, social, and economic power dynamics ingrained in agrarian conflict. World Bank analysts assumed that all economic actors were equally able to acquire land and overlooked peasants' and Indians' limited resources and the unbalanced relations of power they faced historically. Proponents of market-led agrarian reform assumed that purely legal and technical measures would alter existing social, political, and economic structures. In the 2000s, the powerful social movements of the landless and the indigenous emerged to protest land policies in many countries in Latin America including Mexico, Brazil, Peru, Ecuador, and Bolivia. These movements emerged in response to the inability of the 1990s reforms to resolve peasant and Indian land struggles with deep historical roots.

The Bolivian agrarian reformists were guilty of some of the criticisms raised by market-led agrarian reform advocators. The reform was slow, inefficient, and poorly implemented. Miguel Urioste has rightly pointed out that the implementation of the process was bureaucratic and often corrupt and that the government allocated an insignificant percentage of the national budget for its implementation. The agrarian reform was also unable to grant new economic opportunities to peasants. Since 1952, most governments have privileged investment in the cities over the countryside. They promoted the expansion of education or health primarily in the urban areas, and new programs for rural investment mainly benefited the emerging landlord elite in the lowlands.[32] Finally, as scholars such as Deere and Léon have noted, Bolivian land reform solidified gender hierarchies by granting land only to the heads of families who, with the exception of widows, were usually men. Thousands of former colonos, landless workers, and comunarios became landholders, but most women remained excluded from this process.[33] Yet, these flaws should not prevent us from highlighting the reform's outstanding accomplishment in transferring lands to peasants who had been fighting for them for decades, if not centuries, before the revolution. The success of the program of land distribution outlasted the MNR, two decades of military regimes, and two decades of neoliberal rule.

The contemporary strength of the indigenous and peasant movements in Bolivia derives from the particular relationship that developed between those communities and the state after 1952. The effective territorial control that peasants and Indian communities secured in the rural highlands and valleys allowed them to hold political influence in these regions. Access to land gave peasants access to power, as the classic work of Barrington Moore suggests.[34] To this day, the political support of the peasant unions remains a key factor for any political party or candidate to maintain power at the national level. Such dense political organization from below helps explain the emergence of a leader such as Evo Morales, the first indigenous president of Bolivia. In much of Latin America, indigenous voices have been marginalized or play only a minor role in national politics. In Bolivia, indigenous movements have been at the core of national politics. They are not only allies of progressive political parties, as in the case of Ecuador, but the other way around.

NOTES

Introduction

1. Subsecretaría de Prensa, Informaciones y Cultura, "Discurso del Primer Mandatario de la Nación, Víctor Paz Estenssoro," *El libro blanco de la reforma agraria* (La Paz: Subsecretaría de Prensa, Informaciones y Cultura, 1953), 123.

2. The term "Indian" has different connotations that vary enormously depending on its historical and geographical context. In mid-twentieth-century Bolivia, "Indian" referred to people living in an indigenous community (ayllu) and to those people who were subject to servitude in the hacienda. The first ones called themselves "comunarios," and those who lost access to their land called themselves "ex-comunarios." The second group were the colonos (also identified as peons or *peguleros*). When it was possible, I use the terms "comunarios" and "colonos" to make these distinctions evident. Since the onset of the revolution, the MNR tried to erase the word "Indian" from the national political discourse so as to escape the derogatory connotation the word had in the country's political debate. Instead, the party promoted the use of class-based identities. Despite MNR's attempt, the terms "Indian" and "peasant" continued to appear in political discourse as interchangeable.

3. The yungas of La Paz are predominantly situated in the provinces of Nor Yungas, Sud Yungas, and Inquisivi. The subtropical ecoregion of yungas constitutes a series of valleys extending along the upper eastern front of the Andes in a sector north and east of the altiplano. In this region elevations range from four hundred to thirty-five hundred meters. These highland valleys form a transition zone between the moist forests of the Amazon and the Andean altiplano. In this study I focus on the province of Sud Yungas. For a thoughtful study of this province, see Spedding, *Wachu Wachu*, 33.

4. Carlson, "Agrarian Structure and Underdevelopment," 678–79.

5. Bolivian legal nomenclature signals the origin and the context in which a legal order was signed. For instance, a decree is an executive order issued by the president. A law is signed by the president and approved by Congress. A decree-law is a rule of law that has the importance and relevance of a law, but it has not been approved by Congress. Usually, decree-laws are signed by a de facto president or in a revolutionary context. This was the case of the iconic Agrarian Reform Decree-Law

3464 signed on August 2, 1953 (hereafter Agrarian Reform Decree-Law). Finally, a supreme resolution is signed by the head of a ministry. Bolivian legislation from independence in 1825 to the present can be found at the Gaceta Oficial del Estado Plurinacional de Bolivia (hereafter Gaceta Oficial) or on the legal website Lexivox.org.

6. Dozens of headlines in the newspapers reiterated peasants' thankfulness to Paz Estenssoro. In the first two years after the revolution (1952 and 1953), *La Nación*, the MNR's most important media organ, published almost daily reports about peasants entering the city of La Paz to celebrate the revolution and thank the president for enacting the agrarian reform. See, for instance, "La reforma agraria: Liberación del indio," *La Nación*, April 9, 1953; "La reforma agraria destruye la opresión secular de los trabajadores en el campo," *La Nación*, August 13, 1953; "La reforma agraria es la mano firme que arranca de nuestra historia páginas de sangre y de dolor," *La Nación*, August 3, 1953; "Campesinos agradecen por la reforma," *La Nación*, August 13, 1953. Guillermo Bedregal, in his biography of President Paz, reinforces the view that the MNR woke the Indians from their slumbers. Bedregal, *Víctor Paz Estenssoro*, 444.

7. Robert Alexander's was one of the earliest and most influential accounts of the Bolivian Revolution in English. Alexander, *Bolivian National Revolution*, 6. Subsequently, other scholars continued to underscore that peasants were passive before and during the revolution. See, for example, Malloy, *Bolivia*, 282. This view was also prevalent among Bolivian scholars. Guillermo Lora argues peasant were prepolitical parasites of the workers' movement. Lora, "La clase obrera," 186. René Zavaleta Mercado argues that the cultural isolation and exile to which the landowners had subjected the peasants resulted in their practical inferiority. For him, the indigenous uprisings of the first decades of the twentieth century were terror without any promise (or any goal), and the undisputed actor of the Bolivian revolution was the mining proletariat. Zavaleta Mercado, "El desarrollo de la conciencia nacional," in Zavaleta Mercado and Souza Crespo, *Obra completa* 1:151–52.

8. Patch, "Social Implications," 51. See also Patch, "Bolivia: The Restrained Revolution," 128.

9. Heath, Erasmus, and Buechler, *Land Reform*, 371.

10. Heath, Erasmus, and Buechler, *Land Reform*, 227. Guillermo Lora also believes that the peasant union form came from outside, from the proletarian. Lora, "La clase obrera," 184–85.

11. Heath, Erasmus, and Buechler, *Land Reform*, 371. Dwight Heath with the assistance of Manuel Carballo directly addresses the debate initiated by Patch, in Heath and Carballo, "Bolivia's Law of Agrarian Reform," 37, 49.

12. Dandler, *El sindicalismo campesino*, 7, 17–23, 39.

13. Dandler, *El sindicalismo campesino*, 47–48, 51, 58–62.

14. Reinforcing the view of the political brokers, Malloy highlights the role of the Federación Obrera Local (FOL), the Local Workers Federation, in La Paz. Malloy, *Bolivia*, 188, 196–97, 200.

15. This was, of course, a more general tendency that went beyond academia. Court cases regarding agrarian reform show that the topographers in charge of writing reports usually wrote "none" under the rubric of peasant political organization if they did not find a union.

16. See, for example, Zavaleta Mercado, "Las masas en noviembre" 28, 34. The work of Luis Antezana-Ergueta and Hugo Romero-Bedregal is a unique example that lists the formation of peasant unions in Tarija prior to the revolution. Yet, they believe that the unions of Tarija followed the same pattern that Dandler found in Cochabamba: unions were organized by mixed-raced peasants led by political brokers. See Antezana Ergueta and Romero Bedregal, *Historia de los sindicatos campesinos*, 8, 11, 52, 74–77.

17. For a history of THOA, see Stephenson, "Forging an Indigenous Counterpublic Sphere," 101. For a recent study of indigenous leaders' struggles to recover and to popularize histories of past rebellions, see Dangl, *Five Hundred Year Rebellion*.

18. Rivera Cusicanqui, *Oprimidos*; Mamani, *Taraqu*; Taller de Historia Oral Andina, *El indio Santos Marka T'ula*; Choque Canqui and Ticona Alejo, *Jesús de Machaqa*.

19. Condarco Morales, *Zárate, el "temible" Willka*. For further research on Zárate Willka's rebellion, see Hylton, "Reverberations of Insurgency," and Mendieta, *Entre la alianza y la confrontación*.

20. Rivera Cusicanqui, "Luchas campesinas contemporáneas," 129; Rivera Cusicanqui, "Liberal Democracy and Ayllu Democracy," 115.

21. Laura Gotkowitz, examining this long cycle of rebellions from 1880 to 1952, argues that Indians and peasants in fact led a revolution before the Bolivian revolution. Gotkowitz, *Revolution for Our Rights*, 67–100.

22. Platt, *Estado boliviano*, 60–61, 163–65. Platt states that the law of 1874 and the Decree-Law of 1953 were very similar in terms of goals, treatment of the indigenous communities, and tax policy. When referring to the landlord elite, Platt states: "the main absentee is the great landowner who acted notoriously in the few areas where he had become an effective force before the 1952 revolution." Platt, *Estado boliviano*, 179.

23. Rivera Cusicanqui, "Liberal Democracy," 115. See also the work of anthropologist María Lagos on the relations of class and identity in Tiraque (Cochabamba). She argues that a rural merchant class was ultimately the new beneficiary of the post-1952 reconfiguration of local political power. Lagos, *Autonomy and Power*, 3. The most recent work exploring the role of Indian and peasant communities in the altiplano in the twentieth century is Waskar Ari. He also saw the 1952 revolution as a consolidated effort by local elites to modernize and westernize Bolivia's Indian population. He argues that the MNR-sponsored unions—controlled by the mestizo (or mixed-race) provincial elite—became an instrument for racial assimilation in the countryside. Ari, *Earth Politics*, 149.

24. Richard Patch's particular account of the role of peasants during the revolutionary period comes from his firsthand experience in Cliza and Ucureña in 1952. Patch describes this experience in "The Progress of Land Reform in Bolivia," Land Tenure Center Discussion Paper no. 2 (1963), 5.

25. Gordillo, *Campesinos revolucionarios*, 21–22.

26. Antezana-Ergueta and Romero-Bedregal, *Historia de los sindicatos campesinos*, 27. Lehm and Rivera Cuscicanqui refer to the key role of urban activists in organizing unions in the countryside before the revolution. Lehm and Rivera Cusicanqui, *Los artesanos libertarios*, 84–86.

27. In August 23, 1943, President Enrique Peñaranda enacted a new law on labor, the Ley General del Trabajo, which banned colonos from organizing unions.

28. Unions, as William Carter shows, reproduced the same patterns of political participation and selection of authorities as in the traditional indigenous communities. Carter, *Aymara Communities*, 59.

29. The prefect of Cochabamba wrote a private letter to the Ministry of Government in which he argued: "Although the MNR succeeded in organizing peasants into unions almost everywhere in the countryside, I must tell you that ninety per cent of them no longer answer to the MNR." Letter dated December 17, 1952, in Archivo y Biblioteca Nacionales de Bolivia (Bolivian National Archive), Collection Walter Guevara Arze (hereafter ABNB-WGA), box 30. Unless otherwise noted, all translations to English from the original documents in Spanish are mine.

30. This view differs from that presented by Tristan Platt. He finds that in Norte Potosi there was a direct articulation between ethnicity and political organization. The mestizos supported the unions, and the comunarios supported the ayllus. Platt, *Estado boliviano*, 60–62. My study of Omasuyos shows that support for these political organizations was linked to specific economic demands: colonos tended to join the unions, and the comunarios or ex-comunarios the ayllus (see Chapter Five for an analysis of the conflict between colonos and comunarios in Omasuyos).

31. Alison Spedding's rich ethnography outlined economic differences among peasants in Sud Yungas. Spedding, *Wachu Wachu*, 15,17, 31, 37, 45. Madeline Barbara Léons points to the rivalries between peasants who held land before the agrarian reform (*sayañeros*) and the beneficiaries of the agrarian reform (former colonos). Léons, "Political Economy of Agrarian Reform," 95.

32. Bolivia's map of rural property contrasts, for example, with the maps created by what James Scott calls the "Authoritarian High Modernist experiments" (top-down) led by the Soviet or the Tanzanian state. Scott, *Seeing like a State*, 3,6–7, 11.

33. The most recent work that analyzes the United States–Bolivia relation in the context of the Cold War is Young, *Blood of the Earth*, 11–12.

34. Zavaleta Mercado, "Las masas en noviembre," 31–32; Lora, "La clase obrera," 186; Jetté, *De la toma del cielo*, 27–28.

35. Almaraz Paz, *Réquiem para una república*, 17–20; Malloy, *Bolivia*, 263; Dunkerley, *Rebellion in the Veins*, 84–85; Young, *Blood of the Earth*, 59–60; Stephen Cote, *Oil and Nation*, 141.

36. James Clark argues that, contrary to what landlords had expected, Barrientos ratified the spirit of the law on agrarian reform. James Clark, *Temas sobre la propiedad rural y reforma agraria en Bolivia*, 9. The Decree-Law 07189 of May 24, 1965, states that ordinary tribunals of justice cannot revise decisions made by agrarian courts. Decree-Law 07260 of August 2, 1965, states that all land titles that peasants had already received were legal and that they were to be registered in the Derechos Reales, the office that registers property rights.

37. General Bánzer decided to cancel peasants' debts over indemnification in January 7, 1972. Decree-Law 10067, *Gaceta Oficial*. In 1985 the newly reelected President Paz Estenssoro continued to sign decrees for land redistribution.

38. Scott, *Weapons of the Weak*.

39. My notion of everyday forms of revolution also draws from the influential edited volume on Mexico by Joseph and Nugent, *Everyday Forms of State Formation*, 3–4, 12.

40. Scott, "Resistance without Protest"; Thomson, *We Alone Will Rule*, 287; Roseberry, "Beyond the Agrarian Question," 318; Stern, *Resistance, Rebellion, and Consciousness*.

41. I want to thank historian Hernán Pruden for introducing me to this collection.

Chapter One: The Liberal Project in the Countryside

1. Grieshaber, "Survival of Indian Communities," 225. See also Ministerio de Asuntos Campesinos y Agropecuarios, *Censo Agropecuario, 1950*, ii.

2. Malloy, *Bolivia*, 25.

3. García, "Agrarian Reform and Social Development," 305–6; Carter "Revolution and the Agrarian Sector," 233; Léons and Léons, "Land Reform and Economic Change," 271.

4. Assadourian, *El sistema de la economía colonial*. At the turn of the twentieth century, Bolivia relied heavily on tin exports. In 1904, tin represented 40 percent of Bolivia's exports, and in the 1920s over 70 percent. See Langer, *Economic Change and Rural Resistance*, 31.

5. Albó, "¿Por qué el campesino qhochala es distinto?" 2; McEwen, *Changing Rural Society*, 143; Léons and Léons, "Land Reform and Economic Change," 270.

6. Mendieta, *Entre la alianza*, 86; Klein, *Concise History of Bolivia*, 103.

7. Langer, *Economic Change*, 14. The mining industry and commerce were in total collapse because of fifteen years of war. Sanchez-Albornoz, *Indios y tributos*, 198.

8. Platt, "Andean Experience of Bolivian Liberalism," 307–9.

9. Law dated September 28, 1868, Article 1, Gaceta Oficial.

10. Langer, *Economic Change*, 18–20. See also Rivera Cusicanqui, "La expansión del latifundio"; Platt, *Estado boliviano.*

11. Gotkowitz, *Revolution for Our Rights*, 20. See also Sanchez-Albornóz, *Indios y tributos*, 209–10.

12. Mamani, *Taraqu*, 15–16.

13. Tristán Marof denounced the president's illegal appropriation of communal lands in Marof. Marof, *La tragedia del altiplano*, 39. See also Mendieta, *Entre la alianza*, 95; Rivera Cusicanqui, *Oprimidos*, 87; Choque Canqui and Ticona Alejo, *Jesús de Machaqa*, 11–14; Choque Canqui, Albó, and Ticona Alejo, *Cinco siglos de historia.*

14. Ministerio de Asuntos Campesinos y Agropecuarios, *Censo Agropecuario, 1950*, ii.

15. Klein, *Haciendas and Ayllus*, 35.

16. Langer, *Economic Change*, 33.

17. Law dated November 23, 1911, signed by President Eliodoro Villazón. The government gave Simón I. Patiño a new concession one year later to build the railway from Chimoré to Santa Cruz. Law dated November 20, 1912, signed by President Eliodoro Villazón. Simón I. Patiño had a company that was importing livestock, which he sold to the state-owned companies. Law dated March 11, 1929, signed by President Hernando Siles. All laws are in Gaceta Oficial.

18. Law dated December 21, 1901. The government granted to the company of Felix Avelino Aramayo the concession of this area to export rubber and represent the country with companies in the United States and Europe. Ultimately, Bolivia lost this territory to Brazil in 1903.

19. Mauricio Hochschild and Simón I Patiño received concessions for the construction of roads. On September 2, 1942, President Peñaranda granted Hochschild y Cia the concession to build a road between Pacuani and Lambate in La Paz. Supreme Resolution dated September 2, 1942. The *Revista Campo*—the most important magazine on agrarian affairs in Bolivia in the 1940s—often published propaganda offering fertilizers from Hochschild's Company.

20. For Soligno's property, see INRA-La Paz (LP), Sud Yungas Province, box 12, file Iquico y Totoral.

21. Langer, *Economic Change and Rural Resistance*, 74.

22. Brooke Larson demonstrated that economic downturns provoked the fragmentation of the hacienda system already in the late colonial period in the valleys of Cochabamba. Larson, *Cochabamba, 1550–1900*, 302, 401. Historians Gustavo Rodríguez Ostria and Robert Jackson pointed out that the hacienda system further decayed in the late nineteenth century in the valleys of Cochabamba as an effect of the 1874 Disentailment Law. Rodríguez Ostria, *Elites, mercado y cuestión regional*; Jackson, "Decline of the Hacienda," 275–76; Jackson, *Regional Markets*, 259–60.

23. INRA-Cochabamba (CBBA), Germán Jordán Province, file La Alcoholería, box 9, and file Liquinas o El Rosario, box 7.

24. Benton, *Agrarian Reform*, 42. Based on the same census, Melvin Burke argued: "Before 1952 land concentration was very great . . . approximately 6 percent of the largest agricultural units constituted 92 percent of the land, while 80 percent of the smallest held only 1 percent of the land." Burke was merging in the same category private large estates and indigenous communities. Burke, *Land Reform*, 411. See also Carter, "Revolution and the Agrarian Sector," 238. Antonio García presented a fair reading of distribution of land prior to 1953. He argued that both latifundios and minifundios covered 80 percent of land recorded by the census. He also remarks that, prior to the revolution, communities owned 7.2 million hectares. García, "Agrarian Reform and Social Development," 306.

25. Herbert Klein highlighted the ongoing internal stratification within free communities. He stated that the elimination of the mita (Indian obligatory labor in the mines) favored *originarios* with the greatest access to lands. *Agregados* with land constituted 42 percent of the communities' population and *forasteros* without land about 23 percent of all Indian communities. Klein, *Concise History of Bolivia*, 122.

26. Ministerio de Asuntos Campesinos y Agropecuarios, *Censo Agropecuario, 1950*, ii. The same information broken down by regions is offered on page iv. In the Bolivian altiplano (La Paz, Oruro, and Potosi), there were 2,832 large estates that controlled more than 4 million hectares, and 3,267 communities that controlled 6.8 million hectares. In the valleys (Cochabamba, Tarija, and Chuquisaca), there were 4,266 large estates that controlled 6 million hectares and only 387 Indian communities who controlled 305,868 hectares. This shows that Indian communities were still predominant on the altiplano and that large estates had aggressively controlled the valleys. In the valleys, landlords controlled 57 percent of the land, and a growing number of landlords without colonos controlled 28 percent of the land. Ministerio de Asuntos Campesinos y Agropecuarios, *Censo Agropecuario 1950*, page iv.

27. Left and nationalist intellectuals such as Tristán Marof, Carlos Montenegro, Augusto Céspedes, José Antonio Arze, Ricardo Anaya, Walter Guevara Arze, and Víctor Paz Estenssoro popularized the term and turned it into a crucial political weapon against the elite that allegedly ruled only in favor of the mineowners' interests.

28. Writing about the colonial rural elite in Sud Yungas, Klein demonstrated that the hacendado class exhibited important variations from the colonial period—from landlords who held a few hundred of hectares to those who owned vast sections of the province, such as the famous Tadeo Diez de Medina. Klein, *Ayllus y haciendas*, 21.

29. See INRA-LP, Sud Yungas, box 12, file Charvina Grande.

30. Ministerio de Agricultura, Ganadería y Colonización, *Estudio Agro económico de la provincias Los Andes, Omasuyos e Ingavi*, 4. See also Saavedra, *El problema integral del indio*, 2.

31. Leaders of the indigenous movements in present-day Bolivia often use the phrase "our uses and customs" to defend judicial practices, ritual, and political

practices against state-imposed practices. It is surprising to find this phrase used by landlords in the first decades of the twentieth century to defend the colonato system. Eduardo del Granado, lawyer and representative of the Bolivian Rural Society defended colonato as a protection of Bolivian traditions and customs in his conference. "El presente estudio crítico," 77. Landowners individually made similar claims. For example, when referring to the system of work in his hacienda, landlord Maximo Mendoza claimed that it was based in "our uses and customs." INRA-LP, Omasuyos Province, box 26, file Merke Achacachi. Also, the testimonies of property sale usually assess that the sale includes all "uses and customs," a masked way of specifying that colonos are included in the sale. Testimony of sale of *sayaña* in Chulumani from Enriqueta viuda de Farrachol and Modesta Enriqueta y Maria Candelaria Faffachol to Eloy Álvarez Plata, December 14, 1923, in INRA-LP, Sud Yungas Province, box 2, file Cuchu Chajno. See also INRA-CBBA, Germán Jordán Province, box 5, file Monte Redondo.

32. Ronald James Clark neatly describes colonos' obligation in the hacienda. Clark, "Land Reform and Peasant Market Participation," 154–57. See also Gotkowitz, *Revolution for Our Rights*, 136; Dandler and Torrico, "From National Indigenous Congress," 338. Court cases offer vivid details of the system of work in the haciendas. Colonos of hacienda Kehuiñal San Antonio reported they worked under the whip of the majordomo four times a week. They worked both in the hacienda in the countryside and in the town in Tarata. On top of that, they had to deliver eggs and chickens for the owner, and they had to run all her errands. They had to pay the landlord for the use of the pastures. INRA-CBBA, Germán Jordán Province, box 6, file Kehuiñal San Antonio.

33. Claim of Víctor Patiño Flores representing the peasant union claims that they were allowed to use a tractor only once and they had to pay for the fuel. June 29, 1954. See INRA-CBBA, Germán Jordán Province, box 1, file Laloma.

34. "Bolivian landlords relied on an especially severe system of service tenantry known as colonato. As haciendas became more market-oriented in the post–Chaco War era, the burdens of an already arduous system multiplied. Landlords in certain parts of the country violated long standing customary arrangements by heightening labor and service duties and transferring taxes to resident workers." Gotkowitz, *Revolution for Our Rights*, 134.

35. Archivo Historico de la Prefectura de Cochabamba, Expedientes de Prefectura, booklet titled "Libro de convenios entre propietarios y colonos" (Totora, 1888).

36. Since the 1940s the government of Enrique Peñaranda expropriated a number of haciendas and turned them into agricultural farms that operated under the control of the military, the university, or the Ministry of Agriculture. All of them continued using the system of colonato. See Supreme Resolution, February 26, 1942, Gaceta Oficial. For a detail description of Peñaranda's policies, see US Agency for International Development, *Preliminary Historical Review.*

37. In his study of the hacienda in Peru, Joan Martínez-Alier argues that despite their subordination colonos' income was higher than that of waged peasants. Colonos' access to a plot of land and pastures within the hacienda granted them economic security that was unavailable to salaried laborers. Martínez-Alier, *Haciendas, Plantations, and Collective Farms*, 72–78.

38. See INRA-CBBA, Germán Jordán Province, box 4, file Liquinas.

39. Léons and Léons, "Land Reform and Economic Change," 276.

40. Pledge of landlord Maria Salinas refused to grant a plot of land after the agrarian reform to her former majordomo who had received, she argued, one-fifth of the production prior to the revolution. Then she added that this practice was common in the region. Statement from May 18, 1956, in INRA-CBBA, Germán Jordán Province, box 5, file Lote 14.

41. Pledge of Esteban Mamani, February 5, 1955, in INRA-LP, Omasuyos Province, box 11, file Tari.

42. Gotkowitz details the rise of colonos' and comunarios' protests in the countryside, demanding that local authorities enforce the Toro and Busch decree in favor of the peasantry. Gotkowitz, *Revolution for Our Rights*, 132, 146–59. Jorge Dandler and Juan Torrico recount the case of hacienda Yayani, where "campesinos of the suyo of Tirita filed a suit in 1940 against the overseer and patron based on a labor-related incident: a peasant was viciously assaulted by the overseer and threatened with death. His workmates defended him and interposed themselves to avoid further problems. The entire group and the assaulted man were imprisoned in Cochabamba." Dandler and Torrico, "From the National Indigenous Congress," 340.

43. Dandler and Torrico, "From the National Indigenous Congress," 338.

44. In Omasuyos, the files of the prefectura are packed with judicial pleas between landlords Eulogio Franco and Imaña. Although the fight started as a debate about the limits of the properties, it escalated when both landlords declared that there had been deadly encounters between the colonos of both sides. See, for example, the telegram in which Eduardo Imaña declares: "Last Sunday colonos from hacienda Murumamani instigated by their landlord Eulogio Franco seized and burned my property in Collpani. I ask for guarantees and protection. Signed by Eduardo Imaña." Statement, Prefect to Subprefect, in Archivo de La Paz–Expedientes de Prefectura (hereafter, ALP-PE), box 111, May 19, 1949.

45. Colonos from hacienda Compi (Omasuyos Province) filed a judicial plea (to the prefectural office) against the mayordomo, Julio Coca, stating he had whipped them. Telegram from prefect of La Paz to subprefect of Omasuyos, ALP-PE Correspondencia, box 110, April 10, 1945. Alberto Rivera documents colonos' complaints against their landlords in Cochabamba. See Rivera, *Los terratenientes de Cochabamba*, 117–99.

46. In every demand for land expropriation (recorded in agrarian files in the National Institute for Agrarian Reform), colonos had to declare how long they had been working for the hacienda. According to the law, they had to prove they

had served at the hacienda for more than two years. Agrarian Reform Decree-Law 3464, August 2, 1953, Article 82, Gaceta Oficial.

47. Dandler and Torrico, "From the National Indigenous Congress," 338.

48. Analysis of the court cases reveals that many of the colonos working in the haciendas in Sud Yungas came from Peru, some from indigenous background and some of African descent.

49. Ministerio de Agricultura, Ganadería y Colonización, Dirección General de Economía Rural, Bolivia, *Estudio agro económico*, 4.

50. Congressman Salmón defended this argument in the parliament. *La Calle*, August 14, 1943.

51. See INRA-LP, Omasuyos Province, box 11, file Pajchani Grande. In a similar vein, the colonos of hacienda Huallpero in Germán Jordán referred to having good work conditions. They declared they had from one to three months a year of vacation time. Whenever they went to the city to work at the landlord's home, they were offered food, and they had their afternoons free. Since the landlord owned a movie theater, they could also have free tickets to get into the cinema. And they were not physically mistreated. INRA-CBBA, Germán Jordán Province, box 3, file Huallpero 2222. See also INRA-LP, Sud Yungas Province, box 11, file El Calvario.

52. Carter, "Revolution and the Agrarian Sector," 233.

53. Knight, *Mexican Revolution*, 1:3.

54. Barragán, "Entre polleras, lliqllas y ñañacas," 96.

55. Harris and Albó, *Monteras y guardatojos*, 49–53.

56. Dandler, *El sindicalismo campesino en Bolivia*, 57.

57. Soruco, *La ciudad de los cholos*, 48, 51, 77.

58. James Malloy depicts the social status people acquired by becoming landowners before the revolution: "the possession of land was fundamental, almost mystical." Malloy, *Bolivia*, 189.

59. See INRA-CBBA, Germán Jordán Province, box 2, file Monte Redondo, 1553–, 1, and box 3, file Chullpas Banda Arriba.

60. Qayum, Soux, and Barragán, *De terratenientes a amas de casa*, 16–17, 75.

61. Leinaweaver, *Circulation of Children*, 5.

62. ALP-PE, boxes 109, 110, 111, 112 (years 1939 to 1952); ALP-Ministerio de Agricultura (years 1939 to 1944); and Archivo Historico de la Prefectura de Cochabamba, years (1944–1952). Hundreds of telegrams between Corregidor and Subprefectura refer to cases of violence among landlords.

63. Serulnikov, *Subverting Colonial Authority*, 14–15; Lucca, *El sistema de la tenencia*, 7; Léons, "Political Economy of Agrarian Reform," 91–93; Ari, *Earth Politics*, 230.

64. Léons and Léons, in "Land Reform and Economic Change," contend that in Yungas there were three type of workers in the haciendas—that is, colonos, chiquiñeros, and yanaperos: "*Colonos* were the backbone of the hacienda force" (273). "A *colono* received a house and land for his own use on which he cultivated

both subsistence and cash crops. Colonos were subject to *pongueaje*. Although the landlord owned all the land, the usufruct of the *peons* over their own parcels was quasi permanent and was transferred to their heir" (275). "*Chiquiñeros* were the small but steady stream of migrants from the altiplano to the Yungas haciendas. An individual new to the area could be given a small plot of land dedicated to the cultivation of coca leaves and some land for subsistence but not house in return for one day of labor per week" (275). "*Yanapero* also received land for labor but in this case the terms were formalized in a contract since he did not live on the estate. The labor obligation owed by the *yanapero* was calculated in terms of so many days' labor per *mita*" (276).

65. Léons and Léons, "Land Reform and Economic Change," 273. At the time of the hacienda regime these different categories implied different conditions of work. The person who could fully work for the landowner could receive a plot of land. To do so, this probably meant he had other relatives who could help him fulfil his duties at the hacienda and at their own plot.

66. William Carter and Xavier Albó note that, in the Bolivian and Peruvian altiplano, haciendas encapsulated entire Indian communities that remained almost intact after the 1953 agrarian reform. Carter and Albó, "La comunidad aymara," 460.

67. Gotkowitz argues that in Cochabamba "*arrimantes* were landless men and women—often extended family members—who owed their obligation directly to the *colono*." Gotkowitz, *Revolution for Our Rights*, 138.

68. The size of a plot varied considerably from one region to another and from one hacienda to the other.

69. *Originario* and *agregado* were terms widely used on the altiplano and in the yungas.

70. INRA-CBBA, Germán Jordán Province, box 08.09.08, file Monte Redondo 11310 N Contori 5509, Owner Sandalio Salzar Velasquez and Honorina Ochoa. A *pegujal* is a plot of land for colonos' usufruct in a hacienda.

71. Robert Smale referrs to the flexible character of the mining workforce in *I Sweat the Flavor of Tin*, 28, 30–31. For testimonies of former colonos both on the altiplano and in the valleys, see *Tenemos pechos de bronce*; and Ranaboldo, *El camino perdido*.

72. The slogan "To Cultivate Is to Be Patriotic" appeared on the front page of the Banco Agrícola Magazine, *Revista Campo* 1, no. 3 (July 1947).

73. Alcalde, *La vida de Alberto Rodriguez Ríos, Colono*, 9; Unzueta, *Valle*, 65; Marof, *La tragedia del altiplano*; Céspedes, *Sangre de mestizos*.

74. Gotkowitz, *Revolution for Our Rights*, 142–43.

75. Supreme Decree, February 11, 1942, Gaceta Oficial.

76. Supreme Resolution, February 26, 1942, Gaceta Oficial, orders the creation of the experimental farm of Carangas (Oruro). Decree, May 27, 1942, Gaceta Oficial. orders the creation of the agricultural colonies of Warnes (Santa Cruz) and

Santa Ana (Beni). Supreme Decree, June 12, 1942, Gaceta Oficial, orders the creation of a school of agriculture in La Paz and Chuquisaca, each of them with their own experimental farm. See also US Agency for International Development, *Preliminary Historical Review.* The US State Department sent a mission to Bolivia led by Merin Bohan, and the Bohan Report recommended diversifying the Bolivian economy to steer investment away from tin and toward petroleum and agricultural development. Lehman, *Bolivia and the United States*, 78, 117.

77. Supreme Decree, February 11, 1942, Gaceta Oficial.

78. Sanjinés, *La reforma agraria* (1945).

79. General manager's report, September 9, 1955, INRA-LP, Omasuyos Province, box 11, file Pajchani Grande.

80. "Una visita a la provincia Los Andes," *Revista Bolivia* 10, no. 93 (September 1945): 18–19.

81. Bolivia showed in the early twentieth century and in smaller scale tendencies that were similar to those that took place in Chile and Peru from the late nineteenth century onward: the orientation of the hacienda production to the markets, landlord accumulation of land and political power, and the ferocious repression of all peasant demands in the countryside or political debates at the national level concerning conditions of work in the countryside. Although landlords in Bolivia had a number of mechanisms to coerce their labor force, Loveman's description of the hacienda in Chile—such as gated haciendas to control the entry and exit of the workers or haciendas private jails—seemed to expose an even more violent and controlled system in Chile than in Bolivia. Loveman, *Struggle in the Countryside*, 29–34. For a comparison of the Bolivian, Chilean, Cuban, Peruvian, Mexican, and Venezuelan cases, see Hogan, "Agrarian Reform and the Modernization of Agriculture." See also Albertus, *Autocracy and Redistribution*, 142–89.

Chapter Two: The Indian Problem and the Agrarian Question under Debate

A previous version of this chapter was published in Spanish as "La modernidad esquiva: debates políticos e intelectuales sobre la reforma agraria en Bolivia (1935–1952)," *Revista Historia y Cultura*, no. 29 (2012): 23–50.

1. Gotkowitz, *Revolution for Our Rights*; Hylton "Tierra común," 133–95; Langer, *Economic Change*; Langer, "Andean Rituals of Revolt"; Larson, *Trials of Nation Making*, 202–45; Lehm and Rivera Cusicanqui, *Los artesanos libertarios*; Mamani, *Taraqu*; Mamani, Alejo Ticona, and Condori Chura, *El escribano de los caciques apoderados*; Rivera Cusicanqui, *Oprimidos.*

2. Kevin Young underscored that, in contrast with MNR's paternalistic views of the Indian, the urban anarchists and followers of some Marxist currents had a more respectful approach to indigenous demands. Young, *Blood of the Earth*, 18.

3. Marta Irurozqui suggested that the idea of a race war was more likely to be the product of Creole fear than Indian aspirations. Irurozqui, "Sound of the Pututos," 100.

4. Barragán, "Los títulos de la corona," 26.

5. Gotkowitz, *Revolution for Our Rights*, 48.

6. In their study of the Jesus de Machaca rebellion, Roberto Choque and Esteban Ticona pointed out that the causes of the rebellion were the landlords' illegal appropriation of Indians' communal lands and local authorities' common and daily mistreatments. Choque Canqui and Ticona Alejo, *Sublevación*, 12, 14. Langer presented a more complicated scenario when studying the rebellion of Chayanta. He argued that comunario rebels were not looking to undermine the hacienda system but, rather, to replace the landlords (becoming the new landlords of those lands). By highlighting colonos' poor conditions of work, comunarios hoped they would be recognized as the legal owners of the land and secure colonos' labor for themselves. According to Langer, the process that obliged some members of Indians to become colonos of other comunarios was already taking place in several indigenous communities. Langer, "Andean Rituals of Revolt," 229. Also focused on the analysis of the Chayanta rebellion of 1927, Forrest Hylton analyzed the urban-rural connection between comunario leaders, radical artisans, and urban intellectuals in the making of the revolt. Hylton, "Tierra común," 137–42, 170–75.

7. John S. Sandor, *Bolivia's Radical Tradition: Permanent Revolution in the Andes* (Tucson: University of Arizona Press, 2011), 21; Malloy, *Bolivia*, 67. Young argued that, although most "of the writers and formal leaders . . . were male, urban, and mestizo, some also concerned themselves with the exploitation of women, peasants, and Indians." Young, *Blood of the Earth*, 19.

8. Klein, *Parties and Political Change*, 89–90.

9. Malloy, *Bolivia*, 95–96.

10. Marof cited in Schelchkov, "En los umbrales," 6.

11. Marof, *La tragedia del altiplano*, 26. See also Schelchkov, "En los umbrales," 13.

12. Alfredo Sanjinés was a prominent Bolivian politician and writer prior to the revolution. He published *Más fuerte que la tierra* and *El Quijote mestizo*.

13. Sanjinés, *La reforma agraria* (1932), 365. The text was republished in 1945. In the new edition, Sanjinés included his 1937 interview with Trotsky about the agrarian question in Bolivia. One of the most interesting elements of the interview is his reading of Bolivia based on Trotsky's observations. When Trotsky proposed "using" the indigenous community structure to collectivize land tenure under the state's auspices, Sanjinés noted that such collectivization would be met with resistance not only from the landlord elite but among Indians themselves since they were deeply tied to their individual plots [*sayañas*]. Sanjinés described the "Indian" as "individualistic, egoistic, and exclusionary." Trotsky also suggested that a gradual expropriation of the latifundia could be achieved through a stricter taxation policy that would force owners to turn over uncultivated lands.

14. Klein, *Orígenes*, 123.

15. Mendieta, *Entre la alianza*, 280–81.

16. Schelchkov, "La izquierda en la posguerra del Chaco," 76.

17. Cote, *Oil and Nation.*

18. Malloy, *Bolivia*, 87.

19. Dandler, *El sindicalismo campesino*, 64–66.

20. Dandler pointed out that the monastery sold large portions of its property during the first decades of the twentieth century. It sold three hundred hectares in 1905 and one thousand hectares in 1915. Dandler also stated that in many cases these transfers created harder work conditions for the colonos. Dandler, *El sindicalismo campesino*, 63–64.

21. The colonos Desiderio Delgadillo and Pedro Delgadillo, from the league of ex-combatants, met with Dávalos, Revuelta, and Cuellar and all of them together met with Eduardo Arze Loureiro, the recently named secretary of peasant affairs in the Ministry of Labor. Dandler, *El sindicalismo campesino*, 66, 68, 69. A second case that gained media attention was the one that involved the municipality of Vacas, also in Cochabamba. There, the colonos organized a union and petitioned to lease a hacienda that belonged to the municipality. Sanchez, "Hacienda, campesinado," 177–79; Antezana-Ergueta and Romero-Bedregal, *Historia de los sindicatos campesinos.*

22. Historians Forrest Hylton, Gabrielle Kuenzli, Carlos Mamani, among others, have demonstrated that non-Indian and Indian alliances were neither unprecedented nor unusual. Their work referred to the earlier alliances between Indian leaders and the Liberals at the end of the nineteenth century, with the Republicans during the first decades of the twentieth century, and with radical intellectuals in the 1920s. Hylton, "Tierra común," 161; Kuenzli, *Acting Inca*, 3, 7, 28; Mamani, *Taraqu*, 72–73; Mendieta, *Entre la alianza*, 150–57; Young, *Blood of the Earth*, 18–19.

23. Waldo Alvarez, then minister of labor, recounted in his memoir how a delegation of colonos from Santa Clara approached him to ask for his help in the quest for recognition for the recently organized peasant unions. He agreed to support the colonos. In an official visit to the city of Cochabamba, he visited the rural town of Cliza, and he encouraged local officials to protect peasants' rights. Local officers, who usually sided with landlords, were surprised to receive such an order from a government minister. Álvarez Plata, *Memorias del Primer Ministro Obrero*, 211–13.

24. Decree, January 22, 1937, Gaceta Oficial.

25. The elites' program to civilize the Indian through education is outlined in Brienen, "Clamor for Schools," 617.

26. The decree was actually signed by President Carlos Quintanilla in September 9, 1939, because of the abrupt death of President Germán Busch.

27. Antezana-Ergueta and Romero-Bedregal, *Historia de los sindicatos campesinos*, 27. It is not surprising that landlords organized the SRB, the national association that represented landlords from all departments, the same year President Toro forced the Santa Clara Monastery to sell its plots to the colonos. It was a direct response to the government's action.

28. Antezana-Ergueta and Romero-Bedregal, *Historia de los sindicatos campesinos*, 27.

29. Malloy, *Bolivia*, 92.

30. Barragán, *Asambleas constituyentes*, 140–41, 145–46. See also Gotkowitz, *Revolution for Our Rights*, 167–82; República de Bolivia, *Constitución Política del Estado*, October 28, 1880, Gaceta Oficial.

31. Klein, *Parties and Political Change*, 289. Also Klein, *Orígenes*, 328.

32. Honorable Roman F., República de Bolivia, *Redactor de la Honorable Convención Nacional*, 1938, 255. In the same vein, congressman Lijerón Rodriguez argues that Bolivia is very different from Mexico, thus Bolivia cannot copy Mexican legislation. República de Bolivia, *Redactor de la Honorable Convención Nacional*, 1938, 259, BAH-ALP.

33. Bilbao Llano, República de Bolivia, *Redactor de la Honorable Convención Nacional*, 1938, 285, BAH-ALP.

34. Walter Guevara Arze, República de Bolivia, *Redactor de la Honorable Convención Nacional, 1938*, 285, BAH-ALP. See also Klein, *Parties and Political Change*, 289–90. Walter Guevara Arze had a long political career, and his political affiliations changed greatly over time. In the 1938 national convention, he was one the most radical left-wing voices demanding to return land to indigenous communities. In 1941, along with Paz Estenssoro, he founded the MNR. After the 1952 National Revolution, which granted power to the MNR, Guevara was often seen as the most conservative voice within the party, repeatedly clashing with left-wing Juan Lechín Oquendo. Disillusioned with the MNR, he founded the MNR-Authentic in 1960. In 1964, Guevara supported the military coup d'état of General René Barrientos that toppled the MNR from power.

35. Klein, *Orígenes*, 334.

36. Barragán, *Asambleas constituyentes*, 140; Gotkowitz, *Revolution for Our Rights*, 128. Both authors point out that the 1938 constitution was crucial as it gave legal recognition to the indigenous communities for the first time in Bolivian legislation.

37. Antezana and Romero, *Historia de los sindicatos campesinos*, 48.

38. Primer congreso intermaericano de indianistas, *Reglamento, temario y agendas*.

39. Elizardo Pérez along with Avelino Siñani were the founders of the *escuela-ayllu* of Warisata, "which was intended to provide a curriculum especially geared towards the needs of the indigenous peoples of the Bolivian highlands." As Brienen indicates, the government later adopted this model for use in the lowland regions of Santa Cruz, La Paz, Beni, and Pando departments. Brienen. "Clamor for Schools," 616.

40. Primer congreso interamericano de indianistas, *Reglamento, temario y agendas*, 3.

41. Gotkowitz, *Revolution for Our Rights*, 160.

42. Finot, "Discurso pronunciado." Carlos Gonzalo de Saavedra, the son of Abdón Saavedra, made this same argument in his book *El problema integral del indio*, 2. What is noteworthy in the text is not so much the proposal itself but the fact that the author calls it a truly socialist proposal.

43. Gotkowitz argues: "in most general terms indigenismo constitutes a field of dispute over national identity, regional power, and rights that places 'Indians' at the center of politics, jurisprudence, social policy, or study." In Bolivia, "an important cohort of Republican Party politicians . . . championed indigenista policy initiatives, especially in congressional sessions of the 1920s." Gotkowitz, *Revolution for Our Rights*, 44.

44. Antezana and Romero, *Historia de los sindicatos campesinos*, 74. Aside from the peasants' unions of Cliza and Vacas, peasants organized several unions in Higuera-Huayco (Tarija), Coca Marco (Arque, Cochabamba), Kochi (Punata), and Iscayachi (Tarija). These unions were all created on municipal or ecclesiastical rural properties.

45. Landlords and merchants were organized in powerful regional societies, such as the Sociedad de Propietarios de los Yungas (SPY). Yet, the creation of the SRB at the national level in 1940 was the conservative response to the organization of unions on the left.

46. Decree, September 9, 1939, Gaceta Oficial.

47. Gotkowitz, *Revolution for Our Rights*, 146, 153.

48. University Federation of Oruro and SRB cited from *Tierra*, August 21, 1942.

49. Coati was created by the Supreme Resolution of July 17, 1942, Gaceta Oficial. The Supreme Decree of July 18, 1942, enacted the creation of the three penal colonies: Coati, for prisoners coming from La Paz, Oruro, and Potosí; another one without specific geographic location for Cochabamba, Tarija, and Chuquisaca departments, and Ichilo for prisioners from Santa Cruz, Beni, and Pando departments. Gaceta Oficial.

50. *La Calle*, August 14, 1943.

51. *La Calle*, August 15, 1943.

52. Supreme Decree, May 18, 1943, Gaceta Oficial.

53. Supreme Decree, December 20, 1946, Gaceta Oficial. President Villarroel also reviewed the concessions of land in the lowlands for the extraction of lumber and quinine, threatening to withdraw those concessions that had not met their productive goals.

54. *El Diario*, August 28, 1944.

55. "Habló Tamayo en la Convención sobre temas de Política Agraria" *La Calle*, November 30, 1944. The left-wing Tristán Marof described Franz Tamayo as a "landlord and poet" in the prologue of his book *La tragedia del altiplano*, 4.

56. "Habló Tamayo en la Convención sobre temas de Política Agraria," *La Calle*, November 30, 1944.

57. *El Diario,* September 2, 1944. Videla was afraid that Paz and Guevara's proposal would challenge the principles of the Disentailment Law enacted in 1874.

58. *El Diario,* September 2, 1944.

59. Paz Estenssoro, *Discursos parlamentarios,* 312.

60. Agrarian Law for Tarija (Ley Agraria para Tarija), December 15, 1944, Gaceta Oficial.

61. Gotkowitz contends that peasants' demands were only a marginal element of the MNR's political agenda. She argues that, "of the three anti-oligarchic parties that were established after the Chaco War, the MNR was the least indigenista. The party's closest supporters were mineworkers, urban laborers, and the middle class; its manifesto made no explicit call to mobilize Indians." Gotkowitz, *Revolution for Our Rights*, 195.

62. A similar congress took place in Ecuador in 1944. See Becker, *Indians and Leftists,* 78.

63. Hylton, "Tierra común," 175. Lehm and Rivera also highlight the connections between the recently organized unions of workers and artisans and the caciques apoderados. Lehm and Rivera Cusicanqui, *Los artesanos libertarios,* 40–42.

64. Lehm and Rivera Cusicanqui, *Los artesanos libertarios,* 22–29; Young, *Blood of the Earth,* 18–23.

65. Antezana-Ergueta and Romero-Bedregal, *Historia de los sindicatos campesinos,* 53.

66. Reported in *Inti,* May 17, 1941.

67. Reported in *El Diario,* February 10, 1946.

68. *Tierra,* August 11, 1942.

69. *Tierra,* August 11, 1942.

70. *La Calle,* August 21, 1943.

71. *Primer congreso indígena boliviano. Principales ponencias,* La Paz, May 10–15, 1945.

72. *La Calle,* September 22, 1944. Caciques apoderados have been demanding protection to their rights to the Comisión de Asuntos Indígenas in Congress.

73. From *El País,* February 16, 1945, in Gotkowitz, *Revolution for Our Rights,* 207.

74. Gotkowitz, *Revolution for Our* Rights, 207.

75. *Revista Bolivia* (founded by the Bolivian writer Gustavo Adolfo Otero) 9, no. 89 (May 1945).

76. *Revista Bolivia* 9, no. 89 (May 1945): 29–31.

77. Gotkowitz, *Revolution for Our Rights,* 221.

78. Arze, *Bolivia bajo el terrorismo,* 34.

79. Arze, *Bolivia bajo el terrorismo,* 34–35.

80. Anaya, *Unidos venceremos,* 39.

81. Reported in *La Razón,* April 3, 1945.

82. Anaya, *Unidos venceremos,* 39–40.

83. Gotkowitz, *Revolution for Our Rights*, 268–306.

84. Anaya, *Unidos venceremos*, 42.

85. "Hilacata Grabriel Cruz from Chayanta was forced to declare and denounce in the Parliament that members of the PIR Aberlardo Villalpando and Alfredo Arratia were subverting the Indians in this area. They told Indians not to accept white people on their lands and that land belonged to the Indians since the Incaic period" República de Bolivia. *Redactor de la Honorable Cámara de Diputados. Congreso Ordinario de 1943*, 1:499.

86. Klein, *Parties and Political Change*, 381–82.

87. Klein, *Parties and Political Change*, 384.

88. Dandler and Torrico, "From the National Indigenous Congress," 363–70.

89. Anaya, *Cuestiones de derecho agrario*, 9.

90. Decree, April 4, 1879, Gaceta Oficial.

91. Anaya, *Cuestiones de derecho agrario*, 18.

92. Anaya, *Cuestiones de derecho agrario*, 19.

93. The Socialist Party formulated a similar proposal in 1944. Partido Socialista, *Bases y programa de acción*.

94. Del Granado, "El presente estudio," 46, 46-47.

95. Del Granado, "El presente estudio," 49, 51.

96. Del Granado, "El presente estudio," 72.

97. Del Granado, "El presente estudio," 75.

98. Del Granado, "El presente estudio," 77.

99. Rolón-Anaya, "La evolución del derecho," 105–6.

100. Rolón-Anaya, "La evolución del derecho," 115.

101. Reyeros, *El pongueaje*.

102. Ministerio de Educación, "Encuesta del Departamento de Asuntos Indígenas," 7, 8, 9.

Chapter Three: Revolution Comes to the Countryside

1. The conservative presidents were Tomás Monje Gutiérrez (1946–1947), Enrique Hertzog, and Mamerto Urrolagoitia. Indian and peasant rebellions sparked in La Paz, Oruro, the west of Cochabamba, and North Potosí. As a response to indigenous and peasant uprisings that spread across the altiplano, President Enrique Hertzog sent troops to the countryside and ordered the imprisonment and confinement of hundreds of peasant leaders as well as members of the FOL, the POR, and the MNR. Gotkowitz describes in great detail this wave of indigenous and peasant rebellion in the countryside following the overthrow of President Villarroel. Gotkowitz, *Revolution for Our Rights*, 233–67.

2. During the first two years of the revolution, President Paz Estenssoro signed three historic decrees that transformed the politics and the economy of the country: universal suffrage (in July 1952), which extended formal political participation to women and indigenous populations; nationalization of the mines (in October

1952), through which the state gained control over the most important export economy; and agrarian reform (in August 1953), which dismantled feudal haciendas in the western highlands, abolished the system of forced peasant labor, and redistributed expropriated lands to peasants.

3. "Mañana sera firmado el decreto de reforma agraria en un acto acorde con su trascendencia histórica," *La Nación*, August 1, 1953; "En Ucureña culminó ayer la revolución nacional," *La Nación*, August 3, 1953; "Hemos echado al suelo un régimen feudal que impedía el progreso de Bolivia, declaró el Primer Mandatario," *La Nación*, August 3, 1953; "Ecos del grandioso acontecimiento en Ucureña," *La Nación*, August 3, 1953.

4. James Wilkie interviewed Víctor Paz Estenssoro in 1966. To understand the origins of the country's agrarian reform, Wilkie asked about the differences between his proposal to Congress in 1944 and the text of the Agrarian Reform Decree-Law enacted in 1953. Paz Estenssoro answered that there were no differences. In 1944, he argued, he had already stated that the principle the country should follow was that of giving land "to those who work it," and this was the major principle that guided the decree of 1953. Wilkie asked if the fact the government enacted the decree of Agrarian Reform Decree-Law eighteen months after Estenssoro assumed power meant that the peasant problem was less a priority for his party, the MNR, compared with the problem of mining. Estenssoro responded: "Immediately after we assumed power—realizing that the gravest problem in Bolivia was the condition in which the peasant found himself—we created a special ministry: the Ministry of Peasant Affairs, was empowered to carry out land reform. But even if we carried out land reform, we could not acquire, overnight, the miraculous power to bring the peasants up to the cultural level of the other social sectors. Therefore, there was going to be a delay as a result of centuries-old domination and exploitation to which the peasant had being subjected. . . . Besides carrying out the land reform . . . , [the Ministry of Peasant Affairs] was charged with peasant education, which could not be compared to education in the cities precisely because of the state of cultural backwardness in which the peasants found themselves, beginning with the language problem." But in the end, the redistribution began anyway, without waiting for Indians to be educated, Wilkie interrupted. Wilkie, *Measuring Land Reform*, 28.

5. James Kohl surveyed this initial period of the revolution between April 1952 and the moment the government enacted the agrarian reform in August 1953. He argues: "During these few months a revolutionary movement seized power and began the dismantling of a regime entrenched for centuries." Kohl, "Peasant and Revolution," 238–39. In this article, Kohl shows the MNR's initial agenda focused primarily on regulating labor relations in the haciendas.

6. In one such letter, Remigio Ramos, a petitioner from Isla del Sol, La Paz, stated that he had been imprisoned in 1947 and 1948, when his landlord discovered he was collecting money from other colonos to buy school supplies for the peasants' children. ABNB-PR 765, Letter from Remigio Ramos Ticona, September 5, 1952.

Colonos from the Los Andes province of La Paz demanded the release of Carmelo Quispe, Martín Condori, and Clemente Chávez. In their petition, they referred to how landlord Jorge Loza put some of their leaders in jail and murdered others. They recounted the death of Marcela Chávez de Quispe who was "whipped to death by the majordomo as per Loza's orders." See ABNB-PR 765, petition from Carmelo Quispe Chávez, August 1, 1952.

7. "Amnesty for Workers, Miners, and Peasants," Decree, July 22, 1952. *Gaceta Campesina*, (August 1952), 78.

8. *Los Tiempos*, September 9, 1952; Tapia from "Ayer, en acto sencillo, fueron liberados los indigenas de Yayani," *Los Tiempos*, September 12, 1952.

9. After 1945 peasant leaders organized other national political meetings where they mainly ratified the rights peasants had won under President Villarroel. For instance, in 1947 the press noticed that forty-eight hundred comunarios and colonos leaders met in Caranguillas (Oruro) to ratify those rights. "4.800 delegados asistieron a un congreso indigenal llevado a cabo en Caranguilla," *La Noche*, February 5, 1948.

10. The pact secured peasant support for the MNR and was ratified by peasant assemblies in Azanaques, Machacamarca in Oruro, and Cohoni, Titicaca, and Pallamarca in La Paz.

11. "Campesinos hacen conocer el pacto suscrito con el MNR," *El Diario*, January 13, 1953.

12. Laura Gotkowitz summarizes pre-1952 peasant and indigenous petitions as "a revolution for our rights," which is the title of her book in English. The diverse demands that colonos and comunarios raised to the president after 1952 can also be viewed as a general plea for their rights. Gotkowitz, *Revolution for Our Rights*, 247.

13. Decrees 318, 319, 320, dated May 1945, in Ministerio de Asuntos Campesinos, *Gaceta Campesina* 1 (August 1952): 38–44.

14. The government enacted new decrees regulating the working conditions of former colonos, detailing the new institutions (*inspectores de trabajo agrario*) in charge of supervising labor on the haciendas, and specifying the allowable modes of punishment for peasants who failed to fulfill their duties. Decree 3281, December 16, 1952, and Decree 3376, April 30, 1953.

15. To track POR activities in the countryside, see John Sándor, *Bolivia's Radical Tradition*, 121.

16. Following the words of Chavez Ortiz, Minister Lechín Oquendo cautiously said: "We will not follow foreign models, we need to look to our own reality." See "La concentración campesina del domingo. Palabras del ministro de asuntos campesinos," *Los Tiempos*, December 24, 1952.

17. "Los dirigentes sindicales son los únicos responsables de las diferencias en el agro," *Los Tiempos*, January 14, 1953.

18. The government implemented the contracts in the three regions analyzed in this book—Yungas, Omasuyos, and Germán Jordán. Although the Ministry of

Labor did not have a record of these contracts, I found a few inserted in the agrarian reform files. Landlords used them as evidence that they were willing to reach agreements with their former colonos. See Agrarian Court files in the INRA in La Paz and Cochabamba. There are also references to these contracts in ABNB-PR, letters sent to the president or the Ministry of Peasant Affairs.

19. Labor contract between landholder and colonos, dated July, 16, 1954. INRA-LP, Omasuyos Province, box 26, file Merke Achacachi.

20. Agrarian reform court cases can be found in INRA-LP, Sud Yungas Provinces, box 3, file Machacamarca; box 3, file Quiaconi el rancho; box 4, file Coca Yapu; box 5, file Guayrapata; box 7, file El Calvario; box 7, file Chica.

21. Gotkowitz, *Revolution for Our Rights*, 89–91.

22. Paz Estenssoro stated in a personal talk with journalist Drew Pearson that he was afraid of finishing his days being hung as President Gualberto Villarroel had been in 1946. See Bedregal, *Víctor Paz Estenssoro*, 441.

23. Telegram from the Minister of Government to the Ministry of Peasant Affairs, January 5, 1953, ALP-PE, Ministry of Peasant Affairs correspondence, Los Andes Province, box 138 (1952–1957).

24. Letter from the Capinota Peasant Union to the Ministry of Peasant Affairs, May 11, 1953. ABNB-PR, file 803.

25. Letter from Ministry of National Defense to the President, May 20, 1953. Letter initially sent from the commander of the third ministry region in Cochabamba on April 29, 1953. ABNB-PR, file 803.

26. A law passed on October 15, 1927, directed coca taxes to the construction of roads operated under the supervision of the Sociedad de Propietarios de los Yungas (SPY), the Yungas Landlords Society. See also the laws from June 6, 1931, from December 21, 1948, and from January 4, 1950. In 1950, President Urrolagoita made a concession to the Rural Landlords Society of Provincia Carrasco granting it public loans from the Central Bank for the construction of the road from Montepuco to Chimore.

27. "Erróneo comportamiento de la Sociedad de Propietarios de los Yungas," *La Nación*, February 13, 1953; "Las poblaciones yungueñas piden la intervención de la Sociedad de Propietarios," *La Nación*, April 16, 1953; "Está al servicio de contados latifundistas la Sociedad de Propietarios de los Yungas," *La Nación*, March 31, 1953; "Piden disolución de la junta de propietarios," *La Nación*, October 6, 1953; "Con la intervención de la sociedad de propietarios de Yungas cúmplese un justificado anhelo popular," *La Nación*, May 12, 1953.

28. The FRC of Cochabamba published an op ed at least once a week in the newspaper *Los Tiempos* of Cochabamba, and the same happened in Oruro with the newspaper *La Patria*.

29. "Se apresan a falangistas," *Los Tiempos*, February 3, 1953. The article reports that Hugo del Granado, who was one of the most important lawyers of the SRB, was detained. "Varias detenciones politicas se produjeron ayer en esta

ciudad," *Los Tiempos*, March 22, 1953; "Detenidos politicos fueron confinados a Corque [Oruro]," *Los Tiempos*, April 14, 1953; "Detenidos politicos en Sucre," *Los Tiempos*, April 18, 1953.

30. Rivera Cusicanqui, *Oprimidos*, 142; Lagos, *Autonomy and Power*, 3. Fernando Calderón also stressed the corporatist top-down character of peasant unionization. Calderón, "Un siglo de luchas sociales," 434. See also Ari, *Earth Politics*, 149.

31. Albó argues that unions often got their name from indigenous communities that used to be former haciendas and independent communities. Communities became unions to obtain perks from the government (the translation is mine). Albó, "Etnias y pueblos originarios," 468.

32. Calderón, "Un siglo de luchas sociales," 429.

33. Ley General del Trabajo, dated August 23, 1943, Article One.

34. Gordillo, "Modernity, Politics and Identity," 23. In this same vein Albó argues that, although the agrarian question was already in debate, there was no initial consensus on launching a program of agrarian reform. He also highlights the existing division within the MNR between the left wing, which pushed for land redistribution, and the right wing, which warned about the dangers of implementing an agrarian reform. Albó, "Etnias y pueblos originarios," 467.

35. Gordillo, "Modernity, Politics and Identity," 33.

36. Lagos, *Autonomy and Power*, 3.

37. Gordillo recounts how MNR top leaders such as Víctor Zannier, peasant coordinator in Cochabamba, started to appear in public with armed peasants, showing off the power and support that the government had in the countryside. Gordillo, "Modernity, Politics, and Identity," 64.

38. "Primer ejército del campesinado," *Los Tiempos*, March 25, 1953; "Campesinos de Cochabamba organizaron un regimiento," *Los Tiempos*, April 1, 1953. There was another Gualberto Villarroel Regiment in Cochabamba that had five thousand members, with its seat in Tiquipaya. "Una concentración de 25.000 campesinos se hará el día 29 en la zona de Tiquipaya," *La Nación*, June 3, 1953.

39. The Germán Busch First Cavalry Regiment in Patamanta, with six thousand members, was conformed by colonos of Churiaque, Santa Ana, Chirioco, Paxiamaya, Corapata, and communities Seguenca, Chacuha, Peñas, Suriqueña, Esuquellario, Cruzani, Carbeza Catacora, Bayrocondo, Yaurechambi Patamanta, Chapamaya, Cotoca, Carabellque, Tomoyo, Capacazé, and Quella-quella. For the Gualberto Villarroel First Infantry Regiment in Aroma Province, see "Más de 100.000 campesinos asistirán a los festejos de la revolución nacional," *La Nación*, April 8, 1953. Letter from the secretary of the president to the Ministry of Peasant Affairs, letter initially sent from Eusebio Vega et al. to the president. ABNB-PR Letter from April 21, 1953. For the 9 de Abril Regiment in Collantaca, Los Andes, see "Concentración campesina habrá hoy en Collantaca, canton Laja," *La Nación*, July 28, 1953.

40. Gordillo, who documented peasant activities in the upper and lower valleys of Cochabamba, showed how concerned government officials were because they were losing the control of peasant unions. Gordillo, "Modernity, Politics and Identity," 63.

41. Letter from the Prefect Froilán Calderón to the Ministry of Peasants Affairs, January 27, 1953, ALP-PE, Ministry of Peasant Affairs correspondence, box 138 (1952–1957).

42. Patch describes the powerful impression made on him by the sight of "a solid mass of campesinos with rifles over their shoulders" in a *chichería* (a rustic rural bar) in Ucureña, Cochabamba, in 1954. "The Progress of Land Reform in Bolivia," Land Tenure Center, Discussion Paper 2, 1963, 5.

43. "El POR incita a la ocupacion directa de las tierras por los campesinos," *Los Tiempos*, February 24, 1953; "Levantamiento armado de masas, ocupación de tierras bajo gobierno obrero campesino," *Los Tiempos*, February 25, 1953. Both articles referred to the radical agenda they claimed ignited the recent peasant upheavals in Pojo and Colomi (Cochabamba).

44. To track MNR's campaign against POR in 1953, see Sándor, *Bolivia's*, 124.

45. "Informe del jefe de policia sobre la sublevación de Colomi," *Los Tiempos*, November 9, 1952.

46. "Agitadores Poristas pretenden sabotear la reforma agraria," *La Nación*, April 23, 1953. See also "Enérgica prevención de la prefectura de Cochabamba a los agitadores indigenas," *La Nación*, January 29, 1953; "El POR en connivencia con la rosca trata de impedir la reforma agraria," *La Nación*, February 1, 1953; "Arresto de agitadores indigenales poristas," *La Nación*, February 3, 1953; "Contra la desorientación de los campesinos," *La Nación*, February 3, 1953; "Cuando la fraseología izquierdizante es estupidez y reacción," *La Nación*, February 6, 1953.

47. Letter from Minister of Peasant Affairs Ñuflo Chavez Ortiz to the President, March 23, 1953, ABNB-PR, file 803.

48. "Hemos expulsado a los extremistas dice la federación de campesinos," *Los Tiempos*, January 27, 1953; "Agitadores campesinos arrestados por la policía," *Los Tiempos*, January 31, 1953; "Centenares de indigenas de Ucureña y, en actitud hostil, pidieron libertad de varios dirigentes," *Los Tiempos*, February 1, 1953.

49. Sándor, *Bolivia's*, 125, 141–44.

50. The leading forces behind these demands in the 1940s were the PIR, POR, MNR, Federación Obrera Sindical (FOS), the Workers Union Federation, and FOL. "The Indian uprisings and the political turmoil had destroyed this year's harvests: The Bolivian Rural Society in a letter to the Minister of Economy states that the harvest of potatoes of this year is lost: This chaos is the direct consequence of the government's demagogues attitude who had not imposed discipline in the countryside: The government needs to stop the crisis that threats the country." *El Diario*, May 19, 1946.

51. "La producción agrícola. El rendimiento disminuirá a un 50 por ciento," *Los Tiempos*, November 6, 1952; "Agitación campesina causa la ruina de la agricultura," *Los Tiempos*, April 28, 1953. See also "Desolación en los campos," *Los Tiempos*, January 24, 1953.

52. "Los campesinos fueron exhortados a elevar la producción agrícola," *La Nación*, January 25, 1953; "Campesino regala su cosecha de papas para la revolución nacional," *La Nación*, March 29, 1953; "Empezó la cosecha agrícola que en algunos casos sera recogida directamente por el campesinado," *La Nación*, April 30, 1953; "El gobierno encomienda la cosecha de este año y la preparación de tierras a los sindicatos campesinos," *La Nación*, May 1, 1953.

53. Letter from Moisés Castro to Irene Riveros, March 29, 1953. INRA-LP, Omasuyos Province, box 11, file Tari.

54. Several authors have looked at the regional impact of the agrarian reform in Bolivia. See, for example, McEwen, *Changing Rural Society*; Heyduk, *Hacienda System*, 2–8. Heath, Erasmus, and Buechler, *Land Reform*.

55. Moisés Castro, letter to Irene Riveros, September 13, 1954, INRA-LP, Omasuyos Province, box 11, file Tari.

56. Cornelio Chávez, Supervisor de Tecnificación Agraria, October 21, 1954, INRA-LP, Omasuyos Province, box 11, file Tari. Chávez visited haciendas Pajchani Molino, Pajchani Grande, Chijipina Chico, Chijipina Grande, Taramaya, Putuni, Jahuira Lacka in Omasuyos.

57. Cornelio Chávez, Supervisor de Tecnificación Agraria, October 21, 1954, INRA-LP, Omasuyos Province, box 11, file Tari.

58. Cornelio Chávez, Supervisor de Tecnificación Agraria, October 21, 1954, INRA-LP, Omasuyos Province, box 11, file Tari. We find similar problems in Los Andes province in La Paz: "We, comunarios from Tujjuyu in Pucarani [Los Andes province], submit a complaint that our lands are now under the control of Carlos Ponce de León who refuses to pay the salaries according to the laws president Víctor Paz Estenssoro had established in favor of the colonos." *La Nación*, May 1, 1954.

59. INRA-LP, Sud Yungas Province, box 2, file Colonia San Pedro; box 5, file San Jose de Chaui; box 5, file Poxi; box 6, file Colimpampa; box 8, file San Isidro; box 10, file San Martin y San Martin Chico.

60. INRA-LP, Sud Yungas Province, box 8, file San Isidro.

61. Letter from Nataniel Aspiazu to Minister of Peasant Affairs, August 14, 1954, ABNB-PR, file 836.

62. Moisés Castro, letter to Irene Riveros, September 13, 1954, INRA-LP, Omasuyos Province, box 11, file Tari.

63. Letter from Patricio Huaylluco, Secretario General, Celso Bautista, Secretario de Relaciones, and Hilario Hillaquita, Secretario de Actas, Sindicato Agrario de Chillamani (Coripata), October 20, 1953, ABNB-PR, file 803.

64. "En Ucureña culminó ayer la revolución nacional," *La Nación*, August 3, 1953.

65. Letter from September 24, 1953, ABNB-PR, file 803.

66. "Potosi: Tranquilidad en el Agro," *La Nación*, March 7, 1953; "Excesos aislados (Cochabamba)," *La Nación*, April 25, 1953; "Hay completa tranquilidad en el campo, declara el Prefecto (La Paz)," *La Nación*, July 31, 1953.

67. "Campesinos no sitiaron a la poblacion de Tacopaya," *Los Tiempos*, May 1, 1953.

68. "Centenares de indígenas sembaron pánico en Tarata," *Los Tiempos*, May 12, 1953.

69. "Alarmantes noticias de Anzaldo hicieron vivir momentos de angustia a Cochabamba," *Los Tiempos*, May 12, 1953; "Retorno de Anzaldo. Comisión que fue para constatar sucesos sangrientos," *Los Tiempos*, May 13, 1953.

70. Gotkowitz describes colonos' and comunarios' demands for their rights. When looking at the wave of rebellions in 1947, she quotes peasant leaders who defended "a revolution against exploitation and misery . . . and abuses" and advocated for "a revolution in defense of our rights." Gotkowitz, *Revolution for Our Rights*, 3. See also pages 89, 91, 146.

71. Harris and Albó, *Monteras y guardatojos*, 83. Also Harris and Albó recalled the complicated relations between miners and peasants. Displaying in front of peasants their mestizo identity, their proficiency in Spanish, and their skill in urban manners, miners tried to reproduce hierarchical relations with peasants in the countryside. When talking about miners and peasant rivalries, Gordillo assesses that in the valleys of Cochabamba 554 mining and 623 peasant families benefited from land. He continues: "the fact that so many miners had benefited with land was not well received by the peasant leadership." Gordillo, "Modernity, Politics and Identity," 81. Gordillo argues that the former miners sought to organize farming cooperatives under their leadership, which also sparked peasant distrust. Gordillo, "Modernity, Politics and Identity," 84.

Chapter Four: Redistribute Land Soon

1. "Con la reforma agraria no se pretende asaltar a nadie, dijo el Dr. Vera Tapia," *La Nación*, April 11, 1953.

2. A handful of studies identify Achacachi (Omasuyos Province) and Ucureña (Germán Jordán Province) as the epicenter of the political conflict in the initial years of the agrarian reform. In 1958 the conflict would move to the town San Pedro de Buena Vista (North Potosí). See Rivera Cusicanqui, *Oprimidos* (2010), 146, 150–51; Albó, "Etnias y pueblos originarios," 468.

3. "Principios de Acción del Movimiento Nacionalista Revolucionario," *La Nación*, January 19, 1953.

4. The prefect of Cochabamba wrote a private letter to the Ministry of Government, in which he argued: "Although the MNR succeeded in organizing peasants into unions almost everywhere in the countryside, I must tell you that 90 percent of them no longer respond to the MNR." The prefect argued that (irresponsible,

mercenary) "agitators have helped to create the confusion in the countryside. The peasants now believe that a more powerful man will come to implement land redistribution." Letter dated December 17, 1952, in ABNB-WGA, box 30.

5. The Cochabamba Rural Society (FRC) called for a meeting to analyze the question on agrarian reform. Participants complained that the MNR had not consulted them. The members of this meeting were Eduardo Tardío, Eduardo del Granado, Miguel Mercado Moreira, David Paz Mendez, Juan Suarez. To focus on social issues: José Ramirez Velarde, Raimundo Gregoriú, Carlos Antezana Lozada, Carlos Zabalaga, Luis Villaroel. To analyze economic issues: Agustín Villegas, Rafael Gumucio Irigoyen, Octavio Lafaye, Simón Paz. For technical issues: Ricardo Rivero Torres, Rene Saavedra, Jose Coca Achá, Abel Coronel, and Humberto Gandarillas. *El Diario*, January 6, 1953. See ABNB- WGA, box 30, Agrarian Reform.

6. Arze Cuadros, *Bolivia*, 160.

7. "Se crea comisión de reforma agraria," *La Nación*, January 21, 1953; "El decreto supremo sobre la reforma agraria sera firmado el 2 de agosto, dia del indio," *La Nación*, March 28, 1953; "Con doce miembros quedó constituida por decreto la comisión que estudiará la reforma agraria," *La Nación*, March 21, 1953.

8. The newspaper *La Nación* published a letter that designated Federico Álvarez Plata as their representative to the Commission for Agrarian Reform, allegedly signed by delegates of the peasant federations such as Gabino Apaza, Toribio Salas, Modesto Escobar, Gregorio Perez, and many others. "Delegados de los campesinos ante la comisión de reforma agraria," *La Nación*, March 6, 1953.

9. In her study of the government of President Gualberto Villaroel, Gotkowitz highlights the strikingly paternalistic posture of the government toward the majority of the Indian population, which usually implied the negation of Indian agency. Gotkowitz, *Revolution for Our Rights*, 229. See also Gordillo, "Modernity, Politics and Identity," 63. In the 1950s dozens of newspaper articles referred to the need to civilize, rehabilitate, or assimilate the Indian to the nation. See, for example: "Rehabilitación del indio," *La Nación*, January 4, 1953; "Factores para incorporar al indio a la vida civilizada," *La Nación*, February 13, 1953. An article published in *La Nación* assesses the work of the revolution as follows: "Our President is seeking to redeem the Indian from his degrading, illiterate, and unconscious condition and to integrate him into society as a citizen with rights." *La Nación*, April 15, 1953. This view was not a prerogative of the MNR, the Trotskyist Left also shared this point of view. See for example the speech of Ernesto Ayala Mercado, a prominent representative of the POR who was a member of the Commission for Agrarian Reform. Ayala Mercado, "Qué sucede con la reforma agraria?" 6–7.

10. "Credenciales de delegados campesinos rechazados en la IV Convención del MNR," *Los Tiempos*, February 10, 1953.

11. Speech by Federico Álvarez Plata, Secretario Ejecutivo del Comité Político Nacional del MNR, MNR National Convention. "Inauguración de la convención nacional del MNR," *La Nación*, February 4, 1953.

12. "Hemos logrado la total unidad del partido dijo el vice-presidente al clausurar la convención," *La Nación*, February 3, 1953.

13. Salmón quoted from "Punto de Vista sobre la Reforma Agraria," *La Nación*, April 27, 1953.

14. "Reforma agrarian técnica y social," *Los Tiempos*, September 17, 1952.

15. "Reforma o revolución agraria," *Los Tiempos*, January 31, 1953. See also "El dereho de propiedad," *Los Tiempos*, April 11, 1953.

16. "Reforma agraria en la China roja," and "El fracaso de las granjas colectivas es lección util digna de estudio en Yugoslavia," both in *Los Tiempos*, April 8, 1953.

17. "Consideraciones sobre el discurso revolucionario," *Los Tiempos*, October 7, 1952.

18. "La reforma agraria es una necesidad historica en Bolivia," *Los Tiempos*, October 24, 1952; Juan Rodriguez Iriarte, "Hacia la reforma agraria en Bolivia," *Los Tiempos*, February 8, 1953.

19. "Régimen impositivo en relación con el agro," *Los Tiempos*, February 4, 1953; "Acotationes a la reforma agraria," *Los Tiempos*, March 25, 1953.

20. "Por la reforma agraria," *Los Tiempos*, January 27, 1953.

21. Pablo Cardona, "La reforma agraria en Bolivia será copia de la de Guatemala?" *Los Tiempos*, January 31, 1953.

22. "Director de núcleos indigenales hace sugerencias para la reforma agraria," *La Nación*, January 13, 1953.

23. "De los objetivos de la reforma agraria habló el ingeniero Valdivia," *La Nación*, January 27 1953.

24. Alberto Mendoza López, "Consejo de colonización y agricultura nacional: Banco Agrícola, educación campesina y abolición del latifundio improductivo," *La Nación*, March 14, 1953.

25. "Planteamiento del problema agrario y la crisis actual," *La Nación*, February 16, 21, 1953.

26. Edwin Moller, "Tercer proyecto de reforma agraria discute la Central Obrera Bolivia. Tesis presentada en forma de proyecto de resolución ante la COB por el miembro de la comisión designada al efecto, señor Edwin Moller," *La Nación*, July 5, 1953.

27. "El POR, en connivencia con la rosca trata de impedir la reforma agraria. En Cochabamba soliviantó con mentiras a grupos campesinos," *La Nación*, February 1, 1953; "Cuando la fraseología izquierdizante es estupidez y reacción," *La Nación*, February 6, 1953; "La revolución boliviana y la demagogia del POR," *La Nación*, March 29, 1953.

28. "Seminario latinoamericano sobre el problema de la tierra," *Gaceta Campesina* 3 (August 1953): 200. The meeting was organized by the FAO in May and June 1953.

29. "Bolivia enviará tres delegados al seminario sobre agrarismo," in a meeting in which they were expected to discuss issues of land fragmentation, latifundio,

state land, indigenous communities, policies to improve rural structure of property. *La Nación*, March 24, 1953. Ernesto Galarza explains the deplorable condition of work in the countryside in south of the United States. "El movimiento campesino sindical en los EEUU," *La Nación*, April 17, 1952. "Chile impulsaría la reforma agraria," *La Nación*, May 6, 1953; "General Perón reveló que la Argentina realizará una amplia reforma agraria," *La Nación*, June 13, 1953; "Expúsose el problema agrario de Bolivia en la reunión de Campina," *La Nación*, June 15, 1953.

30. "La comisión de reforma agraria recibió al doctor Edmundo Flores. El economista mexicano explicó la experiencia de la reforma agraria en su país," *La Nación*, May 12, 1953.

31. Flores, "Economics of Land Reform," 151–52.

32. "Eminente político guatemalteco llegó ayer de visita a La Paz," *La Nación*, January 14, 1953. See also "Habla el doctor Estrada de la Hoz," *La Nación*, January 18, 1953; "Con la reforma agraria se consolidó la revolución nacional en Guatemala," *La Nación*, January 23, 1953.

33. "Eminente político guatemalteco llegó ayer de visita a La Paz," *La Nación*, January 14, 1953.

34. "La reforma agraria en Bolivia será copia de la de Guatemala?" *Los Tiempos*, January 31, 1953.

35. Adolfo García Montenegro, ambassador from Guatemala said: "We suppressed about 60 plots, and we may have to suppress even more." *La Nación*, January 16, 1953.

36. Edmundo Flores, in a memoir of his work as a Bolivian advisor on agraria reform, states that he warned President Paz Estenssoro that economic compensation for landlords was going to be purely symbolic and that it would cause substantial food shortages in the cities. Flores, "Progress of Land Reform," 5.

37. López Bermudez, "La reforma agraria en Bolivia en concepto del secretario del departamento agrario de México," *La Nación*, July 24, 1953.

38. Agrarian Reform Decree-Law, August 2, 1953, Articles 11–14, Gaceta Oficial.

39. Agrarian Reform Decree-Law, August 2, 1953, Articles 156–57, Gaceta Oficial.

40. It seems that Bedregal saw in Paz Estenssoro a much more radical leader than he probably was. It is important to remember that the PIR and the MNR had been fiercely fighting with one another since the 1940s. Both claimed that the other party was not revolutionary enough. Bedregal's book was part of this political dynamic. Bedregal, *Victor Paz Estenssoro*, 455–56.

41. "En Sicasica o Ucureña sería firmado el decreto de la reforma agraria," *Última Hora (La Paz)*, July 17, 1953. The author discusses the various motivations behind the choice of Sicasica in La Paz or Ucureña in Cochabamba.

42. "En Santiago de Huata habrá el 2 [de agosto] una segunda concentración campesina," *La Nación*, August 1, 1953; "Una magna asamblea hubo en Tarija

de apoyo a la reforma," *La Nación*, August 1, 1953; "En Copacabana hubo una manifestación de campesinos en apoyo de la reforma agraria," *La Nación*, August 3, 1953; "Alcanzó vastas proporciones en Camiri la concentración agraria," *La Nación*, August 9, 1953.

43. Agrarian Reform Decree-Law, August 2, 1953, Gaceta Oficial.

44. Benton, *Agrarian Reform*, 52

45. Decree 3525, October 15, 1953, about agrarian bonds, Gaceta Oficial. In the decree, the emission of bonds was ruled to pay indemnifications.

46. Agrarian Reform Decree-Law, August 2, 1953.

47. Agrarian Reform Decree-Law, August 2, 1953, Article 78, cited in Benton, *Agrarian Reform*, 55.

48. Decree-Law 4008, March 30, 1955, Gaceta Oficial. According to this decree, landowners of provinces Iturralde, Tipuani (Province of Larecaja) Caranavi (Province Nor Yungas), and Province Caupolicán in La Paz; the east provinces of Chapare and Carrasco in Cochabamba, all the provinces of Santa Cruz with the exception of Vallegrande, Florida, Ñuflo Chávez, and Andrés Ibañez; Luis Calvo Province in Chuquisaca, Gran Chaco, O'Connor in Tarija, and Ballivian Province in Beni could sell their plots without facing expropriation.

49. Decree-Law 3471 mandated the creation of Servicio Nacional de Reforma Agraria (SNRA), August 27, 1953, Articles 31–48.

50. "Lázaro Cardenas aplaude la reforma agraria en Bolivia," *La Nación*, September 19, 1953; Portes Gil (former president of Mexico), "La reforma agraria en Bolivia," *La Nación*, August 2, 1953.

51. "*El Combate* de Quito comenta la reforma agraria en Bolivia," *La Nación*, September 24, 1953.

52. Flores, "Progress of Land Reform," 5; Francisco Martínez de la Vega, "Bolivia y Guatemala ante la conciencia de America," *La Nación*, December 11, 1953.

53. "Reforma agraria en Bolivia por Luis Alberto Sánchez," *La Nación*, November 3, 1953. Luis Alberto Sanchez is one of the most renowned intellectuals of Peru in the twentieth century. Coronado states that Sanchez was one of the early proponents of cultural mestizaje in the Andes. See Coronado, *Andes Imagined*, 60.

54. James Dunkerley points out the political role that US academics played during the 1960s in broadcasting the positive but moderate features of Bolivia's reform. Dunkerley notes how, in the context of virulent US operations in Latin America at the time of the Cold War, US academics preferred to highlight Bolivia's reformist and social democratic character: "While the MNR was still in office, sympathetic US academics stressed its reformist, social democratic qualities, not least to stave off a full Cold War offensive by Washington of the type that succeeded so well against Guatemala in 1954 and failed so spectacularly against Cuba from 1960." Dunkerley, "Bolivian Revolution," 332n31.

55. "Las masas campesinas serán la más sólida plataforma para la economía." *La Nación*, January 4, 1953.

56. Although the Bolivian and Guatemalan agrarian reforms shared the same principles, the MNR did not face some of the obstacles that Arbenz faced even before a covert operation by the CIA overthrew him. A month after President Arbenz signed his first verdicts for land expropriation, Guatemala's Supreme Court declared the Agrarian Reform Decree 900 unconstitutional and ordered the lower courts to suspend their work. Neither did Bolivia have to challenge such a powerful landowner as the United Fruit Company. Gleijeses, *Shattered Hope*, 155; Gleijeses, "Agrarian Reform of Jacobo Arbenz," 459–60.

57. Decree dated November 16, 1939, Gaceta Oficial.

58. "La finca de las carmelitas en Cliza sera vendida a los mismos colonos," *La Nación*, May 3, 1953.

59. "En Cochabamba parcelarán tierras de una orden religiosa en beneficio de colonos," *La Nación*, May 7, 1953.

60. Judicial petition from Jorge Soliz, July 7, 1954, INRA-CBBA, Germán Jordán Province, box 12, file acumulado, Santa Clara.

61. Judicial petition from Rosa Valenzuela, abbess of the Santa Clara Monastery, and Antonio Cabrerizo, power of attorney of the monastery, June 22, 1954, INRA-CBBA, Germán Jordán Province, box 12, file acumulado Santa Clara.

62. Judicial petition from Rosa Valenzuela, abbess of the Santa Clara Monastery, and Antonio Cabrerizo, power of attorney of the monastery, July 15, 1954, INRA-CBBA, Germán Jordán Province, box 12, file acumulado Santa Clara. It is worth noting that Guatemalan landlords attempted a very similar strategy—inflating the supposed value of their estates. They got caught because they had previously been deflating the price of estates for years so as to pay lower taxes. Gleijeses, *Shattered Hope*, 20n61.

63. Walter Guevara Arze, letter to the Bolivian bishop, October 10, 1955, AB-NB-WGA, box 30.

64. Jorge Soliz responded to Nélida Araoz on July 20, 1954, and to Eloina Lobo on July 26, 1954, INRA-CBBA, Germán Jordán Province, box 12, file acumulado Santa Clara.

65. Verdict of agrarian judge, October 9, 1954, INRA-CBBA, Germán Jordán Province, box 12, file acumulado Santa Clara.

66. Albó, *Achacachi*, 41. Founded in 1931, Warisata arose out of Aymara demands for education. Its leaders saw literacy as a crucial tool to fight the landowners' continued expansion over indigenous communities: "schools would enable Indians to gain access to the law as well as to legal documents for use in litigation and legal battles over land." Gustafson, *New Languages of the State*, 247.

67. Gustafson, *New Languages of the State*, 247. See also Brienen, "Clamor for Schools," 630–31.

68. Luciano Quispe was head of the rural council in the demands for expropriation in at least eight cases in Achacachi: INRA-LP, Omasuyos Province, box 17,

file Ckasina; box 33, file Tihimpampa-Taramaya; box 3, file CalaCala; box 3, file Antacollo; box 11, file Pajchani Grande; box 15, file Ocorani; box 41, file Taramaya Chico; box 98, file Pajchani.

69. INRA-LP, Omasuyos Province, box 17, file Ckasina.

70. INRA-LP, Omasuyos Province, box 3, file Cala-Cala.

71. Decree-Law 3471 Servicio Nacional de Reforma Agraria, August 27, 1953, Article 105.

72. Consuelo Millán quoted in Official Report from Cornelio Chávez, October 21, 1954. Luis Escobari cites the report in his pledge of January 23, 1956, INRA-LP, Omasuyos Province, box 98, file Pajchani.

73. Carlos Luis Terrezas demands that the judge stop the process of expropriation in Casamaya, February 11, 1955, INRA-LP, Omasuyos Province, box 1, file Casamaya.

74. Cornelio Chávez reported on the situation of six estates: Pajchani Molino, Jahuira Lacka, Taramaya, Pajchani Grande, Putuni, and Chijipina Chico.

75. Cornelio Chávez, Supervisor de Tecnificación Agraria, October 21, 1954, INRA-LP, Omasuyos Province, box 11, file Pajchani Grande.

76. Cornelio Chávez, Supervisor de Tecnificación Agraria, October 21, 1954, INRA-LP, Omasuyos Province, box 11, file Pajchani Grande.

77. Albó, *Achacachi*, 41–52.

78. Cornelio Chávez, Supervisor de Tecnificación Agraria, October 21, 1954, INRA-LP, Omasuyos Province, box 11, file Pajchani Grande.

79. Saravia's judicial petition, November 21, 1955, INRA-LP, Omasuyos Province, box 19, file Corpa Calachaca.

80. The emphasis is mine. See INRA-LP, Omasuyos Province, box 11, file Tari. See also in Omasuyos Province, box 31, file Chococopa Chico; box 17, file Ckasina; box 15, file Ocorani; box 28, Chahuira Chico.

81. Most peasant unions began presenting their demands for expropriation by May or June 1954, and rural councils set the public hearings between September and December 1954. A series of demands began in the late 1950s (1957–1958). In general, these demands were presented by small or medium-sized landowners who petitioned for the consolidation of their properties. These small or medium-sized landowners expected that, once the initial revolutionary impulse had passed, they would be able to consolidate their property legally. However, if there were colonos working on these properties, the colonos demanded that the authorities transform the case into one for land expropriation.

82. Cornelio Chávez, Supervisor de Tecnificación Agraria, October 21, 1954, INRA-LP, Omasuyos, box 11, file Pajchani Grande.

83. Dunkerley, "Bolivian Revolution," 332n31.

84. Flores, "Progress of Land Reform," 5.

Chapter Five: Land to Its Original Owners

A previous version of this chapter was published in *Hispanic American Historical Review* 97, no. 2 (2017): 259–96.

1. Santos Cornejo et al. to Víctor Paz Estenssoro, September 4, 1952, ABNB-PR, file 765. The term *cacique principal* comes from the colonial period, when it referred to the native lord of a community. It is possible that the term was preserved in local community practice during the early republican period, but it appears that indigenous community leaders who engaged in land struggles in the late nineteenth and early twentieth centuries recovered the term after encountering it in the colonial documents and land titles that they found to defend their properties against hacienda encroachment. To track the genealogy of comunario leaders, see Ari, *Earth Politics*, 31–33.

2. The sharpest critique comes from Rivera Cusicanqui, *Oprimidos*, and her "Democracia liberal y democracia del ayllu." See also Albó, "Andean People in the Twentieth Century." Choque Canqui, Albó, and Ticona, *Cinco siglos de historia.*

3. Ari, *Earth Politics*, 149.

4. Decree-Law 3732, May 19, 1954, Gaceta Oficial.

5. Various caciques to Minister of Peasant Affairs Ñuflo Chávez Ortiz, July 10, August 14, 1953, ABNB-PR, file 803.

6. Santos Cornejo et al. to Ñuflo Chávez Ortiz, September 4, 1952, ABNB-PR, file 765. While most comunario petitions I have found were from La Paz department, Cornejo's letter suggests that Indian leaders claimed to represent a network that transcended the altiplano, where indigenous political coordination was most evident.

7. As Ari has shown, it was not new for indigenous leaders to refer to an Aymara republic. During the 1899 civil war, caciques apoderados named Indian leader Zárate Willka the president of the republic. Ari argues that this Aymara discourse was a nineteenth-century reinterpretation of the sixteenth-century Spanish law that created separate and distinct legal regimes, or republics, for the Spanish and the Indians. Ari, *Earth Politics*. 1–2, 37. Although these two legal realms were formally abolished after independence, several scholars have pointed out how the divisions they codified continued to be in force in postcolonial societies. Mark Thurner, *From Two Republics to One Divided.* Indian leaders like Willka found in the republic of Indians a powerful ideological tool amid ongoing racist and segregationist postcolonial practices that privileged ethnic distinctions despite the legal equality allegedly implemented after independence, which Silvia Rivera Cusicanqui has described as internal colonialism. Rivera Cusicanqui, *Violencias (re)encubiertas*, 39, 100.

8. Choque Canqui, "De la defensa"; Choque Canqui, Soria, Mamani, Ticona, and Conde, *Educación indígena*; Soria, "Los caciques apoderados"; Choque Canqui and Ticona, *Jesús de Machaqa*, 11–14; Gotkowitz, *Revolution for Our Rights*, 43–68; Rivera Cusicanqui, *Oprimidos* (2010), 99–100.

9. Gotkowitz reports having found restitution petitions in the provinces of Tapacarí and Arque, in Cochabamba, "precisely where the caciques apoderados had been based." Gotkowitz focuses on the first half of the twentieth century, but in her epilogue she notes that "although the agrarian reform privileged private over communal property, and ignored Indian communities' historic grievances, the outcome was neither inevitable nor easily imposed by the MNR. Available evidence indicates that Indian communities used the provision allowing the reinstatement of usurped communal land more frequently than previously thought." Gotkowitz, *Revolution for Our Rights*, 280–81.

10. Zulema Lehm A. and Silvia Rivera Cusicanqui recall the dispersion of the anarchist movement in La Paz city after the Chaco War. Lehm A. and Rivera Cusicanqui, *Los artesanos libertarios*, 11.

11. Gotkowitz, *Revolution for Our Rights*, 46–47, 192–93, 224–25.

12. Santos Cornejo to Víctor Paz Estenssoro, October 14, 1952, ABNB-PR, file 765.

13. Daniel Barreto, Samuel Aguilar, and Angel Durán to Víctor Paz Estenssoro, May 27, 1953, ABNB-PR, file 803.

14. Law September 28, 1868 Art 1, Gaceta Oficial.

15. Barreto, Aguilar, and Durán to Paz Estenssoro, May 27, 1953, ABNB-PR, file 803.

16. Cornejo et al. to Paz Estenssoro, September 4, 1952, ABNB-PR, file 765.

17. "Tres cuartas partes de la actual hacienda Taraco fueron arrebatadas a los indígenas por la fuerza," *La Nación*, January 14, 1953; "Denuncian usurpación de tierras la junta de vecinos de Taraco," *La Nación*, January 25, 1953.

18. Pedro Quispe and Juan Quispe (representing the Sindicato Agrario de Ex-comunarios de Guyahuani y Utavi) to Ñuflo Chávez Ortiz, September 8, 1953, ABNB-PR, file 803.

19. "Grave queja de comunarios," *El Diario*, December 10, 1952.

20. Letter "From all comunarios of Tamampaya" to Ñuflo Chávez Ortiz, March 27, 1953, ABNB-PR, file 803; letter, July 14, 1954, ABNB-PR, file 836. Scholars have shown that before the revolution, Indian and peasant uprisings threatened landlords' control in the countryside. See, for example, Gotkowitz, *Revolution for Our Rights*, 131–63, 233–67; Rivera Cusicanqui, *Oprimidos*, 99–100, 116–17, 123–28.

21. Gotkowitz, *Revolution for Our Rights*; Dandler and Torrico A., "From the National Indigenous Congress."

22. The dichotomy between rhetoric of nation and anti-nation had strong political resonance in Bolivia. The very influential writings of Carlos Montenegro and Augusto Céspedes—journalists, intellectuals, and founders of the MNR—used this dichotomy to give shape and content to Bolivian nationalism in the 1940s. Montenegro, *Nacionalismo y coloniaje*; Céspedes, *Metal del diablo*.

23. Francisco Paxifrati Luna (secretary general of the Sindicato Agrario de la Ex-comunidad Achaca) and Juan Quispe (secretary general of the Sindicato de la

Ex-comunidad Kasa Achuta) to Víctor Paz Estenssoro, August 14, 1953, ABNB-PR, file 803.

24. "Campesinos de Chivo reclaman sus sayañas," *La Nación*, July 31, 1953. The term *sayaña* implies that the land belonged to a member of an indigenous communities. The term would not be used to refer to the property of a non-Indian person.

25. Roseberry, "Hegemony and the Language of Contention."

26. Cornejo et al. to Paz Estenssoro, September 4, 1952, ABNB-PR, file 765.

27. Mariano Mayta to Paz Estenssoro, August 12, 1952, ABNB-PR, file 765.

28. Soria, "Los caciques apoderados"; Gotkowitz, *Revolution for Our Rights*, 15, 284. See also Mamani Condori, *Taraqu*, 127–30; Ari, *Earth Politics*, 107.

29. Lehm A. and Rivera Cusicanqui, *Los artesanos libertarios*, 40–43, 90–96; Gotkowitz, *Revolution for Our Rights*, 49. See also Rivera Cusicanqui, *Oprimidos*, 117, 125, 127, which highlights the links between rural insurrections, the FOL, and the Federación Agraria Departamental (FAD), the Departmental Agrarian Federation.

30. Ari, *Earth Politics*, 39, 42; Kuenzli, *Acting Inca*, 7–8, 19–20.

31. Dunkerley, "Bolivian Revolution," 338.

32. Almost every day, *La Nación* reported that numerous peasant representatives from all over the country had come to visit the president and the Ministry of Peasant Affairs. Several headlines described the specific character of the comunario petitions. See, for example, "Denuncian usurpación de tierras la junta de vecinos de Taraco," *La Nación*, January 25, 1953; "Representantes de 12 comunidades visitaron ayer *La Nación*," *La Nación*, January 25, 1953.

33. Paz Estenssoro used the dichotomy of the nation and anti-nation in multiple speeches when he was in Congress in the 1940s, in his political writing in exile from 1946 to 1952, and in his early speeches as president. See Paz Estenssoro, *Discursos y mensajes*, 15, 33, 43; Paz Estenssoro, *Discursos parlamentarios*, 109, 121, 133.

34. In April 1952, Paz Estenssoro created the Ministry of Peasant Affairs (MAC). On the first anniversary of the revolution, Minister Germán Vera Tapia explained that the government used the word "peasant" for this new ministry because it fit better with the revolutionary nationalist doctrine that rural workers' problems were class-based. Vera Tapia added: "the problem is that the ones who work the land are tied to an exploitative landlord." See "Homenaje ardiente a este día en el que Bolivia recién comenzó a gozar de su independencia y liberó a sus hijos del yugo atróz de la rosca," *La Nación*, April 9, 1953.

35. "Mensaje presidencial," *La Nación*, January 1, 1953. In this speech Paz Estenssoro also reappraised the government's most important accomplishments in rural areas: "rural courts to attend peasants' unfair dismissals," "new rural schools," and "encouraging the mechanization of agriculture and the organization of new cooperatives among peasants." This rather mild agenda shows the MNR's reluctance to make radical changes.

36. Eguino Zaballa, one of the most prominent indigenista intellectuals in Bolivia, participated at the First Inter-American Indigenista Congress in Pátzcuaro, Mexico, in 1940 along with a generation of artists, intellectuals, and politicians who would play a strong public role in the 1940s and 1950s, such as Eduardo Arze Loureiro, Yolanda Bedregal, Vicente Donoso Torres, Ernesto Fricke Lemoine, Cecilio Guzmán de Rojas, Tristán Marof, Alberto Mendoza López, Marina Núñez del Prado, Arturo Posnansky, and Alipio Valencia Vega. See *Primer Congreso*, 3. Eguino Zaballa also served on the official organizing committee for Bolivia's 1945 National Indigenous Congress. Gotkowitz, *Revolution for Our Rights*, 195. As head of the Bolivian Indigenista Institute he organized the Third Indigenista Congress in 1953. Unlike the 1945 congress, which included twelve hundred Indian delegates, the Third Indigenista Congress invited intellectuals and politicians to discuss the situation of Indian peoples. *Gaceta Campesina (La Paz)*, August 1952. The biannual *Gaceta Campesina* documented the work of the Bolivian Indigenista Institute, publishing the MNR's decrees in favor of the peasants and public speeches made by MNR leaders in the countryside in addition to recent linguistic, archaeological, and folklore research about Aymara or Quechua cultures.

37. Eguino Zaballa, "Contribución al planeamiento," 36.

38. Rivera Cusicanqui, *Violencias (re)encubiertas*, 27, 41–42, 126. Ari, *Earth Politics*, 15.

39. On the commission, see Supreme Decree 3301, January 21, 1953, Gaceta Oficial; "Por Decreto Supremo se crea la comisión de reforma agraria," *La Nación*, January 21, 1953; "La comisión de reforma agraria tiene un plazo de 120 días para presenter su informe al presidente," *La Nación*, January 21, 1953. On the peasant delegations, see Dunkerley, *Rebellion*, 68–69.

40. "Algo fundamental en el caso de la hacienda Taraco," *La Nación*, January 18, 1953.

41. "Cómo fueron adquiridas las propiedades que integran la hacienda Taraco," *El Diario*, January 11, 1953.

42. "Algo fundamental en el caso de la hacienda Taraco," *La Nación*, January 18, 1953.

43. "Representantes indígenas visitan *La Nación*," *La Nación*, January 24, 1953. See also "Dos simpáticos campesinos quechuas trajeron sus quejas a *La Nación*," *La Nación*, July 26, 1953; "5.000 indígenas expresaron ayer su incondicional apoyo al gobierno," *La Nación*, February 26, 1953; "Delegados indígenas retornan a sus bases," *La Nación*, January 26, 1953.

44. "5.000 indígenas expresaron ayer su incondicional apoyo al gobierno," *La Nación*, February 26, 1953; "Delegados indígenas retornan a sus bases," *La Nación*, January 26, 1953.

45. "Demandan que se firme el decreto de reforma agrarian en Taraco," *La Nación*, July 3, 1953. The last names are those of renowned and well-off families

in Bolivia. The article referred specifically to the Taraco communities of Pequeri, Chiara, Aymaya Chiripa, Calacala Chambi, Chivo, and Higuagui.

46. Larson, *Cochabamba*, 171–88.

47. "Antes de viajar, el presidente de la comisión de reforma agraria planteó numerosas sugerencias," *La Nación*, May 21, 1953.

48. Agrarian Reform Decree-Law, August 2, 1953, Article 42, Gaceta Oficial.

49. Decree-Law 3732, May 19, 1954, Gaceta Oficial.

50. Although the PIR had little political force in 1952, once the MNR emerged as the revolution's unquestionable head some former PIR leaders played a prominent role in the new government. See Field, *From Development to Dictatorship*, 3.

51. Arturo Urquidi to Víctor Paz Estenssoro, Cochabamba, June 10, 1954, ABNB-WGA, box 30, file Reforma Agraria.

52. In reference to Ecuador, Kim Clark argues that racialized perceptions of the Indian workforce often provided justifications for appropriating Indian lands for agroexport production. Clark, "Racial Ideologies," 373–74. See also Gould, "¡Vana Ilusión!"; Frank Safford, "Race, Integration, and Progress."

53. For example, "Tierras comunarias y sus poseedores," *La Nación*, May 21, 1954. A year later Paz Estenssoro enacted a new decree stressing that comunarios did not have the right to simply expel the colonos; they had to follow the procedures of the land restitution decree.

54. "Having noticed the constant attacks of comunarios and ex-comunarios against colonos, the Ministry of Peasant Affairs encourages them to use the law to reclaim their rights; otherwise they will be punished by the Penal Law." "Prevención a comunarios and ex-comunarios del Ministerio de Asuntos Campesinos," *La Nación*, August 25, 1953.

55. A rich and dense scholarship has documented Indian communities' robust defense of their communal lands during the republican period, especially after the 1874 Disentailment Law (Ley de Ex-vinculación) abolished communal landholding. Communities launched a broad movement led by their traditional authorities, the caciques apoderados, to defend their corporate land rights via their colonial corporate titles. Platt argues that Indian communities insisted on paying the colonial tribute to the Bolivian state in order to guarantee the state's recognition of their communal property. Platt, "Andean Experience," 307–9. See also Irurozqui Victoriano, *"A bala,"* 70; Langer, "El liberalismo y la abolición"; Klein, *Bolivia: The Evolution*, 152; Larson, *Trials*, 229–42; Gotkowitz, *Revolution for Our Rights*, 18–42; Ari, *Earth Politics*, 32–40.

56. The land restitution decree stated that the colonos already working the land would be able to stay on the property but would have to pay compensation to the original owners. Decree-Law 3732, May 19, 1954, article 7, Gaceta Oficial.

57. Ayala Mercado does not analyse the demands on land restitution. He transcribed the statistics from the CNRA. Ayala Mercado, *Qué sucede*, 14.

58. Servicio Nacional de Reforma Agraria (SNRA), "Evaluación de la Reforma Agraria 1964," 1964, ABNB-PR, file 1932. Unfortunately, the SNRA does not offer information about cases of restitution prior to 1960 or after 1964.

59. INRA-LP, Omasuyos Province, box 36, file Pongon Huyo Circapata.

60. INRA-LP, Omasuyos Province, box 15, file Suntía Grande.

61. INRA-LP, Omasuyos Province, box 10, file Challuyo.

62. See, for example, judicial petition, August 22, 1955, INRA-LP, Omasuyos Province, box 7, file Pacharía.

63. INRA-LP, Omasuyos Province, box 3215, file Pongon Huyo, no. 3382, Suntía Grande.

64. Juan Lanza Heredia, local judge's verdict. February 1, 1955, INRA-LP, Omasuyos Province, box 10, file Challuyo, vol. 2.

65. INRA-LP, Omasuyos Province, box 10, file Challuyo.

66. Judicial petition from Hilario Jallasi Colque, Gregorio Colque Guasco, July 23, 1956, INRA-LP, Omasuyos Province, box 25, file Pongon Huyo.

67. Judicial petition from Fabián Condori, July 7, 1955, INRA-LP, Omasuyos Province, box 25, file Pongon Huyo.

68. Judicial sentence by the *juez agrario móvil*, July 2, 1957, INRA-LP, Omasuyos Province, box 25, file Pongon Huyo. On November 22, 1962, a CNRA auto de vista established that the former colonos had bought their last piece of property from Mollinedo in 1959. After this, the legal battle involved only colonos and ex-comunarios.

69. INRA-LP, Omasuyos Province, box 25, file Pongon Huyo.

70. INRA-LP, Omasuyos Province, box 32, file Warisata.

71. Legal claim by Valentín Chuca, *hilacata*, March 1, 1961, INRA-LP, Omasuyos Province, box 48, file Comunidad Pallareti.

72. Albó refers to the bitter political disputes among peasant leaders in Achacachi in the late 1950s and 1960s. I suspect that the political conflict between leaders aligned with Paz Estenssoro versus the ones aligned to Walter Guevara or René Barrientos masked a more profound struggle for land between comunarios and colonos. Albó, *Achacachi*, 68–78.

73. Antezana, "Sistema," 60–61. Antezana's discussion of revolutionary nationalism also resonates with Roseberry's comments on hegemony, which he thinks of "not as a finished and monolithic ideological formation but as a problematic, contested, political process of domination and struggle." Roseberry, "Hegemony," 358.

Chapter Six: Land for Those Who Work It

1. INRA-LP, Omasuyos Province, box 35, file Pallareti.

2. Agrarian Reform Decree-Law, August 2, 1953, Articles 35, 36, 39.

3. Article 12 defines a latifundio as a combination of many factors: it is an unproductive, un-invested large estate based on servile labor relations. Agrarian Reform Decree-Law, August 2, 1953.

4. Agustín Villegas's judicial petition, July 20, 1954, INRA-CBBA, Germán Jordán Province, box 7, file Santa Lucía de Liquinas.

5. Peasant union's judicial claim, July 20, 1954, INRA-CBBA, Germán Jordán Province, box 7, file Santa Lucía de Liquinas.

6. Agustín Villegas's judicial petition, July 20, 1954, INRA-CBBA, Germán Jordán Province, box 7, file Santa Lucía de Liquinas.

7. On December 1, 1955, the Ministry of Agriculture issued Supreme Decree 4247, which allotted land to peasants who had been displaced because of the construction of the Angostura Dam in neighboring haciendas. The decree created severe conflicts among peasants. Colonos refused to receive displaced peasants on lands they had hoped to receive after the expropriation. These conflicts exploded primarily in the 1970s between the offspring of the colonos and the displaced peasants. See, for example, the case in INRA-CBBA, Germán Jordán Province, box 10 (CBA.08.10.13), file 18916.

8. Judge's verdict, April 4, 1959, INRA-CBBA, Germán Jordán Province, box 7, file Santa Lucía de Liquinas.

9. At the time of writing (2016) the value of this amount is US$167,667.

10. The case started in 1954, the president signed his verdict in 1960.

11. There is no reliable information on agricultural production in the country. The Bolivian government led the first agricultural census in 1950, and the second in 2013. Studies of the Comisión Económica para America Latina y el Caribe (CEPAL), the UN Economic Commission for Latin America and the Caribbean in the 1950s point out the challenge of building statistical data for agricultural prices or production, if not based on some qualitative data. CEPAL, *Campesinado y desarrollo agricola*, 1.

12. In general, most landlords on the altiplano put most of their capital into buying purebred cattle and the construction of barns, stables, and water troughs for the animals. In the valleys of Cochabamba, some built water pipes, deployed agricultural machinery, and used fertilizers. In Yungas, many invested in building and repairing roads and pathways from their property to the main roads and sawmills.

13. INRA-LP, Omasuyos Province, box 35, file Pallareti.

14. Putuni was a section in hacienda Taramaya. INRA-LP, Omasuyos Province, box 38, file Taramaya Grande.

15. INRA-LP, Omasuyos Province, box 28, file Chahuira Chico.

16. Cornelio Chavez, the CNRA's supervisor técnico, reported on the situation of eight haciendas in Omasuyos (Taramaya, Putuni, Chijipina Chico, Chijipina Grande, Pajchani Grande, Ckasina, Masaya y Pacharia). He informs peasant unions and peasant regiments of breakage on all these haciendas. Report from October 21, 1954, INRA-LP, Omasuyos Province, box 11, file Pajchani Grande.

17. See Maria Salinas's judicial petition, November 7, 1957, INRA-CBBA, Germán Jordán Province, box 5, file Lote 14. See also INRA-CBBA, Germán Jordán Province, box 9, file La Alcoholería.

18. Agrarian Judge's verdict. The exact date of the verdict is unclear because the second page of this document was missing. However, because of the previous and following reports we can tell that the judge ordered the verdict around December 1955. INRA-LP, Omasuyos Province, box 11, file Tari.

19. Technical Report October 24, 1956, INRA-LP, Omasuyos Province, box 11, file Tari.

20. Technical Report October 24, 1956, INRA-LP, Omasuyos Province, box 11, file Tari.

21. The situation was similar in Omasuyos and Sud Yungas (see charts in Appendix 6.1).

22. Agrarian Reform Decree-Law, August 2, 1953, Articles 32, 33. These articles established that colonos who had a plot on the estate could retain it, and the landlord could retain the rest. If a colono's plot was too small, the state would grant them land in the areas marked out for colonization (settlement).

23. Erasmus, "Land Reform and Social Revolution," 112, 114.

24. INRA-CBBA, Germán Jordán Province, box 2, file Monte Redondo, 1046.

25. In Germán Jordán, I found two cases of peasant landholders who faced claims for the expropriation of their properties. Peasants from Mizque in Cochabamba made similar claims. They argued that peasants who had never worked on those properties were seizing their lands. Letter to President Barrientos, November 27, 1965, ABNB-PR 1099.

26. Fermín Ayala, leader of the peasant union, October 19, 1954, rural council conclusive report, January 31, 1955, and judge's verdict, August 1, 1956, INRA-CBBA, Germán Jordán Province, box 2, file Monte Redondo, 1553-1.

27. Severino Fuentes's judicial petition, June 18, 1957, and CNRA's verdict, July 5,1957, INRA-CBBA, Germán Jordán Province, box 2, file Monte Redondo, 1553-1.

28. Verdict RS 103418, May 8, 1961, signed on May 8, 1961, by President Víctor Paz Estenssoro, Minister Roberto Jordán Pando, and Oficial Mayor de Asuntos Campesinos Eduardo Rosso Valdivia, INRA-CBBA, Germán Jordán Province, box 2, file Monte Redondo 1553-1.

29. Larson, *Cochabamba*, 172.

30. Hector Lorini's judicial pledge, November 28, 1955, INRA-LP, Sud Yungas Province, box 1, file Naranjani.

31. Mercedes Franco's pledge, September 3, 1956, INRA-LP, Omasuyos Province, box 31, file Cocani. In a similar vein, Juan Monterey, another landholder from Omasuyos, quoted the proverb "troubled waters, fisherman's gain" when referring of the several merchants or town villagers who were obtaining plots by taking advantage of the peasant union's demands for land expropriation. Juan Monterrey's pledge, April 7, 1959, INRA-LP, Omasuyos Province, box 41, file Taramaya Chico.

32. Winn and Kay, "Agrarian Reform and Rural Revolution," 137.

33. Seligmann, *Between Reform & Revolution*, 60. See also Seligmann, "Burden of Visions amidst Reform," 30, 36.

34. Mayer, *Ugly Stories*, 112, 134.

35. There were five legal cases related to the expropriation of the Quirogas. See cases INRA-CBBA, Germán Jordán Province, box 5, files Liquinas el Rosario, Liquinas El Rosario y otros, Lulipata Lameo y Ayoma; box 7, file Liquinas el Rosario; box 9, file Lameo y Ayoma. The mother of the siblings, Concepción Ocampo viuda de Quiroga, on her own held a seventy-six-hectare property, called San Isidro, in Germán Jordán province. She also have properties in the city of Cochabamba and in Quillacollo Province. This example shows the even stronger concentration of land in one family. INRA-CBBA, Germán Jordán Province, box 8, file San Isidro.

36. As seen before, the Agrarian Reform Decree certainly established that the beneficiaries would pay a compensation for the land they received in a twenty-five-year term. However, in the end, neither the MNR nor the subsequent military governments did much to enforce this obligation. Peasant-landlord agreement in Gregorio Jordán Corrales's legal petition in the name of the peasants, July 6, 1957, INRA-CBBA, Germán Jordán Province, box 5, file Liquinas y otros.

37. One *arrobada* is 0.89 acres, one-third of a hectare. One and a half *arrobada* might be approximately half a hectare.

38. First public hearing, July 13, 1957, INRA-CBBA, Germán Jordán Province, box 5, file Liquinas el Rosario.

39. Langer uses James Scott's notion on "moral economy" to study the economic transformation that took place in Cuquisaca at the end of the nineteenth. Langer, *Economic Change*, 5–6. The concept allows him to understand how peasants' life changed when landlords broke their tacit agreements with their colonos in relation to the amount of work per week, the size of the plots, and their use of time.

40. Gregorio Jordán Corrales's judicial petition, in the name of the colonos, July 6, 1957, INRA-CBBA, Germán Jordán Province, box 5, file Liquinas y Otros.

41. See also the case of Hacienda Record of Settlement, October 20, 1954, INRA-CBBA, Germán Jordán Province, box 3, file Huallpero 2222. James Clark sees that many landlords maintained their ties with their former colonos because of their continuing role in traditional political parties and because they continue grandfathering colonos' kids. Clark, *Temas sobre la propiedad rural*, 9.

42. On May 22, 1957, Macario Escobari asked the judge to recognize the sale agreements in which he entered with his former colonos prior to the agrarian reform. INRA-LP, Omasuyos Province, box 38, file Taramaya.

43. Pedro Roberto Terrazas asked for an economic compensation of two hundred million bolivianos. He received less than one million bolivianos. Terrazas's judicial petition, May 14, 1959, INRA-LP, Omasuyos Province, box 15, file Ocorani.

44. The National Institute of Agrarian Reform does not offer consistent information in all provinces. In the provinces of Omasuyos, all cases for expropriation reported the canton where the property was located; in Sud Yungas and Germán

Jordán, the divisions between cantons is less clear. For this study, I reviewed all cases on land expropriation of the canton of Achacachi (in Omasuyos Province). In Sud Yungas I reviewed cases of land expropriation in the cantons of Chulumani and Irupana and in Germán Jordan the cantons of Cliza and Toco.

45. The percentage includes all properties in Germán Jordán that were above fifty hectares, the upper limit of the medium-sized property. One of the problems with this percentage is that it includes the case of the Santa Clara Monastery, which was the largest estate of the region, with the highest number of beneficiaries (765) and which already had a lengthy history of fragmentation prior to the agrarian reform. This case raises the percentage for the whole province. If we exclude the Santa Clara case, the amount of property that was redistributed between the former colonos is 64 percent.

46. Emma Mojica studies seventeen haciendas (six on the altiplano's north, four in Yungas, and seven in the valleys of Luribay and Sapahaqui) and argues on the basis of this sample that, before the agrarian reform, colonos had access to 54.2 percent of land and, after the agrarian reform, they had access to 34.8 percent more land. This means that peasants gained control of 89 percent of the land overall. Emma Mojica, *Resumen del estudio*, 50. Citing the works of Carter and Burke, Albó states that colonos had a much more moderate increase in the size of their plots: from 5 to 25 percent. See Albó, *Bodas de plata*, 34.

47. As a number of authors have pointed out, policies of land redistribution varied greatly depending on the geographic, demographic, and historic characteristics of the region. See Malloy, *Bolivia*, 214; Carter, "Revolution and the Agrarian Sector," 249; Mojica, *Resumen del estudio*, 48–50; Albó, *Bodas de plata*, 34; Heyduk, *Hacienda System*, 1, 8–9. Across the three regions, 40 percent of the judicial petitions presented in Achacachi, Cliza, and Toco related to land expropriation. In contrast, in Irupana and Chulumani only 5 percent of the claims are associated with expropriation. This does not mean that there were fewer cases of expropriation in Sud Yungas (in comparison, for example, to Omasuyos Province); the lower percentage is explained by the fact that peasant petitions for the endowment of state land (in areas designated for *colonization*) outnumbered those concerning land expropriation.

48. Paz Estenssoro's final verdict on August 30, 1962. INRA-LP, Omasuyos Province, box 24, file Murumani.

49. One of the most unusual cases I found was that of hacienda Murumani. In this case, Marcelino Cantuta, in the name of all the members of the union, petitioned the government to grant some land to the former landlord, Eulogio Franco. Cantuta claimed that Franco had invested in the property. However, the CNRA (July 29, 1961) and President Paz Estenssoro (August 30, 1962) rejected the petition. Both verdicts ordered the expropriation and distribution of the entire property. INRA-LP, Omasuyos Province, box 24, file Murumani.

50. Enrique Mayer cited in Carter and Albó, "La comunidad aymara," 474. Studies from the Wisconsin Land Tenure Center (LTC), pointed out this unequal

distribution of land and its consequences in strengthening asymmetrical relations of power. Focusing on the implementation of the agrarian reform in Sud Yungas, Leons shows that arrenderos (sharecroppers), yanaperos (migrant workers from the altiplano), and utawawas received different amounts of land and that the arrenderos retained an advantage over the others because they received bigger plots. Leons argues that this unequal distribution of land gave birth to a new economic hierarchy at the top of which stood former hacendados who were able to keep a portion of their properties; below the hacendados we find the middlemen (town dwellers specialized in buying coca from peasants destined to sell it in the markets), and the new elite consisting of the arrenderos who had become owners of larger plots of land. At the bottom, we find former colonos, yanaperos and arrenderos who held less land and were usually forced to work for these new elites who had received more land and capital. Leons, "Political Economy," 84, 95, 106. Lagos has also studied the process of rural differentiation in Cochabamba. Lagos, *Autonomy and Power*, 78.

51. Before the agrarian reform, colonos in Cochabamba, where there was high demographic pressure over land, complained that landlords forced them to pay a fee for the utilization of pasturelands. Attending to these numerous complaints, the conservative President Mamerto Urrologoitia exempted colonos from paying fees for the use of hacienda pasturelands. Decree 2026, May 3, 1949.

52. Deere and León argue that the incorporation of rural women was an explicit state policy only in Cuba and Nicaragua. Deere and León, *Rural Women and State Policy*, 6, 173, 176–177. See also Deere and León, *Empowering Women*; Tinsman, *Partners in Conflict*, 3, 4, 5.

53. Agrarian judge Willy Luna states: "it is impossible to define the size of the individual plots assigned peasants as established in the president's final verdict. Anyway, peasants preferred to keep small individual plots in order to maintain the aynocas [collective lands]." May 20, 1968, INRA-LP, Omasuyos Province, box 21, file Humacha Sullulluni. Renato Fernandez, one of the heads of the SNRA, approved that distribution on October 1, 1968, INRA-LP, Omasuyos Province, box 21, file Humacha Sullulluni. In another case, topographer Carlos Zuleta informs that peasants in this hacienda preferred to receive individual but discontinuous plots of land. See April 6, 1962, INRA-LP, Omasuyos Province, box 21, file Guala-ta Chico.

54. Mexican Edmundo Flores, invited by the government to analyze the Peruvian agrarian reform, describes how the government started to organize cooperatives under direct governmental supervision. "La reforma agraria en el Perú," *El Trimestre Económico* 37, no. 147 (3) (July–September 1970): 516. See also the comparison between the Peruvian and Bolivian agrarian reforms in Carter and Albó, "La comunidad Aymara," 455; Seligmann, "Burden of Visions."

55. Albó argues that the cooperatives failed "because the lawmakers ran the program based on a false and platonic idea of Andean community." Albó, *Bodas de Plata*, 36 (translation mine).

56. Every Bolivian government since 1953 declared that agrarian reform was the state's priority, but Robert Turovsky reveals that less than 1.5 percent of the national budget was designated for the implementation of the agrarian reform, allegedly the crowning jewel of Bolivia's national revolution. "The budget dwindled from 0.8% and 1.5% of the national budget in the first two years of operation to a mere 0.44% and 0.55% during the remaining years of the MNR government and an even less significant percentage in the Barrientos and Bánzer governments of the 1960s and 1970s." Turovsky, "Bolivian Haciendas," 209.

57. James Clark refers to the delays in the implementation of the agrarian reform. He states that in the mid-1960s peasants were afraid that, once President Paz Estenssoro finished his term in office, landlords would be able to recover their former haciendas. Clark, *Problemas y conflictos.*

58. The exception was the infamous and so-called Champa Guerra (the Champa war) that took place in the Cochabamba valleys in the late 1950s. However, this political conflict, incentivized from above, was relatively isolated. In general, tranquility came back to the countryside when colonos took control of the production and management of the haciendas. Kohl, "Cliza and Ucureña War," 616–22.

59. Rivera Cusicanqui, *Oprimidos*, 2010, 47, 76. See also César Soto, *Historia del pacto militar campesino*, 6.

60. Albó, "From MNRristas to Kataristas to Katari," 386. Quote translated by Webber, *Red October*, 88.

61. In a general assessment of the agrarian reform in Bolivia, James Clark argues that because the state took so much time to grant the new owners the legal titles to the properties, some former landlords used peasant judicial insecurity to threaten them with the possibility of recovering their lands, especially after 1964. Clark, *Temas sobre la propiedad rural*, 7.

62. Letter to President General René Barrientos, August 30, 1965, ABNB-PR, file 1099.

63. Decree-Law 07033, January 24, 1965. See also Decree-Law 07189, May 24, 1965, which states that ordinary tribunals of justice cannot revise decisions made by agrarian courts. Decree-Law 07260 of August 2, 1965, states that all land titles that peasants have already received are legal and that they have to be registered in Derechos Reales (the office that registers property rights in Bolivia). James Clark argues that, in contrast with what landlords had expected, Barrientos ratified the spirit of the law on agrarian reform. Clark, *Temas sobre la propiedad*, 9.

64. Constitución Política del Estado, February 2, 1967, Article 7, clause 9, also Articles 165–70.

65. Decree-Law 10067, January 7, 1972, Gaceta Oficial.

66. "25 años de reforma agraria en Bolivia," *El Diario*, March 25, 1973.

67. Albó expresses doubts about the reliability of this data. Albó, *Bodas de plata*, 33.

68. Carlos Luis Terrazas's judicial petition, February 21, 1978, INRA-LP, Omasuyos Province, box 82, file Zona Aruquipa.

69. Severo Quisbert's judicial petition in the name of the appellants. Quisbert argued not only that the land had been abandoned but that the Indians were the legitimate owners of those lands, and they had lost them during the time of the hacienda regime, and it was fair that the government (by implementing the Agrarian Reform Decree) returned those lands to those who were truly working on them. November 23, 1978, INRA-LP, Omasuyos Province, box 82, file Zona Aruquipa.

70. President Paz Estenssoro and Guillermo Justiniano's verdict, September 29, 1987, INRA-LP, Omasuyos Province, box 82, file Zona Aruquipa.

71. Conzelman, "Coca Leaf," 169.

72. James Clark states that many landlords hoped to recover their land after 1964 when Barrientos seized power. They had little chance of doing so in places where the peasant unions were strong. Clark, *Temas sobre la propiedad*, 8.

73. Cristóbal Kay and Miguel Urioste highlight the contradictory effects of the agrarian reform. Land redistribution dominated in the western part of the country, and the eastern part witnessed a new process of land concentration. Kay and Urioste, "Bolivia's Unfinished Agrarian Reform," 42. See also Albó, *¿Bodas de plata?*, 63.

Epilogue: Everyday Forms of Revolution

1. Mariano Ramos, Policarpio Ramos, Eleuterio Ramos, and Samuel Alejandro Cabrera to the Minister of Peasant Affairs, ABNB, PR 1099.

2. Klein, "Social Change in Bolivia," 232.

3. Multiple works have used these adjectives to describe the Bolivian revolution and to highlight, in particular, MNR's undeniable mistakes. Sergio Almaraz scathingly describes the revolution as "abandoned," "vanquished," "betrayed," "kneeling," in *Requiem para una república*. See also Malloy, *Bolivia*; Justo, *Bolivia*; Lehman, "Braked but not Broken."

4. The Spanish title of Gotkowitz's book translates as "The revolution prior to the revolution." See Gotkowitz and Calla, *La revolución antes de la Revolución*.

5. For the legal process of agrarian reform, see the introduction of Miguel Urioste and the article of Rossana Barragan in Urioste, Barragán, and Colque, *Los nietos de la reforma agraria*, liv, 93.

6. See Calderón, "Un siglo de luchas sociales," 436.

7. Joseph, "On the Trail of Latin American Bandits," 22.

8. Grindle, *State and Countryside*.

9. Hale, "Mistados, Cholos, and the Negation of Identity," 267–78; Cadena, *Indigenous Mestizos*.

10. Calderon, "Un siglo de luchas sociales," 434; Ari, *Earth Politics*, 149; Rivera Cusicanqui, *Oprimidos*.

11. Albó, *Bodas de plata*, 32. In the same vein Angel Jemio-Ergueta notes in a 1973 article, "the absence of reliable statistics on agrarian reform in Bolivia." Jemio-Ergueta, "La reforma agraria de Bolivia," 35.

12. Miguel Urioste, *La reforma agraria abandonada*, 22.

13. Clark, *Land Reform in* Bolivia, 36. James Clark at the Land Tenure Center (LTC) in Wisconsin worked in coordination with the CNRA.

14. García, *Diez años*, 44, 48–49. This book was widely circulated in Bolivia. Similar to Raúl Alfonso García's version, Antonio García, a Colombian specialist on agrarian reform in Latin America, reports that Bolivia distributed 4.4 million hectares and 221,304 titles. Antonio García, "Agrarian Reform and Social Development," 313. For the same period, Uri Mendelberg reports that the CNRA distributed an estimated of 7.8 million hectares, which would be almost double the amount that Raúl Alfonso García gives. Mendelberg bases his report on the study of Machicado Saravia (1966), 134. See Mendelberg, "Impact of the Bolivian Agrarian Reform," 47. The SNRA reports that 6.1 million hectares were distributed for the same period. Servicio Nacional de Reforma Agraria, *Estadisticas sobre tenencia de la tierra del SNRA, 1953–1970*, 6.

15. Wilkie, *Measuring Land Reform*, 33. Critics of the inconsistent data or lack of credible data on agrarian reform were not unique to Bolivia. Wassily Leontief notes "that only 1.4% of the articles published between 1977 and 1981 in the *American Economic Review* contained empirical analyses based on data researched by the author, while two-thirds of the articles contained models or analyses without any data and another 23% contained empirical analyses using indirect statistical inference based on data published or researched elsewhere." Barraclough, "Reviewed Work," 641.

16. Robert Turovsky, "Bolivian Haciendas," 209. Joseph Thome points to the precarious budget of the regional CNRA office in Santa Cruz: "The list of deficiencies is staggering: the department offices have no money for mailing case files to La Paz and must charge this to the campesinos; the Council . . . has only two serviceable vehicles for the entire nation, and, as of August 31, 1966, has already used up 80% of its operating budget for 1966, which among other things, means that it will not be able to provide any more paper, stationery or pencils to any of its 386 employees." Thome, "Problems Which Obstruct the Process," 20, cited in Wilkie, *Measuring Land Reform*, 29. See also Richard Patch, "U.S. Assistance"; Kohl, "Peasant," 248.

17. Young, *Blood of the Earth*, 57.

18. Kevin Young states that, starting in the mid-1950s, the MNR sought to redefine revolutionary nationalist priorities and iconography by shifting the emphasis from mine workers and the urban working class to the peasants, the middle class, and the army. Young, *Blood of the Earth*, 107.

19. The Alliance for Progress, based on US funding, had among the ambitious goals: "a minimum annual per capita economic growth rate of 2.5 percent, more

equitable redistribution of national income, tax reform, comprehensive agrarian reform, elimination of adult illiteracy and provision of a six minimum years schooling for all children, a series of public health measures to raise life expectancy . . . a plan for democratic progress." Wright, *Latin America*, 66–67. See also Wilkie, *Measuring Land Reform*.

20. O'Connor, "Agrarian Reforms," 179.

21. CNRA, annual reporting, booklet, 1962.

22. García, *Diez años*, 85.

23. Between 1964 and 1982, a number of military dictators ruled Bolivia—some of them right-wing conservatives, such as General Rene Barrientos and Hugo Bánzer, and the even more violent regime of Luis García Meza. Some of them were progressive, such as Alfredo Ovando (1969–1970), who nationalized the hydrocarbons, and Juan José Torres (1970–1971) who led the Popular Assembly.

24. In Bolivia, the north and east parts of the country (called the lowlands) were home to numerous nomadic indigenous groups. After the nineteenth century, the state enacted laws encouraging the colonization of those areas. The MNR, in the same vein as their predecessors, saw those indigenous groups as savages that the state needed to civilize and the areas as a source of available land to settle. Bolivia's most successful policy of colonization started in the 1950s and deepened in the 1970s when General Hugo Bánzer endowed large concessions of land to the military and their political allies, a process that ended up with the formation of neo-latifundia.

25. While the MNR was in power, the Dirección Nacional de Informaciones, a government office, published *Bolivia:10 años de Revolución* (La Paz: Dirección Nacional de Informaciones, 1962), and Raúl Alfonso García, *Diez años*. Not surprisingly, the LTC's annotated bibliography on agrarian reform describes this work as an "enthusiastic government report on progress in agrarian reform." Land Tenure Center, *Agrarian Reform in Latin America*, 1:177.

26. Postero, *Now We Are Citizens*, 47.

27. President Jaime Paz Zamora signed Decrees 22609, 22610 and 22611, on September 24, 1990, Gaceta Oficial.

28. Calla and Molina, "Los pueblos indígenas La Paz."

29. Colque Fernández, Tinta, and Sanjinés, *Segunda reforma agraria*, 79.

30. Decree 23331, November 24, 1992, Gaceta Oficial.

31. Borras, Kay, and Lahiff, *Market-Led Agrarian Reform*.

32. Urioste has pointed to the contradictory impact of the 1950s agrarian reform. On the one hand, Urioste highlights the radical redistributive character of the reform in the valleys and highlands (which constituted about 35 percent of the territory and was the heart of latifundios in Bolivia). On the other hand, he argues that the Agrarian Reform Decree-Law's vague definition of latifundios allowed new concentration of land in the lowlands, which constitute about 65 percent of the territory and were primarily home of a number of indigenous groups prior to the

agrarian reform. Urioste also highlights the slow pace of the process, the state and bureaucratic corruption, and the limited government budget allocated for implementation. Urioste reveals how loans and credits benefited rural elites in the lowlands, while the state's basic services for peasants such as health and education were either mediocre or nonexistent. Urioste, *Bolivia.*

33. Deere and Léon, *Empowering Women*, 63, 74.

34. Moore, *Social Origins of Dictatorship.*

BIBLIOGRAPHY

Archival Sources

Cochabamba

Archivo Histórico de la Prefectura de Cochabamba
    Expedientes de Prefectura (PE)
Archivo Histórico Municipal
Biblioteca Simón I. Patiño
Instituto Nacional de Reforma Agraria, Cochabamba (INRA-CBBA)

La Paz

Archivo de La Paz (ALP)
    Expedientes de Prefectura (PE)
Biblioteca Universidad Mayor de San Andrés
Biblioteca y Archivo Histórico de la Asamblea Legislativa Plurinacional (BAH-ALP)
Centro de Estudios para el Desarrollo Laboral y Agrario
Centro de Información de la Fundación Flavio Machicado Viscarra
Centro de Investigación y Promoción del Campesinado
Gaceta Oficial del Estado Plurinacional de Bolivia
Instituto Nacional de Reforma Agraria, La Paz (INRA-LP)

Sucre

Archivo y Biblioteca Nacionales de Bolivia (ABNB)
    Collection Walter Guevara Arze (WGA)
    Collection of Political Pamphlets
    Presidential Official Correspondence (PR)

United States

Land Tenure Center, University of Wisconsin, Madison
The Research Institute for the Study of Man, New York University, Elmer Holmes Bobst Library

Newspapers and Magazines

La Calle, La Paz
El Diario, La Paz
Gaceta Campesina, La Paz
Gaceta Oficial, La Paz
La Nación, La Paz
La Razón, La Paz
Revista Bolivia, La Paz
Revista Campo, Bolivia
Los Tiempos, Cochabamba
Tierra, La Paz
Ultima Hora, La Paz

Secondary Sources

Abrams, Philip. "Notes on the Difficulty of Studying the State." *Journal of Historical Sociology* 1, no. 1 (1988): 58–89.
Adams, Richard. *Social Change in Latin America Today, Its Implications for United States Policy.* New York: Published for the Council on Foreign Relations, 1961.
Albertus, Michael. *Autocracy and Redistribution: The Politics of Land Reform.* New York: Cambridge University Press, 2015.
Albó, Xavier. *Achacachi. Medio siglo de lucha campesina.* La Paz: Centro de Investigación y Promocion del Campesinado, 1979.
Albó, Xavier. "Andean People in the Twentieth Century." In *The Cambridge History of the Native Peoples of the Americas*, edited by Frank Salomon and Stuart B. Schwartz, vol. 3, part 2, 756–872. Cambridge: Cambridge University Press, 2008.
Albó, Xavier. *¿Bodas de plata? O, réquiem por una reforma agraria.* La Paz: Centro de Investigación y Promocion del Campesinado, 1979.
Albó. Xavier. "Etnias y pueblos originarios. Diversidad étnica cultural y linguística." In *Bolivia en el siglo XX. La formación de la Bolivia contemporánea*, edited by Fernando Campero, 451–82. La Paz: Harvard Club Bolivia, 1999.
Albó, Xavier. "From MNRristas to Kataristas to Katari." In *Resistance, Rebellion, and Consciousness in the Andean Peasant World, 18th to 20th Centuries*, edited by Steve Stern, 379–419. Madison: University of Wisconsin Press, 1987.
Albó, Xavier. "¿Por qué el campesino qhochala es distinto? Brochazos de una historia rural diferente en Cochabamba." Paper for the conference "Economía Comunitaria e Identidades Étnicas," 2, Cochabamba, November 1986.
Albó, Xavier. *Raíces de América. El mundo aymara.* Madrid: Alianza Editorial, 1988.
Albro, Robert. 2005. "The Indigenous in the Plural in Bolivian Oppositional Politics." *Bulletin of Latin American Research* 24, no.4 (October 2005): 433–53.

Alcalde, Alfonso. *La vida de Alberto Rodriguez Ríos, Colono*. La Paz: Subsecretaría de Prensa, Informe y Cultura, 1956.

Aldunate Romero, José. *Luces nuevas, nuevos horizontes. En homejane al cuarto centenario de la fundación de Potosí*. Potosí: Universo, 1945.

Alexander, Robert J. *Agrarian Reform in Latin America*. New York: Macmillan, 1974.

Alexander, Robert J. *The Bolivian National Revolution*. New Brunswick, NJ: Rutgers University Press, 1958.

Almaraz Paz, Sergio. *Réquiem para una república*. La Paz: Los Amigos del Libro, 1980.

Álvarez Plata, Waldo. *Memorias del Primer Ministro Obrero*. La Paz: Ministerio de Trabajo, 2016.

Anaya, Ricardo. *Consideraciones sobre la reforma agraria en Bolivia*. Cochabamba: Jurídica, 1948.

Anaya, Ricardo. *Cuestiones de derecho agrario. En torno al proyecto de creación del instituto de reforma agraria*. Cuaderno no. 40. Cochabamba: Universidad Autónoma de Cochabamba. Publicaciones de la facultad de derecho, 1949.

Anaya, Ricardo. *Democracia y revolución. Publicaciones del Partido de la Izquierda Revolucionaria*. La Paz, La Época, 1945.

Anaya, Ricardo. *Imperialismo rosca y miseria*. La Paz: Publicaciones del Partido de la Izquierda Revolucionaria, 1947.

Anaya, Ricardo. *Unidos venceremos. PIR, mensaje al pueblo boliviano*. Santiago de Chile: n.p., 1945.

Antezana, Luis. *Proceso y sentencia a la reforma agraria en Bolivia*. La Paz: Puerta del Sol, 1979.

Antezana, Luis. "La reforma agraria campesina en Bolivia (1956–1960)." *Revista Mexicana de Sociología* 31, no. 2 (April 1969): 245–321.

Antezana, Luis, and Consejo Nacional de Reforma Agraria. *Reorientación de la Reforma Agraria, 1987*. La Paz: Consejo Nacional de Reforma Agraria, 1987.

Antezana, Luis, and Hugo Romero. *Historia de los sindicatos campesinos. Un proceso de integración nacional en Bolivia*. La Paz: Ministerio de Asuntos Campesinos, Consejo Nacional de Reforma Agraria, Dpto. de Investigaciones Sociales, 1973.

Antezana, Luis H. *Bolivia, hoy*. Mexico City: Siglo XXI, 1983.

Antezana, Luis H. "Sistema y proceso ideológicos en Bolivia." In *Bolivia, hoy*, edited by René Zavaleta Mercado, 60–84. Mexico City: Siglo Veintiuno Editores, 1983.

Aráoz, Mario C. *Nuevo digesto de legislación boliviana*. La Paz: Renacimiento, 1929.

Argañarás, Fernando Garcia. "Bolivia's Transformist Revolution." *Latin American Perspectives* 19, no. 2 (April 1992): 44–71.

Ari, Waskar. *Earth Politics: Religion, Decolonization, and Bolivia's Indigenous Intellectuals*. Durham, NC: Duke University Press, 2014.

Arnold, Denise, Rossana Barragán R., David Llanos, Carmen B. Loza, and Carmen Soliz. *¿Indígenas u obreros? La construcción política de identidades en el Altiplano boliviano.* La Paz: Fundación UNIR, 2009.

Arze, José Antonio. *Bolivia bajo el terrorismo nazifascista. Un llamado a la ciudadanía boliviana y a la conciencia democrática internacional para reforzar la acción de la Unión Democrática Boliviana.* Lima: Empresa Editora Peruana, 1945.

Arze, José Antonio. *Proceso de la educación boliviana.* La Paz: Universo, 1947.

Arze, José Antonio, Abelardo Villalpando, Víctor de Sanjinés, Adan Rojas, Luis Are amayo, Mario Cornejo, militantes del PIR desterrados a Chile por el gobierno de Mamerto Urrolagoitia. "Bolivia. Una democracia degollada." Carta abierta a ONU. Santiago de Chile, February 21, 1951.

Arze Aguirre, René Danilo. *Guerra y conflictos sociales. El caso rural boliviano durante la campaña del Chaco.* La Paz: Ceres, 1987.

Arze Cuadros, Eduardo. *Bolivia, el programa del MNR y la revolución nacional. Del movimiento de reforma universtaria al ocaso del modelo neoliberal (1928–2002).* La Paz: Plural Editores, 2002.

Assadourian, Carlos Sempat. *El sistema de la economía colonial. Mercado interno, regiones y espacio económico.* Lima: Instituto de Estudios Peruanos, 1982.

Avis, Julio Alberto d'. *Los errores administrativos de la reforma agraria de Bolivia.* Cochabamba: Imprenta Universitaria, 1959.

Ayala Mercado, Ernesto. *Qué sucede con la reforma agraria?* La Paz: Subsecretaría de Prensa, Informaciones y Cultura, 1955.

Baciu, Stefan. *Tristán Marof de cuerpo entero.* La Paz: ISLA, 1987.

Barcelli, Agustín. *Medio siglo de luchas sindicales revolucionarias en Bolivia, 1905–1955.* La Paz: Editorial del Estado, 1956.

Barnadas, Josep. *Apuntes para una historia aymara.* La Paz: Centro de Investigación y Promoción del Campesinado, 1978.

Barnadas, Josep M., Guillermo Calvo, Juan Ticlla, and Grupo de Estudios Históricos. *Diccionario histórico de Bolivia.* Sucre: Grupo de Estudios Históricos, 2002.

Barnes de Marschall, Katherine. *Revolution and Land Reform in Chuquisaca and Potosi.* La Paz: Servicio Nacional de Reforma Agraria, 1970.

Barraclough, Solon. "Reviewed Work: The Agrarian Question and Reformism in Latin America by Alain de Janvry." *Economic Development and Cultural Change* 32, no. 3 (1984): 641.

Barraclough, Solon. *Reviews: Alain de Janvry, the Agrarian Question, and Reformism in Latin America.* Geneva: United Nations, 1985.

Barragán, Rossana. *Asambleas constituyentes. Ciudadanía y elecciones, convenciones y debates (1825–1971).* La Paz: Muela del Diablo Editores, 2006.

Barragán, Rossana. "Entre polleras, lliqllas y ñañacas. Los mestizos y la emergencia de la *tercera república*," In *Etnicidad, economía, y simbolismo en los Andes*, edited by Silvia Arze, Rossana Barragán, Laura Escobari, et al., 85–127. Lima: Institut français d'études andines, 1992.

Barragán, Rossana. "Los títulos de la corona de España de los indígenas. Para una historia de las representaciones políticas, presiones y negociaciones entre Cádiz y la república liberal." *Boletin Americanista* 65 (2012): 15–37.

Barragán, Rossana, and Carmen Soliz. "Etnografía de la justicia estatal. La violación como prisma de las relaciones de género." In *Justicia y diversidad en América Latina. Pueblos indígenas ante la globalización.* edited by Victoria Chenaut, Magdalena Gómez, Héctor Ortiz, and María Teresa Sierra, 313–34. Mexico City: Centro de Investigaciones y Estudios Superiores en Antropología Social, Facultad Latinoamericana de Ciencias Sociales, 2012.

Bartra, Roger. *Agrarian Structure and Political Power in Mexico.* Baltimore, MD: Johns Hopkins University Press, 1993.

Baud, Michiel. "Indigenous Politics and the State: The Andean Highlands in the Nineteenth and Twentieth Centuries." *Social Analysis* 51, no. 2 (2007): 19–42.

Blasier, Cole. *The United States, Germany, and the Bolivian Revolutionaries, 1941–1946.* Pittsburgh, PA: University of Pittsburgh Press, 1973.

Blasier, S. C. *The Hovering Giant: U.S. Responses to Revolutionary Change in Latin America, 1910–1985.* Pittsburgh, PA: University of Pittsburgh Press, 1989.

Becker, Marc. *Indians and Leftists in the Making of Ecuador's Modern Indigenous Movements.* Durham, NC: Duke University Press, 2008.

Bedregal, Guillermo. *Víctor Paz Estenssoro, el político. Una semblanza crítica.* Mexico City: Fondo de Cultura Económica, 1999.

Benton, Jane. *Agrarian Reform in Theory and Practice: A Study of the Lake Titicaca Region of Bolivia.* Aldershot, UK: Ashgate, 1999.

Bernstein, Henry, and Terence J. Byres. "From Peasant Studies to Agrarian Change." *Journal of Agrarian Change* 1, no. 1 (January 2001): 1–56.

Bethell, Leslie. *The Cambridge History of Latin America* Vol. 6, Pt. 1. Cambridge: Cambridge University Press, 1994.

Blanco, J. *Antonio Alvarez Mamani. Historia de un dirigente campesino.* La Paz: n.p., 1969.

Bobrow-Strain, Aaron. *Intimate Enemies: Landowners, Power, and Violence in Chiapas.* Durham, NC: Duke University Press, 2007.

Bolivia. "Gaceta oficial." *Gaceta oficial*, 1960.

Bolivia. Dirección Nacional de Informaciones. *Bolivia. 10 años de revolución.* La Paz: Dirección Nacional de Informaciones, 1962.

Bonifáz, Miguel. *El problema agrario-indígena en Bolivia.* Sucre: Salesiana, 1948.

Borras, Saturnino M. "Questioning Market-Led Agrarian Reform: Experiences from Brazil, Colombia and South Africa." *Journal of Agrarian Change* 3, no. 3 (2003): 367–94.

Borras, Saturnino M., Cristóbal Kay, and Edward Lahiff. *Market-Led Agrarian Reform: Critical Perspectives on Neoliberal Land Policies and the Rural Poor.* London: Routledge, 2008.

Boyer, Christopher. *Becoming Campesinos: Politics, Identity, and Agrarian Struggle in Postrevolutionary Michoacán, 1920–1935.* Stanford, CA: Stanford University Press, 2003.

Brienen, Marten. "The Clamor for Schools: Rural Education and the Development of State-Community Contact in Highland Bolivia, 1930–1952." *Revista de Indias* 62, no. 226 (2002): 615–50.

Buechler, Judith-Maria. "The Dynamics of the Market in La Paz, Bolivia." *Urban Anthropology* 7, no. 4 (December 1978): 343–59.

Buechler, Judith-Maria. "Trade and Market in Bolivia before 1953: An Ethnologist in the Garden of Ethnohistory." *Ethnohistory* 30, no. 2 (April 1983): 107–19.

Burga, Manuel. *De la encomienda a la hacienda capitalista. El valle del Jequetepeque del siglo XVI al XX.* Lima: Instituto de Estudios Peruanos, 1976.

Burke, Melvin. *Land Reform in the Lake Titicaca Region.* In *Beyond the Revolution: Bolivia since 1952*, edited by James Malloy and Richard Thorn, 301–40. Pittsburgh, PA: University of Pittsburgh Press, 1971.

Cadena, Marisol de la. *Indigenous Mestizos: The Politics of Race and Culture in Cuzco, Peru, 1919–1991.* Durham, NC: Duke University Press, 2000.

Cadena, Marisol de la. "Las mujeres son más indias. Etnicidad y género en una comunidad del Cuzco." *Estudios y debates* 1 (July 1991): 7–47.

Calderón, Fernando. "Un siglo de luchas sociales." In *Bolivia en el siglo XX. La formación de la Bolivia contemporánea*, edited by Fernando Campero, 427–50. La Paz: Harvard Club Bolivia, 1999.

Calla, Ricardo, and Ramiro Molina. "Los pueblos indígenas y la construcción de una sociedad plural." In *Movimientos indígenas y pactos de género*, edited by Ricardo Calla Ortega, Ramiro Molina Barrientos, and Cecilia Salazar de La Torre, 9–38. Cuadernos del Futuro no 5. La Paz: Programa de Naciones Unidas para el Desarrollo, 2000.

Canessa, Andrew. "Reproducing Racism: Schooling and Race in Highland Bolivia." *Race, Ethnicity and Education* 7, no. 2 (2004): 185–204.

Capriles Rico, Remberto, and Gastón Ardúz Eguía. *El problema social en Bolivia. Condiciones de vida y de trabajo.* La Paz: Fénix, 1941.

Carlson, Chris. "Agrarian Structure and Underdevelopment in Latin America: Bringing the Latifundio 'Back In.'" *Latin American Research Review* 54, no. 3 (2019): 678–93.

Carter, William. "Revolution and the Agrarian Sector." In *Beyond the Revolution: Bolivia since 1952*, edited by James Malloy and Richard S. Thorn, 233–68. Pittsburgh, PA: University of Pittsburgh Press, 1971.

Carter, William, and Xavier Albó. "La comunidad aymara. Un mini-estado en conflicto." In *Raíces de América. El mundo aymara.*, edited by Xavier Albó, 451–92. Madrid: Alianza Editorial, United Nations Educational, Scientific and Cultural Organization, 1988.

Carter, William E. "Agrarian Reform in Latin America." *Proceedings of the Academy of Political Science* 30, no. 4 (August 1972): 1–14.

Carter, William E. *Aymara Communities and the Bolivian Agrarian Reform.* Gainesville: University of Florida Press, 1964.

Carter, William E, and Mauricio Mamani. *Coca en Bolivia.* La Paz: Juventud, 1986.

Carter, William E, and Mauricio Mamani. *Irpa Chico. Individuo y comunidad en la cultura aymara.* La Paz: Juventud, 1989.

Castillo Avendaño, Wálter del (editor). *Compilación legal de la reforma agraria en Bolivia.* La Paz: Editorial Fénix, 1955.

Céspedes, Augusto. *El Dictador suicida. 40 años de historia de Bolivia.* Santiago de Chile: Editorial Universitaria, 1956.

Céspedes, Augusto. *Metal del diablo.* La Paz: Libreria editorial Juventud, 1987.

Céspedes, Augusto. *Sangre de mestizos. Relatos de la guerra del Chaco.* La Paz: Juventud, 1969.

Chenaut, Victoria. *Justicia y diversidad en América Latina. Pueblos indígenas ante la globalización.* Mexico City; Quito: Centro de Investigaciones y Estudios Superiores en Antropología Social, Facultad Latinoamericana de Ciencias Sociales, 2011.

Choque Canqui, Roberto. "De la defensa del ayllu a la creación de la República del Qullasuyu. Historia del movimiento indígena en Bolivia (1912–1955)." In *Historia y evolución del movimiento popular* edited Luís Antezana, 465–504. Encuentro de Estudios Bolivianos. Cochabamba: Centro de Estudios de la Realidad Económica y Social, 1986.

Choque Canqui, Roberto. "La escuela indigenal. La Paz (1905–1938)." In *Educación indígena: ciudadanía o colonización?* edited by Choque Canqui et al., 19–40 La Paz: Ediciones Aruwiyiri, 1992.

Choque Canqui, Roberto. *La masacre de Jesús de Machaca.* La Paz: Ediciones Chitakolla, 1986.

Choque Canqui, Roberto, and Cristina Quisbert. *Líderes indígenas aymaras. lucha por la defensa de tierras comunitarias de origen.* La Paz: Unidad de Investigaciones Históricas UNIH-PAKAXA, 2010.

Choque Canqui, Roberto, Vitaliano Soria, Humberto Mamani, Esteban Ticona Alejo, and Ramón Conde. *Educación indígena. Ciudadanía o colonización?* La Paz: Ediciones Aruwiyiri, 1992.

Choque Canqui, Roberto, and Esteban Ticona Alejo. *Sublevación y masacre de Jesús de Machaqa de 1921.* La Paz: Diálogos, 1998.

Clark, A. Kim. "Racial Ideologies and the Quest for National Development: Debating the Agrarian Problem in Ecuador (1930–1950)." *Journal of Latin American Studies* 30, no. 2 (1998): 373–93.

Clark, Ronald James. "Land Reform and Peasant Market Participation on the North Highlands of Bolivia." *Land Economics* 44, no. 2 (1968): 153–72.

Clark, Ronald James. *Land Reform in Bolivia.* Madison: Land Tenure Center, University of Wisconsin, USAID Bolivia, 1970.

Clark, Ronald James. *Problemas y conflictos sobre propiedad de tierras en Bolivia.* Madison: Land Tenure Center, University of Wisconsin, 1969.

Clark, Ronald James. *Temas sobre la propiedad rural y la reforma agraria en Bolivia.* La Paz: Servicio Nacional de Reforma Agraria, Sección Investigaciones, 1970.

Claure, Toribio, and Arturo Urquidi Morales. *Una escuela rural en Vacas.* La Paz: Universo, 1949.

Colburn, Forrest D. *Everyday Forms of Peasant Resistance.* Armonk: M. E. Sharpe, 1989.

Collier, John. "United States Indian Administration as a Laboratory of Ethnic Relations." *Social Research* 12, no. 3 (September 1945): 265–303.

Colque Fernández, Gonzalo, Tinta G, Efraín, and Esteban Sanjinés. *Segunda reforma agraria. Una historia que incomoda.* La Paz: Fundación Tierra, 2016.

Comisión Económica para América Latina y el Caribe. *Campesinado y desarrollo agricola en Bolivia.* Santiago de Chile: Comisión Económica para América Latina y el Caribe, 1982.

Comité Nacional del Sesquicentenario de la República. *Monografía de Bolivia.* La Paz: Biblioteca del Sesquicentenario de la República, 1975.

Condarco Morales, Ramiro. *Zárate, el "temible" Willka. Historia de la rebelión indígena de 1899 en la República de Bolivia.* La Paz: Renovación, 1983.

Consejo Nacional de Reforma Agraria. Annual reporting booklet, 1962.

Conzelman, Caroline Sommer. "Coca Leaf and Sindicato Democracy in the Bolivian Yungas: The Andeanization of Western Political Models and the Rise of the New Left." PhD diss., University of Colorado, Boulder, 2007.

Cooper, Frederick. *Confronting Historical Paradigms: Peasants, Labor, and the Capitalist World System in Africa and Latin America.* Madison: University of Wisconsin Press, 1993.

Coronado, Jorge. *The Andes Imagined: Indigenismo, Society, and Modernity.* Pittsburgh, PA: University of Pittsburgh Press, 2009.

Corporación Boliviana de Fomento. *Informe Final de Préstamo.* La Paz, 1970.

Cote, Stephen C. *Oil and Nation: A History of Bolivia's Petroleum Sector.* Morgantown: West Virginia University Press, 2016.

Cottyn, Hanne. "Mantener la exvinculación a raya: reformas liberales y derechos comunitarios en Carangas, 1860–1930." *Umbrales* 29 (July 2015): 97–132.

Cuestiones de derecho agrario. En torno al proyecto de creación del Instituto de Reforma Agraria. Cochabamba: Universidad Autónoma de Cochabamba, 1949.

Dandler, Jorge. *Campesinado y reforma agraria en Cochabamba (1952–1953). Dinámica de un movimiento campesino en Bolivia.* La Paz: CIPCA, 1975.

Dandler, Jorge. *El sindicalismo campesino en Bolivia. Los cambios estructurales en Ucureña.* Mexico: Instituto Indigenista Inter-americano, 1969.

Dandler, Jorge, and Juan Torrico A. "From the National Indigenous Congress to the Ayopaya Rebellion: Bolivia, 1945–1947." In *Resistance, Rebellion, and Consciousness in the Andean Peasant World, 18th to 20th Centuries*, edited by Steve Stern, 334–78. Madison: University of Wisconsin Press, 1987.

Dangl, Benjamin. *The Five Hundred Year Rebellion: Indigenous Movements and the Decolonization of History in Bolivia*. Chico, CA: AK Press, 2019.

De Janvry, Alain. *The Agrarian Question and Reformism in Latin America*. Baltimore, MD: Johns Hopkins University Press, 1981.

De la Fuente, Alejandro. *A Nation for All: Race, Inequality, and Politics in Twentieth-Century Cuba*. Chapel Hill: University of North Carolina Press, 2011.

Del Granado, Eduardo. "El presente estudio crítico del Dr. Eduardo del Granado ha sido aprobado por la federación rural de Cochabamba como expresión de la defensa de los derechos del agricultor contra el comunismo." Cochabamba: n.p. 1949.

Deere, Carmen Diana. *Empowering Women: Land and Property Rights in Latin America*. Pittsburgh, PA: University of Pittsburgh Press, 2007.

Deere, Carmen Diana, and Magdalena León. *Empowering Women: Land and Property Rights in Latin America*. Pittsburgh, PA: University of Pittsburgh Press, 2001.

Deere, Carmen Diana, and Magdalena León. *Rural Women and State Policy: Feminist Perspectives on Latin American Agricultural Development*. Boulder, CO: Westview Press, 1987.

Díaz Villamil, Antonio. *La niña de sus ojos, novela*. La Paz: Juventud, 1956.

Dorner, Peter. *Land Reform in Latin America: Issues and Cases*. Madison: Land Tenure Center, University of Wisconsin, 1971.

Dunkerley, James. "The Bolivian Revolution at 60: Politics and Historiography." *Journal of Latin American Studies* 45, no. 2 (2013): 325–50.

Dunkerley, James. *Rebellion in the Veins: Political Struggle in Bolivia, 1952–1982*. London: Verso, 1984.

Dunkerley, James. *Studies in the Formation of the Nation-State in Latin America*. London: Institute of Latin American Studies, 2002.

Edelman, Marc. "Bringing the Moral Economy Back In . . . to the Study of 21st-Century Transnational Peasant Movements." *American Anthropologist* 107, no. 3 (September 2005): 331–45.

Eguino Zaballa, Felix. "Una contribución al planeamiento de la reforma agraria," *Gaceta Campesina* (August 1952): 34–37.

Eisenhower, Milton Stover. *The Wine Is Bitter: The United States and Latin America*. Garden City: Doubleday, 1963.

Eiss, Paul K. *In the Name of El Pueblo: Place, Community, and the Politics of History in Yucatán*. Durham, NC: Duke University Press, 2010.

Enríquez, Laura J., and Marlen I. Llanes. "Back to the Land: The Political Dilemmas of Agrarian Reform in Nicaragua." *Social Problems* 40, no. 2 (May 1, 1993): 250–65.

Erasmus, Charles. "Land Reform and Social Revolution in Southern Bolivia: The Valleys of Chuquisaca and Tarija." In *Land Reform and Social Revolution in Bolivia*, edited by Dwight Heath, Charles Erasmus, and Hans Buechler, 61–165. New York: Praeger, 1969.

"El II congreso indigenista interamericano." *B.B.A.A. Boletín Bibliográfico de Antropología Americana* 12, no. 1 (January 1949): 16–23.

Fabricant, Nicole. "Between the Romance of Collectivism and the Reality of Individualism: Ayllu Rhetoric in Bolivia's Landless Peasant Movement." *Latin American Perspectives* 37, no. 4 (July 2010): 88–107.

Fabricant, Nicole. *Mobilizing Bolivia's Displaced: Indigenous Politics and the Struggle over Land.* Chapel Hill: University of North Carolina Press, 2012.

Falange Socialista Boliviana. *La revolución ha sido traicionada. Carta abierta al presidente Villaroel.* La Paz, November 4, 1944.

Farcau, Bruce W. *The Chaco War: Bolivia and Paraguay, 1932–1935.* Westport: Praeger, 1996.

Field, Thomas. *From Development to Dictatorship: Bolivia and the Alliance for Progress in the Kennedy Era.* Cornell: Cornell University Press, 2018.

Finot, Enrique. "Discurso pronunciado en representación de las delegaciones latinoamericanas en la sesión inaugural del primer Congreso Indigenista Interamericano, Apr. 14, 1940." In *Sobre el Problema del Indio*, 1–20. Mexico City, 1940.

Finot, Enrique. *El problema integral del indio. Una solución socialista.* La Paz, 1946.

Flores, Edmundo. "Un año de reforma agraria en Bolivia." *El Trimestre Económico* 23, no. 90(2) (April 1, 1956): 241–61.

Flores, Edmundo. "The Economics of Land Reform." In *Agrarian Problems and Peasant Movements in Latin America*, edited by Rodolfo Stavenhagen, 139–58. New York: Doubleday, 1970.

Flores, Edmundo. "Land Reform in Bolivia." *Land Economics* 30, no. 2 (May 1, 1954): 112–24.

Flores, Edmundo. "The Progress of Land Reform in Bolivia." Discussion Paper 2 (May 1963): 4–5. Land Tenure Center, University of Wisconsin, Madison.

Foland, Frances M. "Agrarian Reform in Latin America." *Foreign Affairs* 48, no. 1 (October 1969): 97–112.

Frontaura Argandoña, María. *Hacia el futuro del indio.* La Paz, Intendencia de Guerra, 1932.

García, Antonio. "Agrarian Reform and Social Development in Bolivia." In *Agrarian Problems and Peasant Movement in Latin America*, edited by Rodolfo Stavenhagen, 301–46. New York: Anchor Books, 1970.

García, Antonio. *El nuevo problema agrario de la América Latina.* Mexico City: Universidad Nacional Autónoma de México, Instituto de Investigaciones Económicas, 1981.

García, Antonio. "Proceso y frustración de las reformas agrarias en América Latina." *Estudios Internacionales* 1, no. 3–4 (October 1967): 353–410.

García, Raúl Alfonso. *Diez años de reforma agraria en Bolivia.* La Paz: Dirección Nacional de Informaciones, 1963.

García Linera, Álvaro. *El retorno de la Bolivia plebeya.* La Paz: Muela del Diablo, 2007.

García Linera, Álvaro, and Pablo Stefanoni. *La potencia plebeya acción colectiva e identidades indígenas, obreras y populares en Bolivia.* Buenos Aires: Consejo Latinoamericano de Ciencias Sociales, 2015.

Gildner, Matthew. "La historia como liberación nacional. Creando un pasado útil para la Bolivia pos-revolucionaria." *Ciencia y Cultura. La revolución nacional. Sesenta años después* 29 (December 2012): 103–26.

Giraudo, Laura, and Juan Martín Sánchez. *La ambivalente historia del indigenismo. Campo interamericano y trayectorias nacionales, 1940–1970.* Lima: Instituto de Estudios Peruanos, 2011.

Gleijeses, Piero. "The Agrarian Reform of Jacobo Arbenz." *Journal of Latin American Studies* 21, no. 3 (1989): 453–80.

Gleijeses, Piero. *Shattered Hope: The Guatemalan Revolution and the United States, 1944–1954.* Princeton, NJ: Princeton University Press, 2006.

González Casanova, Pablo. *El estado en América Latina. Teoría y práctica.* Mexico City: Siglo XXI, 1990.

González Casanova, Pablo. *Historia política de los campesinos latinoamericanos.* Mexico City: Siglo XXI, 1984.

Gootenberg, Paul, and Luis Reygadas. *Indelible Inequalities in Latin America: Insights from History, Politics, and Culture.* Durham, NC: Duke University Press, 2010.

Gordillo, José M. *Arando en la historia. La experiencia política campesina en Cochabamba.* La Paz: Plural Editores, Centro de Estudios de la Realidad Económica y Social, 1998.

Gordillo, José M. *Campesinos revolucionarios en Bolivia. Identidad, territorio y sexualidad en el valle alto de Cochabamba, 1952–1964.* La Paz: Promec, Universidad de la Cordillera, Plural Editores, 2000.

Gordillo, José M. "Modernity, Politics and Identity: Post-revolutionary Peasant Struggles in the Upper Valley of Cochabamba (Bolivia), 1952–1964." PhD diss., State University of New York, Stony Brook, 1999.

Gordillo, José M., Alberto Rivera P., and Ana Evi Sulcata Guzmán. *¿Pitaq kaypi kamachiq? Las estructuras de poder en Cochabamba, 1940–2006.* Cochabamba, La Paz: Centro de Estudios Superiores Universitarios–Universidad Mayor de San Simón, Dirección de Investigación Científica y Tecnológica–Universidad Mayor de San Simón, Fundación PIEB, 2007.

Gotkowitz, Laura. *A Revolution for Our Rights: Indigenous Struggles for Land and Justice in Bolivia, 1880–1952.* Durham, NC: Duke University Press, 2008.

Gotkowitz, Laura, and Fernando Calla. *La revolución antes de la Revolución. Luchas indígenas por tierra y justicia en Bolivia, 1880–1952.* La Paz: Plural, 2011.

Goudsmit, Into A. "Exploiting the 1953 Agrarian Reform: Landlord Persistence in Northern Potosí, Bolivia." *Journal of Latin American and Caribbean Anthropology* 13, no. 2 (November 2008): 361–86.

Gould, Jeffrey L. *To Lead as Equals: Rural Protest and Political Consciousness in Chinandega, Nicaragua, 1912–1979.* Chapel Hill: University of North Carolina Press, 2014.

Gould, Jeffrey L. "'¡Vana Ilusión!' The Highlands Indians and the Myth of Nicaragua Mestiza, 1880–1925." *Hispanic American Historical Review* 73, no. 3 (1993): 393–429.

Graham, Richard, Thomas E. Skidmore, Aline Helg, and Alan Knight. *The Idea of Race in Latin America, 1870–1940.* Austin: University of Texas Press, 1990.

Grandin, Greg. *Empire's Workshop: Latin America, the United States, and the Rise of the New Imperialism.* New York: Metropolitan Books, 2006.

Grieshaber, Erwin P. "Hacienda-Indian Community Relations and Indian Acculturation: An Historiographical Essay." *Latin American Research Review* 14, no. 3 (1979): 107–28.

Grieshaber, Erwin P. "Survival of Indian Communities in Nineteenth-Century Bolivia: A Regional Comparison," *Journal of Latin American Studies* 12, no. 2 (November 1980): 223–69.

Grindle, Merilee S. "Agrarian Class Structures and State Policies: Past, Present, and Future." *Latin American Research Review* 28, no. 1 (January 1993): 174–87.

Grindle, Merilee Serrill. *State and Countryside: Development Policy and Agrarian Politics in Latin America.* Baltimore, MD: Johns Hopkins University Press, 1986.

Grindle, Merilee Serrill, and Pilar Domingo. *Proclaiming Revolution: Bolivia in Comparative Perspective.* Cambridge, MA: Institute of Latin American Studies, David Rockefeller Center for Latin American Studies, Harvard University, 2003.

Guardino, Peter F. *Peasants, Politics, and the Formation of Mexico's National State: Guerrero, 1800–1857.* Stanford, CA: Stanford University Press, 2001.

Guardino, Peter F. *The Time of Liberty: Popular Political Culture in Oaxaca, 1750–1850.* Durham, NC: Duke University Press, 2005.

Gueiler Tejada, Lydia. *La mujer y la revolucion.* La Paz: Los Amigos del Libro, 1983.

Guerrero, Andrés. "The Construction of a Ventriloquist's Image: Liberal Discourse and the 'Miserable Indian Race' in Late 19th-Century Ecuador." *Journal of Latin American Studies* 29, no. 3 (1997): 555–90.

Guevara Arze, Walter. *Manifiesto a los campesinos de Ayopaya.* La Paz: Subsecretaría de Prensa, Informaciones y Cultura, 1953.

Gustafson, Bret D. *New Languages of the State: Indigenous Resurgence and the Politics of Knowledge in Bolivia.* Durham, NC: Duke University Press, 2009.

Gutierrez-Aguilar, Raquel, and Stacey A. D. Skar. *Rhythms of the Pachakuti: Indigenous Uprising and State Power in Bolivia.* Durham, NC: Duke University Press, 2015.

Hahn, Dwight R. *The Divided World of the Bolivian Andes: A Structural View of Domination and Resistance.* New York: Crane Russak, 1992.

Hale, Charles. "Mistados, Cholos, and the Negation of Identity in the Guatemalan Highlands." In *Histories of Race and Racism: The Andes and Mesoamerica from Colonial Times to the Present*, edited by Laura Gotkowitz, 254–77. Durham, NC: Duke University Press, 2011.

Handy, Jim. *Revolution in the Countryside: Rural Conflict and Agrarian Reform in Guatemala, 1944–1954.* Chapel Hill: University of North Carolina Press, 1994.

Harris, Olivia, and Xavier Albó. *Monteras y guardatojos. Campesinos y mineros en el norte de Potosí.* La Paz: Centro de Investigación y Promoción del Campesinado, 1986.

Havet, José. *The Diffusion of Power: Rural Elites in a Bolivian Province.* Ottawa: University of Ottawa Press, 1985.

Heath, Dwight, and Manuel Carballo. "Bolivia's Law of Agrarian Reform." In *Land Reform and Social Revolution in Bolivia*, edited by Dwight B Heath, Charles J Erasmus, Hans C Buechler, 29–62. New York: Praeger, 1969.

Heath, Dwight B. "New Patrons for Old: Changing Patron-Client Relationships in the Bolivian Yungas." *Ethnology* 12, no. 1 (January 1973): 75–98.

Heath, Dwight B., Charles J. Erasmus, and Hans C. Buechler. *Land Reform and Social Revolution in Bolivia.* New York: Praeger, 1969.

Henderson, Timothy J. *Worm in the Wheat: Rosalie Evans and Agrarian Struggle in the Puebla-Tlaxcala Valley of Mexico, 1906–1927.* Durham, NC: Duke University Press, 2012.

Hertzog. Enrique, Presidente Constitucional de la República. *Mensaje al honorable congreso ordinario.* La Paz: n.p., 1948.

Heyduk, Daniel. *The Hacienda System and Agrarian Reform in Highland Bolivia: A Re-evaluation.* Madison: Land Tenure Center, University of Wisconsin, 1974.

Hines Sarah. "The Power and Ethics of Vernacular Modernism: The Misicuni Dam Project in Cochabamba, Bolivia, 1944–2017." *Hispanic American Historical Review* 98, no. 2 (2018): 223–56.

Hinojosa, Roberto. *La revolución de Villazón.* La Paz: Universal, 1945.

Hogan, Andrew J. "Agrarian Reform and the Modernization of Agriculture in Latin America: A Study of the Mid-Twentieth Century Agrarian Reform Programs in Mexico, Bolivia, Cuba, Venezuela, Chile and Peru." MA thesis, University of New Mexico, 1974.

Holtey, Robert C. *Víctor Paz Estenssoro: A Political Biography.* Prescott, AZ: Createspace Independent, 2012.

Huber, Evelyne, and Frank Safford, eds. *Agrarian Structure and Political Power: Landlord and Peasant in the Making of Latin America.* Pittsburgh, PA: University of Pittsburgh Press, 1995.

Humerez, Walker. *El cuantioso litigio sobre la finca vacas, juicio por el señor Walker Humerez contra el honorable consejo municipal de Cochabamba.* Cochabamba: Universitaria, 1938.

Hylton, Forrest. "Reverberations of Insurgency: Indian Communities, the Federal War of 1899, and the Regeneration of Bolivia." PhD diss., New York University, New York, 2010.

Hylton, Forrest. "Tierra común. Caciques, artesanos e intelectuales radicales y la rebellión de Chayanta (1927)." In *Ya es otro tiempo el presente*, edited by Forrest Hylton, Felix Patzi, Sergio Serulnikov, and Sinclair Thomson, 133–95. La Paz: Muela del Diablo, 2005.

Hylton, Forrest, Felix Patzi, Sergio Serulnikov, and Sinclair Thomson, eds. *Ya es otro tiempo el presente. Cuatro momentos de insurgencia indígena.* La Paz: Muela del Diablo, 2005.

Hylton, Forrest, Sinclair Thomson, and Adolfo Gilly. *Revolutionary Horizons: Past and Present in Bolivian Politics.* London: Verso, 2007.

Instituto Nacional de Reforma Agraria. *Breve historia del reparto de tierras en Bolivia. De la titulación colonial a la reforma agraria y Ley INRA. Certezas y proyecciones de la Ley de reconducción comunitaria en Bolivia.* La Paz: Instituto Nacional de Reforma Agraria, 2010.

Iriarte, Gregorio. *Sindicalismo campesino.* La Paz: CIPCA, 1974.

Irurozqui Victoriano, Marta. *"A bala, piedra y palo": La construcción de la ciudadanía política en Bolivia, 1826–1952.* Sevilla: Diputación de Sevilla, 2000.

Irurozqui Victoriano, Marta. "The Sound of the Pututos: Politicization and Indigenous Rebellions in Bolivia, 1826–1921." *Journal* of *Latin American Studies* 32, no. 1, Andean Issue (February 2000): 85–114.

Jacobsen, Nils, and Cristóbal Aljovín de Losada. *Political Cultures in the Andes, 1750–1950.* Durham, NC: Duke University Press, 2005.

Jackson, Robert H. "The Decline of the Hacienda in Cochabamba, Bolivia: The Case of the Sacaba Valley, 1870–1929." *Hispanic American Historical Review* 69, no. 2 (1989): 259–81.

Jackson, Robert H. *Regional Markets and Agrarian Transformation in Bolivia Cochabamba, 1539–1960.* Albuquerque: University of New Mexico Press, 1994.

Jemio-Ergueta, Angel. "La reforma agraria de Bolivia." *Nueva Sociedad* 7 (July–August 1973): 19–37.

Jetté, Christian. *De la toma del cielo por asalto a la relocalización. Movimiento popular y democracia en Bolivia, 1976–1986.* La Paz: Hisbol, 1989.

Joseph, Gilbert M. "On the Trail of Latin American Bandits: A Reexamination of Peasant Resistance." *Latin American Research Review* 25, no. 3 (January 1, 1990): 7–53.

Joseph, Gilbert M. *Revolution from Without: Yucatán, Mexico, and the United States, 1880–1924.* Cambridge: Cambridge University Press, 1982.

Joseph, Gilbert Michael, and Daniel Nugent. *Everyday Forms of State Formation: Revolution and the Negotiation of Rule in Modern Mexico*. Durham, NC: Duke University Press, 1994.

Justo, Liborio. *Bolivia. La revolución derrotada. Del Tahuantinsuyu a la insurrección de abril de 1952*. Buenos Aires: Juárez, 1971.

Kay, Cristóbal, Saturnino M. Borras, and A. Haroon Akram-Lodhi. *Land, Poverty and Livelihoods in the Era of Globalization Perspectives from Developing and Transition Countries*. London: Routledge, 2007.

Kay, Cristóbal, and Graciela Salazar. "Estructura agraria, conflicto y violencia en la sociedad rural de América Latina." *Revista Mexicana de Sociología* 63, no. 4 (October 2001): 159–95.

Kay, Cristóbal, and Miguel Urioste, "Bolivia's Unfinished Agrarian Reform: Rural Poverty and Development Policies." In *Land, Poverty and Livelihoods in the Era of Globalization Perspectives from Developing and Transition Countries*, edited by Cristóbal Kay, Saturnino M. Borras, and Haroon Akram-Lodhi, 41–79. London: Routledge, 2007.

Kelley, Jonathan, and Herbert S. Klein. *Revolution and the Rebirth of Inequality: A Theory Applied to the National Revolution in Bolivia*. Berkeley: University of California Press, 1981.

Klein, Herbert. *Ayllus y haciendas en el mercado boliviano en los siglos XVIII y XIX*. Buenos Aires: Biblos, 1988.

Klein, Herbert. *Bolivia: The Evolution of a Multi-ethnic Society*. New York: Oxford University Press, 1992.

Klein, Herbert. *A Concise History of Bolivia*. New York: Cambridge University Press, 2011.

Klein, Herbert. *Haciendas and Ayllus: Rural Society in the Bolivian Andes in the Eighteenth and Nineteenth Centuries*. Stanford, CA: Stanford University, 1993.

Klein, Herbert. *Orígenes de la revolución nacional boliviana. La crisis de la generación del Chaco*. La Paz: Editorial Juventud, 1968

Klein, Herbert. *Parties and Political Change in Bolivia, 1880–1952*. Cambridge: Cambridge University Press, 1969.

Klein, Herbert. "Social Change in Bolivia since 1952." In *Proclaiming Revolution: Bolivia in Comparative Perspective*, edited by Merilee Grindle and Pilar Domingo, 232–58. London: Institute of Latin American Studies, 2003.

Klein, Herbert S. "German Busch and the Era of 'Military Socialism' in Bolivia." *Hispanic American Historical Review* 47, no. 2 (May 1, 1967): 166–84.

Knight, Alan. *The Mexican Revolution: Porfirians, Liberals, and Peasants*. Vol. 1. Lincoln: University of Nebraska Press, 1990.

Knight, Alan, ed. *Racismo, revolución e indigenismo. México, 1910–1940*. Puebla: Universidad Autónoma de Puebla, Instituto de Ciencias Sociales y Humanidades, Consejo Estatal de Ciencia y Tecnología, 2004.

Knight, Alan. "Social Revolution: A Latin American Perspective." *Bulletin of Latin American Research* 9, no. 2 (January 1990): 175–202.

Kohl, James V. "The Cliza and Ucureña War: Syndical Violence and National Revolution in Bolivia." *Hispanic American Historical Review* 62, no. 4 (November 1982): 607–28.

Kohl, James V. "Peasant and Revolution in Bolivia, April 9, 1952–August 2, 1953." *Hispanic American Historical Review* 58, no. 2 (1978): 238–59.

Kourí, Emilio. *A Pueblo Divided: Business, Property, and Community in Papantla, Mexico.* Stanford, CA: Stanford University Press, 2004.

Kuenzli, Gabrielle. *Acting Inca: Identity and National Belonging in Early Twentieth-Century Bolivia.* Pittsburgh, PA: University of Pittsburgh Press, 2013.

Lagos, María L. *Autonomy and Power: The Dynamics of Class and Culture in Rural Bolivia.* Philadelphia: University of Pennsylvania Press, 1994.

Lahiff, Edward, Saturnino M. Borras Jr., and Cristobal Kay. "Market-Led Agrarian Reform: Policies, Performance and Prospects." *Third World Quarterly* 28, no. 8 (January 2007): 1417–36.

Land Tenure Center. *Agrarian Reform in Latin America: An Annotated Bibliography.* Vol. 1. Madison: Land Tenure Center, University of Wisconsin, 1974.

Land Tenure Center. *Bolivia: Problems and Promise. A Series of Speeches by Víctor Andrade, Ambassador of Bolivia.* Washington, DC: Embassy of Bolivia, 1956.

Langer, Erick. "Andean Rituals of Revolt: The Chayanta Rebellion of 1927." *Ethnohistory* 37, no. 3 (1990): 227–53.

Langer, Erick. *Economic Change and Rural Resistance in Southern Bolivia, 1880–1930.* Stanford, CA: Stanford University Press, 1989.

Langer, Erick. "El liberalismo y la abolición de la comunidad indígena en el siglo diecinueve." *Historia y Cultura* 14 (1988) 59–95.

Langer, Erick, and Robert Jackson. "El liberalismo y el problema de la tierra en Bolivia (1825–1920)." *Siglo XIX, Revista de Historia* 10 (1990): 9–33.

Larson, Brooke. "Bolivia Revisited: New Directions in North American Research in History and Anthropology." *Latin American Research Review* 23, no. 1 (January 1988): 63–90.

Larson, Brooke. "Capturing Indian Bodies, Hearts, and Minds: The Gendered Politics of Rural School Reform in Bolivia, 1920s–1940s." In *Natives Making Nation: Gender, Indigeneity, and the State in the Andes,* edited by Andrew Canessa, 32–59. Tucson: University of Arizona Press, 2005.

Larson, Brooke. *Cochabamba, 1550–1900: Colonialism and Agrarian Transformation in Bolivia.* Durham, NC: Duke University Press, 2012.

Larson, Brooke. "Exploitation and Moral Economy in the Southern Andes: A Critical Reconsideration." Paper presented at the Consortium of Columbia University Institute of Latin American and Iberian Studies and New York University Center for Latin American and Caribbean Studies, 1988.

Larson, Brooke. *Trials of Nation Making: Liberalism, Race, and Ethnicity in the Andes, 1810–1910*. Cambridge: Cambridge University Press, 2004.

La Serna, Miguel. *The Corner of the Living: Local Power Relations and Indigenous Perceptions in Ayacucho, Peru, 1940–1983*. Chapel Hill: University of North Carolina Press, 2012.

Lefevbre, Georges. *The Great Fear of 1789: Rural Panic in Revolutionary France*. Princeton, NJ: Princeton University, 1973.

Lehm A., Zulema, and Silvia Rivera Cusicanqui. *Los artesanos libertarios y la ética del trabajo*. La Paz: Gramma, 1988.

Lehman, Kenneth Duane. *Bolivia and the United States: A Limited Partnership*. Athens: University of Georgia Press, 1999.

Lehman, Kenneth Duane. "Braked but not Broken: The United States and Revolutionaries in Mexico and Bolivia." In *Proclaiming Revolution: Bolivia in Comparative Perspective*, edited by Pilar Doming and Merilee S. Grindle, 91–113. London: Institute of Latin American Studies, 2003.

Leinaweaver, Jessaca. *The Circulation of Children: Kinship, Mobility, and Morality in Ayacucho*. Durham, NC: Duke University Press, 2008.

Leonard, Olen E. *Cantón Chullpas. Estudio económico social en el valle de Cochabamba, Bolivia*. La Paz: Ministerio de Agricultura, Ganadería y Colonización, 1947.

Léons, Bárbara, and William Léons. "Land Reform and Economic Change in the Yungas." In *Beyond the Revolution: Bolivia since 1952*, edited by James Malloy and Richard S. Thorn, 269–300. Pittsburgh, PA: University of Pittsburgh Press, 1971.

Léons, Madeline Barbara. "The Political Economy of Agrarian Reform in the Bolivian Yungas." In *New Directions in Political Economy: An Approach from Anthropology*, edited by Madeline Barbara Léons and Frances Rothstein, 83–111. Westport: Greenwood Press, 1979.

Lora, Guillermo. "La clase obrera después de 1952." In *Bolivia hoy*, ed. René Zavaleta Mercado, 169–281. Mexico: Siglo XXI, 1987

Lora, Guillermo. *Historia del movimiento obrero boliviano*. La Paz: Los Amigos del Libro, 1967.

Loveman, Brian. *Struggle in the Countryside: Politics and Rural Labor in Chile, 1919–1973*. Bloomington: Indiana University Press, 1976.

Lucca D., Manuel de. *El sistema de la tenencia de la tierra en las comunidades originarias de la Provincia Manco Capac, Departamento de La Paz*. La Paz: Servicio Nacional de Reforma Agraria, 1970.

Machicado Saravia, Flavio. "Ensayo crítico sobre la reforma agraria: (una interpretación teórica del caso boliviano)." Santiago: Facultad de Ciencias Económicas, Universidad de Chile, 1966.

Mallon, Florencia. "Entre la utopía y la marginalidad. Comunidades indígenas y culturas políticas en México y los andes, 1780–1990." *Historia Mexicana* 42, no. 2 (October 1992): 473–504.

Mallon, Florencia E. *Peasant and Nation: The Making of Postcolonial Mexico and Peru.* Berkeley: University of California Press, 1995.

Malloy, James. *Bolivia: The Uncompleted Revolution.* Pittsburgh, PA: University of Pittsburgh Press, 1970.

Malloy, James, and Richard S. Thorn. *Beyond the Revolution; Bolivia since 1952.* Pittsburgh, PA: University of Pittsburgh Press, 1971.

Mamani, Carlos, Esteban Ticona Alejo, and Leandro Condori Chura, *El escribano de los caciques apoderados.* La Paz: Hisbol/Taller de Historia Oral Andina, 1993.

Mamani Condori, Carlos B. *Taraqu, 1866–1935. Masacre, guerra y renovación en la biografía de Eduardo L. Nina Qhispi.* La Paz: Ediciones Aruwiyiri, 1991.

Marof, Tristán. *La tragedia del altiplano.* Buenos Aires: Editorial Claridad, 1935.

Martínez-Alier, Joan. *Haciendas, Plantations and Collective Farms: Agrarian Class Societies, Cuba and Peru.* London: Frank Cass, 1977.

Mayer, Enrique. *Ugly Stories of the Peruvian Agrarian Reform.* Durham, NC: Duke University Press, 2009.

McEwen, William J. *Changing Rural Society: A Study of Communities in Bolivia.* New York: Oxford University Press, 1975.

Medinaceli, Carlos. *La chaskañawi. Novela de costumbres bolivianas.* La Paz: Los Amigos del Libro, 1971.

Medinaceli, Ximena, Eugenia Bridikhina, María Luisa Soux, Rossana Barragán, Ana María Lema, Pilar Mendieta, Magdalena Cajías, Florencia Durán, and Ana María Capra de Seoane. *Bolivia, su historia.* La Paz: Coordinadora de Historia, 2015.

Medrano Ossio, José. *Responsabilidad penal de los indígenas.* Potosi: Tipografía Magne, 1941.

Mendelberg, Uri. "Immobilization and Peasant Class Consciousness." PhD diss., University of Wisconsin, 1980.

Mendelberg, Uri. "The Impact of the Bolivian Agrarian Reform on Class Formation." *Latin American Perspectives* 12, no. 3 (1985): 45–58.

Méndez G., Cecilia. *The Plebeian Republic: The Huanta Rebellion and the Making of the Peruvian State, 1820–1850.* Durham, NC: Duke University Press, 2005.

Mendieta, Pilar. *Entre la alianza y la confrontación. Pablo Zárate Willka y la rebelión indígena de 1899 en Bolivia.* La Paz: Instituto Francés de Estudios Andinos, Plural Editores, ASDI, Instituto de Estudios Bolivianos, Agencia de Cooperación Sueca, 2010.

Ministerio de Agricultura, Ganadería y Colonización. Dirección General de Economía Rural. *Estudio agro económico de la provincias Los Andes, Omasuyos e Ingavi.* La Paz: Ministerio de Agricultura. June 1946.

Ministerio de Asuntos Campesinos. *Gaceta campesina* (August 1952).

Ministerio de Asuntos Campesinos. *Gaceta campesina* (April 1953).

Ministerio de Asuntos Campesinos. *Gaceta campesina* (August 1953).

Ministerio de Asuntos Campesinos. *Gaceta campesina* (August 1954).

Ministerio de Asuntos Campesinos y Agropecuarios, Instituto Nacional de Estadística, Organización de las Naciones Unidas para la Agricultura y la Alimentación. *Censo Agropecuario 1950*. La Paz: Instituto Nacional de Estadística, 1985.

Ministerio de Educación, "Encuesta del Departamento de Asuntos Indígenas del Ministerio de Educación, Bellas Artes y Asuntos Indígenas led by the Jefe del Departamento de Asuntos Indígenas, Rafael Reyeros." September 1941. Government publication.

Ministerio de Educación. *Memoria de instrucción y agricultura*, 1911.

Ministerio de Educación. *Memoria del ministerio de instrucción pública y agricultura*. La Paz: Artística, 1915.

Ministerio de Educación. *Memoria y anexos que presenta el ministro de instrucción pública y agricultura presentado al congreso ordinario*. La Paz: Moderna, 1918.

Ministerio de Educación Pública y Bellas Artes, and Consejo Nacional de Educación. *Informe del director general de educación, 1941–1942*. La Paz: n.p., 1942.

Ministerio de Educación y Bellas Artes y Asuntos Indigenas. *Tercer congreso nacional de maestros*. La Paz: Ministerio de Educacion, Bellas Artes y Asuntos Indigenas, 1947.

Ministerio de Guerra y Colonización. *Memoria de guerra y colonización*, 1913.

Ministerio de Hacienda. Dirección General de Estadística. *Industria fabril y manufactura*. La Paz: Editorial Argote, 1941.

Ministerio de Hacienda y Estadística. *Censo demográfico 1950*. La Paz: Editorial Argote, 1955.

Ministerio de Obras Públicas and Justo Rodas Eguino. *Memoria presentada al honorable congreso nacional*. La Paz: n.p., 1941.

Ministerio de Trabajo, Salubridad y Previsión Social. *Leyes sociales de Bolivia*. La Paz: Publicación Oficial, 1945.

Mojica, Emma. *Resumen del estudio de la estructura agraria en Bolivia*. La Paz: Ministerio de Asuntos Campesinos y Agropecuarios, Consejo Nacional de Reforma Agraria, 1978.

Montenegro, Carlos, *Nacionalismo y coloniaje*. La Paz: Los Amigos del Libro, 1982.

Moore, Barrington. *Social Origins of Dictatorship and Democracy: Lord and Peasant in the Making of the Modern World*. Boston: Beacon Press, 1966.

Mörner, Magnus. *El sector agrario en América Latina. Estructura económica y cambio social*. Stockholm: Instituto de Estudios Latinoamericanos de Estocolmo, 1979.

Movimiento Nacionalista Revolucionario. Instituto de capacitación política del MNR. *Lecciones de propaganda, organización y agitación*. La Paz: Subsecretaría de Prensa, Informaciones y Cultura, 1953.

O'Connor, James. "Agrarian Reforms in Cuba, 1959–1963." *Science & Society* 32, no. 2 (1968): 169–217.

Olcott, Jocelyn. *Revolutionary Women in Postrevolutionary Mexico*. Durham, NC: Duke University Press, 2005.

Olsson, Tore C. *Agrarian Crossings. Reformers and the Remaking of the US and Mexican Countryside.* Princeton, NJ: Princeton University Press, 2017.

Orías Osorio, José. *Notas del ministerio publico.* La Paz: n.p., October 1947.

Ostria Gutierrez, Alberto. *Una revolución tras los andes.* Santiago de Chile: Nacimiento, 1944.

Partido Comunista de Bolivia. *Segundo congreso nacional del Partido PCB.* La Paz: Publicaciones PCB, 1964.

Partido de la Izquierda Revolucionaria. *Conclusiones del Séptimo pleno del PIR.* December 1950.

Partido de la Izquierda Revolucionaria. *Proyecto de ley para la creación del instituto de reforma agraria.* April, 24, 1947.

Partido Social Democratico. *Programa de acción politica.* Sucre: Escuelas gráficas salesianas, 1950.

Partido Socialista. *Bases y programa de acción partido socialista.* La Paz: n.p. October 1944.

Patch, Richard. "An Anthropologist's Approach to Economic Aid." West Coast South America Series 8 no. 7. New York: American Universities Field Staff, Reports Service, 1961.

Patch, Richard. "Bolivia: US Assistance in a Revolutionary Setting." In *Social Change in Latin America Today,* edited by Richard N. Adams, John P. Gillin, Allan R. Holmberg, Oscar Lewis, Richard N. Patch, and Charles Wagley, 108–76. New York: Harper, 1960.

Patch, Richard W. "Bolivia: The Restrained Revolution." *Annals of the American Academy of Political and Social Science* 334, no. 1 (March 1961): 123–32. Reprint no. 33. Land Tenure Center, University of Wisconsin.

Patch, Richard W. *Bolivia, the Seventh Year: A Letter from Richard W. Patch.* New York: American Universities Field Staff, 1959.

Patch, Richard W. "Social Implications of the Bolivian Agrarian Reform." PhD diss., Cornell University, Ithaca, New York, 1956.

Paz Ballivián, Danilo. *Cuestión agraria boliviana, presente y futuro.* La Paz: Academia Nacional de Ciencias de Bolivia, 1997.

Paz Estenssoro, Víctor. *Discursos parlamentarios.* La Paz: Canata, 1955.

Paz Estenssoro, Víctor. *Discursos y mensajes.* Buenos Aires: Meridiano, 1953.

Paz Estenssoro, Víctor. *Proceso y sentencia contra la oligarquía boliviana.* Buenos Aires: n.p., 1948.

Paz Estenssoro, Víctor. "La ultima carta de la oligarquía, Honor a los caidos del 1 de mayo en La Paz." Buenos Aires, May 1949.

Pearse, Andrew. *The Latin American Peasant.* London: Cass, 1975.

Petras, James F., and Robert LaPorte. *Cultivating Revolution: The United States and Agrarian Reform in Latin America.* New York: Random House, 1971.

Platt, Tristan. "The Andean Experience of Bolivian Liberalism, 1825–1900." In *Resistance, Rebellion, and Consciousness in the Andean Peasant World, 18th to 20th*

Centuries, edited by Steve Stern, 280–326. Madison: University of Wisconsin Press, 1987.

Platt, Tristán. *Estado boliviano y ayllu andino. Tierra y tributo en el norte de Potosí.* La Paz: Centro de Investigaciones Sociales, 2016.

PNUD-Bolivia. *Informe nacional sobre desarrollo humano 2007. El estado del estado en Bolivia.* La Paz: Programa de las Naciones Unidas para el Desarrollo, 2007.

Postero, Nancy Grey. *Now We Are Citizens: Indigenous Politics in Postmulticultural Bolivia.* Stanford, CA: Stanford University Press, 2008.

Powell, John Duncan. "Peasant Society and Clientelist Politics." *American Political Science Review* 64, no. 2 (June 1970): 411–25.

Priegue Romero, F. *La cruz de Bolivia. Crónica de la revolución de julio.* La Paz: Renacimiento, 1946.

Primer congreso indígena boliviano. Principales ponencias. La Paz, May 1945.

Primer congreso interamericano de indianistas. Reglamento, temario y agendas. La Paz: Fenix, 1939.

Pruden, Hernán. "Las luchas cívicas y las no tan cívicas. Santa Cruz de la Sierra (1957–1959)." *Ciencia y cultura. La revolución nacional. Sesenta años después* 29 (December 2012): 127–74.

Qayum, Seemin, María Luisa Soux, and Rossana Barragán R. *De terratenientes a amas de casa. Mujeres de la élite de La Paz en la primera mitad del siglo XX.* La Paz: Ministerio de Desarrollo Humano, Secretaría de Asuntos Étnicos, de Género y Generacionales, Subsecretaría de Asuntos de Género, 1997.

Ramos Quevedo, Luis. *Plan sintético. La salvación de Bolivia y la felicidad del pueblo. "Pueblo boliviano, uníos, para reclamar por todos los medios la reivindicación de vuestros derechos ururpados por el capitalismo imperialista."* Colquiri: Federación Obrera Local del departamento de Oruro, 1947.

Ranaboldo, Claudia. *El camino perdido. Chinkasqa ñan Thakhi chhagayata. Biografía del dirigente campesino kallawaya Antonio Álvarez Mamani.* La Paz: Servicios Múltiples de Tecnologías Apropiadas, 1988.

República de Bolivia. *Constitución Política del Estado*, 1880.

República de Bolivia. *Constitución Politica del Estado*, 1938.

República de Bolivia. *Constitución Politica del Estado*, 1967.

República de Bolivia. *Redactor de la Honorable Convención Nacional de 1938.* La Paz: Universo, 1938.

República de Bolivia. Redactor de la Honorable Camara de Diputados. *Congreso Ordinario de 1943* (August–September) Volume 1. La Paz: Escuela Tipográfica Salesiana, 1944.

Reyeros, Rafael A. *Caquiaviri. Escuelas para los indígenas bolivianos.* La Paz: Universo, 1946.

Reyeros, Rafael A. *El pongueaje. La servidumbre personal de los indios bolivianos.* La Paz: Universo, 1949.

Reynaga, Fausto. *Víctor Paz Estenssoro.* La Paz: Editorial La Paz, 1949.

Rivas Antezana, Sinforoso, and José Miguel Gordillo Claure. *Los hombres de la revolución. Memorias de un líder campesino.* La Paz: Plural Editores, 2000.

Rivera, Alberto. *Los terratenientes de Cochabamba.* Cochabamba: Centro de Estudios de la Realidad Económica y Social, Facultad de Ciencias Económicas, 1992.

Rivera Cusicanqui, Silvia. "La expansión del latifundio en el altiplano boliviano. Elementos para la caractarización de una oligarquía regional." *Avances* 2 (1978): 95–117.

Rivera Cusicanqui, Silvia. "Liberal Democracy and Ayllu Democracy in Bolivia: The Case of Northern Potosí." *Journal of Development Studies.* 26, no. 4 (1990): 97–121.

Rivera Cusicanqui, Silvia. "Luchas campesinas contemporáneas en Bolivia. El movimiento Katarista, 1970–1980." In *Bolivia, hoy*, edited by René Zavaleta Mercado, 129–68. Mexico City: Siglo XXI, 1987.

Rivera Cusicanqui, Silvia. *Oprimidos pero no vencidos. Luchas del campesinado aymara y qhechwa, 1900–1980.* La Paz: Mirada Salvaje, 2010.

Rivera Cusicanqui, Silvia. *Violencias (re) encubiertas en Bolivia.* La Paz: Mirada Salvaje, 2010.

Rodríguez Ostria, Gustavo. *Elites, mercado y cuestión regional en Bolivia. Cochabamba.* Quito: Facultad Latinoamericana de Ciencias Sociales, 1994.

Rojas Ortuste, Gonzalo. *Lo público en la pluralidad. Ensayos desde Bolivia y América Latina.* La Paz: CIDES, 2015.

Rolón-Anaya, Mario. "La evolución del derecho y el problema de la reforma agraria." Paper presented at the auditorium of Radio Popular, March 30, 1949.

Roseberry, William. "Beyond the Agrarian Question in Latin America." In *Confronting Historical Paradigms: Peasants, Labor, and the Capitalist World System in Africa and Latin America*, edited by Frederick Cooper, Allen Isaacman, Florencia E. Mallon, William Roseberry, and Steve J. Stern, 318–68. Madison: University of Wisconsin Press, 1993.

Roseberry, William. "Hegemony and the Language of Contention." In *Everyday Forms of State Formation: Revolution and the Negotiation of Rule in Modern Mexico*, edited by Gilbert Joseph and Daniel Nugent, 355–66. Durham, NC: Duke University Press, 2012.

Rosset, Peter, Raj Patel, and Michael Courville. *Promised Land: Competing Visions of Agrarian Reform.* Oakland, CA: Food First, 2006.

Roxborough, Ian. *Theories of Underdevelopment.* London: Macmillan, 1979.

Saavedra, Carlos Gonzalo de. *El problema integral del indio. Una solución socialista.* La Paz: n.p., November 1946.

Safford, Frank. "Race, Integration, and Progress: Elite Attitudes and the Indian in Colombia, 1750–1870." *Hispanic American Historical Review* 71, no. 1 (1991): 1–33.

Sánchez, Walter. "Hacienda, campesinado y estructura agraria en el Valle Alto." BA thesis, Universidad Mayor de San Simón, 1992.

Sánchez-Albornoz, Nicolas. *Indios y tributos en el Alto Peru*. Lima: Instituto de Estudios Peruanos, 1978.

Sandor, John S. *Bolivia's Radical Tradition: Permanent Revolution in the Andes*. Tucson: University of Arizona Press, 2011.

Sanjinés, Alfredo. *Más fuerte que la tierra. Ensayo social del indio boliviano*. La Paz: Editorial Renacimiento, 1933.

Sanjinés, Alfredo. *El Quijote mestizo. Historia novelada de Belzu y Melgarejo, con el proceso de la demagogia y de la dictadura en Bolivia*. La Paz: Editorial Centenario, 1951.

Sanjinés, Alfredo. *La reforma agraria en Bolivia*. La Paz: Universo, 1932.

Sanjinés, Alfredo. *La reforma agraria en Bolivia*. La Paz: Universo, 1945.

Sarmiento, Gerardo. *Dos años de labor efectiva en el parlamento*. La Paz: Escuela Tipográfica Salesiana, 1925.

Schelchkov, Andrey. "En los umbrales del socialismo boliviano. Tristán Marof y La Tercera Internacional Comunista." *Revista Izquierdas*, no. 5 (July 2009): 1–24.

Schelchkov, Andrey. "La izquierda en la posguerra del Chaco." In *Historia de las izquierdas bolivianas: Archivos y documentos* (1920–1940), edited by Andrey Schelchkov and Pablo Stefanoni, 76–83. La Paz: Centro de Investigaciones Sociales, 2016.

Schelchkov, Andrey. "Roberto Hinojosa. ¿revolucionario Nacionalista o Goebbels Criollo?" *Izquierdas* 2 (December 2008): 1–21.

Scott, James. *The Moral Economy of the Peasant: Rebellion and Subsistence in Southeast Asia*. New Haven, CT: Yale University Press, 1978.

Scott, James. "Resistance without Protest and without Organization: Peasant Opposition to the Islamic Zakat and the Christian Tithe." *Comparative Studies in Society and History* 29, no. 3 (July 1987): 417–52.

Scott, James. *Seeing like a State: How Certain Schemes to Improve the Human Condition Have Failed*. New Haven, CT: Yale University Press, 1998.

Scott, James C. *Weapons of the Weak: Everyday Forms of Peasant Resistance*. New Haven, CT: Yale University Press, 1985.

Seligmann, Linda. *Between Reform and Revolution: Political Struggles in the Peruvian Andes, 1969–1991*. Stanford, CA: Stanford University Press, 1995.

Seligmann, Linda. "The Burden of Visions amidst Reform: Peasant Relations to Law in the Peruvian Andes." *American Ethnologist: The Journal of the American Ethnological Society* 20 (February 1993): 25–51.

Senior, Clarence. "Review of *Agrarian Reform in Latin America* by Robert J. Alexander." *Annals of the American Academy of Political and Social Science* 416, no. 1 (November 1974): 208.

Serulnikov, Sergio. *Subverting Colonial Authority Challenges to Spanish Rule in Eighteenth-Century Southern Andes.* Durham, NC: Duke University Press, 2003.

Servicio Nacional de Reforma Agraria. *Estadísticas sobre tenencia de la tierra del SNRA, 1953–1970.* La Paz: Centro Nacional de Computación, 1972.

Siekmeier, James. "Latin American Economic Nationalism and United States–Latin American Relations, 1945–1961." *Latin Americanist* 52, no. 3 (2008): 59–76.

Siekmeier, James F. *The Bolivian Revolution and the United States, 1952 to the Present.* University Park: Pennsylvania State University Press, 2011.

Smale, Robert L. *"I Sweat the Flavor of Tin": Labor Activism in Early Twentieth-Century Bolivia.* Pittsburgh, PA: University of Pittsburgh Press, 2010.

Smith, Stephen M. "Labor Exploitation on Pre-1952 Haciendas in the Lower Valley of Cochabamba, Bolivia." *Journal of Developing Areas* 11, no. 2 (January 1977): 227–44.

Smith, T. Lynn. *Agrarian Reform in Latin America.* New York: Knopf, 1965.

Soliz, Carmen. "Agrarian Reform in Bolivia in the 20th and 21st Centuries." *Oxford Research Encyclopedia of Latin American History.* August 2018.

Soliz, Carmen. "'Land to the Original Owners': Rethinking the Indigenous Politics of the Bolivian Agrarian Reform." *Hispanic American Historical Review* 97, no. 2 (2017): 259–96.

Soliz, Carmen. "La modernidad esquiva. Debates políticos e intelectuales sobre la reforma agraria en Bolivia (1935–1952)." *Ciencia y Cultura. La revolución nacional. Sesenta años después* 29 (December 2012): 23–50.

Soria, Vitaliano. "Los caciques apoderados y la lucha por la escuela (1900–1952)." In *Educación indígena. ¿Ciudadanía o colonización?* edited by Roberto Choque Canqui et al., 51–78. La Paz: Aruwiyiri, 1992.

Soruco, Ximena. *La ciudad de los cholos. Mestizaje y colonialidad en Bolivia, siglos XIX y XX.* La Paz: IFEA, 2012.

Soto, César. *Historia del pacto militar campesino.* Cochabamba: Centro de Estudios de la Realidad Económica y Social, 1984.

Spedding, Alison. *Wachu wachu. Cultivo de coca e identidad en los Yunkas de La Paz.* La Paz: Hisbol, Centro de Investigación y Promoción del Campesinado, Cocayapu, 1994.

Stavenhagen, Rodolfo. *Agrarian Problems and Peasant Movements in Latin America.* Garden City: Anchor Books, 1970.

Stavenhagen, Rodolfo. "Indigenous Peoples and the State in Latin America: An Ongoing Debate." In *Multiculturalism in Latin America: Indigenous Rights, Diversity and Democracy,* edited by Rachel Sieder, 24–44. Institute of Latin American Studies Series. London: Palgrave, 2002.

Stefanoni, Pablo. *Los inconformistas del centenario. Intelectuales, socialismo y nación en una Bolivia en crisis (1925–1939).* La Paz: Plural Editores, 2015.

Stefanoni, Pablo. *¿Qué hacer con los indios? y otros traumas irresueltos de la colonialidad.* La Paz: Plural Editores, 2010.

Stephenson, Marcia. "Forging an Indigenous Counterpublic Sphere: The Taller de Historia Oral Andina in Bolivia." *Latin American Research Review* 37, no. 2 (2002): 99–118.

Stern, Steve J. *Resistance, Rebellion, and Consciousness in the Andean Peasant World, 18th to 20th Centuries.* Madison: University of Wisconsin Press, 1987.

Subsecretaría de Prensa, Informaciones y Cultura. *Antología de poemas de la revolución.* La Paz: SPIC, 1954.

Subsecretaría de Prensa, Informaciones y Cultura. *El libro blanco de la reforma agraria.* La Paz: Subsecretaría de Prensa, Informaciones y Cultura, 1953.

Taborga, Alberto. *Al pueblo de Bolivia. Impreso por el comité de liberación nacional.* N.p., February 1945.

Tadic, Vicente. *"Aporte al estudio y solución del problema del indio." Conferencia masónica leída en la tenida ordinaria del 21 de octubre de 1929.* Oruro, October 1929.

Taller de Historia Oral Andina. *El indio Santos Marka T'ula. Cacique principal de los ayllus de Qallapa y apoderado general de las comunidades originarias de la República.* La Paz: Taller de Historia Oral Andina, 1988.

Tamayo, Franz. *Creación de la Pedagogía Nacional.* La Paz: Editorial Juventud, 1986.

Tapia, Luis. "Los escritos sobre el 52." *Ciencia y Cultura. La revolución nacional. Sesenta años después* 29 (December 2012): 9–18.

Tenemos pechos de bronce . . . pero no sabemos nada. Memoria de la Conferencia Internacional Revoluciones del siglo XX, Homenaje a los cincuenta años de la Revolución Boliviana. La Paz: Programa de Naciones Unidas, FES-ILDIS, Plural Editores, 2003.

Tenth Inter-American Conference, Resolutions. March 1–28, 1954, Caracas.

Thiesenhusen, William C. *Broken Promises: Agrarian Reform and the Latin American Campesino.* Boulder, CO: Westview Press, 1995.

Thome, Joseph R. "Problems Which Obstruct the Process of Title Distribution under the Bolivian Agrarian Reform." In manuscript, 1966.

Thomson, Sinclair. "Bull Horns and Dynamite: Echoes of Revolution in Bolivia—The Explosions of Miners' Dynamite in October 2003." *NACLA Report on the Americas* 42, no. 2 (2009). https://nacla.org/article/bull-horns-and-dynamite-echoes-revolution-bolivia/.

Thomson, Sinclair. *We Alone Will Rule: Native Andean Politics in the Age of Insurgency.* Madison: University of Wisconsin Press, 2002.

Thomson, Sinclair, Rossana Barragán, Xavier Albó, Seemin Qayum, and Mark Goodale. *The Bolivia Reader History, Culture, Politics.* Durham, NC: Duke University Press, 2018.

Thurner, Mark. *From Two Republics to One Divided: Contradictions of Postcolonial Nation-Making in Andean Peru.* Durham, NC: Duke University Press, 2012.

Thurner, Mark, and Andrés Guerrero. *After Spanish Rule: Postcolonial Predicaments of the Americas.* Durham, NC: Duke University Press, 2003.

Tinsman, Heidi. *Partners in Conflict: The Politics of Gender, Sexuality, and Labor in the Chilean Agrarian Reform, 1950–1973.* Durham, NC: Duke University Press, 2002.

Tuma, Elias H. "Agrarian Reform in Historical Perspective Revisited." *Comparative Studies in Society and History* 21, no. 1 (January 1979): 3–29.

Tuma, Elias H. *Twenty-Six Centuries of Agrarian Reform: A Comparative Analysis.* Berkeley: University of California Press, 1965.

Turovsky, Paul Robert. "Bolivian Haciendas: Before and After the Revolution." PhD diss., University of California, Los Angeles, 1980.

Universidad Mayor de San Simón, and Facultad de Derecho. *Cuestiones de derecho agrario en torno al proyecto de creación del Instituto de Reforma Agraria.* Cochabamba: Imprenta Universitaria, 1949.

Universidad Técnica de Oruro. *Antecedentes para la reforma agraria en Bolivia.* Departamento de extensión cultural. Oruro: Universitaria, 1953.

University of Wisconsin. Land Tenure Center. "The Progress of Land Reform in Bolivia." Discussion Paper 2 (May 1963), 1–23. Land Tenure Center, University of Wisconsin, Madison.

Unzueta, Mario. *Valle.* Cochabamba: Época, 1945.

Urioste, Miguel. *Bolivia. La reforma agraria abandonada. Valles y altiplano.* La Paz: Plural Editores, CIDES, 2003.

Urioste, Miguel, Rossana Barragán, and Gonzalo Colque. *Los nietos de la reforma agraria. Acceso, tenencia y uso de la tierra en el altiplano de Bolivia.* La Paz: Fundación Tierra, 2007.

Urquidi, Arturo. *La comunidad indígena. Precedentes sociológicos. Vicisitudes históricas.* Cochabamba: Universitaria, 1941.

Urquidi, Arturo. "Consideraciones de orden doctrinal sobre la reforma agraria en Bolivia." *Revista Mexicana de Sociología* 18, no. 1 (January 1, 1956): 65–95.

Urquidi Morales, Arturo. *El feudalismo en America y la reforma agraria boliviana.* Cochabamba: Imprenta Universitaria, 1966.

Urrolagoitia, Mamerto. Presidente Constitucional Interno de la República. *Mensaje al honorable congreso ordinario.* La Paz: n.p., 1949.

US Agency for International Development. Rural Development Division. *Preliminary Historical Review of Rural Development Division.* La Paz: n.p., 1970.

Valencia Cabrera, Pastor. *Pensemos en el indio. Ensayos acerca de la situación actual del aborigen en Bolivia.* La Paz: Fenix, 1945.

Van Young, Eric. *Hacienda and Market in Eighteenth-Century Mexico: The Rural Economy of the Guadalajara Region, 1675–1820.* Berkeley: University of California Press, 1981.

Villalpando Retamozo, Abelardo. "La cuestión del indio. Tesis presentada al primer congreso nacional de facultades de derecho." Potosí: Universidad Tomás Frías, June 1939.

Villamor, Germán G. *Historia de la gran revolución popular del 21 de julio de 1946 en la ciudad de La Paz*. La Paz: Popular, 1946.

Villarroel López, Gualberto, Franz Tamayo, and Cástulo Chávez. *Conferencia de los presidentes de los tres poderes del Estado. Efectuada del 23 de abril al 2 de mayo de 1945, en el palacio de gobierno de la ciudad de La Paz*. La Paz: Dirección General de Propaganda e Informaciones, 1945.

Webber, Jeffery R. *Red October: Left-Indigenous Struggles in Modern Bolivia*. Chicago: Haymarket Books, 2012.

Wiarda, Howard J. *Politics and Social Change in Latin America: The Distinct Tradition*. Amherst: University of Massachusetts Press, 1974.

Wilkie, James Wallace. *Measuring Land Reform*. Los Angeles: UCLA Latin American Center, 1974.

Willard, William. "The Ninth Inter-American Indian Congress Historical Overview." *Wicazo Sa Review* 2, no. 1 (April 1986): 21–27.

Winn, Peter, and Cristobal Kay. "Agrarian Reform and Rural Revolution in Allende's Chile." *Journal of Latin American Studies* 6, no. 1 (1974): 135–59.

Wolfe, Mikael. *Watering the Revolution: An Environmental and Technological History of Agrarian Reform in Mexico*. Durham, NC: Duke University Press, 2017.

Womack, John. *Zapata and the Mexican Revolution*. New York: Knopf, 1969.

Wright, Thomas C. *Latin America in the Era of the Cuban Revolution*. Westport: Praeger, 2000.

Young, Kevin. *Blood of the Earth: Resource Nationalism, Revolution, and Empire in Bolivia*. Austin: University of Texas Press, 2017.

Young, Kevin. "From Open Door to Nationalization: Oil and Development Visions in Bolivia, 1952–1969." *Hispanic American Historical Review* 97, no.1 (February 2017): 95–129.

Zanatta, Loris, and Mariano Aguas. "Auge y declinación de la tercera posición. Bolivia, Perón y la guerra fría, 1943–1954." *Desarrollo Económico* 45, no. 177 (April–June 2005): 25–53.

Zavaleta Mercado, René. *Bolivia, hoy*. México City: Siglo XXI, 1983.

Zavaleta Mercado, René. *El estado en América Latina*. La Paz: Los Amigos del Libro, 1990.

Zavaleta Mercado, René. "Las masas en noviembre." In *Bolivia, hoy*, edited by René Zavaleta Mercado. México City: Siglo XXI, 1983.

Zavaleta Mercado, René, and Mauricio Souza Crespo. *Obra completa*. Vol. 1. La Paz: Plural Editores, 2011.

Zilveti Arce, Pedro. *Bajo el signo de la barbarie. Matanzas de noviembre*. Santiago de Chile: Editorial Orbe, 1946.

Zulawski, Ann. "The National Revolution and Bolivia in the 1950s: What Did Che See?" In *Che's Travels: The Making of a Revolutionary in 1950s Latin America*, edited by Paulo Drinot, 181–209. Durham, NC: Duke University Press, 2010.

Zulawski, Ann. *Unequal Cures: Public Health and Political Change in Bolivia, 1900–1950*. Durham, NC: Duke University Press, 2007.

INDEX

Achacachi, 16, 95, 113–18, 122, 36, 223n44; land restitution cases in, 135, 138
agrarian court cases, 13, 25, 27, 33, 116, 147–48, 167, 174, 185n15; and expropriation, 132, 136; on land distribution, 18, 10, 159, 162. *See also* judges
agrarian reform, 8–9, 31, 48, 165, 172, 201n2; across Latin America, 108–10; continued salience of, 178–81; definition of the term, 47; delays in implementing, 225nn56–57, 225n61; lack of data on, 227nn14–15; presidential verdicts, 168–69, 175; trials, 145, 158–59, 164
Agrarian Reform Decree-Law (August 2, 1953), 68, 70, 84, 86–87, 95, 103–8, 130, 136; Article 32, 135; Article 42, 131; and colonos' rights, 139; enactment of, 13, 14, 109, 115–16, 121, 141–42, 201n4; and political landscape, 168; various interpretations of, 114, 118–19, 139, 228n32. *See also* decree-laws
agregados, 34, 35, 36, 142, 159, 160, 177
Agricultural Bank, 39–40, 42, 72, 96, 103, 106
agronomists, 94, 99, 143, 144, 146, 147
Albó, Xavier, 33, 116, 165, 175
Alexander, Robert, 5
Allende, Salvador, 3, 153
Alliance for Progress, 176, 227n19
Almaraz, Sergio, 12
Alvarez, Waldo, 49, 50, 196n23
Álvarez Plata, Federico, 16–17, 96, 97
Anaya, Ricardo, 62–63, 64, 65, 189n27
Antezana, Luis H., 52, 50, 140
anthropologists, 5, 32, 80–81, 167, 179
Aramayo, Carlos Victor, 24
Arbenz, Jacobo, 3, 95, 101, 117, 212n56
Ari, Waskar, 121, 127
arrenderos. *See* sharecroppers
arrimantes, 35, 91, 144, 145, 193n67; different from originarios, 142, 159; and expropriation, 147, 150–55, 160; sitiajeros, 142, 159
Arze, José Antonio, 62, 63, 64, 65–66, 189n27
Ayala Mercado, Ernesto, 96, 133, 208n9, 218n57
ayllus, 23, 122–26, 138, 183n2, 186n30
aynocas. *See* collective lands

Bánzer, General Hugo, 12, 142, 169, 177, 179, 228nn23–24; and peasants, 165, 166
Barragán, Rossana, 33, 51
Barrientos, General René, 11–12, 166, 171, 197n34, 219n72, 225n63, 228n23; overthrew President Paz Estenssoro, 142, 165
beneficiaries. *See under* land distribution
Bolivian Indigenista Institute, 128, 217n36
Bolivian National Revolution (1952), 3, 184n7
Bolivian Rural Society. *See* Sociedad Rural Boliviana (SRB)

Bolivian Society of Agronomists, 94, 99
Bolivian Workers Federation. *See* Central Obrera Boliviana (COB)
Busch, Germán Busch, 38, 51, 52, 59, 79, 126, 166, 196n26; death of, 53

caciques apoderados, 60, 120, 122, 124–25, 199n72, 214n7, 215n9, 218n55; network of, 6, 58, 129. *See also* Indian community leaders
Carter, William, 32, 33, 186n28, 193n66
Castro, Moisés, 84–85, 86
census data, 26, 33, 37, 189n24, 220n11; absence of, 10, 164
Central Obrera Boliviana (COB), 4, 57, 59, 88, 96
Céspedes, Augusto, 189n27, 215n22
Chaco War, 32, 38, 46, 49, 81, 122
Chávez, Cornelio, 85, 115–18, 213n74, 220n16
Chávez Ortiz, Ñuflo, 73, 82, 97
Chayanta rebellion, 48, 195n6
chicha (maize beer), 28, 39, 72–73
Chile, 12, 21, 42; agrarian reform in, 3, 4, 153, 165, 194n81
Chipana, Basilio, 113–14
Chipana Ramos, Francisco, 61–62
chiquiñeros, 34, 37, 192n64
Choque Canqui, Roberto, 6, 122
Chulumani, 45, 156, 190, 223n44, 223n47
Central Intelligence Agency (CIA), 109, 117, 119
Clark, James, 175, 187n36, 190n32
Cliza, 33, 54, 65, 151, 186n24, 196n23, 223n44, 223n47; peasant union in, 198n44; Santa Clara monastery in, 12, 111, 112
CNRA. *See* Consejo Nacional de Reforma Agraria (CNRA)
COB. *See* Central Obrera Boliviana (COB)
coca leaves, 31, 39, 68, 208n26; cultivation of, 34, 162, 193n64; sale of, 21, 153, 224n50
Cochabamba Rural Society. *See* Federación Rural de Cochabamba (FRC)
collective lands, 153, 160, 161, 224n53
colonato system, 32, 38, 41, 58, 84, 190n31, 190n34, 190n36; eliminated by decree, 106. *See also* colonos
colonization, 39, 40, 53, 68, 99; areas for, 54, 106, 119, 221n22, 223n47, 228n24; settlement, 95, 96, 177
colonos, 9, 12, 14, 132, 151, 224n50; and agrarian reform, 120, 172, 175; and Agustín Villegas, 143–44; and comunarios, 71, 90, 173; conditions of work, 28–29, 30, 59, 191n45, 202n6, 202n14; and contracts, 92, 202n18; definition of term, 183n2; and ex-comunarios, 10, 122, 132, 133, 137–38, 140; included in land sales, 20, 190n31; and landlords, 27, 34, 49, 98, 129, 147, 158; and peasants, 144–45, 191n37, 220n7; and petitions, 58, 87; and politics, 13, 53–57, 75, 213n81; and the Quirogas, 154, 155; unionization of, 18, 49, 138, 186n30, 196n21; union leaders, 76, 106, 119; and unions, 8, 186n27; and the whip, 89, 190n32, 191n45, 202n6; and working on hacienda, 124, 191n46, 192n64
Colque, Natalio, 113–14
Comité Indigenal Boliviano, 60, 62
Commission for Agrarian Reform, 17, 94, 95–104, 128, 208nn8–9
communal lands, indigenous, 21–23, 47, 58, 67, 139, 218n55; appropriation of, 188n13, 195n6; restitution of, 122, 124, 131–32
comunarios, 130, 131, 135, 139, 172, 186n30, 195n6; and colonos, 61, 177; definition of term, 183n2; leaders of, 76, 120, 121, 214n1; petitions, 75, 122, 127, 206n58, 214n6, 216n32, and restitution decree, 218n53; Samuel Alejandro Cabrera, 171; and unions, 8. *See also* ex-comunarios
Consejo Nacional de Reforma Agraria (CNRA), 9, 17, 85, 121, 152, 158, 180; appeals to, 115, 137, 145, 151; auto de vista, 219n68; established, 106; and expropriation cases, 107–8, 146–47, 150; and land distribution, 143, 160, 169–70; offices of, 141, 146, 179, 227n16; reports and propaganda, 166, 175, 176–78
constitutions: in 1880, 52; in indigenous communities (1953), 92; in Latin America, 174; liberal, 51; Mexican,

48; in 1938, 46, 52, 55, 68, 197n36; in 1967, 166
corregidores, 31, 69, 76–77, 79, 81–82, 88, 175, 192n62
Cote, Steven, 12
Cuba, 3, 163, 174, 176, 211n54, 224n52
Cuellar, Doctor, 50, 196n21

Dandler, Jorge, 5–6, 31, 33
Dávalos, Andrés, 50, 196n21
de Daza, Benita, 129, 130
de la Cadena, Marisol, 174–75
decree-laws: number 07189 (May 24, 1965), 187n36, 225n63; number 07260 (August 2, 1965), 187n36, 225n63; number 3471, 114, 211n49; number 4008 (March 30, 1955), 211n48; number 7033 (1965), 166. *See also* Agrarian Reform Decree-Law (August 2, 1953)
decrees, 49, 53, 62, 106, 125, 202n14; Melgarejo's, 23; in 1942, 193n76; in 1945, 29, 61, 70, 72, 73; in 1955, 106; Paz Estenssoro's, 131, 200n2; for the restitution of communal land (1954), 11, 121–22, 131–32, 136, 139, 171, 218n56; Toro's, 50, 99, 110. *See also* Agrarian Reform Decree-Law (August 2, 1953); decree-laws; laws
Deere, Carmen Diana, 163, 180
Dunkerley James, 12, 127

Ecuador, 107, 108, 180, 181, 199n62, 218n52
Eguino Zaballa, Félix, 128, 131, 217n36
Erasmus, Charles, 5, 149
Escobari, Macario, 32, 40, 85, 146, 156, 222n42
Estrada de la Hoz, Julio, 101–2
ex-comunarios, 121–22, 125, 127–30, 132, 134–40; definition of term, 183n2; petitions from, 123, 126; political agenda of, 9–10. *See also* comunarios; Indians

Falange Socialista Boliviana (FSB), 78–79
FAO. *See* Food and Agricultural Organization (FAO)
Federación Departmental de Campesinos de Cochabamba (FDCC), 78, 82–83
Federación Obrera Local (FOL), 127, 184n14, 200n1, 205n50, 216n29
Federación Obrera Sindical (FOS), 60, 205n50
Federación Rural de Cochabamba (FRC), 66–68, 72, 98, 208n5
Finot, Enrique, 46, 52–53
Flores, Edmundo, 101, 108, 119, 210n36, 224n54
FOL. *See* Federación Obrera Local (FOL)
Food and Agricultural Organization (FAO), 95, 101, 109, 119
forasteros, 34, 36, 144, 189n25
FOS. *See* Federación Obrera Sindical (FOS)
Franco family, 157–58; Eulogio, 23, 134, 191n44, 223n49; Mercedes, 153
FRC. *See* Federación Rural de Cochabamba (FRC)
Frías, President Tomas, 22–23
FSB. *See* Falange Socialista Boliviana (FSB)
Fuentes, Severino, 33–34, 151, 152

García Meza, Luis, 169, 228n23
gender disparities, 74, 163, 168, 180–81. *See also* women
Goitia, Benedicto, 125, 130
Gordillo, José, 8, 80, 90
Gotkowitz, Laura, 6–7, 22, 53, 60, 62, 63, 122, 124; and peasant mobilization, 76, 89, 127, 172
Gregoriú, Raimundo, 96, 208n5
Grindle, Merilee, 174
Guatemala, 106, 108, 109, 119, 165, 212n56, 212n62; advisors from, 95, 101
Guevara Arze, Walter, 15, 51, 55, 87, 111, 189n27, 197n34, 219n72

haciendas, 87, 113–14, 115; Alcoholería, 29, 43, 148; Callisaya, 23, 45; Casamaya, 23, 27, 44–45, 115, 213n73; Cariquina, 126; Challuyo, 136; Charvina Grande, 27; Chijipina Chico, 85; Chillachirca, 86; Chillamani, Coripata Nor Yungas, 87; Chiquero, 159, 160, 162; Chirapaca, 40; Compi, 191n45; Cucuntupa, 149; Huallpero, 192n51; Jahuira Lacka, 118; Karhuisa,

40; Kehuiñal San Antonio, 190n32; Merke Achacachi, 74; Monte Redondo, 36, 148, 149, 150, 151; Murumani, 27, 44–45, 158, 191n44, 223n49; Naranjani, 152; Ocorani, 156; Pajchani Grande, 113–14, 160–61; Pajchani Molino, 85, 213n74; Santa Clara, 112, 154; Santa Lucía de Liquinas, 143–44, 145, 147, 149, 154; Taramaya Grande, 156; Taramaya, 85; Tari, 30, 86, 89, 117–18, 146–47, 149; Toco Viejo, 149; Yayani, 31, 65, 72, 191n42. *See also* latifundios
hacienda system, 19–20, 28–29, 34, 115, 188n22, 190n32, 193nn65–66
Hale, Charles, writings, Guatemala, 174–75
Harris, Olivia, 33
Herrera, Oscar, 99–100
Hertzog, Enrique, 55, 64, 126, 200n1
hilacatas, 29–30, 125, 126, 130, 138
Hochschild, Mauricio, 24, 188n19
Hylton, Forrest, 57

Imaña family, 24, 44, 191n44
indemnification, 99–103, 131, 136, 145, 154, 211n45; colonos and, 112, 137, 156; and land expropriation, 52, 68, 109; peasants and, 9, 106, 187n37
Indian communities. *See* indigenous communities
Indian community leaders, 7, 10, 47–48. *See also* caciques apoderados
Indian problem, the, 47–53, 57, 68–69, 96, 97
Indians, 32, 105, 109, 127, 184n6, 195n6, 196n22; definition of term, 183n2; and education, 127, 212n66; and mixed races, 6, 32, 150–51; uprisings of, 64–65. *See also* indigenistas
indigenistas, 47, 69, 88, 128, 198n43, 199n61; congresses, 52, 57–58, 59, 61–63, 217n36; definition of term, 53, 69; Inter-American Indigenista Congress, 217n36
indigenous, 34, 47, 69, 124, 128; Comisión de Asuntos Indígenas, 199n72; Comité Indigenal Boliviano, 60, 62; Confederación Indígena del Oriente Boliviano (CIDOB), 179; congresses, 57, 58, 59, 62; leaders, 15–16, 63, 126; National Indigenous Congress (1945), 7, 60; and politics, 49, 173, 180, 181, 200n2; property, 124, 125, 129; schools, 57–58, 68. *See also* indigenistas; Quechua
indigenous communities, 10–11, 26, 76, 98, 113, 120, 124, 125, 128, 130, 139, 140, 167; Antarani community, 171; boundaries of, 164; cooperatives among, 56; del Granado and, 67; indigenous contribution, 22; Jesus de Machaca community, 48, 130, 195n6; and land restitution, 105, 122, 131; legal existence of, 52, 197n36; MNR and, 69, 121; and the national revolution, 122–28; by 1950, 19, 37; nullified, 135; original members of, 34; Pallareti community, 138; and peasant unions, 79, 92–93, 174, 181, 186n28; Pongon Huyo community, 137–38; and unions, 92
INRA. *See under* laws
intendants, 31, 76, 77, 79, 82, 88
investment, agricultural, 141–51, 155, 156, 159
Irupana, 45, 156, 223n44, 223n47

Joseph, Gilbert, 174
Kay, Cristobal, 153, 226n73
Klein, Herbert, 23, 48, 172, 189n25, 189n28
Knight, Alan, 33
Kuenzli, Gabrielle, 127

labor contracts, 29, 71, 73, 74–75, 76, 83–88, 91
land: property, 168, 174, 179; property reform, 21, 65, 175; redistribution, 14, 70, 96, 139, 158, 168, 169; restitution, 121, 126, 132–39; surveys, 120, 124, 135; titles, 12, 21, 162–63, 169, 179, 187n36, 214n1, 225n63. *See also* land distribution; land expropriation; land tenure
land distribution, 73, 75–76, 95, 142, 169–70, 172; beneficiaries of, 142, 153, 159, 160, 162–64, 178; and inequality, 157–65

land expropriation, 107, 110–13, 118–19, 149, 156; cases, 112–13, 133–34, 150, 158, 159–60. *See also* Santa Clara monastery
landless peasants. *See* arrimantes
landlords, 9, 17, 27–28, 89, 97, 106, 115–16, 117, 138, 147–49, 150, 153, 154; and Agrarian Reform Decree-Law, 117, 141, 168; Antonio Rivera, 150; and Barrientos, 12, 165–66, 226n72; caciques apoderados and, 6; and colonos, 34, 54, 147, 152, 156, 166, 222n39, 222n41; elite, 7, 14; and expansion into communal land, 124, 125–26, 138; and investment, 18, 21, 141, 143, 145, 148; and peasants, 4, 154, 155, 156; political power of, 13, 75, 76, 141–42, 143; rivalry among, 24, 30–31; and rural societies, 78, 94; unions and, 81–82. *See also* colonato system; Imaña family; Lorini, Héctor; Mollinedo family; Quiroga family; Riveros de Oviedo, Irene; Terrazas, Carlos; Terrazas, Pedro Roberto; Terrazas, Roberto; Vilela, Samuel; Villarroel, Juan; Villegas, Agustín
land tenure, 3, 21–22, 23, 101, 120, 195n13, 223n50; changes in, 83, 96
Langer, Erick, 25, 155
latifundios, 21, 48, 136, 146, 157, 189n24; classified, 118, 119, 150; declared illegal, 106, 166; denounced, 48, 149–52
laws, 71, 188n17, 203n26; agrarian, 56–57, 179, 180; Disentailment Law (1874), 7, 23, 52, 135, 185n22, 188n22, 199n57, 218n55; Institute of Agrarian Reform (INRA) law, 14, 67, 68, 180; Ley General del Trabajo, 186n27; supreme decrees, 194n76, 198n49, 220n7; supreme resolutions, 184n5, 188n19, 193n76, 198n49. *See also* decree-laws; decrees
Lechín Oquendo, Juan, 73, 197n34
León, Magdalena, 163, 180
liberals, 7, 47, 48, 65, 126, 127, 129, 196n22
literacy, 33, 126, 172, 212n66, 228n19
López Avila, Hugo, 96, 129
López Bermudez, José, 102–3
Lorini, Héctor, 23, 152
Loureiro, Eduardo Arze, 54, 96, 196n21, 217n36
LTC. *See* Wisconsin Land Tenure Center (LTC)

MAC. *See* Ministerio de Asuntos Campesinos (MAC)
majordomos, 17, 28, 65, 82, 87, 190n32, 191n40, 202n8; Moisés Castro, 84, 86, 89; role of, 29–30
Malloy, James, 6, 12
Mamani, Carlos, 6, 7
Mariátegui, José Carlos, 48
Marof, Tristán, 48, 188n13, 189n27, 217n36
Martínez de la Vega, Francisco, 108
Mayer, Enrique, 153, 160
Melgarejo, Manuel Mariano, 22, 23, 120, 125
mestizos, 29, 69, 150, 185n23, 186n30, 195n7, 207n71; among landlord elite, 32–33, 121, 177
Mexico, 3, 18, 51, 119, 180, 197n32; advisors from, 95, 101; agrarian reform in, 48, 56, 101–2, 106, 174; Lázaro Cárdenas, 107; Emilio Portes Gil, 107; indigenous congress in, 52, 57, 217n36
military dictators, 177, 180, 228n23
military regimes, 70, 142, 165, 169, 172, 179
military socialism, 49, 50, 51, 57
Military-Peasant Pact, 12, 165–67, 169
mines nationalization, 4–5, 100, 111, 176, 201n2
mine workers, 12, 17, 33, 57, 71, 159, 207n71
mining economy, 14, 19, 20–22, 24, 25, 187n7
minister of foreign affairs, 87, 111
Ministerio de Asuntos Campesinos (MAC), 17, 71, 78, 91, 177, 201n4, 216n32, 218n54; agents, 75, 76, 83; commissioners, 88; created, 73–74, 216n34; first convention (1953), 97–98; and hacienda Casamaya, 115; inspectors, 77, 117; minister of, 82, 97, 107, 115, 123, 143, 171, 202n16;

Office of Peasant Affairs, 73, 77; and petition for land expropriation, 107–8; representatives from the, 128; and Santa Lucía de Liquinas, 145
Ministry of Agriculture, 29, 38, 44, 50, 61, 62, 73, 190n36, 220n7; minister of, 72, 94, 118, 144
Ministry of Government, 76, 90, 186n29, 207n4
Ministry of Labor, 50, 61, 62, 196n21, 202n18; minister of, 49, 196n23
Ministry of Peasant Affairs. *See* Ministerio de Asuntos Campesinos (MAC)
mita, the, 22, 189n25, 193n64
mitanis, 28, 37
MNR. *See* Movimiento Nacionalista Revolucionario (MNR)
Mollinedo family, 24, 135, 137
Montenegro, Adolfo García, 102, 210n210
Montenegro, Carlos, 189n27, 215n22; Peasant Regiment, 80, 81
Montenegro, Mario, 77–78
Montes, President Ismael, 23, 120, 125, 130
Moore, Barrington, 181
Morales, Evo, 4, 181
Movimiento Nacionalista Revolucionario (MNR), 3, 7–8, 46, 71, 137, 172–73, 205n50; agendas, 199n61, 201n5, 216n35; agrarian program, 17–18, 70–71, 78, 96; and Catholic Church, 111; and control of information, 5, 109, 176; downfall of the, 142, 204n34; founders of the, 215n22; and FRC, 208n5; and FSB, 78–79; and indigenous groups, 62, 139, 228n24; and land distribution, 87–88, 94, 168, 181; and legal procedures, 110, 116, 117; members of the, 16, 24, 58, 64, 70, 97, 130; and Mexican example, 101, 102; nationalist, 49, 124, 132, 227n18; and peasants, 9, 57, 76, 95, 96–97, 159, 200n1, 202n10; and peasant unions, 90, 157, 207n4; PIR and, 210n40; and POR, 73, 80; and private property, 141

national constitutional convention (1938), 46, 51–52, 56, 57, 65, 197n34
National Council of Agrarian Reform. *See* Consejo Nacional de Reforma Agraria (CNRA)
National Institute of Agrarian Reform, 14, 65, 67–68, 191n46, 222n44
national press, 55, 60, 88, 89, 117, 175, 184n6. *See also* newspapers
newspapers: *La Calle*, 50, 55, 59, 60; *El Combate*, 108; *El Diario*, 72, 88; *Gaceta Campesina*, 94, 128; *La Nación*, 88, 92–93, 94, 102, 104, 128–30, 132; *Revista Bolivia*, 40, 60–61; *Los Tiempos*, 88–89, 98, 102; *Tierra*, 58; *Ultima Hora*, 88
Nicaragua, 163, 224n52

Office of Peasant Affairs. *See under* Ministerio de Asuntos Campesinos (MAC)
originarios, 34, 35, 36, 154, 160, 189n25; different from utawawas, 142, 159, 168

Pando, José Manuel, 24, 127
Partido de la Izquierda Revolucionaria (PIR), 5–6, 46, 62, 69, 173, 205n50, 218n50; and agrarian policy, 63–64, 65–66, 78, 96; and the Commission for Agrarian Reform, 103–4; members of, 67–68, 96, 103, 131; and the MNR, 210n40; Stalinist, 49
Partido Obrero Revolucionario (POR), 49, 75, 88, 90, 173, 200n1, 205n50; and agrarian reform, 95, 96, 100; militants of the, 73, 82
Patch, Richard, 5, 8
Patiño, Simón I., 24, 25, 188n17, 188n19
Paz Estenssoro, Víctor, 51, 105, 126, 158–59, 189n27, 219n72; and agrarian reform, 3, 94, 170, 177; and commission, 103, 128; and decrees, 104, 131, 200n2, 218n53; and Guevara Arze, 55–56, 197n34; interviewed, 201n4; and landlords, 78, 166; and MNR, 55, 70; overthrown, 142, 165; as president, 11, 72–73, 167, 176, 187n37; speeches of, 216n33, 216n35
Paz Zamora, Jaime, 179, 228n27
peasant regiments, 78, 81; Carlos Montenegro Regiment, 80, 81; Germán Busch First Cavalry Regiment

(Patamanta), 81, 204n39; Gualberto Villarroel First Infantry Regiment (Aroma Province), 81, 85
peasants, 53–56, 74, 117, 143, 177, 181; appeals, 141, 145; Aymara, 21–22, 34, 59, 72, 136, 174; and education, 201n4, 201n6; and landownership, 18, 139, 142, 221n25; leaders of the, 77, 96, 219n72; and petitions, 4, 71–73, 202n12, 223n47; Quechua, and court cases, 152; and the Quirogas, 156; and Reform Decree, 168; unionization of, 5, 95, 204n30. *See also* colonos; peasant regiments; peasant unions
peasant unions, 17, 78–82, 90, 103, 153, 198n44, 226n72; and land expropriation, 149–50, 213n81, 221n31; and land redistribution, 9, 10–11, 163–64, 172–73; leaders of (called secretary generals), 110, 126, 138, 151, 166; leading role of, 12, 18, 111, 159, 169, 174; organization of, 7, 173, 185n16, 196n23; and political power, 4, 71, 166, 167, 181, 205n40; recognized, 15
penal colonies, 55, 198n49
Peñaranda, Enrique, 39, 40, 59, 186n27, 188n19, 190n36; and peasants, 53–54, 55, 79
peonage system, 14, 50, 63, 67–69
Pérez, Elizardo, 52, 197n39
Peru, 21, 108, 114, 164; intellectuals in, 48, 56, 108, 211n53; military regimes in, 4, 12, 165; Peruvian Aprista Party (APRA), 56; reforms in, 3, 153, 174–75, 180, 193n66, 224n54; workers in, 31, 42, 153, 191n37, 192n48, 194n81
petitions, 4, 107–8, 121, 134, 164. *See also under* peasants
PIR. *See* Partido de la Izquierda Revolucionaria (PIR)
Platt, Tristan, 7, 22, 185n22, 186n30
pongueaje, 31, 58, 127, 143, 155, 193n64; abolition of, 48, 55, 72
POR. *See* Partido Obrero Revolucionario (POR)
progressives, 38, 47, 52, 69, 181, 228n23; progressive landowners, 42, 66, 137, 177
property: agendas, 137; private, 7, 95, 98; rights, 63, 172; rural, 55, 96; taxes, 73
Provincial Agrarian Federation, 72, 113–14, 216n29

Quechua, 34, 72, 87, 174, 217n36; congresses, 58–59, 124
Quintanilla, Carlos, 38, 52, 53, 54, 55–56, 110, 196n26
Quiroga family, 24, 25, 154–56, 222n35
Quispe, Luciano, 16, 113–17, 118, 212n68

republicans, 47, 48, 65, 196n22
revisita de tierra, 58, 59, 124, 135, 136
Revolutionary Nationalist Movement. *See* Movimiento Nacionalista Revolucionario (MNR)
Revuelta, Antonio, 50, 196n21
Reyeros, Rafael, 68, 69
Rivas, Sinforoso, 77, 78
Rivera Cusicanqui, Silvia, 6, 7, 12, 122
Riveros de Oviedo, Irene, 30, 84–85, 86, 146, 147
Rojas, Carlos Augusto, 113–14
Roman Catholic Church, 11, 30, 32, 80, 110–11, 112
rural councils, 79, 81, 113–19, 171, 175; and land expropriation, 107, 213n81; MNR and, 11, 86, 90, 106. *See also* Quispe, Luciano

Salas, Toribio, 16, 116–18, 208n8
Salmón, Hugo, 55, 192n50
Salmón, José, 97–98
Sánchez, Luis Alberto, 108, 109, 211n53
Sanjinés, Alfredo, 48, 195nn12–13
Santa Clara monastery, 23, 43, 49–50, 53, 148, 154, 196n20; and expropriation of land, 110–13, 119, 196n23, 196n27, 223n45
Santos Cornejo, 122, 124, 126
schooling, 172, 174, 228n19
schools, 61, 167; on haciendas, 32, 84, 86, 144, 160; indigenous, 52, 57–58, 59, 60, 68, 94, 98, 212n66; landlords and, 73, 201n6; rural, 15, 63, 72, 113, 126–27, 129, 194n76, 216n35. *See also* teachers

Scott, James, 13–14, 155
Seligmann, Linda, 153
settlement, 39, 95, 96, 177, 221n22, *See also* colonization
sharecroppers, 31–32, 154, 224n50
Siles Zuazo, Hernán, 12, 62, 97, 158, 159, 188n17; and agrarian reform, 176, 177; and landlords, 166, 169–70
Sociedad de Propietarios de los Yungas (SPY), 198n45, 203n26
Sociedad Rural Boliviana (SRB), 39, 42, 55, 56, 69, 83, 190n31, 196n27; and Congress, 60, 64; creation of, 198n45; dismantled, 11; PIR and, 47, 66; proposals for agrarian reform of, 68, 78; rural societies, 78, 98, 143; Villarroel and, 53
Solar, Jorge Del, 41
Soliz, Jorge, 16, 110, 112
Soria Choque, Vitaliano, 122, 127
SPY. *See* Sociedad de Propietarios de los Yungas (SPY)
SRB. *See* Sociedad Rural Boliviana (SRB)
students, 32, 46, 48, 64, 102, 120
subprefects, 31, 69, 76, 79, 81–82, 88, 113, 175
supreme decrees and resolutions. *See under* laws

Taller de Historia Oral Andina (THOA), 6, 7
Tamayo, Franz, 56, 198n55
Taraco, 81,128,129, 130, 217n45
taxes, 39, 73, 76, 98, 111, 203n26, 228n19; landholders and, 55, 67, 190n34, 212n62; levied on haciendas, 29, 42; and policy, 185n22, 195n13; rural, 55, 68
teachers, 57, 32, 64, 84, 113; rural, 5–6, 50, 59, 99
Terrazas, Carlos, 115, 166, 167
Terrazas, Pedro Roberto, 115, 222n43
Terrazas, Roberto, 115, 156
THOA. *See* Taller de Historia Oral Andina (THOA)
Thompson, Sinclair, 13–14
Ticona Alejo, Esteban, 6, 122
tin economy, 24, 38, 187n4
Toco, 150, 156, 223n44, 223n47
Toro, David, 49, 50, 51–53, 54, 59, 110, 111
Turovsky, Robert, 176

Ucureña, 5, 15, 83, 95, 103, 130
unions, 8, 49, 50, 111, 167, 199n63; and traditional indigenous communities, 92–93, 186n28. *See also* peasant unions; Salas, Toribio
universities, 29, 32, 41, 55, 72, 190n36. *See also* students
Urioste, Miguel, 175, 179, 180
Urquidi, Arturo, 96, 103, 131
Urriolagoitía, Mamerto, 70, 126, 200n1, 203n26, 224n51
utawawas, 34, 36, 37, 38, 160, 224n50; different from originarios, 142, 159, 168

Vera Tapia, Germán, 72, 94, 118, 216n34
Vilela, Samuel, 141, 146, 150
Villarroel, Gualberto, 39, 53, 55, 61, 62, 76, 198n53; agenda (1945), 71–75; and agrarian law, 56–57; Barrientos, and, 166; decrees of, 63, 74; murder of, 64; and peasants, 29, 60, 113, 126, 202n9
Villarroel, Juan, 134–35
Villegas, Agustín, 143–44, 147, 154, 208n5

Warisata, 16, 113, 135, 138, 212n66
Wilkie, James, 175
Winn, Peter, 153
Wisconsin Land Tenure Center (LTC), 223n50, 227n13, 228n25
Wolf, Eric, 5, 172
women, 24, 74, 125, 193n67, 224n52; exploited, 37, 74, 91–92, 195n7; indigenous, 58, 69, 72, 96; not among beneficiaries, 163, 181; and suffrage, 3, 200n2
Workers Union Federation, 57, 205n50

yanaperos, 34, 36–38, 92, 141, 152, 168, 192n64, 224n50
Young, Kevin, 12

Zárate Willka, 6, 47, 127
Zavaleta Mercado, René 12, 184n7